WORK PLACES

Environment and Behavior Series

Editors

DANIEL STOKOLS
University of California, Irvine

IRWIN ALTMAN
University of Utah

WORK PLACES
The psychology of the physical environment in offices and factories

ERIC SUNDSTROM
University of Tennessee, Knoxville

in collaboration with
MARY GRAEHL SUNDSTROM
Knoxville, Tennessee

CAMBRIDGE
UNIVERSITY PRESS

CAMBRIDGE UNIVERSITY PRESS
Cambridge, New York, Melbourne, Madrid, Cape Town, Singapore, São Paulo, Delhi

Cambridge University Press
The Edinburgh Building, Cambridge CB2 8RU, UK

Published in the United States of America by Cambridge University Press, New York

www.cambridge.org
Information on this title: www.cambridge.org/9780521319478

First published 1986
Reprinted 1989, 1993
Re-issued in this digitally printed version 2009

A catalogue record for this publication is available from the British Library

ISBN 978-0-521-26545-4 hardback
ISBN 978-0-521-31947-8 paperback

CONTENTS

PART II.   THE INDIVIDUAL WORKER

PART III.   INTERPERSONAL RELATIONS

SERIES FOREWORD

In recent decades the relationship between human behavior and the physical environment has attracted researchers from the social sciences – psychology, sociology, geography, and anthropology – and from the environmental-design disciplines – architecture, urban and regional planning, and interior design. What is in many respects a new and exciting field of study has developed rapidly. Its multidisciplinary character has led to stimultion and cross-fertilization, on the one hand, and to confusion and difficulty in communication, on the other. Those involved have diverse intellectual styles and goals. Some are concerned with basic and theoretical issues; some, with applied real-world problems of environmental design.

This series prefers a common meeting ground. It consists of short books on different topics of interest to all those who analyze environment-behavior links. We hope that the series will provide a useful introduction to the field for students, researchers, and practitioners alike, and will facilitate its evolutionary growth as well.

Our goals are as follows: (1) to represent problems the study of which is relatively well established, with a reasonably substantial body of research and knowledge generated; (2) to recruit authors from a variety of disciplines with a variety of perspectives; (3) to ensure that they not only summarize work on their topic but also set forth a "point of view," if not a theoretical orientation – we want the books not only to serve as texts but also to advance the field intellectually; and (4) to produce books useful to a broad range of students and other readers from dif-

ferent disciplines and with different levels of formal professional training. Course instructors will be able to select different combinations of
books to meet their particular curricular needs.

Irwin Altman
Daniel Stokols

PREFACE

This book explores psychological and social-psychological influences of the physical environment in offices and factories. Its purpose is to provide a coherent, focused overview of current knowledge on the basis of empirical research and relevant theory.

Students and professionals interested in offices, factories, or the built environment in general comprise the audience envisioned for this book. The book is directed primarily toward the field of environmental psychology, but also toward such related disciplines as applied experimental psychology, architecture, engineering psychology, ergonomics, facilities management, human factors engineering, human factors psychology, industrial engineering, industrial hygiene, industrial-organizational psychology, interior design, management science, occupational psychology, office planning, organizational behavior, and social psychology.

Our approach represents an attempt to serve readers from diverse backgrounds, who are not necessarily familiar with environmental psychology. We define our terms, particularly those that carry special meanings for psychologists; wherever possible, however, we try to avoid technical language. Examples from actual offices and factories are provided. For heavily studied topics, research findings are condensed into tables. In an effort to concentrate on the central issues, empirical studies are described only in sufficient detail to indicate their contribution to current knowledge.

Although this book deals more with basic knowledge than with practical application, the two are not always distinct. Examples often involve discussions of current practices or actual cases. Even so, we provide little advice on the design of offices or factories. We do outline, in general terms, the practical issues involved in the topics addressed here.

This book should interest professional designers, but it makes no attempt to provide practical guidelines or standards for offices or factories. However, selected sources are cited where readers can find them. We offer no procedures, algorithms, or flowcharts for use in making decisions about design. Nor do we analyze or criticize the processes by which the design of offices or factories occurs. (For a discussion of this topic, see Becker's *Workspace*.) We offer no advice on the conduct of applied research, whether as an adjunct to design or as a tool for evaluation (see Zeisel, 1981). We explore basic knowledge that should prove useful in the design of work places, but we do not try to close the gap between knowledge and application.

For coherence, the book is planned around an analytic framework on the influences of the work environment. The framework includes three units of analysis, which differ in size and scale: individual workers, interpersonal relationships, and organizations. For each unit of analysis, we identify critical facets of the physical environment and try to link them with important outcomes through psychological, social-psychological, or organizational processes.

The scope of the book is largely defined by the outcomes and facets of the physical environment included in the framework. For the individual worker, we emphasize the outcomes of satisfaction and performance and their connections with the ambient environment (light, air, temperature, sound) and with the work-station. For interpersonal relationships, we focus on the outcomes of communication and group formation and cohesion, as well as their connections with features of workspaces and the layout of work areas. For the organization, we focus on the outcome of organizational effectiveness and its connections with the features and layouts of buildings.

The scope of this book does not include the physiological or medical influences of the work place, nor does it deal with its impact on the health of workers or its connection with safety and security. However, these issues are sometimes difficult to separate from those we do emphasize. For instance, the discussion occasionally raises issues related to health. Recommended sources for a fuller treatment of physiological and health-related effects of offices and factories are the textbook on human engineering by McCormick (1976) and the textbook on industrial hygiene by Allen, Ellis & Hart (1976).

This book attempts to provide an historical perspective on the work place. Although this approach may be unusual for a text on environmental psychology we believe it is essential to the subject matter. Offices and factories have changed during their history, as have ideas about their influences. An understanding of today's offices and factories calls for an understanding of their past. Furthermore, we speculate about the future of the work place, and our forecasts are based in part on the trends in their past evolution.

ACKNOWLEDGMENTS

We are grateful for all the help and support we received during the eight years since starting this book. Many people contributed of their time and expertise.

The editors of the series, Daniel Stokols and Irwin Altman, provided encouragement and inspiration from the beginning. They read and commented in detail on several drafts and made suggestions on every chapter. We especially appreciate their continuing patience. We are indebted to many colleagues who graciously reviewed earlier versions of the manuscript. Several commented in detail on the whole manuscript and wrote pages of valuable suggestions: Alan Hedge, Stephen Margulis, H. McIlvaine Parsons, Ralph B. Taylor, and Lawrence Wrightsman. Others gave suggestions on one or more specific chapters: Michael Brill, William Calhoun, Ellen Konar, David Mandel, Gere Picasso, Robert W. Rice, and Jerry Town. We tried to incorporate the suggestions and hope that we succeeded.

The University of Tennessee has been an ideal setting for the research and writing for this book, thanks in large part to the continued support of William Calhoun, Head of the Department of Psychology, and office co-managers Karen Fawver and Polly Johnson. Our project has benefited from the timely efforts of a succession of capable secretary-typists, including Margaret Garrett, Debbie Myers, Connie Ogle, Mary Richards, Ann Smith, and Deanna Tilley. The university also provided the services of graphic artist Carlene Malone, who executed all the original graphic art. Several graduate students in psychology assisted with the library research, including David W. Brown, Robert E. Burt, Andrew Forman, William Johnson, and Donald Windham. We had invaluable help from the University of Tennessee Library, where Flossie Wise and the staff at the Interlibrary Loan Department and Robert Bassett and the staff at the Reference Department are probably glad to see the book finished.

We thank the staff at Cambridge University Press, especially psychology editor Susan Milmoe, who oversaw the project.

Our gratitude also goes to Alexander, now five years old, who has patiently tolerated his father's working during many evenings and weekends.

1
INTRODUCTION

This book addresses the question, What is known about certain psychological and social-psychological influences of the physical environment in offices and factories? The opening chapter describes the general approach that guides the remainder of the book. It presents a framework for analyzing environmental influences in offices and factories, defines key terms, and identifies central themes. The chapter ends with a summary of the plan of the book.

Framework for analysis

The framework of this book grows out of two premises. First, people and their physical environments exert mutual influence, and together form interdependent systems. Second, relationships between people and physical settings differ, depending on whether the unit of analysis is the individual, the interpersonal relationship, or the entire organization. These three units of analysis are interrelated in that individuals participate in interpersonal relationships and interpersonal relationships are elements of organizations. However, the units of analysis operate within the context of physical environments of different size and scale. In consequence, each unit of analysis involves different facets of the physical environment, different outcomes, and different underlying processes.

1

Mutual influence of people and settings

The term *physical environment* as used in this book refers to buildings and their interiors. This includes the appearance and layout of buildings, the arrangement of rooms, furnishings, and equipment, as well as ambient conditions (lighting, sound, temperature, and air). Examples of the mutual influence of people and physical environments are easy to find. Consider the operator of an electronic word processor in a new office. Bright overhead lights create glaring reflections in the video screen, which constantly distract him. He is dissatisfied with his working conditions, and his output suffers. He tolerates the effects of these adverse conditions for only a few hours before complaining to the office manager. Meanwhile he fashions a cardboard hood, which he tapes around his video screen to block the light; it is ugly but effective. He tapes newspaper onto the window to block the sunlight. The building engineer soon removes some of the overhead lamps; the office manager orders a commercially produced glare shield for the worker's video screen (and all others in the office), replacing the jury-rigged cardboard one. Venetian blinds are installed on the windows to replace the newspaper. These changes in the physical environment help the worker (and his peers) to feel more comfortable and satisfied in the new office. He is able to produce more work.

The example illustrates some of the influences that physical settings can have on occupants, and it illustrates Rene Dubos's (1980) observation that people never submit passively to environmental forces. This suggests a picture of the relationship between people and their settings as one of give and take.

People and their environments may be regarded as interdependent elements of a system, as has become traditional in branches of psychology that deal with the physical environment (e.g., Altman, 1973; McCormick, 1976; Proshansky, Ittelson & Rivlin, 1976). The systems perspective implies, among other things, that repetitions of the cycle of mutual influence tend toward a mutual accommodation between people and settings, as the occupants try to bring their environment into congruence with their needs and activities. This process can occur through modification of the environment. It can also occur through changes in occupants or their activities, defined here as *adaptation*. (See Dubos, 1980, for a discussion of this concept.) In effect, much of this book concerns adaptation in offices and factories.

Orientation toward outcomes

Although our preferred model of relationships between people and environments rests on the concept of a system, most of the available research uses a different approach. Empirical studies have generally investigated the connections of specific environmental variables with important *outcomes*. These consist of psychological, social-psychological, and organizational criteria, such as individual satisfaction or interpersonal communication.

This book focuses on empirical rsearch, and reflects the orientation of the research toward outcomes. The choice of outcomes to treat as part of the model hinges on the unit of analysis.

Units of analysis

Shifting the focus from the individual to the interpersonal relationship to the organization is like changing the lenses on a camera. A picture of the organization as a whole calls for the wide-angle lens, with a focus broad enough to encompass the entire membership and the technological infrastructure of the organization. For interpersonal relationships the picture is less inclusive, narrowing to a few people at a time. Focusing on the individual calls for a closeup view of just one person. Figure 1.1 illustrates the analogy between units of analysis and width of focus.

Definitions. The term *individual* means a person who works in an organization, analytically separate from his or her social context. Interpersonal relationship refers to any transient or lasting bond between individuals, either job related or friendly. An important type of interpersonal relationship manifests as *group* – that is, two or more people interacting in such a way as to influence one another (Shaw, 1981). The type of group of interest here is the small group, usually fewer than 20 to 30 people. An *organization* includes a collection of people working in concert toward a common goal, with each person having a specified role and position in the hierarchy of authority. (By this definition, the members of an organization comprise a group with a complex and differentiated social structure.) The term organization as used here also includes the buildings, machinery, equipment, materials, and information under the control of its members. This definition of an organization approximates a *sociotechnical system*, or a marriage of a social system with a technological one (see Katz & Kahn, 1978). The definition applies particularly to organizations that operate offices or factories, many of which are private businesses or manufacturing firms.

Outcomes. Understanding environmental influences on individuals, interpersonal relationships, and organizations calls for an identification of key outcomes and specification of dynamic processes that mediate their

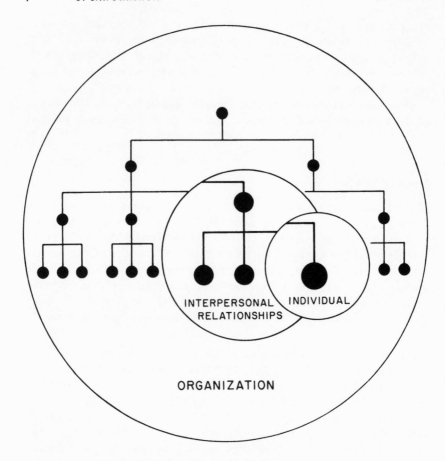

Figure 1.1. Three units of analysis: the individual worker, interpersonal relationships, and the organization.

influences. Table 1.1 shows the outcomes emphasized for each unit of analysis, and the general types of processes involved.

With the individual worker as the unit of analysis, psychologists have traditionally emphasized two outcomes: satisfaction and performance. The term *job satisfaction* refers to the worker's evaluation of his or her job as a whole or of the general quality of life at work (see Landy & Trumbo, 1976; Locke, 1983). Job satisfaction represents an amalgamation of many types of satisfaction, including satisfaction with the physical environment. The term *job performance* refers to the effectiveness with which the individual accomplishes assigned tasks, according to such criteria as quantity, quality, or efficiency. The physical environment can influence these outcomes through psychological processes. For example,

Table 1.1. *Units of analysis, dynamic processes, and outcomes*

Units of analysis	Dynamic processes	Outcomes
Individual	Psychological	Satisfaction; performance
Interpersonal relationship	Social-psychological	Communication; group formation and cohesion
Organization	Organizational	Effectiveness

a factory worker in uncomfortably hot conditions may exercise psychological stress and consequently perform a complex task less effectively than at a comfortable temperature. At the same time, the worker probably feels dissatisfied with the working conditions, and perhaps with the job itself.

When analysis focuses on the interpersonal relationship, the picture becomes more complicated, because the outcomes relevant to the individual remain important, whereas others emerge in the interpersonal domain. For example, a manager receives a promotion and moves from a shared office to a private office. The office symbolizes her new status, enabling her to conduct confidential conversations regarding subordinates' work and personal concerns. Her satisfaction with the environment increases, as does her communication with other workers. Here the outcomes include satisfaction (an individual outcome) and communication (an interpersonal outcome). The underlying processes are interpersonal: information concerning her status conveyed through the workspace, and the conduct of personal conversations. (Communication is a process as well as an outcome, which illustrates the difficulty in specifying outcomes at the level of interpersonal relationships.)

Critical outcomes at the interpersonal level of analysis include the formation of groups and the develoment of group cohesion. For example, a dozen factory workers are placed in a segregated work-area, where they assemble automobile engines as a team. Their physical separation from other workers makes it inconvenient to seek social stimulation outside the work area, and close proximity during the performance of work creates opportunities for conversation. Their common work area also helps define them as a group. As they work and talk together, they eventually develop into a cohesive team. The existence of a cohesive team contributes to their job satisfaction, and to their efficiency as a work-unit. The process underlying group formation is face-to-face conversation, made convenient by the physical environment.

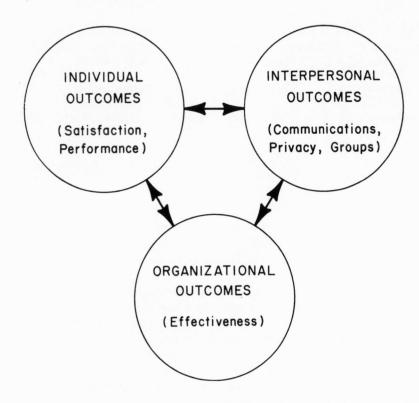

Figure 1.2. Interconnections among outcomes at three levels of analysis.

Focusing on the organization as the unit of analysis creates still greater complexity, because outcomes for the organization encompass inter-personal and individual outcomes, and the three types of outcomes are interdependent. As shown in Figure 1.2, outcomes at the three levels of analysis are all linked, in that an outcome at any level of analysis can influence outcomes for the other two. For example, an insurance com-pany measures its success at least partly in terms of the volume of sales of insurance policies. This outcome at the level of the organization depends on the performance of salespersons (an individual outcome) and on the coordination of effort within sales teams, which depends in turn on communication (interpersonal outcome). Communication and individual performance may be mutually dependent in this situation in that effective communication contributes to performance, and good per-formance leads to a worker's being sought out for communication by peers.

The key outcome for the largest unit of analysis is organizational effectiveness, which includes not only productivity, but other criteria of success as well. Organizational psychologists disagree about the definition of effectiveness (see, e.g., Katz & Kahn, 1978, chapter 8), although a few common themes can be discerned in the various definitions. For present purposes, the definition of organizational effectiveness refers to its success at maintaining satisfaction and commitment among its members, communication and coordination among its work-units, adequate production, and a mutually supportive relationship with its external environment. These outcomes depend on many factors, including the physical environment in the offices and factories of the organization.

Facets of the physical environment

A central proposition of our model is that the individual, interpersonal, and organizational levels of analysis emphasize different aspects of the physical environment. The difference concerns the relative size or scale of the environment for the three units of analysis.

At the smallest scale, the physical environment of the individual comprises his or her immediate surroundings during the workday, which consist primarily of a workspace or work-station and its ambient conditions. We define *work-station* as a place designated for an individual to work, such as a desk and chair in an office or a position at a production line in a factory. The term *workspace* is more restrictive; it refers here to a work-station assigned to a specific individual. Workspaces and work-stations include furniture, machinery, equipment, supplies, decorative items, and other things that occupy the area designated for the person who works there. *Ambient conditions* refer to the atmosphere of a working environment, both literally and figuratively. These conditions include the quality and movement of the air, the temperature, the humidity, the ambient sound, and the lighting (see Parsons, 1976). (The individual's environment also includes areas surrounding the work-station designed to support the work, such as locker rooms, restrooms, hallways, conference rooms, libraries, lounges, gymnasia, cafeterias, and parking garages.

The interpersonal level of analysis involves a larger-scale environment, including features of workspaces with symbolic value, the layout of rooms, and the layout of buildings. Symbolic qualities of workspaces concern the occupant's status or self-identity. The layout and arrangement of rooms in the layout of buildings influences the convenience of face-to-face conversations, through the physical proximity of workers and barriers that separate their workspaces.

In analyzing the organization as a whole, the scale of the physical

Table 1.2. *Levels of analysis, facets of the environment, processes, and outcomes*

Level of analysis	Facets of physical environment	Key processes	Outcomes

Individual workers	Ambient conditions
	  Temperature
	  Air quality
	  Lighting
	  Noise
	  Music
	
	Work-stations
	  Color
	  Equipment
	  Chair
	  Floorspace
	
	Supporting environment
	  Hallways
	  Restrooms
	  Work areas, etc.
		Adaptation
		Arousal
		Overload
		Stress
		Fatigue
		Attitudes
			Satisfaction
			Performance

Interpersonal relationships	Workspaces
	  Differentiation
	
	Room layout
	  Seating arrangements
	  Furniture
	
	Building layout
	  Inter-workspace proximity
	  Enclosure of workspaces
	  Gathering places
		Self-identity
		Status
		
		Regulation of immediacy
		Self-presentation
		Choices in communication
		Regulation of interaction (privacy)
			Adequacy of communication
			Group formation
			Group cohesion

Organizations	Buildings
	  Separation of work-units
	  Differentiation of work-units
		Congruence of organizational process and structure with the physical environment	Organizational effectiveness

environment is larger still, encompassing entire buildings. Details of the buildings and their design express the values of the organization and determine its flexibility. The layout of the work-areas in the buildings symbolically defines work-groups and establishes their accessibility.

Table 1.2 summarizes the facets of the physical environment emphasized for each unit of analysis. Also listed are the specific psychological and social-psychological processes that may mediate the influence of the environment on the outcomes.

Dynamic processes that mediate the influences of the environment at the individual level of analysis are psychological responses evoked under a variety of conditions. Perhaps the simplest is the individual's attitude concerning the environment, which includes an evaluative judgment as well as certain beliefs. Other responses include arousal, or the individual's degree of alertness or excitation, and psychological stress, a mobilization of a person's capacities to deal with adversity, challenge, threat, or demand. The environment can distract attention and create overload, which arises when an individual receives stimulation or information at a rate that exceeds his or her capacities. The environment can also create discomfort or fatigue. However, all these psychological responses can change with continued experience in an environment, particularly through perceptual adaptation (extreme environmental conditions such as loud noise appear less extreme as time passes).

Dynamic processes at the interpersonal level concern interactions between people. Symbolic properties of the individual workspace involve the display of the individual's personal identity or status in the organization. When people converse, the environment is involved through the regulation of immediacy, the psychological closeness or distance between individuals. Through the convenience of face-to-face conversation between people, the environment may influence a person's choices regarding communication, including the medium or the person with whom to communicate. Through its influence on the accessibility of people to one another, the environment enters the process of regulation of social interaction. The convenience of conversation may also provide opportunities for the formation of new groups and the development of cohesion in existing groups.

At the level of the organization, dynamic processes concern the operation of the system as a whole. The principal relevance of the physical environment occurs through its support of the organization's structure, within which its activities proceed. (The term organizational structure refers here to enduring relationships among work-roles, and their relationships with the organization's technology.) In particular, the organization's definition of values, roles, and work-units can involve the physical environment. Our premise is that organizations strive for congruence between their structure and the physical environment of their offices and factories.

In summary, the framework underlying this book proposes that people and their physical environments exert mutual influence, and represent interdependent elements of systems. Key results of the mutual influence are labeled as outcomes. The framework defines three interrelated units of analysis – individuals, interpersonal relationships, and organizations – and emphasizes different outcomes for each. Specific facets of the physical environment are identified for each unit of analysis as sources of influence on the outcomes. Processes that mediate the influences of the environment are psychological, social-psychological, and organizational.

Themes

Our exploration of the psychology of the physical environment in offices and factories incorporates two central themes. The first is evolution, or the idea that offices and factories can best be understood within the context of their development. The second theme is differential impact, the idea that an environment affects people in different ways.

Evolution

A central premise of our approach holds that offices and factories represent the products of constantly evolving technology, but that they continue to accommodate the needs of the occupants. Although the work environments have changed, they raise a collection of recurrent issues: comfort and efficiency for the individual; accessibility and symbolic meanings for interpersonal relationships; and congruence with the structure of the organization.

Differential impact

A second premise is that a given feature of the work environment influences its occupants in different ways, depending on characteristics of the person, the job, the group, and the organization. For instance, lighting adequate for performance of an office task by an individual of age 30 may be far too dim for someone age 60 doing the same task. Responses to the ambient conditions are particularly variable, but essentially all aspects of the work environment seem to have differential impact.

Plan of the book

The plan of this book reflects the use of the framework to organize the relevant research and theory, as well as an orientation toward the themes of evolution and differential impact. It contains five sections: one on the past, one on each of the three units of analysis, and one on the future. Part I develops the theme of evolution, in two chapters. The first chapter traces the history of factories and offices; the next outlines the evolution of the study of the psychology of work places. Part II concerns the individual and opens with a chapter on the psychological processes that mediate the influence of the physical work environment as a whole. (Included is a discussion of practical considerations, a common feature of later chapters.) The ambient conditions are treated next, in chapters on lighting and windows, temperature and air, noise, and music. The section ends with chapters on color and the work-station and some of its elements, including floor space, chairs, and equipment. Part III examines interpersonal relationships in four chapters, which concern self-identity, status, and the symbolic aspects of workspaces; communication and the layout of buildings, inter-workspace proximity, and the arrangement of rooms; privacy and the limitation of social interaction through workspaces; and groups and the role of the environment in their formation and cohesion. Part IV concerns the organization as a whole and consists of a single chapter on the congruence between the physical environment and properties of the organization. Part V returns to the theme of evolution, this time dealing with the future. It comprises two chapters: one speculating on the future and one summarizing conclusions that grew out of the earlier discussion, raising unanswered questions, and setting priorities for future research.

PART I
THE PAST

This part looks backward, to provide the historical perspective essential to an understanding of today's work places. Chapter 2 gives a brief history of offices and factories and identifies recurrent issues that concern the psychology of the work place. Chapter 3 traces the evolution of the psychology of work places. It outlines past and present approaches taken by three branches of psychology to the study of the physical environment. It describes the principal types of empirical research and summarizes the extent of their application to different aspects of the work environment. These historical sketches set the stage for the review of theory and research presented in the rest of the book.

2

HISTORICAL VIEW OF OFFICES AND FACTORIES

While factories and offices have changed over the past century, they have always had to accommodate people who handle machinery or information. The evolution of work places reflects change attributable to development of technology and organizations, as well as continuity in the relationship between workers and work places.

This chapter sets the stage for exploration of the psychology of factories and offices by tracing their past, and by noting parallel developments in ideas about their influences on people. We begin by outlining the evolution of the factory building and its working conditions; we then turn to the office building, its interior, and its working conditions. History suggests some recurrent issues for the psychology of the work place, which we discuss at the end of the chapter.

If the evolution of factories and offices has a central theme, it is the continued emphasis on the work place as a resource for efficiency and productivity. This theme manifests itself in different ways, reflecting changing conceptions of workers, advancing technology, and emerging properties of the physical environment.

Factories

Before the Industrial Revolution, production occurred on a small scale, usually in houses or adjoining workshops (Chapman, 1974). Manufacturers were literally people who worked with their hands in their cottages. The term *cottage industry* still refers to the production of goods in workers' homes.

The word *factory* is an abbreviation of *manufactory* (Sturgis, 1904). The factory evolved from a room in a house, to an existing building such as a shed or barn, to a separate building designed specifically for production. The first was probably John Lombe's silk-throwing mill, built in England in 1719. Descriptions vary, but it apparently resembled a huge barracks; it was about 500 feet long and four to six stories high, and it had more than 400 windows (Nelson, 1975; Pierson, 1949).

The factory building

The location and shape of the earliest factories conformed to limitations set by their reliance on water power. A factory was built on a river, where a shaft extending from the water wheel reached the entire length of the building. Machines operated from belts on the shaft. The long rectangular form of the first factory dominated early textile mills; dimensions of 300 feet to 600 feet by 50 or 60 feet and heights of five to seven stories were fairly common (Nelson, 1975). The need for sunlight limited the width of the buildings, as it only penetrated about 30 feet from windows. Consequently, buildings were seldom wider than 60 feet.

The long, narrow, multistory "block" building persisted through the late 1800s, even though the steam engine permitted other forms. In the United States some steam-powered machine shops were built near early textile mills and resembled them quite closely.

Single-story buildings soon replaced multistory construction. For instance, the Willimantic Linen Company built a one-story building in 1881. It was inexpensive to build and relatively unsusceptible to fire hazard, and it permitted convenient transportation inside the factory. Furthermore, it gave flexibility in supervision of the work area. In place of the traditional gable roof was one that incorporated skylights. The new roofs removed one of the main restrictions on width, so single-story factories of the late 1800s were considerably wider than the early textile mills. However, the width of buildings was still limited by the use of windows for ventilation.

The factories of the 1800s not only looked different but had begun to accommodate a wide range of industries. Accurate machine tools became available in the early 1800s, and firearms factories had begun to use interchangeable parts. In 1835, Samuel Colt started what was apparently the first assembly line to manufacture pistols, presaging the automobile assembly lines of the early 1900s (see Konz, 1979).

Developments of the 1890s revolutionized the factory building. Steel-frame construction and reinforced concrete made it possible to build

Figure 2.1. Multistory factory building typical of early twentieth century architecture. This building includes parts built before 1900 and additions as recent as 1968.

factories of practically any size and shape. The electric motor came into widespread use, and the electric light became available. Now machines could be located practically anyplace in a building because the electric motor freed them from a central power shaft, and the electric light removed the need for sunlight. Multiple buildings became common, especially for operations that gave off heat, smoke, or dust. The large open spaces of the new buildings allowed almost endless variety in designing factory buildings to conform to the requirements of the technology. (See Table 2.1 for some key developments of the factory.)

Throughout its history, the factory building has reflected a utilitarian design, sometimes described as "austere and grim" (Pierson, 1949, p. 1). For example, see Figure 2.1. However, many industrial buildings incorporated architectural ornamentation, often at least partly in the belief that attractive buildings produced better work. One expert wrote "for psychological reasons it is desirable that the building presents a pleasing appearance rather than that of an ugly monster or prison" (Diemer, 1921, p. 107). This idea seems to have gained wide acceptance shortly before World War I.

Nevertheless, factory buildings still accommodated manufacturing

Table 2.1. *Some key developments in the evolution of the factory*

Date	Development
1719	First factory building (Lombe silk-throwing mill, England)
1776	Watt steam engine in industrial use
1798	Interchangeable parts (Eli Whitney's musket factory)
1800	Improved lathe and machine tools (Henry Maudsley)
1831	Electric motor (Michael Faraday)
1835	Assembly line (Colt pistols)
1860s	Iron construction of buildings
1880s	Steel-frame construction
1879	Electric light bulb (Edison)
1899	Oldsmobile assembly line
1911	First Workman's Compensation Act
1930s	Refrigerated air-conditioning
1930s	Early industrial robots
1960s	Programmable computerized controllers
1970	Occupational Safety and Health Act
1980s	Fully automated robot factory for manufacturing robots (Japan)

processes more than they reflected architectural fashion. According to one estimate, the requirements of technology determined perhaps 75% of the factory building, leaving only 25% to the discretion of the architect (Fitch, 1948).

Today factory buildings usually employ steel frames and reinforced concrete in single-story construction, often with several buildings in a complex. Shapes and sizes vary with the manufacturing process. The utilitarian orientation persists. Appearance has remained important to many industrial firms, although the definition of beauty has done an about-face: a building seems to be judged attractive to the extent that it represents utility – beauty is as beauty does. However, in what has been called the postmodern era of architecture, ornamentation is beginning to see a return; with hard lines and sharp contrasts becoming less common. If so, beauty may be undergoing another redefinition, and factory buildings later may take on a different appearance.

Interior arrangements

The typical factory of the mid-1800s drew power from water wheel or steam engine and had long power shafts attached to the ceilings with rows of machines below, run by belts. Workers operated the machines in gloomy, dirty interiors (Nelson, 1975). Figure 2.2 shows the interior of an early factory.

The factory of 1900 was a different place. The electric motor allowed practically unlimited flexibility in arrangement of machines. Steel-frame construction had reduced interior supports to a few narrow pillars and permitted large windows. Electric lighting provided uniform illumination. These developments culminated in the feasibility of huge, well-lit, nearly unobstructed work areas.

Managers quickly noticed the advantages of open spaces.

[U]nquestionably the open floor is in every way to be preferred to the sep-arate-room plan for operations that do not interfere with each other. Sep-arate rooms entail a vast amount of needless labor and lost time, even when workmen do their best; where workmen are not more than commonly honest and earnest in their toil, they fall before the temptation of convenient obscurities, and drop into easy habits of chatting and loitering in spots where the eye of the foreman is not likely to find them. (Arnold, 1896a, p. 265)

The premise reflected in this quote – that workers shirk when left unsupervised – reflects the predominant philosophy of management of the time. Managers considered factory work an unpleasant chore that workers would only do under close supervision. (Only later did the philosophy of management include the idea that people experience intrinsic satisfaction from their work.) So when open areas appeared in factories, managers welcomed the opportunity for convenient supervision.

The open factory floor roughly coincided with the development of a set of ideas called scientific management around 1900, which dominated the philosophy of management for the next three decades, and remained influential thereafter (see Nelson, 1974). The originator, Frederick W. Taylor (1895; 1911), claimed that efficient production demanded the objective analysis of work activities into their smallest components, in order to develop standard procedures that would minimize effort and maximize efficiency. The primary vehicle for such analysis was the time study, which only became practical with the advent of large, open areas. It developed quickly (see Gilbreth, 1931) and remains important today (see Konz, 1979).

The open floor also allowed factory managers to arrange machinery for efficient production, using the *straight-line flow of work*, in which a product travels the shortest distance from one process to the next. According to a 1915 text,

the ideal order of industrial management is the straight industrial line. The ideal order of the assembling industry may be regarded as a river fed from

Figure 2.2. An early factory interior. *Source:* "As They Used to Look." *System.* (1917, November). *32,* p. 728.

many sources, the shipping room corresponding to the mouth of a stream. The ideal plant is one which will make the rivulets flow into the main channel as soon as possible, and yet not flow until all is ready for their absorption. (Duncan, 1915, pp. 123–124)

The straight-line flow of work soon dominated all facets of the interior layout of factories. Managers located departments with most business with each other closest together to minimize the distance that people and materials had to travel (Nelson, 1975). Similarly, within departments offices were connected by shortest "line of travel" (Arnold, 1896a, p. 263). The principle of *work-flow*, as it is now called, still governs the layout of manufacturing operations, departments, machinery, and desks in modern factories (see, for example, Hicks, 1977).

The next major development in the layout of factories came with the European movement toward industrial democracy, and the accompanying redesign of some factories for work by groups. The idea was to assign workers to more satisfying and motivating jobs by replacing a single specialized operation for each individual with a series of inter-related tasks that could be divided among the members of a work-group. The groups were quite often autonomous and had the responsibility of dividing the labor and producing a product. The factory became a "*socio-technical system*" in which the building and physical arrangements had to support the social system (e.g., Trist, Higgins, Murray & Pollack, 1963). Factories with autonomous work groups were arranged to reinforce the groups' boundaries through the physical environment. For instance, the Volvo factory in Kalmar, Sweden, was especially designed to accommodate work-groups and did so by providing each group with its own work area and locker room (see Katz & Kahn, 1978). Meshing the technical system with the social system poses perhaps a more complex problem than designing work-flow by itself. However, new factory organizations seem likely to continue to make it necessary.

Working conditions

Early factories earned a reputation for abominable working conditions. They were dark, dirty, poorly ventilated, and often infested with rats or cockroaches; extreme temperatures were commonplace; amenities such as restrooms, lockers, and cafeterias were rare. Conditions in textile mills, for instance, were sometimes terrible:

At first the noise is fierce, but you get used to it. Lots of us is deaf – weavers – that's one reason I couldn't get that second girl's place. The lady said I couldn't hear the doorbell if it would ring, but you never think of the noise after the first, in the mill. Only its bad one way: when the bobbins flies out and a girl gets hurt, you can't hear her shout. . . . She's got to wait till you see her. (Barnum, 1971, p. 29)

The textile industry ran infamous sweat shops in which immigrants produced more than 90% of the garments. A visitor gave the following description of one sweat shop:

perhaps twenty by thirty feet, three dirt-curtained windows at one end, three dirt-curtained windows at the other. The ceiling was dingy, the floor dingy, rubbish covered. The air, heavy, sticky, breathed over again and again seemed to smear me over with filth. Two score girls bent over the whizzing machines – bu-u-z-z! and a seam was done. . . . The hovering little boss wore a look of high geared worry. The girls were very stupid, he told me – spoiled many waists by their blunders – were very slow – would loaf if he didn't watch them. (Scott, 1905, p. 6408)

Working conditions in the United States during the 1880s varied greatly from one factory to another, but only a few exceptional factories were comfortable (see Phillips, 1900). In Great Britain and Europe, working conditions in factories had begun to improve during the 1800s, due in large measure to the activities of social reformers (see P.G. Hall, 1975).

Miserable working conditions in the United States persisted through about 1900 for several reasons. Labor was plentiful – the huge population of uneducated immigrants usually could not hope to obtain anything better than a factory job. Those who complained were often dismissed, therefore few complained. The technology at the time, though rapidly advancing, sometimes offered few alternatives to the processes used in the factories. Some managers were unaware of the effects of poor working conditions. Others claimed that they bought only a worker's labor and bore no responsibility for their persons. And improved working conditions were expensive. So around the turn of the century conditions in U.S. factories were so bad that "the accident rate was higher in all probability . . . than at any other time or place" (Lescohier & Brandeis, 1935, p. 366).

Working conditions in the United States began a period of rapid and dramatic improvement after 1900. The popular press brought pressure to bear on industry by publicizing the problems in the factories. (e.g., Hard, 1907). Thomas Oliver's book *Dangerous Trades* (1902) focused attention on industrial disease. Journalists harshly criticized factory owners, especially those who had the technology available to prevent injuries but did not install it because of the cost. For example, in 1906, 100 men were killed or maimed in the state of Illinois when their clothing caught on set screws that projected from whirling shafts. For 35¢ each of the screws could have been sunk flush with the shafts (Hard, 1908). Such avoidable injuries prompted public outrage.

A major tragedy occurred in 1911 – the so-called Triangle Fire that broke out on the eighth floor of the Triangle Shirtwaist Company in New York City. When the firm's 1,000 employees tried to escape, they found the doors locked – a measure designed to keep employees from leaving early and to maintain the high temperature and humidity ideal for fabric. Fire-fighters could not prevent the 146 deaths and hundreds of injuries. The Triangle Fire was by one account "a torch that lighted up the whole industrial scene" (Cahn, 1972, p. 189).

Partly as a consequence, states soon began to adopt tough laws to regulate the work place. Workmens' Compensation Acts came before state legislatures during the year of the fire. These laws placed responsibility for accidents squarely on employers, forcing them to create better working conditions. This in turn affected insurance rates, which gave another incentive for clean, safe factories.

While many factory owners improved working conditions in response to public and legal pressures, others did so in hopes of increasing their profits. This reflected the growing belief that comfortable working conditions led to greater output by workers (see, e.g., Adams, 1896). As early as the 1890s, companies experimented with what they called "welfare work" – programs designed to make workers "satisfied, contented, and happy, and to improve their condition physically" (Nimmons, 1919). A spokesperson for the National Cash Register Company explained such programs this way:

In 1892 registers worth over $50,000 were returned because of defective workmanship. We decided that more interest would have to be taken in our employees to make them better workers and we then started welfare work and found that it paid in a better product. (Lescohier & Brandeis, 1935, p. 323)

The idea that a comfortable worker does better work grew out of the analogy of the worker to the machine, which at the time was taken quite literally:

[I]t is only where high spirits and enthusiasm enter the human machine that, like a well-oiled engine, all parts work smoothly and produce the greatest effect with the least friction. (Meakin, 1905, p. 203)

This view guided the management of an early garment shop, which, in contrast with nearby sweat shops, had clean walls and ceiling, plentiful windows, good lighting, clean floors, and excellent ventilation. The superintendent explained,

"It's dollars and cents. . . . The air and light keep the girls at their best."
They did better and more rapid work than if in a poor room – and the
difference more than paid for the light and ventilation. They made no
costly blunders; and the well-made goods commanded a ready market and
a superior price. (Scott, 1905, p. 6408)

Another writer expressed the same view:

The nearer we approach the 100 percent mark in ideal conditions for our
people, the nearer they will approach the 100 percent mark of efficiency.
(Dempsey, 1914, p. 496)

This belief was well accepted until the 1950s, when the weight of research
evidence began to cast doubt on the association between satisfaction
and performance (see Chapter 4). But despite the lack of evidence to
support it, the belief still seems to be fairly common.

World War I brought another incentive to improve working conditions
in the factories: scarcity of labor. Companies began to compete for
skilled workers, and the competition often took the form of improved
physical conditions: installation of electric fans, frequent cleaning, installation of toilets and cafeterias, hot lunch programs, and so on. Many
improvements were introduced specifically to accommodate women,
who entered the factories in large numbers during the war. At the time,
women were thought to have more delicate natures than men and to
require cleaner and more comfortable work places (Lescohier & Brandeis, 1935).

The labor union movement of the early 1900s added more pressure
as employers improved working conditions to avoid strikes. The labor
laws passed during the first two decades of the twentieth century, especially 1915–1920, contained provisions demanded by labor unions.
Sometimes welfare work represented an attempt to avoid giving employees reason to join unions. A few companies even installed work
councils, which gave workers representation in decisions about working
conditions. This was hailed as a step toward industrial democracy, but
the impact of workers on decisions by management was limited. Still
the work councils set an important precedent (Lescohier & Brandeis,
1935). Industrial democracy apparently played a much stronger role in
Europe, especially in Norway and Sweden, where work councils eventually gained considerable influence (see Katz & Kahn, 1978).

By the 1930s, working conditions in the factory had become far more
hospitable than they had been in the 1890s. However, the factory environment since the 1930s is difficult to characterize. This is partly because so many different types of factories have emerged and partly

because so few accounts of factory environments have appeared. Legal developments undoubtedly stimulated improvements in working conditions: in 1949 the last state without a Workmen's Compensation Law adopted one (Vaughn, 1977), and in 1970 the Occupational Safety and Health Act (OSHA) credited stringent regulations on U.S. work places to control noise, ventilation, temperature, lighting, and amenities. But a factory was apparently still less than an ideal place to work the year after OSHA went into effect. In 1971, a survey by the U.S. Bureau of Labor Statistics recorded work-related injury, illness, or death for 12 of every 100 employees during the first 6 months (Allen, Ellis & Hart, 1976). The 1977 *Quality of Employment Survey* of a national sample of employees found that about one-half of all factory operatives and craft workers reported "unpleasant physical conditions" and that about one-third of those who reported a problem said it was either a sizeable or great problem (Quinn & Staines, 1979).

Working conditions in modern factories can hardly compare with the comfort of modern offices. This could reflect the relatively low status of blue collar workers, perhaps as a carryover from times when clerks in white collars were few and had substantial authority (see Becker, 1981; Duffy, 1980). But the distinction between blue and white collar blurs – some factory jobs require years of training and experience, and some office jobs require little more than the ability to read. Nevertheless, a double standard still seems to exist – one for factories, another for offices. Unfortunately for factory workers, it may be necessary to some extent. The factory environment has to accommodate a wide range of technology, which may preclude the kind of environment possible in an office. For example, carts and motorized carriers may make carpeting unsafe, finished surfaces may be marred by rough or sharp materials; and rapid air circulation may make air-conditioning impossible. So factories may be inherently less comfortable than offices. On the other hand, advanced technologies are setting new standards for factory environments. For instance, manufacturers of microscopic computer chips must take extraordinary precautions to keep their operations clean, as just one mote of dust spoils an expensive computer chip (M. Chase, 1982).

Offices

Offices differ from factories in the activities they house. People "assemble to cope with the millions of details involved in planning, directing, and recording industrial activity" (Shultz & Simmons, 1959, p. 13).

Office workers keep records and files, conduct conferences and discussions, perform calculations, compose written text, and do other tasks involved in the handling of information and the making of decisions and plans.

In its earliest form the office was simply a place where lawyers, brokers, merchants, bankers, and the like conducted their business (Pile, 1976). It was sometimes a room in a house, sometimes a desk in the corner of a shop (Logan, 1961), sometimes a bench or table at a tavern or public house. For example, Lloyd's of London had its first "offices" in a coffee house, where agents and customers negotiated contracts (Duffy, 1980).

Office buildings appeared in the mid-1800s in Europe, providing rooms for rent to small firms. In 1864 the Oriel Chambers of Liverpool, England, consisted of separate one-room units, each with its own fireplace. During the same period, prosperous companies erected their own office buildings, such as the three-story Sun Insurance Company headquarters in London, built in 1849 (see Duffy, 1980).

A major impetus for the development of office buildings in the United States came from the emergence of large corporations. Up to the time of the Civil War, businesses were relatively small and served only local markets. They were typically managed by their owners, had minimal staff, and kept few written records. However, during the period of economic growth following the Civil War, organizations of unprecedented size and complexity were established, such as the Standard Oil empire in 1879, and the Woolworth company. Such large enterprises needed extensive records, and required a larger proportion of their staffs to do office work than smaller firms. A rapid expansion of office work was possible because of simultaneous expansion in technology to support it. In the two decades between 1880 and 1900, the telephone, the typewriter, and the mechanical calculator all appeared and all came into general use (Armstrong, 1972).

The office building

The office building appeared in the United States during the late 1800s primarily in the largest cities – New York City, Philadelphia, and Chicago. It was "a mammoth structure of many stories" (G. Hill, 1893, p. 445), "intended for renting to tenants for the purpose of transacting clerical or executive business" (Sturgis, 1904, p. 19). One of the earliest examples in the United States was the Arcade Building in New York City, built in 1849 in the architectural style of residences of the period. But office buildings soon began to acquire a style of their own, as shown by the Mutual Life Insurance Building, built in 1865 specifically for the firms located there (Weisman, 1953; see Fig. 2.3).

Figure 2.3. Office building of the late nineteenth century: The Mutual Life Insurance Building, New York City, as of 1870–1871. *Source*: Reprinted from the *Journal of the Society of Architectural Historians*. (1953). *12*(1), 13–21.

The office building evolved because of competition for the increasingly expensive space in central business districts. Locations on major downtown thoroughfares were valuable for the "efficiency of proximity" with other business and potential customers (Shultz & Simmons, 1959, p. 13). For example, the stockbrokers of New York City rarely rented offices anywhere but on Wall Street (Steffans, 1897).

As space grew scarce in central business districts, two choices remained for expansion: build up or build out. Early businesses did expand horizontally:

When a ground floor firm found its business really flourishing, it would expand sidewise, knocking passages through the walls of the adjacent structures, and sometimes this process would go on, through house after house, until an entire block front of buildings had been drawn together into one intricate warren. (Logan, 1961, p. 140)

But eventually there was no place to go but up. Owners of buildings found they could rent more space than three- or four-story walkups had to offer. So they built up to six stories or added onto existing structures (Steffans, 1897). Upper floors brought less rent because businessmen preferred the ground floor. As new arrivals to the financial community "rose in the world, [they] descended at a corresponding pace toward the choicer and more expensive quarters at street level" (Logan, 1961, p. 140). The sixth floor was as high as anyone cared to climb.

In 1853 Elisha Graves Otis invented a safety brake for the freight hoist, which led to the development of the passenger elevator. Seeing the possibilities, Equitable Life Insurance Company introduced two elevators into their office building, which opened in 1870. Other companies followed suit and, within a few years, preferences for office space had shifted from the lower to the upper floors (Webster, 1959). Lawyers were among the first to appreciate the upper stories for their light and freedom from the dust and noise of the streets (Logan, 1961). "There are men called 'high livers' who will not have an office unless it is up where the air is cool and fresh, the outlook broad and beautiful, and where there is silence in the heart of business" (Steffans, 1897, p. 44). Later an office management text described the ideal location for an office as the seventh floor or higher, with the fifth floor as a lower limit for buildings near noisy streets (Galloway, 1919).

The elevator had removed one limit on the height of the buildings, but another remained. With masonry construction, each added story increased the thickness needed in the walls at the base. For instance, a 10-story building required walls four feet thick in the bottom story (Shultz & Simmons, 1959). Taller buildings of masonry brought prohibitive costs for thick walls, and a sacrifice of space on lower floors. This set a practical limit of about 10 stories, which was very tall at the time (Steffans, 1897). The 10-story skyscrapers rose above the steeples of nearby churches and were sometimes called "cathedrals of commerce."

Beginning in about 1865, office buildings incorporated iron girders and pillars, first to carry the weight of the walls and later to support the floors. Structural steel replaced iron in the 1880s (Webster, 1959). The height of buildings was then theoretically unlimited and "buildings in New York shot skyward in rocket-like fashion" (Weisman, 1953, p. 18). The Manhattan skyline reached 30 stories in 1899 with the Park Row Building, 50 stories in 1909 with the Metropolitan Life Insurance Building, and 58 stories in 1913 with the Woolworth Building (Armstrong, 1972).

The shape of the early office building, like that of the early factory, reflected the use of windows as the primary source of light. Buildings were limited to 40 to 60 feet in width because sunlight only penetrated 25 to 30 feet from the windows (Leffingwell, 1925). Many buildings incorporated wings or courts, resulting in L, T, I, U, or O shapes. This practice continued up to the 1930s, when electric lighting finally found its way into common usage in offices (Shultz & Simmons, 1959). (Factories had begun widespread use of electric lights in the 1890s, shortly after they became commercially available.)

Tall buildings created problems, because they blocked the light and air that reached neighboring buildings. As such, they were sometimes called "sunlight blotters." Darkness in the lower floors made them difficult to rent, which in turn encouraged more tall buildings (see Robinson, 1891). In New York City the streets soon seemed like chasms between sheer walls and were even described as "'disease-breeding canyons" (Clark & Kingston, 1930, p. 95). In New York in 1885 a law came before the state legislature to prohibit "preternaturally tall buildings," which were even blamed for malaria (Logan, 1961). The law failed, but buildings soon came under state regulation. For example, a 1916 ordinance in New York restricted buildings through setbacks. They could go as high as the neighborhood limit, which varied, and the size of higher stories was restricted even further (Arnaud, 1952). The result was sometimes a large building with a smaller tower, or a building shaped something like a wedding cake. Similar ordinances help explain the shapes of many buildings still standing today.

After the advent of steel construction, the evolution of office buildings brought only minor changes. In the 1930s, central ventilation systems freed buildings of limitations on width, and electric lights made windows only a secondary source of light and air (Shultz & Simmons, 1959). More recently, companies such as the New York Telephone System occupy windowless office buildings (Mills, 1972, p. 120). The glass and steel towers standing in most large cities of the United States rely on the same basic practices of construction that molded the skyscrapers of the early 1900s. Their appearance has changed only slightly as styles of architecture have until lately favored straight lines and austere silhouettes. (See Fig. 2.4 for an example.) However, the 1980s seem to be ushering in a modest return to architectural ornamentation.

Working conditions

Along with the office building, the interior of the office has changed considerably during the past 100 years. In 1894 a writer for *The Engineering Magazine* described his first office this way:

Figure 2.4. A modern office building: The Plaza Building, Knoxville, Tennessee.

Imagine a room with its floor some steps below the level of the sidewalk;
a small and dusty room, ill-lighted by an abortive skylight, and two windows upon one side; worse ventilated by one door opening into an equally
dismal office, and another communicating directly with the foundry,
whence drifted in a dull and heavy air, laden with smoke and evil odors,
ornamented with graceful festoons of cobwebs, thrice magnified by accu-
mulated grime and soot. Side windows, facing the west, opened upon a
narrow driveway on the opposite side of which were a dirty boiler room
and a noisy engine . . . this unattractive picture, far from being overdrawn,
really serves to give but a faint idea of the drawing office of a large and
famous establishment in New York City. (MacCord, 1894, p. 855)

Other offices of the time shared similar problems. Workers often suffered from poor light, despite the narrowness of the buildings. Farther
than 16 feet from a window the light was inadequate even by the modest
standards of the period (Hill, 1893). On the lower floors of tall masonry
buildings, light was restricted even by windows because of the thick
walls and small openings necessary for strength (Shultz & Simmons,
1959).

   Working conditions in the early office may have been unpleasant but
were seldom as bad as conditions in factories. This was at least partly
because offices were usually separated from dangerous machinery and
noxious chemicals. Even so,

productivity of the office worker is viewed in a quite different light from
productivity of the industrial worker. These "step-children" struggle along
in humid, ill-lighted and ugly offices in the midst of the clatter of typewriters or the distracting jibber of fellow employees, surrounded by the
wasted effort that poor layout inevitably fosters. (Wylie, 1958, p. 72)

Office workers of the early 1900s seldom benefited from the welfare
programs that factory workers enjoyed; programs to relieve harsh physical labor took priority. For instance, office workers often had to walk
several flights of stairs to a restroom (if there was one), while in many
factories clean, up-to-date facilities were located for quick access.

   Inattention to working conditions in the office may have been partly
attributable to their locations in cities. By contrast, factories of the time
were built on cheap rural land far from the amenities of cities; they
often had their own company towns with houses, schools, and churches,
besides offering comfortable working environments. This occurred especially during periods of scarce labor.

   Office workers did experience improved conditions in the 1920s and

1930s, as reports of gains in productivity came from the factories. The improvements directly concerned the efficiency of work: better lighting, better ventilation, and better chairs. Cafeterias, gymnasia, and the like did not come until later.

The offices of the 1940s represented a considerable improvement in working conditions. Electric lighting was commonplace; acoustical ceil- ings had begun to appear; some offices had piped-in music; and electrical heating and ventilation systems were coming of age.

By the 1950s the term "recreation management" replaced the more patronizing "welfare work." The journal *Recreation Management* pub- lished articles about elaborate recreational facilities in office complexes – usually located some distance from large cities, but not always. For instance, the Xerox Corporation in downtown Rochester, New York, installed elaborate recreation facilities, including executive exercise fa- cilities on the 13th floor, gymnasia, and even a skating rink.

Office work was influenced in the 1960s and 1970s by the spread of the computer and its more recent companion, the video display terminal, or VDT. Computers developed in the 1960s, and by 1970 there were more than 70,000 in use in the United States (Armstrong, 1972). The cathode ray tube led to the development in the 1960s of the TV-like screen for the display of information (see Cakir, Hart & Stewart, 1980). The VDT and its electronic keyboard permitted office employees to transfer information to and from the computer from their desks. The technology of "word processing" followed, enabling essentially all cler- ical operations to be done on computers. The 1970s witnessed an ex- plosion in the development, marketing, and adoption of word-processing technology (see Kornbluth, 1982; Marbach, Lubenow & Ghinby, 1981; Uhlig, Farber & Bair, 1979). Relatively inexpensive and powerful desk- top computers in the 1980s made the technology accessible to practically any office.

The new office technology transformed many office workers of the 1970s and 1980s into full-time VDT operators. With the possibility of performing most clerical operations from a terminal, some operators began spending most of the day at the keyboard, staring at the VDT screen. Complaints surfaced, reflecting poorly designed equipment (e.g., Gorman, 1982). However, the VDT evolved quickly.

The new technology also brought advances in electronic communi- cation. The combination of telecommunications and computers provided practically instantaneous transfer of written messages – known as *elec- tronic mail*. Other equipment permitted *video-conferences*, in which two or more people talk with televised images of one another. These de- velopments could have an enormous impact on the office of the future

Table 2.2. *Some key developments in the evolution of the office*

Date	Development
1849	Early U.S. office building (Arcade Building, New York City)
1860s	Iron-frame construction of buildings
1870	Office building with elevators (Equitable Life Insurance Co., New York City)
1874	Commercial adaptation of typewriter (Remington)
1876	Telephone patented (Alexander Graham Bell)
1879	Electric light bulb (Edison)
1884	Steel-frame office building (Home Insurance Building, Chicago, 10 stories)
1894	Mechanical calculators commercially available (Burroughs)
1904	Open office building (Larkin Building, Buffalo)
1930s	Refrigerated air-conditioning
1954	Programmable electronic computers
1958	Solid state electronics
1960s	Cathrode ray tube and video display terminal (VDT)
1967	*Burolandschaft* in United States (duPont de Nemours, Wilmington, Delaware)
1970s	Video conferences; electronic mail; advanced telephones
1980s	Microcomputers

(see Chapter 16). Table 2.2 highlights the key developments in the evolution of the office.

Interior arrangements

Probably the most important development for the interiors of offices was steel-frame construction, introduced in the 1880s. The ability to support walls and floors with steel beams resulted in the potential for nearly unobstructed open spaces with only a few narrow support columns. The advantages became immediately obvious:

Large open offices are better than the same space cut into smaller rooms, because they make control and communication easier and provide better light and ventilation. (Barnaby, 1924, p. 400)

Open offices also permitted flexibility. Owners could erect inexpensive partitions to accommodate new tenants, which of course increased the rental value of the space. This encouraged the construction of more buildings with open spaces.

The best-planned modern office building leaves each floor as one great loft to be subdivided by light, interchangeable and easily-moved partitions, to suit the tenants' wishes. (Berg, 1892, p. 463)

The *Architectural Record* criticized the Chicago Title and Trust building in its series "Wasted Opportunities" (1893), because interior bracing partitions made it "extremely difficult to get any large space for the use of more than two tenants per floor" (p. 76).

Architect Frank Lloyd Wright designed one of the early buildings containing open office space – the Larkin Building in Buffalo, New York, which opened in 1904 to accommodate a mail-order firm with a large clerical staff (see Fig. 2.5). The open central court of the building contained rows of built-in desks; each desk seated six clerks, three on each side, facing each other from built-in chairs (see Duffy, 1980).

By one account, Wright had designed the building in an effort to produce a "communal experience" among the workers (Barnett, 1974, p. 128). The open space also provided management with a convenient means of supervision in a company that stressed unity and adherence to rules. Another reason for the design may have been the necessity to accommodate a mechanical ventilation system, which at the time worked only in large spaces (see Duffy, 1980).

A consultant in office management saw the open office at the Larkin Building in still different terms. He saw it as facilitating efficient flow of work for clerical operations, providing unimpeded circulation of paper from desk to desk, department to department (Galloway, 1919). The concept of work-flow that originated in the factory was adapted to the office (see Alford, 1924; Leffingwell, 1925; Schulze, 1919). It guided especially the planning of clerical operations:

Although there is some intercourse among all departments, the work of each one is tied up particularly closely to one or two others and should, of course, be located as near those departments as possible. A stenographic force, for instance, should be on the same floor and as near as possible to the dictators – an elevator or a flight of stairs between them is a serious disadvantage. (Barnaby, 1924, p. 398)

Some offices even used conveyor belts to carry papers from one operation to the next (Leffingwell & Robinson, 1943).

The modern trend in planning offices is entirely in the direction of the *open office principle.* No longer are clerical staffs separated from each other by partitioned spaces which obstruct the flow of work. . . . In the well planned office groups of clerical workers are brought together in large, open, unobstructed areas which strengthen *esprit de corps* and permit of

Figure 2.5. Interior of administration building: *Larkin Building*, 1904, Buffalo, New York, by Frank Lloyd Wright. *Source:* Photograph courtesy of the Collection, The Museum of Modern Art, New York, and reproduced by permission.

planning for expeditious procedure according to the principle of forward movement of work [italics added]. (Hopf, 1931, pp. 753–775)

Private offices grew less common, but the primary occupants of open spaces were still clerical workers. Managers and professionals were usually housed in their own offices for privacy. One architect considered the ideal office space to be a large rectangular area with columns dividing off a strip on one side, the large space for clerical work and the smaller area for private offices (Hopf, 1927).

Management consultants began to analyze the flow of work in offices and recommended rearrangements on the basis of work-flow, which sometimes took precedence over the popular rectilinear layout of an office with desks in rows and columns parallel to the walls. Instead, an office was occasionally arranged with desks separated by minimal distances in apparent disarray (e.g., Conroy, 1933).

By the late 1950s, handbooks of office management were recommending an integrated office layout consisting of open areas adjoining private offices, in which "the open office space would accommodate increases and decreases of personnel by the mere switching of occupants of private offices or by shifting desks" (Ripnen, 1958, p. 619).

Other trends favored open offices. The *human relations movement* of the 1950s and 1960s had revolutionized the philosophy of management (e.g., McGregor, 1960). Managers began to see the importance of two-way communication between workers and supervisors, as well as the benefits of worker participation in decisions. The parallel movement toward industrial democracy called for more equality among employees, greater access by workers to the processes of decision making, and less emphasis on status and authority. The accessibility provided by open offices seemed to promote all of these ideals – communication, participation, and equality.

The time was ripe in the 1960s for *Burolandschaft*, or "office landscape," an entirely open office arranged for efficient work-flow, convenient communication, and minimal indications of status. The concept had originated in Germany, with Wolfgang Schnelle and his brother, who had worked in their father's office furniture business. The Schnelles found their clients eager for guidance in planning offices and opened the Quickborner consulting firm to fill the need (Shoshkes, 1976).

The concept of *Burolandschaft* was revolutionary in that it allowed no private offices. Until the Quickborners, essentially all office planners had advocated a combination of open areas and private offices. However, the Quickborners claimed that completely open offices were more efficient, in addition to avoiding physical symbols of status. Privacy was subordinated to convenient conversation and circulation of paper. To

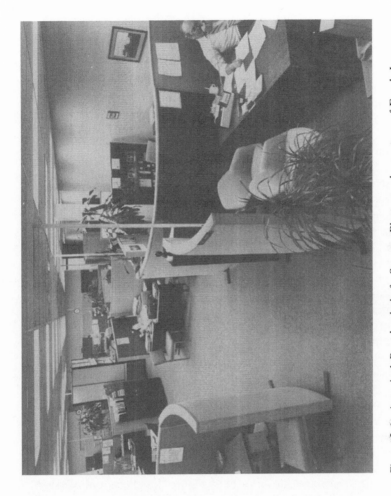

Figure 2.6. A typical *Burolandschaft. Source:* Photograph courtesy of Frank J. Carberry, managing director, Office Landscape Users Group, Philadelphia.

regain some privacy, the Quickborners eventually used curved, free-standing partitions about 5 feet high, as shown in Figure 2.6. These became a kind of hallmark of the *Burolandschaft*, although some early German installations lacked them.

Burolandschaft presented a novel appearance. Like others before them, the Quickborners rejected the conventional arrangement of desks in parallel rows and placed them at odd angles with asymmetrical spacing. The result was an expansive interior "landscape" (see Pile, 1969). (One common feature of these offices was the liberal use of large potted plants to separate workspaces; the term *office landscape* was sometimes misunderstood in the United States to mean an office in which living plants had been liberally distributed.)

Burolandschaft first appeared in the United States in 1967 at the DuPont offices in Wilmington, Delaware, where the new arrangement reportedly gave the organization several advantages (see Fig. 2.7). It allowed fast, inexpensive changes of layout; it saved space – more people could be accommodated – and it saved maintenance costs (see "Mixed Reactions to First Office Landscape," 1968). However, occupants complained about noise and lack of privacy.

Controversy surrounded *Burolandschaft* (e.g., "More Controversy over Office Landscaping at IBD, BEMA, Seminars in New York and Chicago," 1968). It meant giving up two long-standing practices: the location of certain people in private offices (e.g., Leffingwell, 1925) and the use of the physical working environment to symbolize status. Private offices were traditional marks of status, and managers were understandably reluctant to give them up, even to promote egalitarianism.

By the mid-1970s *Burolandschaft* had become common in both Europe and the United States and had evolved in several variations. One variation used "systems furniture," consisting of moveable, interlocking panels with desks and files attached. Figure 2.8 shows one version of what came to be called the *open-plan office*. By 1980, national surveys found that about one of three U.S. office employees worked in an open-plan office (Louis Harris and Associates, 1978; 1980).

Critics of the open-plan office questioned its conceptual basis (e.g., Duffy, Cave & Worthington, 1976) and identified practical problems in its application (e.g., "Office Landscape: Pro & Con," 1968). However, critics went largely unheeded until the late 1970s, when companies began to publicize their problems. In 1978, *Business Week* published an article entitled "The Trouble with Open Offices," which told of discontent. Some employees complained because they could not have an office to signify their status; others complained of the noise of co-workers' conversation, the lack of privacy, and the movement of people. By 1980

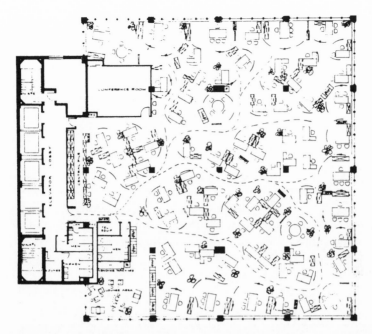

Figure 2.7. Floor plan of duPont's office landscape. *Source*: Reproduced with permission from "Mixed Reactions to First U.S. Office Landscape" (1968), *Contract*, 9(4), 74–79. (*Contract* is a Gralla publication.)

Figure 2.8. An open-plan office. *Source*: Photograph courtesy of Steelcase, Inc., Grand Rapids, MI.

many office planners and designers had become disenchanted with purely open offices and had begun to use private offices again, often in combination with open-plan offices (Ellis & Duffy, 1980; Rout, 1980). However, at least one legacy of the open-plan office remained – the modular workspace.

Recurrent issues

Throughout the history of offices and factories, a handful of issues has repeatedly surfaced in various forms. These issues refer to the problems that people have as they try to adapt to any working environment along with evolving conceptions of the work place. They include comfort and efficiency of individuals, communication and relationships among workers, and productivity for the organization.

Comfort and efficiency

Around 1900, managers in the United States began to show concern for the comfort of workers – at the time believed to be related to production. Workers were seen as analogous to machines, which operated best if kept well oiled. (Health and safety apparently also became issues of concern at the time, for similar reasons.)

The physical comfort of workers later came to be viewed as a component of job satisfaction, and it was often labeled *satisfaction with working conditions*. Researchers sought to show that job satisfaction was associated with efficient performance, but the evidence was not consistent. Later, job satisfaction became a concern in its own right, as part of the quality of work life (see Korman, 1977).

The connection between the physical environment and workers' efficiency has continually been an issue. Early psychologists concentrated on the influences of ambient conditions (temperature, air, lighting, sound) on the performance of jobs. Industrial managers also tried to design work-stations to afford economy of motion and minimal fatigue.

Communication and interpersonal relationships

Early managers and designers used the physical environment to promote accessibility of workers for work-flow and supervision. The principle of work-flow – that work should move the shortest possible distance during processing – dominated early factories as soon as technology allowed it. Similarly, factories were designed for visual accessibility when open work-areas became feasible. Offices followed suit, also focusing on accessibility among workers as a primary issue.

Interpersonal relationships of interest at the time in work organizations consisted primarily of supervision (the direct surveillance and monitoring of workers) and of coordination of work. The physical environment had a central role in both. With the human relations movement, the concept of interpersonal relationships widened, and the issue of physical accessibility was tied to communication. Offices were eventually designed with the idea that visual accessibility and physical proximity create opportunities for face-to-face conversation; workers were thought to communicate more if given such opportunities. Work places came to be viewed as vehicles for defining and reinforcing relationships. In particular, work-groups were delineated by enclosing them and creating physical accessibility among the members. The work place has also had a role as a symbolic means of communication. In particular, it has traditionally been used to symbolize status in organizations.

Productivity and effectiveness of organizations

The physical environment in offices and factories has generally been harnessed in the service of production. At around the turn of the century, managers and designers concentrated on ambient conditions and work-flow, hoping to encourage production through individual efficiency and coordination of work. Late managers saw that productivity called for effective communication, and the physical environment became a tool for the facilitation of communication.

In time it became clear that productivity represented an overly restrictive criterion for the success of an organization; the larger concept of "organizational effectiveness" replaced it (Katz & Kahn, 1978). The physical environment may have a corresponding role, perhaps as part of a sociotechnical system, which defines the work-units of an organization as well as their relationships. However, this role is only beginning to emerge.

These three recurrent issues correspond with the three levels of analysis outlined in Chapter 1. Individual comfort, and its relationship with efficiency and satisfaction, is an issue for the individual level of analysis. Communication and interpersonal relationships are issues for the interpersonal level of analysis, including the increasingly prominent concern over work-groups. For the organizational level, productivity and effectiveness are issues for analysis; at this level, the definition of organizational effectiveness partly determines the scope of questions raised about the physical environment and its role in the organization.

The recurrent issues, like the physical environment in offices and factories, have evolved and changed over time. New evidence, theories, and practical experiences continue to prompt new questions, and to suggest new ways of looking at old questions.

Summary

An historical overview sets the stage for an exploration of the psychology of the work place. Factories evolved as separate buildings in the 1700s, and drew power from water wheels and light and ventilation from windows. The Industrial Revolution brought new technology – steel-frame construction, electric motors for power, electric lighting, mechanical ventilation – which together allowed the factory building to be shaped to fit manufacturing processes. The interior of the factory was arranged for efficient flow of work, and eventually accommodated work groups. Working conditions in U.S. factories were terrible around 1900, but improved in response to pressures from the public and the unions, and by the 1930s were much more comfortable. Current conditions in factories in the United States vary, but since 1970 they have been regulated by federal laws.

Office buildings appeared in the mid-1800s in urban business districts, and maximized the use of valuable real estate by expanding upward. The development of the elevator and steel-frame construction allowed skyscrapers to develop in New York, Chicago, and other large cities. When building technology permitted large, open spaces, they began to house clerical operations, which were arranged for efficient work-flow (applying the concept used in factories). In the 1960s the controversial *Burolandschaft* ("office landscape") represented an attempt to do away with private offices, and to facilitate communication through physical accessibility of co-workers. This development may have grown out of the human relations movement in the philosophy of management. Variations of *Burolandschaft* (called the "open-plan office") spread across Europe and the United States during the 1970s, but problems with noise and lack of privacy led to the reemergence of offices that combined open areas and private offices. The legacy of the open plan office was the modular workspace. Working conditions in the office evolved to a high standard of comfort, especially after the introduction of electric lights, central air-conditioning, and acoustical ceilings in the 1930s. The spread of computers in the 1960s and video display terminals (VDTs) and advanced word-processing technology in the 1970s and 1980s marked a shift away from the use of paper as the medium for exchanging information.

The psychology of the workplace requires an understanding of some recurring issues in the evolution of the office and factory: comfort and efficiency, communication and interpersonal relationships, and the productivity and effectiveness of the organization.

3
PSYCHOLOGY OF THE WORK PLACE

Scientific methods for studying the psychology of the work place have evolved along with conceptions of the relationship between person and environment. This chapter explores the development of concepts of the psychology of the work place, methods of empirical research, and the resulting research literature. We begin by describing perhaps the best known, most influential research project concerning the physical working environment: the Hawthorne studies. We then discuss the approaches to research developed in industrial-organizational psychology, human factors psychology, and environmental psychology. The discussion continues with a summary of four strategies of research used to generate the empirical findings described in the rest of the book and concludes with an overview of current research on offices and factories.

The Hawthorne studies

In 1924, the Western Electric Company initiated a research project sponsored by the National Academy of Sciences, on "the relation of quality and quantity of illumination of efficiency in industry" (Roethlisberger & Dickson, 1949, p. 14). For the next two and a half years, experiments continued at the Hawthorne Works in Chicago, where telephone equipment was assembled. (The details of the experiments were never published in professional journals, but were summarized in a news report and in the widely cited work by Roethlisberger & Dickson, 1941, 1949.)

Experiments on illumination

The first experiment involved groups of employees from three departments that inspected small parts, assembled relays, and wound coils. In each department the researchers began by recording the employees' output under existing conditions of illumination from daylight and artificial lights. Then in each department the intensity of the artificial lighting was systematically increased or decreased while recordings of employees' production continued.

The Hawthorne researchers hoped that the output of the three departments would change in correspondence with the changes in lighting. It did not. In the inspection department the lighting was increased by 3, 6, 14, and 23 footcandles; rates of production "bobbed up and down without direct relation to the amount of illumination" (Roethlisberger & Dickson, 1949, p. 15). In the relay assembly department, lighting was augmented by 5, 12, 25, 44 footcandles; output increased more or less continuously, not only as a function of increased lighting. In the coil-winding department, the lighting was intensified by as much as 46 footcandles; output steadily increased, but did not fall when lighting was reduced.

The results were disappointing, in that something besides the lighting had obviously affected employees' production. At the time it was not clear what, but the researchers suspected competition among employees. Some writers later suggested that output steadily increased in the relay-assembly and coil-winding departments because of the motivating effect of being observed, which came to be called the Hawthorne effect. The term is still sometimes used to describe the unintended influence of researchers on the performance of people under observation. However, a reanalysis of the data from other studies at Hawthorne indicated that the employees, who were paid on a piece rate, received added motivation from the recordings of their output. The recordings apparently gave them detailed knowledge of the results of their performance, which has been found a powerful source of motivation (see Parsons, 1974).

The Hawthorne researchers designed a second experiment to eliminate sources of unwanted influence on employees' output. This time just the coil-winding department took part and was divided into two groups of equal size and comparable records of output. The groups worked in separate buildings to reduce the chances of competition. One group received augmented lighting, while the other served as a control group. The experimental group had lighting of three different intensities (24, 46, and 70 footcandles). The control group had illumination of roughly constant intensity (16 to 24 footcandles, including daylight).

The researchers hoped that output would rise faster in the experimental group than in the control group. It didn't. Instead, the two groups increased their output at comparable rates. If the added lighting had had any influence, the experimental group should have improved at a faster rate – unless perhaps the control group worked harder to compensate for their relative disadvantage (see Cook and Campbell, 1983).

The third experiment eliminated daylight, providing complete control over the illumination. The same two groups from the coil-winding department participated. The control group worked in constant illumination of 10 footcandles; the test group started with lighting of 10 footcandles, but lighting was decreased in increments to only three footcandles. Even so, "The efficiencies of both the test and control groups increased slowly but steadily" (Roethlisberger & Dickson, 1949, p. 17) – that is, until the test group finally complained that they could not see what they were doing. Up to that point, they had maintained their efficiency.

In retrospect, the third experiment demonstrated that the task of winding coils could be done in very limited light, perhaps because skilled workers depended more on touch than sight (Boyce, 1981). However, the fact remains that the studies failed to find any effects of illumination on performance.

A subsequent series of "informal" studies showed that employees' perceptions of illumination could be influenced by suggestion, and did not necessarily correspond with objective conditions. The Hawthorne researchers increased the lighting in one department by increments for a few days and asked the workers' opinions of the changes. The workers said they liked the brighter light. Then the light bulbs were replaced with identical bulbs, and the employees commented favorably on the increased light. Similarly, when the light was decreased for a few days, and the bulbs were again replaced with identical ones, employees said the " 'lesser' light was not so pleasant" (Roethlisberger & Dickson, 1949, p. 17). This demonstration left little doubt of the need to modify the mechanistic view of the work environment that prevailed when the project began.

Importance of the Hawthorne studies

The Hawthorne studies represented a turning point in the history of the psychology of the work place, especially in the United States. When the studies began in 1924, psychologists had been showing increasing interest in the influences of the physical environment on performance, particularly influences of noise, temperature, ventilation, and lighting. Large-scale publicly sponsored projects on some of these topics had been initiated. In Britain, the Industrial Fatigue Research Board had initiated a long series of investigations in industrial settings, and had published its first report only 5 years earlier (Vernon, 1919). In the United States, the New York State Commission on Ventilation started its own series of experiments. The Hawthorne studies began as another step in the same direction.

The failure of the Hawthorne studies to find effects of lighting widened the focus of industrial psychology to include employees' attitudes, interpersonal relationships, and groups. The research at Hawthorne continued for about a decade after the experiments on lighting, first investigating the effects of rest pauses in a small groups of relay-assemblers. The researchers discovered that groups of employees developed their own norms, which apparently influenced output. The experiments also demonstrated the importance of the relationship between employee and supervisor and attitudes about other characteristics of jobs. The Hawthorne studies eventually included interviews with thousands of employees at Western Electric Company in an effort to assess their attitudes. This attempt established a precedent for the use of surveys and interviews among employees to study job satisfaction, attitudes, organizational climate, and other issues. The Hawthorne studies had ushered in the human relations movement in management (e.g., Blum & Naylor, 1968), which had eclipsed the physical environment.

Approaches to the psychology of the work place

This section summarizes the major traditions of theory and research on the psychology of the physical environment. Early researchers labeled themselves simply as applied psychologists. Later, specialties developed: industrial-organizational, human factors, and environmental psychology.

Early applied psychology

Psychologists had begun to apply empirical methods of research to the work environment soon after 1900. Some of the earliest studies were conducted in Britain. For instance, Vernon (1919) recorded the monthly output of five English tinplate factories as well as the corresponding outdoor temperatures, for 6 years. He concluded that output fell as temperature rose, on the basis of the data summarized in Figure 3.1. These and other data pointed to the importance of ventilation in factories, and indirectly led to improved working conditions.

The then-prevailing conception of the relationship of person and environment can perhaps best be described as mechanistic and deterministic. Researchers viewed people as analogous to machines that would operate efficiently if well "oiled." The physical environment was seen

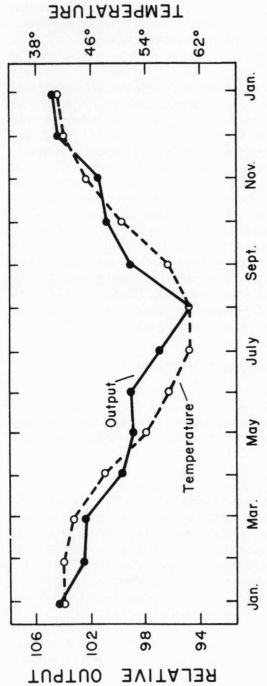

Figure 3.1. Relative production in five tinplate factories; outside temperatures by months of the year. *Source:* Reproduced from Vernon, H.M. (1919). *The Influence of Hours of Work and of Ventilation on Output in Tinplate Manufacture.* Industrial Fatigue Research Board, Report No. 1. London: H. Majesty's Stationery Office, p. 22.

as a source of resistance and of poor performance (e.g., J.J.B. Morgan, 1916). They implicitly assumed that relationship of the environment and its occupants was one sided and deterministic – the environment exerting the influence – and that its effects were uniform from one person to the next. Furthermore, they assumed that they could study the influences of environmental variables in isolation.

Methods of research reflected this mechanistic view of worker and work place. Like Vernon in his study of temperature and output, early researchers singled out specific facets of the environment for study, and measured performance or output under varying environmental conditions. They often relied on the laboratory, studied small samples of people (at least by modern standards), and did not attach enough importance to attitudes and perceptions to assess them. Some of the earliest studies were conducted by industrial psychologists.

Industrial psychology

The first textbook on industrial psychology in the United States (Munsterberg, 1913) included considerable coverage of the physical working environment. Its author later wrote,

The psychologist will never put his confidence in the vague testimonials of the worker himself, but will accompany his self-observations with exact measurements to determine with careful instruments the increase or decrease in efficiency under the influence of lights or sounds or smells or temperatures. (Munsterberg, 1915, p. 191)

This quotation reflects the emphasis on objective measurement, the mistrust of workers' perceptions, and the deterministic view of the environment that pervaded industrial psychology at the time.

Researchers had already begun to conduct laboratory experiments to isolate the effects of environmental conditions on performance. For instance, J.J.B. Morgan (1916) studied the effects of noise by having people work on a decoding task in which they used a kind of typewriter with 10 keys. Participants were alternately exposed to quiet conditions and to loud, irregular noise. Morgan not only measured the speed and accuracy of performance, but recorded participants' breathing and measured the depth of the impressions left as they struck keys on the keyboard. Results indicated that performance was approximately equivalent in noise and quiet, but participants exerted extra effort to maintain their performance in noise (see Chapter 8). Morgan's experiment differed from modern laboratory experiments in that it did not include a randomly assigned control group, and did not include any systematic assessments of participants' attitudes.

Early research in actual work environments had become quite advanced, particularly in Britain, where industrial psychologists sometimes spent months observing factories. They had become sensitive to potential sources of bias. For instance, as representatives of the National Institute of Industrial Psychology noticed:

[S]ometimes the mere presence of the Institute's investigators and the interest which they have shown in the employees' work have served to send up output before any actual changes have been introduced. (Myers, 1925, p. 28)

The Hawthorne studies brought many advances in U.S. industrial psychology, including significant progress in theory and research, but with these changes came a loss of interest in the physical environment. Perhaps the most important change was a widened focus. The Hawthorne studies alerted industrial psychologists to the variety of influences important for workers' experiences on a job. Within a few years, job satisfaction developed into a major topic of research (e.g., Hoppock, 1935), and researchers identified many contributing factors; the physical environment was one such factor, usually called "working conditions" (e.g., Herzberg, Mausner, Peterson & Capwell, 1957).

Post-Hawthorne industrial psychology made extensive use of interviews and questionnaires, in sharp contrast with earlier practice, and developed procedures for assessing attitudes. These methods of research complemented the focus on job satisfaction and permitted investigation of a wider range of topics than before. The physical environment remained only a minor topic of study.

Post-Hawthorne industrial psychology also developed new theoretical models, and went beyond the individual level of analysis. Whereas early industrial psychology concentrated on the individual worker and took a mechanistic, deterministic perspective, after Hawthorne the analogy of worker and machine disappeared. Instead, the worker was viewed as active and communicative, as researchers began to study interpersonal communication, relationships, and groups. The new focus complemented the human relations movement in management (see Chapter 2).

With its widened scope, industrial psychology needed a theoretical model that would encompass many variables at once, a need met by the concept of *systems*. The idea developed in Europe (Bertalanffy, 1950) and was popularized in the United States after World War II (e.g., Wiener, 1948). Systems theory allowed industrial psychologists to picture organizations as entities composed of interrelated elements, and to analyze their dynamics from a new perspective – an organizational level of analysis. Systems theory developed into a dominant view (e.g., Berrien, 1983; Katz & Kahn, 1966; March & Simon, 1958; Seiler, 1967) as the field adopted ideas from sociology (e.g., Weber, 1947) and changed its name to industrial-organizational psychology (see Dunnette, 1976).

From the perspective of systems theory, the physical working environment represented one of many interrelated components of an organization; in Britain it had an explicit role in the concept of *sociotechnical systems* (e.g., Trist et al., 1963). European researchers studied the relationship between physical environments and new forms of social organization, especially autonomous work-groups (Katz & Kahn, 1978; see also Chapter 2). In the United States, however, the physical environment in offices and factories was left to other fields of study, particularly human factors psychology.

Human factors psychology

This specialty combines psychology and engineering in the design of equipment, facilities, and environments (see McCormick, 1976). Its development as a separate discipline came mainly during World War II, as psychologists became involved in the design of military hardware. However, the origins of the field can be traced to earlier times (e.g., Yerkes, 1919). By some accounts, human factors originated as a reaction to scientific management and the tendency to treat workers as pieces of machinery without taking account of psychological effects (Friedmann, 1955). Human factors may have represented a response to some of the same forces that gave rise to the human relations movement in management.

The scope of human factors includes not only the psychological effects of the work environment, but health and safety, physiological effects, information processing, and other topics (see McCormick, 1976; Chapanis, 1976; Parsons, 1976). The European equivalent of human factors psychology is *ergonomics* (*ergos* for "work" and *nomos* for "natural laws"; see Murrell, 1965; Poulton, 1970).

Human factors psychology has sometimes adopted a deterministic model of the effects of the physical environment on the individual but, almost from its inception, relied on a more complex model, called the *man–machine system*. This model pictures the person and his or her equipment as comprising a system, each component exerting reciprocal influence: the operator manipulates the controls, the machine gives feedback, the operator adjusts the controls, and so on (see Chapter 10). This model represents a shift from a mechanistic to an interactive model of the relationship between worker and environment.

Research and practice in human factors have emphasized variability among individuals in developing settings and equipment that comfortably accommodate a wide range of users. The focus has been practical, oriented toward the design of displays, controls, and self-contained environments.

Empirical research from human factors and ergonomics has been varied and eclectic, but specific projects have tended to have a narrow scope. Many studies incorporate precise measurements of a few critical variables. For instance, Burandt and Grandjean (1963) investigated the comfort of chairs in the laboratory by having office workers sit in and rate work-stations with varying combinations of chair-height and work-surface height. The workers' own heights and other dimensions were also measured. Results showed, among other things, that the preferred height of the chair depended on the length of the worker's knee joint, or the distance from floor to knee. The findings suggested guidelines for the design and dimensions of office chairs.

Much of the research from human factors and ergonomics has focused on the relationship of the individual worker and the immediate environment, and most of what is cited in later chapters concerns ambient conditions. However, the 1970s and 1980s have also seen a few studies on the role of the work place in interpersonal relationships (e.g., Conrath, 1973; Allen & Gerstberger, 1973).

Environmental psychology

Apart from those interested in human factors, U.S. psychologists largely ignored the physical environment after the Hawthorne studies, until environmental psychology emerged in the 1960s. It is probably too early to form a clear picture of the influences that fostered it, but environmental psychology seems to represent the convergence of separate developments in the United States and Europe, especially England. Lately, its practitioners have become quite involved in the study of offices (see Wineman, 1982).

Environmental psychology in the United States apparently started as social psychologists began to study connections between physical environments and social relationships (see Festinger, Schachter & Back, 1950; Rosow, 1961). Others studied the role of the physical distance between people in conversations and developed the concept of personal space (Hall, 1966; Sommer, 1969). By 1970, a book of readings had been published by Proshansky, Ittelson & Rivlin (1970).

In Europe, psychologists had continued to study the work environment after the Hawthorne studies, following the precedent set by the Industrial Fatigue Research Board. Ergonomics (the European equivalent of human factors psychology) apparently kept close ties with experimental psychology, and in England the field of applied experimental psychology became prominent. Research on noise, temperature, and lighting continued fairly steadily through World War II and afterward (see Broadbent, 1957a; Pepler, 1963; Weston, 1945). However, after the Hawthorne studies, this research occurred mainly in the laboratory. Perhaps in reaction to the prevalence of laboratory experiments, a group of English researchers in the 1960s began naturalistic studies of buildings as total environments, examining many aspects of buildings at once (e.g., Manning, 1965; Markus et al., 1972). Others investigated workers' responses to open plan offices, which appeared throughout Europe in the 1960s. These studies also assessed many features of the environment (e.g., see Boje, 1971; Boyce, 1973; Lunden, 1972). European environmental psychology issued a book of reading about the same time as its American counterpart (Canter, 1970).

Environmental psychology from its inception operated at multiple levels of analysis. In the United States, it focused on interpersonal and group dynamics. Theories developed around key concepts on the interpersonal use of the environment (Altman, 1975), such as territoriality, personal space, and privacy (see Chapters 11–13). Other theories emerged to describe ecological units consisting of people and their environments (Wicker, 1979; see Chapter 15). European environmental psychology continued to operate at the individual level of analysis, but also employed interpersonal and organizational levels of analysis (e.g., Duffy & Worthington, 1977; Jockusch, 1982).

Research from environmental psychology on work environments has generally focused on offices, particularly open-plan offices (see Wineman, 1982). Whereas basic research on such topics as personal space and crowding has often favored the laboratory, studies related to work environments have usually occurred in natural settings.

Environmental psychology has only recently begun to develop theories specifically for the work environment; but practitioners have tended to take an approach based on ecological concepts. In studying the connection of the physical environment and interpersonal dynamics, they reject a deterministic model (e.g., Duffy, 1974a,b,c) and instead invoke concepts that link people and their settings through social-psychological processes such as privacy, territory, and personal space (Altman, 1973, 1975; Altman & Chemers, 1980).

A recent trend in research in offices favors an approach called *post-occupancy evaluation*, in which buildings are evaluated after their occupants move in. Post-occupancy evaluations assess their occupants' reactions on a wide range of variables, including general satisfaction and specific responses to noise, temperature, lighting, and privacy, communication, and so on (see, e.g., Marans & Spreckelmeyer, 1982b).

Table 3.1. *Approaches to the psychology of the work place*

Fields of psychology	Approaches
	Pre-Hawthorne
Applied psychology	Focus on ambient conditions (especially temperature, noise, lighting)
	Individual level of analysis
	Mechanistic, deterministic model of person–environment relationships
	Post-Hawthorne
Industrial-organizational psychology	Focus on physical environment as component of job satisfaction
	Individual, interpersonal, organizational levels of analysis
	System models (especially sociotechnical system)
Human factors psychology	Focus on equipment design, ambient conditions
	Individual level of analysis, sometimes interpersonal level
	Reciprocal model of person–environment interaction (man–machine system), sometimes deterministic model
Environmental psychology	Focus on offices as total environments
	Interpersonal and organizational levels of analysis
	Social-psychological and ecological models

Such research investigates many properties of a new building all at once, in contrast to studies designed to isolate specific facets of the environment.

In summary, the fields of industrial-organizational, human factors, and environmental psychology have all developed approaches to the psychology of the work place. The approaches use multiple levels of analysis and complex models of the relationship between person and environment. As shown in Table 3.1, the three fields tend to complement one another.

Strategies of empirical research

This section outlines four basic strategies of empirical research used by industrial, human factors, and environmental psychologists to implement their approaches to the study of the office and factory. The strategies include field experiments, laboratory experiments, field studies, and surveys. They differ, but all involve the systematic assessment of behavior or attitudes in relationship to variation in the physical environment.

Field experiments

The purpose of a field experiment is to assess the consequences of a change introduced into the environment, usually on production or workers' attitudes. The environmental variable is treated as a causal agent, and the experiment as a way to determine its effects.

A primitive field experiment involves the introduction of a change into an office or factory, along with measurements taken before and after the change. Before the Hawthorne studies, research on lighting in industry often used this approach and found higher rates of production after the introduction of artificial lighting (see Luckiesh, 1924). Unfortunately, such results do not support the conclusion that the new lighting caused higher productivity – because of the many plausible alternative explanations for a rise in production. The procedure of measurement itself could have caused higher production through motivation spurred by observation. An event that occurred simultaneously with the environmental change could account for higher output, such as a new policy or new manager (see Cook & Campbell, 1983).

The Hawthorne researchers could have conducted a "true experiment" if they had randomly assigned workers to experimental and control groups, introduced the environmental change into just the experimental group, and kept conditions in the two groups otherwise comparable (Cook & Campbell, 1983). They approximated this in the third experiment (in which two groups were isolated in rooms with artificial lighting) but did not use randomly assigned groups, the critical ingredient. A true experiment requires substantial influence in the organization where it is conducted, which is very difficult to achieve. (In fact, we uncovered not one true experiment on the physical environment in an office or factory.)

Laboratory experiments

A true experiment is possible in a laboratory. The conditions of the environment can be precisely controlled; participants can be randomly assigned to treatments; their behavior can be measured under standard conditions. However, the laboratory is artificial, and the participants know it. As a result, their behavior could differ from what they would do in an actual office or factory. The generalizability of laboratory findings to the work place is open to question and can be satisfactorily demonstrated only through field research. For instance, the laboratory experiment by Burandt and Grandjean (1963) had a companion study of the seating habits of workers in their offices, which yielded findings consistent with those from the laboratory.

The principal use of laboratory experiments has been to study individual performance of tasks. We distinguish five types of tasks:

1. *Clerical tasks* involve the identification or transcription of symbols, as in checking numbers or typing, and are roughly analogous to routine office activities done by clerical employees.
2. *Mental tasks* call for the learning or recall of information or its transformation or integration, as in coding or proofreading, and are analogous to duties of professional or technical employees but are rarely as complex.
3. *Motor tasks* call for the coordinated manipulation of materials or controls in response to instructions, signals, or displays, as in the assembly of objects or the tracking of moving objects. (In "compensatory tracking," adjustments of the control that guides a moving object determine not only its position, but its speed or acceleration.) Motor tasks are directly analogous to the operation of industrial equipment (and some military equipment).
4. *Vigilance tasks* call for the monitoring of one or more sources of signals, such as dials or indicator lights. Vigilance resembles some kinds of inspection or monitoring of factory machines.
5. *Dual tasks* call for simultaneous performance of two tasks, usually vigilance plus a motor task. An example in a factory would be operating a machine while monitoring its output.

The five types of tasks are listed in Table 3.2. They are referred to later, particularly in connection with the effects of temperature (Chapter 6) and noise (Chapter 7) on performance.

One difficulty in interpreting the results of a laboratory experiment comes from the possibility that participants react to something in the experimental situation that reveals the researcher's hypotheses, or otherwise seems to call for a particular response. For example, in Morgan's research on noise, participants probably realized they were supposed to be distracted. However, they apparently went to great effort to perform well in spite of the distractions. The noise itself seemed to have little effect, but the way the participants saw the experiment may have motivated them to exert extraordinary effort. (For a discussion of the "demand characteristics" of laboratory experiments, see Aronson & Carlsmith, 1968.)

A second difficulty in drawing conclusions from laboratory experi-

Table 3.2. *Five laboratory tasks for studying performance*

Task	Description	Examples
Clerical	Identifying, recognizing, or transcribing symbols	Letter recognition Number checking Copying
Mental	Learning, recalling, integrating or transforming information; complex calculations	Coding/decoding Mental arithmetic Paired-associate learning Proofreading
Motor	Coordinated manipulation of controls in response to signals or displays; assembly of materials according to instructions	Assembly Pursuit tracking Compensatory tracking Serial reaction-time
Vigilance	Monitoring of one or more sources of signals to detect irregularities	Inspection Three dials 20 dials
Dual	Simultaneous performance of two tasks	Tracking + auditory vigilance Tracking + monitoring visual signal

ments comes from their brief duration. Much of the laboratory research provides less than an hour's exposure to an environmental condition (there are exceptions). Effects that emerge in so short a time might not persist long enough to matter much in a work place, but longer-term effects might not have time to develop in the laboratory.

Although laboratory experiments permit control over the environment and precise measurement of performance of several types of tasks, their artificiality and brief duration might elicit behavior unrepresentative of what occurs in the work place. So, laboratory research is best supplemented with studies conducted in actual offices and factories.

Field studies

A field study, unlike an experiment, only seeks to uncover correlations of properties of environments and behavior or attitudes of the occupants, without trying to identify causes and effects. A field study involves only measurement, not experimental intervention. The most rudimentary field study, a *case study*, involves observation and narrative, and often leads to hypotheses for further investigation. More formal field studies call for systematic measurement of environmental conditions and employees' responses. An example is Vernon's (1919) study involving the measurement of temperature and output in English tinplate factories, which showed that production declined as temperature rose (see Fig. 3.1).

Field studies inevitably leave the possibility that observed correlations reflect the influence of unmeasured factors. In the Vernon study, the association of high temperatures with poor production could reflect the greater difficulty of working with tin at slightly higher temperatures. Or the fact that poor production always came in the summer could reflect a seasonal drop in motivation. However, Vernon also classified the five factories in terms of the adequacy of their ventilation. He found the decline in production with rising temperatures most pronounced in factories with no ventilation, but no decline in the one factory with a new ventilation system. By taking an extra variable into account, Vernon rendered less likely many alternative explanations of the inverse correlation of temperature and production. Even so, unmeasured variables could still account for the observed relationship among temperature, ventilation, and output.

The principal difficulty in field research is the possibility that the procedures of measurement may unintentionally alter the behavior of workers under study. The term "reactivity" refers to changes in behavior attributable to the presence of an observer (see Webb, Campbell, Schwartz & Sechrest, 1966). The Hawthorne researchers apparently induced such a change with their recordings of output, which may have created extra motivation by providing individuals with information about their production (Parsons, 1974).

Surveys

The basis of a survey is a questionnaire or systematic interview that provides workers with a standard series of questions on their work environments. Surveys have been used extensively since the Hawthorne studies to address a wide range of issues concerning the work place.

Surveys usually serve three purposes. First, they provide the opportunity to assess the prevalence of specific attitudes or problems. For example, the national survey of U.S. office workers conducted by Louis Harris and Associates in 1978 found the "ability to concentrate without noise and other distractions" important to a greater proportion of the workers than over a dozen other characteristics of their offices, but less satisfactory than most of the other features. Second, surveys permit assessment of correlations among subjective reactions and reported properties of the environment. For instance, in a small group of office workers, ratings of privacy were correlated with reports of satisfaction with the workspaces (Sundstrom, Burt & Kamp, 1980). Third, surveys provide a vehicle for evaluating a building as a whole by exploring the reactions of occupants on a spectrum of issues, including temperature, air quality, noise, and privacy. For example, Marans & Spreckelmeyer (1982a) surveyed government employees after they had moved into a new federal office building.

A major difficulty in survey research is the possibility of bias in responses to the questions. Bias can come from several sources, including *social desirability* (participants saying what they believe will make them look good or what they think the researcher wants to hear) and the *halo effect* (responding to specific questions in terms of a generalized evaluative reaction; see Babbie, 1975). However, even if a survey could be completely free of bias, its usefulness would be limited by participants' ability to report their own reactions. (Some influences of the work place may occur below conscious awareness, particularly after adaptation; see Chapter 4).

In summary, the strategies of empirical research that have developed for studying the psychology of the work place all have strengths and weaknesses. Field experiments allow the study of people in their offices or factories, and may provide evidence on the influence of an environmental variable on workers' behavior or attitudes. Nevertheless, even carefully designed field experiments may contain some threats to validity. Laboratory experiments provide the control necessary to establish a cause-and-effect relationship between an environmental variable and workers' responses, but the artificial situation and brief duration leave open the question of generalizability of laboratory findings to the work place. Field studies establish relationships among workers' behavior and attitudes in work places but do not allow inference of cause and effect, and may reflect the unintended influences of research procedures on workers. Surveys permit assessment of subjective reactions but are susceptible to bias and are limited by participants' abilities to report their reactions.

Current status of empirical research

The ideal approach to studying the psychology of the work place applies different strategies of research to the same problem, so questions left unanswered by one strategy can be answered by others. For instance, a field study may establish that heat and performance are related in the work place, a laboratory experiment may show a causal connection, a survey could show the prevalence of uncomfortably hot temperatures in a factory, and a field experiment could introduce a modified temperature and assess the impact in an actual work setting.

The research falls short of ideal. For most topics, evidence is scant. Where research is relatively plentiful, it consists primarily of laboratory experiments, as shown in Table 3.3. The list presented certainly underestimates the research evidence. It probably misses some published studies and unquestionably excludes some unpublished or uncirculated work conducted by private organizations. We have no way of knowing how much private or proprietary research has been conducted. However, we do have grounds for speculation. For instance, very little research on the effects of music has been published in the past three decades, but large companies such as Muzak continue to market their programs; they presumably have access to data from their clients and powerful incentives to analyze the data. When a large company does conduct a study, it often commands resources far greater than those available to university researchers, whose studies represent the bulk of those published in professional journals.

One encouraging development of the past two decades is the advent of comprehensive studies of offices that deal with many facets of the environment at once. Early examples occurred in England, combining detailed surveys of office workers with direct, physical measurements of their office buildings (Langdon, 1966; Manning, 1965). This trend continued in studies of open-plan offices (Boyce, 1973; Nemecek & Grandjean, 1973). In the U.S., Steelcase, Incorporated (a manufacturer of office furniture) commissioned Louis Harris and Associates (1978, 1980) to conduct two surveys of representative samples of office workers, and published the results (an exception to the general rule that privately funded research tends to remain private). Another comprehensive project on offices was conducted by a nonprofit research firm called BOSTI (Buffalo Organization for Social and Technological Innovation) with funds provided by the National Science Foundation and other sources. The BOSTI (1980a,b, 1981) project is unique in that it included a survey of the same office workers before and after they changed offices, which allowed the researchers to link changes in the offices with coincident changes in satisfaction and performance. The BOSTI project and other comprehensive studies of offices are cited throughout this book.

In brief, the current status of empirical research on work places is uneven, and in some areas primitive. More evidence almost certainly exists as proprietary data, inaccessible to the public. Encouraging developments include large, federally funded projects like the BOSTI study of offices. Although the research is sparse, it at least allows some tentative conclusions.

Table 3.3. *Empirical studies concerning the physical environment in offices and factories cited in this book*

Level of analysis and topic of study	Numbers of studies cited				
	Laboratory experiments	Field experiments	Surveys	Field studies	Totals
Individual worker					
Lighting	13	1	—	5	19
Windows	—	—	3	1	4
Temperature	27	2	2	8	39
Air quality	4	1	2	1	7
Noise	72	1	1	1	75
Music	9	9	1	—	19
Color	25	—	1	—	26
Work-stations	2	—	5	1	8
Interpersonal relations					
Status	—	—	1	1	2
Personalization and participation	—	1	1	3	5
Ambient conditions and interaction	8	—	—	—	8
Proximity of workspaces and interaction of groups	—	—	—	9	9
Room layout and interaction	11	—	1	9	21
Privacy and enclosure	12	—	4	8	12
Seating arrangement and group discussions	12	—	—	—	12
Organization					
Organization, structural and physical layout	—	—	—	1	1
Comprehensive studies and postoccupancy evaluations	—	2	15	6	23
Totals	183	16	37	54	290

Note: An empirical study is a self-contained report of a research project that involved the collection of original data, with detailed descriptions of methods and results. Each study is counted only once, even if it has multiple experiments. Studies that share a common data base are counted separately if they report separate findings. Studies that deal with more than two of the topics are counted as comprehensive studies.

Summary

This chapter traces the development of empirical research on the psychology of the work place, and provides an overview of the research literature. Before the Hawthorne studies of illumination, researchers held a mechanistic view of the relationship between physical environment and the worker, and conducted limited experiments on the effects of noise, lighting, and temperature on performance. The failure of the Hawthorne studies of illumination and performance led the researchers, and eventually the whole field of industrial psychology, to look beyond the physical environment for influences on workers' behavior. Research began to focus on interpersonal relationships, groups, and workers' attitudes. Industrial psychologists soon adopted the concept of systems to describe organizations; they treated the physical environment as an element of job satisfaction. However, most studies on the influence of the work place after Hawthorne came from human factors psychology and ergonomics, where the concept of the man–machine system described the relationship of worker and work place as a reciprocal one. Environmental psychology developed in the 1960s and 1970s; it built theories on the relationships of the environment and social behavior and developed procedures for assessing the impact of whole buildings.

Current approaches to the study of offices and factories taken in the fields of industrial psychology, human factors, and environmental psychology involve not only the individual level of analysis, but also the interpersonal and organizational levels. Strategies of empirical research have evolved, including field experiments, laboratory experiments, field studies, and surveys. Each method has strengths and weaknesses; the strongest evidence comes from the application of several strategies to one problem. The current status of empirical research on offices and factories leaves much to be desired. It overemphasizes laboratory experiments and underemphasizes field research. For many issues, evidence is scant.

PART II
THE INDIVIDUAL WORKER

This part deals with the first and smallest unit of analysis – the individual worker. This is the longest part, consisting of seven chapters, because research and theory on the influences of the physical environment on the individual have a longer history and larger literature than the other units of analysis. Chapter 4 discusses the psychological processes that mediate the influences of the physical environment on individual performance and satisfaction. The subsequent chapters discuss the ambient conditions separately: lighting and windows (Chapter 5), temperature and air (Chapter 6), noise (Chapter 7), and music (Chapter 8). Chapter 9 concerns color, which is more a feature of the building's interior than of the ambient environment. Finally, Chapter 10 considers the relatively permanent, substantial aspects of work-stations, including equipment, chairs, and floorspace.

4

PSYCHOLOGICAL PROCESSES

This chapter explores psychological processes through which the physical setting might influence the performance or satisfaction of an individual who works in a factory or office. Relevant theories suggest that the physical environment may influence performance through arousal, stress, overload, distraction, or fatigue; these processes are modified by adaptation. Job satisfaction is seen as a combination of many forms of satisfaction, one of which concerns the physical environment.

Influences on performance

Theories of short-term environmental influence

Psychologists have developed theories about four processes that can account for short-term influences of the work place on the performance of individual workers. One pictures the physical environment as a source of psychological *arousal*, which can either help or hinder performance. A related theory treats the environment as a source of *stress*, which includes arousal and can also have either positive or negative effects. Early psychologists also explained adverse effects of the work place in terms of *distraction*, similar to recent theories of *overload*. Early psychologists also relied on the concept of *fatigue* to explain adverse effects of the work place, but fatigue is now more narrowly defined as a physiological consequence of muscular exertion.

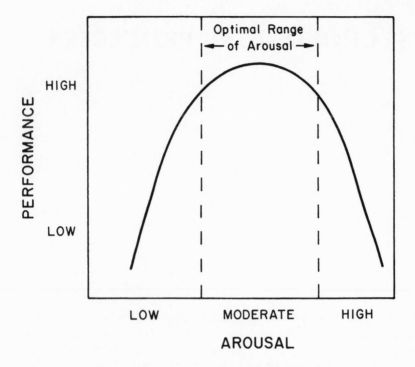

Figure 4.1. The arousal hypothesis: proposed relationship between arousal and performance.

Arousal. The term "arousal," or more recently "activation," refers to a person's general state of alertness or excitation, both physiological and psychological (see Scott, 1966). It ranges from drowsiness through alertness to extreme agitation. Arousal is thought to reflect certain types of electrical activity in the brain (Duffy, 1962). The physiological components of increased arousal include increases in heart rate, blood pressure, blood flow in peripheral vessels, perspiration, skin temperature, and muscular tension – which may or may not occur together (Poulton, 1970). Exactly how arousal works is still not well understood.

The principal hypothesis that relates arousal to performance, advocated by psychologist Donald Hebb (1949) among others, holds that people perform most effectively at moderate levels of arousal. Figure 4.1 illustrates this "inverted-U hypothesis," which shows that performance is thought to decline as arousal departs in either direction from the optimal range. Small deviations from the optimum have relatively minor consequences, but larger departures toward either relaxation or

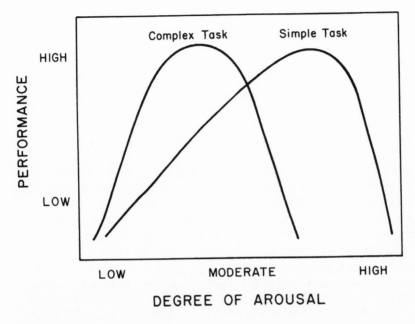

Figure 4.2. The Yerkes-Dodson law: complexity of the task and the relationship between arousal and performance. *Source*: Adapted from Yerkes, R.M. & Dodson, J.D. (1908) The relation of strength of stimulus to rapidity of habit formation. *Journal of Comparative Neurology and Psychology, 18,* 459–483.

excitation are thought to produce sizeable decrements in performance (see also Welford, 1973).

The level of arousal optimal for performance of a task depends upon its complexity, according to an early formulation of the arousal hypothesis. The so-called Yerkes-Dodson Law suggests that optimal arousal is lower for complex tasks than for simple ones (based on Yerkes & Dodson, 1908), as shown in Figure 4.2. If so, someone very stimulated or excited might do well at a simple task like stuffing envelopes, but might not be able to concentrate on a complex task like composing a report.

The importance of arousal for the psychology of the work place comes from the capacity of intense physical stimuli to create arousal, particularly heat and noise. The stimulating properties of a physical environment reflect both physiological and psychological processes. For instance, heat can create arousal at least partly through the body's mechanisms for maintaining constant temperature (see Chapter 6). But an intense environmental stimulus, such as loud noise, bright light, or strong odor, can lead to arousal for psychological reasons, including perceived novelty or threat.

According to the arousal hypothesis, the impact of the physical environment on performance depends upon the demands of the task. If the work place adds to a worker's level of arousal, performance should improve if the added stimulation brings the worker's arousal into the optimal range. On the other hand, performance should decline if the extra arousal takes the worker's arousal beyond what is optimal. For relatively undemanding tasks (such as sewing hems on shirts), added arousal is more likely to help than hurt performance, as such tasks have a relatively high optimal level of arousal. However for complex tasks (such as bookkeeping), added arousal may detract from performance because of the low optimal arousal.

Empirical evidence for the arousal hypothesis comes primarily from the laboratory and is largely consistent with its predictions (see E. Duffy, 1962). However, the hypothesis has rarely been subjected to a full test, in which performance is measured under conditions of low, moderate, and high arousal. Furthermore, research has been complicated by difficulties of measurement, because physiological indexes of arousal do not always correlate with one another (e.g., Lacey & Lacey, 1958). The evidence of increased performance with increasing arousal is considerably stronger than the evidence for a decrease in performance with overarousal (see McGrath, 1976). Even so, the arousal hypothesis is fairly well accepted as an explanation for the impact of physical environments on performance (see Broadbent, 1971; Poulton, 1980).

Environmental stress. Definitions vary, but to a psychologist the term "stress" usually means a form of psychological and physiological mobilization in response to perceived adversity, demand, challenge, or threat. Stress includes arousal and active attempts at coping (see Appley & Trumbull, 1967; Baum, Singer & Baum, 1981; Lazarus, 1966; McGrath, 1970, 1976; Sells, 1970). Stress occurs when people see environmental conditions as threats to their continued well-being or as taxing their abilities to cope. Stress is difficult to distinguish from arousal; the difference seems to be a matter of degree. However, stress usually refers to a stronger or more intense reaction, reserved for environmental conditions perceived as having particularly potent or threatening consequences.

The subjective appraisal of an environment is critical to its capacity to produce stress. For example, a factory worker might experience stress when exposed to air pollution he believes causes cancer. Another worker in the same factory might react to the same air pollution with indifference, if he sees it as benign. Researchers have found stress intensified when aversive or threatening conditions are uncontrollable and unpredictable (Averill, 1973; Glass & Singer, 1972; Baum et al., 1981). Stress also seems to increase with uncertainty about the individual's ability to cope (McGrath, 1976).

If the work place creates stress, the expected influences on performance follow the arousal hypothesis. Mild stress can improve the performance of simple tasks, but may degrade the performance of complex ones. Severe stress may impair a person's ability to do even the simplest task (Berkun, 1964).

One consequence of stress that is not predicted by the arousal hypothesis is a restriction in cognitive capacities that manifests as narrowing of attention. Some research suggests that people under stress show a tendency to focus their attention on the most salient features of their surroundings – especially the source of stress – to the exclusion of other cues they would usually notice. This phenomenon has been demonstrated both in the laboratory (e.g., Solly, 1969) and in natural settings (e.g., Saegert, Mackintosh & West, 1975). The narrowing of attention may even improve the individual's abilities to deal with the cues upon which he or she focuses (Hockey, 1970a), although the evidence that it does is not consistent (see Forster & Grierson, 1978; see also Chapter 7).

An author who worked in a factory provides an example of the narrowing of attention during the first stressful days of the job:

The third morning when I came to work I was much more relaxed and began to notice things that had totally escaped my attention the previous two days. I noticed that a tall wire fence stretched around all but the front of the plant and that I was entering the factory through Gate #9.
As soon as I entered the plant I looked upward and realized just how high the ceiling was. The floor-to-ceiling height was at least twenty feet. Looking out across the floor, I noticed that there were no windows, and that the inside of the plant looked like a giant Quonset hut. . . . I punched in and for the first time was aware of the sound of the clock stamping my card. All this made me realize how nervous I had been. (Balzer, 1976, pp. 17–18)

Balzer initially overlooked the physical environment; his attention focused first on more pressing concerns.

Distraction and overload. Early theorists regarded the environment as a source of distractions, which was regarded as a diversion of attention from the task and as an impediment to performance (e.g., J.J.B. Morgan, 1916). This notion assumes that each person has a finite capacity or span of attention, which he or she allocates according to priority. A distraction, in effect, subtracts attention from that given the task (see Cohen, 1978). Consequences may include lapses in performance during the distractions and shortly afterward, before the individual can shift attention back to the task.

Theories of overload describe distractions as demands that exceed a person's capacities. *Sensory overload* refers to excessive stimulation that contains no specific meaning for the individual (Wohlwill, 1976), such as the flickering of a spent flourescent lamp or the clatter of an air hammer. *Information overload* refers to sources of stimulation that carry meaning and call for a response; overload occurs when information comes faster than it can be assimilated and dealt with (Miller, 1960, 1964).

The tendency for physical settings to contribute to overload probably depends on the worker's job and abilities. In a simple, repetitive job well within the worker's capacities, extra demands created by physical conditions can even aid efficiency if the distractions add to the worker's arousal. But if the job challenges the worker's abilities, any demands added by the environment could lead to decreased performance.

When confronted with sources of overload, a person can cope in several ways, outlined in the theory by psychologist James G. Miller (1960, 1964):

Filtering: selection of only certain signals, usually according to priority
Approximation: simplified response
Queuing: letting work accumulate during periods of demand and catching up during lulls
Omission: failing to respond to certain signals
Error in processing
Escape from the situation

Miller tested the theory in the laboratory, using a machine that presented on a 3- × 4-foot screen a sequence of pictures of arrows in one of eight positions corresponding to points of the compass. The task was to push a button in one of several sets of buttons that corresponded with different positions on the screen, selecting the proper button within the set. When the rate of display was increased to overload participants' capacities, they tried several ways of coping, but preferred filtering – by focusing on selected locations on the screen. When the rate of input exceeded their capacity to watch even one location, they resorted to omission and ignored signals they could not process.

One possible consequence of distraction or overload is what social psychologist Stanley Milgram (1970) called "ignoring low-priority inputs." To the extent that the work place poses salient or compelling distractions, such as loud noise, glaring light, or uncomfortable temperatures, people might attend to the environment and ignore the aspects of their jobs they see as least important. (For example, to a factory worker operating near capacity, overload from the environment might mean paying less attention to the quality of work.)

The physical environment itself may become a low-priority input. A worker may learn to ignore it in favor of other aspects of the job. If so, overload from the environment represents only a temporary influence on performance.

Fatigue. Early psychologists explained the adverse effects of poor ventilation and uncomfortable temperatures as consequences of fatigue. They often distinguished muscular fatigue from mental or psychological fatigue. However, difficulties in defining and measuring mental fatigue led to its abandonment as an heuristic concept (see Blum & Naylor, 1968). Fatigue is now generally defined as a consequence of muscular exertion (Woodson, 1981). Fatigue may occur in work environments that necessitate uncomfortable postures, strenuous movements, or awkward procedures. For instance, a poorly designed typist's chair may force the occupant to hunch over, producing strain on certain muscles of the back and eventually leading to fatigue. The result might be back pain, which could create discomfort, distraction, or even stress and may lead to reduced efficiency through decreased capacity.

In summary, several psychological processes might link the physical environment with effects on individual performance. Intense physical stimuli can create arousal, which may be sufficient to shift a worker's total level of arousal toward or beyond what is optimal for the task, resulting in either better or poorer performance. The environment can create stress by posing a perceived threat to well-being, resulting in arousal and narrowing of attention. The environment can pose distractions, which can overload the worker's capacities, and lead to coping responses such as ignoring low-priority inputs. However, the environment itself may become the low-priority input and lose its distracting quality over time. The work place can create muscular fatigue and discomfort by forcing awkward postures or movements. All these processes involve short-term influences.

Adaptation

Adaptation refers to processes that allow people to adjust to their environments, including changes in perception of the environment and actions taken to cope with problems it creates (see Dubos, 1980). Adaptation is critical to the psychological influences of the work place, because through adaptation the influences of the physical environment change over time.

Perceptual adaptation. One form of adaptation involves a shift in perception after continued exposure to an environment, usually toward evaluating it as less extreme. This can involve automatic physiological processes. Loud sound, for instance, causes a tightening of certain muscles of the inner ear, which attenuates the sensation of the sound. Bright light elicits a constriction of the pupils, permitting less light to enter the eye; darkness elicits a dilation of the pupils, so vision adapts quickly to a variety of conditions of light. Olfactory sensations disappear quickly; some odors can only be detected for a few minutes. The skin shows decreased sensitivity to warm or cold temperatures within a certain range after continued exposure. The metabolism even adjusts after several days in unusually hot conditions, a phenomenon known as *acclimatization* (see McCormick, 1976).

Perceptions of the environment can apparently also shift through purely psychological processes, as outlined in the theory of *adaptation level* (Helson, 1964; see also Wohlwill, 1975). An adaptation level constitutes a psychological benchmark for evaluating new conditions. It represents a person's previous experience with a particular kind of stimulus. The theory suggests that an individual judges any environment against the adaptation level established in the past. For instance, a factory worker accustomed to working around noisy machinery may experience a secretarial typing pool as relatively quiet. On the other hand, an executive used to working in a quiet private office probably has a much lower adaptation level for background sound, and may experience the same typing pool as terribly loud.

The central hypothesis of adaptation-level theory is that after continued exposure to a particular environment, a person's adaptation level gradually moves toward the conditions in that environment (Helson, 1964). What was once extreme and novel is slowly incorporated into a new standard of reference. The stimulus becomes less extreme as the benchmark shifts. The adaptation level hypothesis has substantial empirical support (see the review by Wohlwill, 1975).

The main implication of the adaptation-level hypothesis is that after continued exposure to an environment, its conditions have less capacity to elicit arousal or stress. With stimuli of moderate intensity, adaptation can be very rapid. In one laboratory experiment, loud noise was found to lose its capacity to produce psychological arousal within a few minutes (Glass & Singer, 1972; see Chapter 7). However, as environmental conditions become more extreme – more unfamiliar or different from a person's adaptation level – changes in perceptions may be relatively slight; conditions may still seem extreme after continued exposure. If so, extremely intense conditions might continue to create stress for quite some time (see Bell, Fisher & Loomis, 1978).

Psychologists have described a second form of perceptual adaptation that can occur as a way of coping with stress: *defensive reappraisal.* In this process, environmental conditions first seen as threatening are reevaluated as benign (see Lazarus, 1966). For example, a factory worker who at first fears the effects of air pollution may reevaluate it and decide that if he has stayed healthy this long, the pollution may not be so bad after all. This type of adaptation alleviates potentially disruptive stress. However, if the air pollution actually is harmful, the defensive reappraisal would only blind the worker to its danger.

Behavioral adaptation. Overt behavior designed to cope with an inhospitable environment can make it more bearable or compensate for its unwanted influences. The experiment by J.J.B. Morgan (1916) cited in Chapter 3 provides an illustration. People exposed to loud, distracting noise exerted extra effort to concentrate on their task. In work environments, people can also modify the environment (for instance by changing the thermostat) or alleviate adverse conditions (for instance by wearing extra clothing in a cold office, or wearing ear protectors in a noisy factory). When coping is directed toward changing the environment instead of toward changing the person's responses, the behavior has been called *adjustment* rather than adaptation (see Wohlwill, 1975).

Behavioral adaptation to inhospitable working conditions includes alteration of the environment and alteration of habits of work. Unfortunately, we have little basis for predicting when these occur or what forms they take. A plausible hypothesis is that people need a powerful motivation to maintain peak performance in adverse conditions; in general, workers may establish patterns of work that meet minimal standards while providing maximal comfort.

In brief, adaptation can modify the influence of the physical environment on performance through gradual changes in perception that occur with continued exposure to an environment. Perceptual adaptation can decrease the capacity of an environment to elicit arousal, stress, or distraction. Adaptation may involve coping behavior, but we have little basis for saying just how.

Summary of influences on performance

There are at least five psychological processes through which the physical environment can affect performance. The work place can be a source of arousal, stress, distraction or overload, and fatigue. The influences of these processes upon performance depend on the task. Adaptation is a limiting factor. Performance is also a consequence of motivation and of ability, among other things (see, e.g., Campbell, Dunnette, Lawler & Weick, 1975).

So far, we have analyzed the influences of the work place upon performance by considering its characteristics one at a time, but they do not operate that way. The worker experiences the environment of an office or factory all at once, and many of its effects may be cumulative. For example, moderately loud noise, moderately warm temperatures, and bright lights may each have only minor influences but may combine to have a powerful impact. How they combine and with what effects is not well understood (e.g., Welford, 1973).

Influences on job satisfaction

This section discusses the contribution of the physical working environment to job satisfaction. The first part outlines relevant theories by Abraham Maslow and Frederick Herzberg and a more recent perspective from attribution theory. Next comes a review of empirical evidence on the connection between the physical environment and job satisfaction, and a discussion of psychological processes that might modify the connection.

Theories concerning the physical environment and job satisfaction

The term *job satisfaction* refers simply to the individual's satisfaction with the job, all things considered. Industrial psychologists began to study it in the 1930s (e.g., Hoppock, 1935) and produced a large research literature (Herzberg, Mausner, Peterson & Capwell, 1957; Locke, 1983). One impetus for studying job satisfaction was the long-standing idea that comfortable or satisfied workers perform best on the job. The relationship between job satisfaction and performance has been investigated extensively, but no consistent correlation has emerged (see the review by Porter, Lawler & Hackman, 1975). Research has consistently associated job satisfaction with relatively low rates of absenteeism and turnover (e.g., Davis, 1977), which have practical importance. Lately the term job satisfaction has sometimes been replaced by a more inclusive term, the "quality of work life" (see Korman, 1977).

Job satisfaction represents the individual's attitude toward the job. As an attitude, job satisfaction is a summary evaluative judgment that reflects the individual's past and present experience, including experience with the physical environment. A relatively simple hypothesis on the contribution of the physical environment to job satisfaction is that a worker makes a judgment about the environment, weighs its importance in relationship to other aspects of the job, and arrives at an evaluative judgment about the job. According to this hypothesis, an uncomfortable or harsh environment would detract from job satisfaction (and the quality of work in life in general). A comfortable or pleasing work place would make the job as a whole more satisfying.

Theories on job satisfaction present a more complicated picture. They suggest that in most circumstances people tend to overlook or underemphasize the physical environment in making judgments about their jobs. According to Maslow's and Herzberg's theories, the work place only becomes salient for job satisfaction when it becomes inadequate. In satisfactory environments, people are thought to emphasize other factors in judgments of job satisfaction.

Hierarchy of needs. An influential theory proposed by Abraham Maslow in 1943 suggested that the physical environment can satisfy a person's basic needs but that it only becomes salient when it threatens not to. According to this theory, each person has an ordered hierarchy of needs, the most potent of which are the basic *physiological needs* for air, water, food, and protection from the elements. Once these needs are met, the person focuses on the next step in the hierarchy, which includes *safety and security*. Once the need for a secure environment is satisfied, it loses its motivational force, and the next step takes precedence: needs for *belongingness* or for satisfying social relationships. Finally come *higher-order needs* for recognition and self-development, or self-actualization.

According to Maslow's theory, the physical setting is perceived as most important when it is least satisfactory, that is, when it threatens or fails to meet basic needs. Otherwise, the physical environment psychologically recedes into the background. The theory has great practical appeal but rather limited empirical support (see the review cited by Wahba & Bridwell, 1975).

The main implication of the hypothetical hierarchy of needs is that people in an adequate work environment take it for granted and only pay attention to it when it fails to meet their basic needs. If so, workers may routinely underestimate the extent to which an adequate physical environment contributes to their satisfaction.

Environment as satisfier or dissatisfier. An influential theory proposed by Frederick Herzberg in 1966 classified the physical working environment as a *dissatisfier* (or *hygiene* factor). These terms refer to aspects of the job that lead to dissatisfaction when conditions are inadequate, but only lead to indifference when conditions are satisfactory. Besides the physical environment, the category of dissatisfiers includes pay, supervision, company policies, and other factors not intrinsic to the work. A second category consists of *satisfiers* (or *motivators*), thought to contribute directly to job satisfaction when present, but not to cause dissatisfaction when absent. *Motivators* include the work itself, as well as achievement, advancement, responsibility, and recognition (Herzberg, Mausner & Snyderman, 1959; Herzberg, 1966).

Evidence for the theory came from interviews using the "critical incident" technique, which called for employees to describe incidents that led to exceptionally good or bad feelings about their jobs. Working conditions figured prominently in incidents connected with dissatisfaction, but seldom appeared in satisfying ones (Herzberg et al., 1959). Studies by other researchers using the same method generally supported the theory (see Herzberg, 1966; Locke, 1983). As predicted, physical surroundings emerged more often as sources of dissatisfaction than of satisfaction. Research using methods other than Herzberg's has generally failed to find a clear-cut distinction between dissatisfiers and satisfiers, but the physical setting has generally emerged as a dissatisfier (see Locke, 1983).

Herzberg's theory, like Maslow's, suggests that people take for granted an adequate physical environment, which only affects job satisfaction by failing to create *dis*satisfaction. Both theories reject the idea that a pleasant or satisfying environment can contribute in a positive way to job satisfaction, although office designers would probably argue the point.

Attributions and the environment. Attribution theory suggests that people ignore the physical working environment because they are used to thinking of people, not environments, as the major sources of influence on their experience. Attribution theory is a family of related theories on the cognitive processes by which people identify the causes of everyday events (see, e.g., Harvey, 1981). One theorist suggested that people tend to make a "fundamental attribution error" – that is, they underestimate the role of the situation and overestimate the role of peoples' personalities in influencing behavior (Ross, 1977). If so, people may overlook the physical environment, as it is a relatively static backdrop for the more interesting and varied activities of other people (R. Taylor, 1982). By implication, the tendency of workers to rate the physical environment as relatively unimportant to their job satisfaction could reflect their habits of attribution more than the actual contribution of the physical environment.

Research linking the physical environment with job satisfaction

Studies of job satisfaction. Early research on job satisfaction identified the physical environment as one of several characteristics of the job associated with general satisfaction. The physical environment was usually considered as a whole and was called "working conditions" (which sometimes also included hours of work). In many surveys, participants ranked the importance of each of several characteristics of the job, including working conditions, work itself, pay, and other features. In a summary of 16 such studies that involved a total of more than 11,000 employees, researchers calculated the median rank given the importance of each of 10 job factors, with "working conditions" split into two components – hours of work and others. Working conditions excluding hours ranked eighth in the list, after job security, opportunity for advancement, company and management, wages, intrinsic aspects of the job, supervision, and social aspects of the job (Herzberg et al., 1957, p. 44).

The ranking of working conditions showed greater inconsistency than that of any other job characteristic. Female workers ranked working conditions as more important than men did, and factory workers gave higher rankings than office workers did.

That workers considered their working conditions as relatively unimportant to their job satisfaction is consistent with the theories of Maslow and Herzberg, and with attribution theory. The substantial inconsistency in the ranking of working conditions from one study to another suggests that the perceived importance of the physical environment varied, perhaps with its adequacy and the extent to which workers took it for granted.

Surveys on office environments. At least four surveys among office employees included items that focused specifically on the environment. They generally confirm the early finding that physical working conditions are consistently associated with job satisfaction. As in earlier studies, the environment ranked lower in importance than did many other job characteristics.

A survey of 2,287 London office workers asked them to select from a list of 10 job factors the two most important for "making a job enjoyable and satisfying." In order of popularity these included interesting work (32% of the participants), responsibility (16%), good pay (14%), nice people to work with (13%), plenty to do, security, a pleasant office (4%), a comfortable and convenient office (2%), convenient location of work, and short hours (Langdon, 1966).

A survey of 450 office workers in Sweden included employees from nine office buildings, who ranked 10 job factors on their contribution to contentment in the office. Office environment was seventh (Lunden, 1974).

The magazine *Psychology Today* polled its readers and reported on a sample of 2,300 respondants, predominantly from white-collar jobs. They rated the importance of 18 characteristics of their jobs. The item rated most important was a job that contributes to self-respect. Physical surroundings ranked last on the list. Participants also rated the satisfaction they experienced from each of the 18 factors; physical environment ranked thirteenth (Renwick & Lawler, 1978).

A survey in the United States conducted by Louis Harris and Associates (1978) included a sample of 1,047 office employees who rated the importance of 19 factors in their jobs. Highest ranking was clarity of scope and responsibilities of the job. Two items on the physical environment ranked fourteenth and seventeenth in the list and were rated "very important" by 45% and 37% of participants. These items concerned adequate work surface, chair, storage, and furniture, as well as pleasant physical surroundings in the office.

In all four surveys, office workers attached only minor importance to the work place for their job satisfaction. However, they probably had fairly adequate physical working conditions. Had their basic needs not been met or been threatened by their office environments, these workers might have seen greater importance in the work place.

Field studies. Several studies of office workers included separate measures of satisfaction with the workspace and job satisfaction, and assessed the correlation between the two. For example, Zalesny, Farace & Kurchner-Hawkins (1983) studied 420 state office employees and reported a significant correlation between job satisfaction and satisfaction with the physical environment. Similar correlations were reported by BOSTI (1981), Ferguson (1983), Sundstrom, Town, Brown, Forman & McGee (1982a), and Sundstrom et al. (1980). These studies consistently suggested an association between satisfaction with the environment and job satisfaction.

The BOSTI (1981) project reported that among people who changed offices, shifts in environmental satisfaction were associated with changes in job satisfaction. Specifically, among those whose environmental satisfaction increased, job satisfaction stayed roughly constant. For others it decreased, and the decrease was greatest among those for whom environmental satisfaction had decreased as well.

In summary, theories that link the work place with job satisfaction suggest that the physical environment is either seen as a source of dissatisfaction or is taken for granted. Research suggests that workers consider the physical environment a factor in their job satisfaction, but on average, one of the lesser ones. Physical working conditions clearly represent a component of job satisfaction. Each facet of the physical environment may be seen as contributing to satisfaction with the physical working conditions, as shown in Figure 4.3. The main implication of this diagram is that any single facet of the physical environment is unlikely to influence job satisfaction very much by itself, unless it is a very potent source of dissatisfaction. However, the physical environment as a whole is important to job satisfaction.

Processes that modify the influence of work places on job satisfaction

Equity. One process that can amplify the influence of the physical environment is equity, or the perception of fairness in a social exchange (see J. S. Adams, 1965; Berkowitz & Walster, 1976). In the case of the work place, the exchange occurs between employee and employer. In evaluating equity, the employee considers what he or she receives in return for the investment of effort and expertise. The evaluation is based on a comparison with some other person in similar circumstances, or in reference to some ideal standard. The employee experiences an acceptable degree of equity if the ratio of investments to returns matches the standard set by the comparison person or standard of reference. The work environment represents part of what the worker gets in exchange for his contribution to an organization, and may add to job satisfaction if seen as better than deserved. An apparently inequitable environment, regarded as insufficient or substandard, may create greater dissatisfaction than expected from its physical properties. In a similar vein, psychologist J.A.C. Brown (1954) wrote:

[W]orkers complain about working conditions, not because they are objectively bad, but because they are worse than they need be in the circumstances. If it is in the nature of the job to be dirty or unpleasant, few complaints may be received, but if the job is avoidably dirty or unpleasant, there will be justifiable resentment. (p. 197)

Workers may even complain about apparently adequate conditions if they feel they deserve better.

Equity theory implies the possibility of a tradeoff of work environment for money, or vice versa. If the pay is attractive enough, people may feel very little inequity at having to endure poor conditions. Conversely, if the working conditions are attractive enough, people may endure low pay more cheerfully. An example of a trade of environment for money occurred at the office of Lincoln Electric Company, a small firm with a liberal profit-sharing plan. Employees worked in a crowded, dingy office without air-conditioning, music, or recreation facilities and surrounded by old furniture. Despite these short-comings, morale was high, pro-

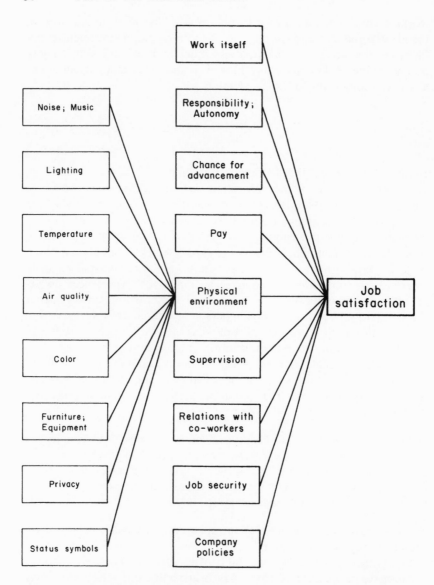

Figure 4.3. The physical environment as a component of job satisfaction.

duction was above the industry's standard, and the company's last layoff had been 19 years earlier. The workers could improve their physical environment, or they could take home the money as cash bonuses. They took the cash (CBS television news special, "Work in America," July 5, 1977).

A tradeoff can involve other compensations besides money. For instance, the camaraderie of a group might offset miserable working conditions; in fact, shared adversity might even add to the cohesiveness of the group. An example occurred in a London slaughterhouse, where a group of six women worked in a small, cold, dimly lit basement room. Their job was to sort the organs of slaughtered pigs. The floor was covered with blood and viscera. Any visitor found the stench was awful, but the women were cheerful and contented in their small room and vigorously resisted a well-meant attempt to have them transferred to a more comfortable environment (Brown, 1954).

Adaptation. Another process that might modify the influence of the physical environment on job satisfaction is adaptation, which can lead to shifts in perception of an environment. With continued exposure, a work place may lose its novelty. One psychologist theorized that people prefer slight novelty – or small departures from adaptation level – over accustomed conditions (Haber, 1958). If so, then after awhile in a constant environment people prefer something slightly different. By implication, practically any minor physical change in a work place should bring a positive reaction, including repainting, new furniture, slight shifts in layout, new decorations, and so on. If satisfaction with the environment does rise, however, the effect is bound to be short lived.

Summary

This chapter identifies four psychological processes thought to account for influences of the physical environment on an individual's performance:

1. *Arousal*, or the general level of physiological and psychological excitation, may change as a consequence of intense physical stimuli, such as noise or heat. The effect on performance depends on whether the added stimulation brings the worker's level of arousal into the range of arousal optimal for the task. If so, it may benefit performance; with over-arousal, performance may suffer.
2. *Stress* may occur in response to conditions seen as threatening to the individual's well-being; stress brings arousal and possibly narrowing of attention, which may adversely affect performance.
3. *Distractions* from the physical environment may divert attention from the task or add lead to overload of the individual's capacities. Workers may cope with overload by ignoring low-priority aspects of their jobs.
4. *Fatigue* may result from poorly designed equipment and may reduce a person's comfort and level of efficiency.

Influences of the work place on performance that occur through these processes are modified by adaptation, including shifts in perception after continued exposure, which can reduce the occurrence of arousal or stress, and shifts in activities or levels of effort.

The physical environment represents one of several facets of the job that contribute to job satisfaction. According to Maslow's theory, the work place is only a factor when it fails to satisfy basic needs. In Herzberg's theory, the work environment functions as a "dissatisfier," capable of creating dissatisfaction if inadequate, but leading only to indifference to the physical environment if adequate. Consistent with these theories, surveys have found that workers place less importance on the physical environment than on other characteristics of their jobs.

The connection of the work place with job satisfaction may be modified by perceptions of equity and by adaptation. If the work place is seen as either over-equitable or under-equitable in comparison to what a worker believes he or she deserves, the influence on job satisfaction may be greater than expected from the physical properties of the work place alone. Through adaptation, an environment may lose its novelty after continued exposure and become taken for granted.

Practical considerations

For the manager or designer interested in the influences of the physical environment on performance, the key concept is adaptation. Theories of environmental influences of ambient conditions are based on short-term psychological processes that may disappear after adaptation has taken place. People can apparently adapt to many conditions. Because of adaptation, the ambient environment is perhaps better viewed as an influence on comfort than a contributor to performance.

Workers apparently take their physical settings for granted unless they have complaints. This may be somewhat demoralizing to facilities managers, because they are likely to hear more about their mistakes than about their successes. (But no news is not necessarily good news, as people can probably adapt to poorly designed environments.)

The environment clearly represents a component of job satisfaction. However, as a consequence of adaptation, the occupants of an environment may be unaware of many of the qualities that affect their satisfaction. This is a particularly thorny problem for the practitioner, because the occupants of an environment are also the best source of information regarding its adequacy. One solution is to systematically observe the behavior of the occupants of an office or factory; another is to ask specific and probing questions. (Unfortunately, behavioral observation and in-depth interviews are both costly and time consuming.)

Any change in the physical environment is likely to attract the occupants' attention, at least for awhile. If it is a welcome change, people may report greater satisfaction with the environment. In any event, change will probably create some disruption until adaptation is underway. It is immediately after a change in the environment that changes in satisfaction or performance are most likely to appear. However, they will probably be short lived.

Workers may tend to take their environments for granted, but they are unlikely to ignore apparent inequities. Particularly for people who have the same job or rank, if one person lacks an amenity that others have, the relative deprivation may be a source of great dissatisfaction.

Managers may decide to use the work place itself as a source of compensation by rewarding good performance through improved workspaces (see Chapter 11). For instance, an office worker who has had a particularly good year may get carpeting for her office or an extra table. Such items may lead to greater satisfaction for the recipient but could also create perceptions of inequity among co-workers who do not receive them.

5
LIGHTING AND WINDOWS

Lighting in offices and factories is important for the performance of most jobs, but it is especially critical in jobs that call for visual discrimination of small details. Lighting may also affect employee satisfaction with the work environment, which may depend to some extent on whether the light comes from windows.

This chapter briefly outlines the history of lighting in the work place – essentially an account of rising standards – and reviews the research on its role in employee performance and satisfaction. A separate section discusses windows and their contribution to illumination. The research suggests that lighting can add to performance and satisfaction but follows a principle of diminishing returns: each added increment of intensity of light brings less and less benefit, until eventually glare introduced by bright light creates discomfort. Research concerning windows suggests that workers value them both for daylight and for a view outdoors.

Rising standards of lighting

Until the advent of electric lights in the 1880s, lighting in factories and offices came primarily from daylight, and buildings were designed accordingly (see Chapter 2). Many factories occupied single-story structures with windows and skylights to admit sunlight. Office buildings had multiple stories, but their width was limited to about 60 feet because sunlight would not penetrate beyond 30 feet from the windows. However, experts recommended office buildings no more than 40 feet wide, with windows on two sides, for best "natural daylight" (Leffingwell, 1925).

Reliance on sunlight also affected the interiors of office buildings. For instance, the "borrowed light partition" evolved in an attempt to illuminate interior offices and corridors:

Of course the boss had to have his private office next to the window with the light coming over his shoulder. In some cases his secretary worked in his office, too, but usually she and other clerical help used the reception room between the office and the corridor wall. To get maximum light into the reception room, the partition dividing it from the private office was glassed. Sometimes this glass was opaqued to prevent people waiting in the reception room from seeing into the private office. In the early buildings even the corridor walls had glass in them to "borrow" light from the offices for the public corridors. This came to be called a "borrowed light partition." (Shultz & Simmons, 1959, p. 130)

Electric lights became commercially available during the 1890s and brought the potential for factories to be adequately lit regardless of size or shape. Factories soon appeared in the United States without windows or skylights; they were electrically lit and were shaped entirely to suit manufacturing processes. Windowless factories became customary but were not completely accepted. For instance, the architect Gropius reacted against the trend toward windowless factories by designing the Fabus Fabric Factory in 1911 with a glass exterior supported by a steel framework; he later advocated "transparency" in all buildings.

One impetus for the rapid spread of artificial lighting through factories of the early 1900s came from reports of dramatic rises in efficiency after its installation. One writer catalogued cases in which management claimed that added lighting had increased production as much as 79% and had decreased accidents as much as 60% (Luckiesh, 1924). By another account,

Where investigations had been made under controlled conditions, output has been found to increase much more rapidly than the cost of the improved lighting. For example, in a series of experiments conducted by the Commonwealth of Edison Company of Chicago it was found [that] the greatly improved lighting increased output in several operations as much as 8 to 27 percent. The average increase was 15 percent, while the average cost of the improvements amounted to only 5 percent of the payroll for the period. (Hollingworth & Poffenberger, 1926, pp. 169–170)

Electric lighting in factories was soon regarded as a good thing that could not be overdone – for employees' morale as well as production.

Well-lighted surroundings promote cheerfulness. . . . There is no danger of overlighting in this respect. Certainly working men are depressed by improper and inadequate lighting. (Luckiesh, 1924, p. 18)

Some employees even demonstrated their preference for well-lighted interiors by removing the shades from lamps in poorly lit factories, apparently willing to tolerate the glare of exposed light bulbs in return for less gloom (Weston, 1952).

Not until the 1930s did electric lighting become commonplace in offices in the United States. Windows remained the principal source of lighting until the technology of electric air-conditioning allowed large interior spaces to be kept at comfortable temperatures all year (see Chapter 6). When electric lighting finally did gain acceptance in offices, it spread quickly. One impetus came from the desire to use office space in which the sunlight was blocked by nearby tall buildings (see Chapter 2).

During the 1930s, electric utility companies in the United States mounted an "educational campaign" on the importance of lighting for good working conditions. (An unpublicized motive may have been to increase the sales of power.) Until then, most experts agreed that lighting of about 5 footcandles was sufficient for reading and office work (Shultz & Simmons, 1959). Within a few years, the standard for lighting in the United States doubled and redoubled, to 25 footcandles and more. (See McCormick, 1976, regarding the footcandle.) Some experts even urged the use of 500-watt lamps, assuming that if bright light was a good thing, more was better. Even the practical limit set by the heat of incandescent lamps disappeared during the 1940s with the availability of inexpensive fluorescent lamps.

As electric lighting gained acceptance in offices, architects designed high-rise buildings with exteriors of glass that maximized the expanse of windows. Glass-sheathed office towers began to appear during the 1930s, and grew increasingly more common (Wotton, 1976).

World War II brought further increases in lighting. Some factories in the United States and England used up to 200 footcandles of illumination, partly because of the complex assembly tasks involved in the production of aircraft and munitions and partly because managers in some wartime factories in which the windows were "blacked out" believed the extra light lifted morale.

Soon after the war, many industrialized countries established standards for lighting. As shown in Table 5.1, standards in the United States are much higher than others. The standards were adopted in 1958 by the U.S. Illuminating Engineering Society, on the basis of extrapolations from laboratory experiments (Blackwell, 1959), and they created considerable controversy among experts on lighting (see Faulkner & Mur-

Table 5.1. *Standards in eight countries for illumination of "difficult" seeing tasks*

Country	Illumination (footcandles)[a]
Australia	28–65
Belgium	23–54
England	28–65
Finland	28
France	28–65
Sweden	28
Switzerland	14–28
United States	93–462

[a] Converted from lux (1 footcandle equals approximately 10.8 lux).
Source: Rapoport, A. & Watson, N. (1967). Cultural variability in physical standards. *Transactions of the Bartlett Society*, 6, 63–83.

phy, 1973). Despite criticisms, however, the Illuminating Engineering Society continued to recommend essentially the same standards.

Whereas in the United States standards have focused on artificial lighting, in Britain they have centered on natural light, or "daylighting." A law called the Permanent Supplementary Artificial Lighting Installation (PSALI) mandated that lighting from windows be the dominant feature of illumination in many work places, supplemented by artificial light where necessary (see Collins, 1975, p. 56). No such law prevails in the United States.

In summary, the past century has witnessed a shift from dependence on daylight to reliance on electric light. The standards for lighting have risen since the 1930s, especially in the United States, where they are higher than those of most other industrial nations.

Lighting and performance

Research on the influence of lighting on performance has emphasized the intensity or brightness of light and the visibility of details. Studies of the quality and distribution of lighting point to the problem of glare, or bright light coming from the object a person is trying to see or from the surrounding area. Glare makes seeing difficult and uncomfortable. This section reviews research on the relationship between lighting and performance of tasks common in office work or assembly. (For a review of research on specialized tasks, see Boyce, 1981.)

Intensity of lighting

Research on the intensity of lighting has followed three more or less distinct phases. The earliest studies were conducted in factories, and linked lighting and performance often enough to prompt further study. A second phase consisted of laboratory studies on visual performance. The laboratory work made some major advances, but eventually drew criticism for its artificiality. More recently, a third phase of research involves attempts to use tasks representative of those in actual work places.

Field studies. While much early research on the brightness of lighting consisted of primitive field experiments in factories (Luckiesh, 1924), the Industrial Fatigue Research Board in England sponsored some careful field studies that linked performance and lighting. One early study concerned a group of silk-weavers, whose only source of light was the windows in their small building. The brightness of the daylight varied with the time of year; sunlight decreased as winter approached, then increased with the approach of spring. Elton (1920) noted the brightness of the daylight inside the building each day and recorded the silk-weavers' daily production of cloth. Production paralleled the brightness of light. Output generally declined during the first 4 weeks of the study, while daylight decreased, but output rose over the following 10 weeks, while daylight increased. Unfortunately, the correlation between output and lighting was far from conclusive, as the dip in production during the winter months may have reflected a seasonal trend independent of the changes in light.

A later study of English linen weavers incorporated hourly measurements of the intensity of daylight and hourly recordings of output, and found that production declined markedly with decreasing daylight. The light approached 2 footcandles in the late afternoons (Weston, 1921). Similar results emerged from a field study of typesetters (Weston & Taylor, 1926). Taken together, the English field studies suggested that, for jobs requiring the visual discrimination of details, performance deteriorated when lighting became inadequate to discern the details. Similarly, European research has shown an association between increased intensity of lighting and improved performance (Sucov, 1973).

Laboratory studies. An early researcher in the United States wondered whether lighting affected performance beyond what would be expected from the effects of lighting on the visibility of details, and found that it did. Students at Harvard University took part in a 3-year laboratory experiment. Once or twice per week for a semester the students did multiplication problems, tapped a telegraph key, learned nonsense syllables, performed a complex reaction-time task, and did other tasks under light of varying hue and brightness. Color had no effects, but participants performed more quickly under relatively bright light during multiplication, a "tapping test," and a test of reaction time (Pressy, 1921). The results cannot easily be explained in terms of visibility of details, but the brighter light may have created arousal, which could account for faster work. Later research largely ignored the possibility that bright light contributes to performance for reasons other than visibility of details.

The Hawthorne studies on illumination (described in Chapter 3) apparently discouraged researchers in the United States for awhile. However, a line of laboratory research was soon established in Britain.

The *analytic approach* assumed that the visual difficulty of tasks could be quantified in terms of size of detail and amount of contrast, that appropriate brightness of lighting could be determined for each level of visual difficulty on the basis of laboratory tests, and that actual jobs could eventually be analyzed for visual difficulty (Beutell, 1934). This approach was pioneered by Weston in 1945, a British researcher who used a laboratory task that called for discrimination of visual stimuli, called "Landolt rings." (These are small circles, each with a small gap pointed toward one of the eight points of the compass.) Participants received sheets of paper printed with Landolt rings and were asked to mark the rings with gaps pointed in a specific direction. The rings came in varying sizes, with varying contrasts produced with shades of gray. (*Contrast* is defined as the difference in the amount of light reflected from a stimulus and its background.) Lighting also varied, from about 5 footcandles to more than 500 footcandles. Weston assessed performance by measuring speed and accuracy in marking certain rings.

Results of the laboratory experiments conformed to a principle of diminishing returns. Added illumination did produce improvements in performance, which became smaller with each increment in lighting. The benefits of added illumination were most pronounced for difficult variations of the task (small details and minimal contrast), but negligible for the least difficult variations (large details, high contrast). Changes in contrast produced marked shifts in performance, especially in discriminating small details. Later research confirmed the early laboratory findings, and demonstrated the importance of *age* in the effect of illumination on performance. In one experiment, with light ranging from about 20 to 150 footcandles, performance by 150 adults on a series of

Landolt rings increased with added illumination. However, the effect was slight for people aged 16 to 30 years and pronounced for people aged 46 to 60. Performance by older participants fell short of that of younger participants at lower levels of lighting, but approximately equaled it in brighter light (Boyce, 1973).

The *"visibility" approach* represented an attempt to extend Weston's analytic technique to develop a single numerical index of visibility that could be used to establish standards for lighting in the work place. Its originator, H. R. Blackwell (1959), criticized earlier research for failing to hold constant the amount of time spent viewing the Landolt rings. To correct this deficiency, he designed a procedure that controlled viewing time. Participants sat in front of a translucent screen onto which lighted disks of a certain size were projected for periods as brief as one-hundredth of a second, with contrast and lighting varied. A typical participant completed several hundred trials. The task was to select one of four periods of time during which a disk appeared on the screen. From the participants' accuracy in detecting stimuli at the threshold of vision, Blackwell developed an index of visibility. The index was based mainly on size of detail, contrast, and brightness of lighting.

Blackwell's research found essentially the same relationship between lighting and performance found in earlier studies. As visual difficulty increased, through smaller details and lower contrasts, more and more light was required to sustain a constant level of performance. Added increments of light brought smaller and smaller gains in performance (see Blackwell, 1959; Blackwell & Smith, 1970).

Blackwell's early research (1959) is important because it formed the basis for the U.S. Illuminating Engineering Society's controversial standards of lighting in the work place, which differed considerably from those of other countries. The index of visibility was based on laboratory data and extrapolated to tasks in factories and offices, where it was used to recommend illumination. For example, the standard for general office work was 100 footcandles.

The standards have been criticized on several grounds. One critic pointed to inconsistencies, for instance that the lighting standard for the reading of printed text with good contrast was far lower than the standard for general office work (Murrell, 1965, p. 304). Others noted that small errors in the laboratory data would lead to large differences in recommended lighting (see Faulkner & Murphy, 1973). However, perhaps the most serious criticisms concern the artificiality of the testing situation. The visibility method involved flashed exposures of fractions of a second, whereas in practice people usually can look at their work for much longer periods of time. The research involved the recognition of a single symbol or detail, while most office and factory tasks provide many details and redundant information. Furthermore, whereas the visibility method called for viewing a target from a single angle and distance, in practice people usually can move their heads to change the angle or distance of vision, and often can move their work or the light. In brief, the direct generalizability of findings from laboratory studies to the work place is questionable, as are the standards of illumination that resulted in the United States.

Later research used tasks that more closely resembled office work. For example, a series of seven experiments called for participants to perform actual office tasks under varying levels of illumination. The tasks included check-reading, reading and typing, a standard reading test, proofreading, and number verification. A total of 58 adults aged 17 to 69 years participated in seven experiments involving more than 2,000 trials. Lighting was measured as *luminance* (the intensity of light reflected back from the visual stimulus to the viewer) and varied from 0.3 to about 900 footlamberts (which probably corresponded to roughly 0.5 to 500 footcandles of illumination). The results, shown in Figure 5.1, suggest progressively smaller improvements in performance with increments in illumination, which held for both younger and older participants (S. Smith, 1978). However, the tasks varied in visual difficulty, and performance of the less difficult tasks probably benefited much less from added light than did the more difficult ones.

Another study using actual office tasks showed that the effects of lighting depended on the age of the worker. Participants, aged 19 to 27 years or 46 to 57 years, worked on clerical tasks during 18 sessions, with illumination of 50, 100, or 150 footcandles. Performance on a number-locating task increased with the brightness of the lighting, but the increase was greater for older workers, whose scores improved 11.7% as lighting rose from 50 to 150 footcandle levels. Participants also rated the adequacy of the light; younger workers found the lowest level of illumination almost as satisfactory as the highest level, but older workers rated the lowest level of lighting much less satisfactory than the highest level (Hughes, 1976).

A third study of office tasks used the laboratory-derived method of flashed presentations. Researchers developed a series of typical office tasks such as reading a handwritten insurance form. To assess the visibility of the tasks, they flashed small segments of each task into view and asked for recognition of a single symbol. The results suggested lighting standards for the tasks, which are limited by the artificial viewing conditions (Henderson, McNelis & Williams, 1975; McNelis, Williams & Henderson, 1975).

One research project simulated a factory task in which participants watched metal washers on a moving conveyor belt and identified de-

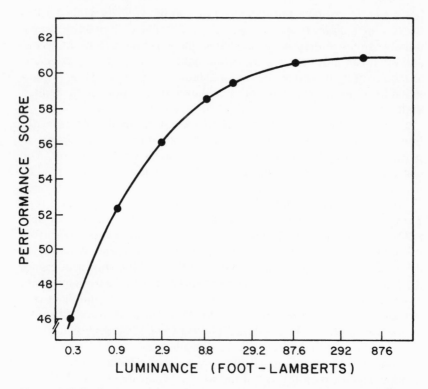

Figure 5.1. Performance of a clerical task as a function of lighting. *Source*: Reproduced with permission from Smith, S.W. (1978). Is there an optimum level of light for office tasks? *Journal of the Illuminating Engineering Society*, 7, 255.

fective ones. Illumination ranging from 20 to 150 footcandles had no effects on performance, regardless of participants' ages (Boyce, 1973). The task of inspecting washers was apparently not visually taxing, probably because the three-dimensional stimulus was moving, which made the details easy to see. Added light did not help at all.

Researchers have generally ignored the hypothesis that bright light stimulates performance for reasons other than the visibility of details. One piece of evidence tangentially relevant to the question comes from a field experiment at a university. Sanders, Gustanski, and Lawton (1974) varied the lighting in an area where students gathered, recorded the noise level resulting from conversation, and found the area quieter in dim light. Louder talking in bright light could reflect arousal, but it could also reflect a feeling of intimacy in dim light as well as a lowering of voices to discuss relatively personal topics. If lighting does produce arousal, and the augmented performance in laboratory studies reflects this influence, the effects could be short lived, because of adaptation. This is an empirical question, yet to be answered.

In summary, research on the intensity of lighting suggests that performance of tasks involving visual discrimination of details deteriorates when the light is not bright enough. Laboratory tasks show that the visibility of details declines with decreasing contrast and size of details. Performance increases with added light, but lighting follows a principle of diminishing returns, that is, each increment in brightness of light brings less benefit, and the benefits are smallest for the least difficult tasks. Older workers apparently need more light than younger ones, especially for visually difficult tasks. There is little evidence that lighting contributes to performance for reasons other than visibility.

Quality and distribution of light

Research has seldom examined the importance of the quality of lighting for performance. However, one experiment demonstrated a critically important phenomenon for the distribution of light: an involuntary *phototropism*, or attraction of gaze to bright sources of light. Hopkinson & Longmore (1959) took unobtrusive photographs of people's eyes as they viewed charts of Landolt rings while sources of light were introduced into their fields of vision. The photos showed that "sharp, intensely bright points of light distracted the attention in a series of jerky eye movements, whereas less bright but larger areas caused more eye movements of longer duration" (p. 321). If bright sources of light can cause distractions, the consequences for some tasks may include impaired performance. For instance, bright overhead lights in the field of vision of draftsmen may cause them to look up and lose track of their drafting.

Phototropism also has beneficial implications for performance: if a person's work is more brightly lit than the surrounding areas, his or her gaze may be naturally drawn to the work. This point is taken into account in recommendations concerning the design of lighting. For instance, current practice in offices calls for a 3 to 1 ratio of brightness of the task to the surrounding area (see McCormick, 1976).

Perhaps the most important consequence of bright light in the field of vision is *glare*, created by light of brightness "sufficiently greater than . . . [that] to which the eyes are adapted to cause annoyance, discomfort, or loss in visual performance and visibility" (McCormick, 1976, p. 324). Glare can be *direct*, from a radiant source of light, or *reflected* from a shiny surface, such as the screen of a video display terminal. Other types of glare sometimes are distinguished: "discomfort glare" allows visibility of the task, and "disability glare" does not (e.g., Cakir et al., 1980). While glare represents a potential source of impaired performance, much of the research evidence related to glare comes from studies of satisfaction.

Lighting and satisfaction

Lighting seems to be one of the features of the work place that people take for granted and ignore, unless they have a reason to notice it. Artificial illumination probably represents one of the more satisfactory aspects of modern offices and factories, but by one account, "whether lighting be good or bad, it is one of the last things people remark upon unless prompted" (Manning, 1965, p. 24; see also Manning, 1968). When researchers have asked people about their lighting, the typical finding has been that more is better, up to a point. As in the studies of performance, satisfaction seems to follow a principle of diminishing returns. However, lighting can be excessive, and can create glare and dissatisfaction. Evidence comes from surveys of office workers, field studies, and laboratory experiments.

Surveys of office workers

The survey of U.S. office workers by Louis Harris and Associates (1978) included the question, "Which two or three characteristics do you feel are most important in helping you get your job done well?" Respondants rated lighting as quite important, and ranked it fifth in importance in a list of 17 aspects of the office environment. They also gave it very high ratings on adequacy, where it ranked third. Similarly, the earlier study of English office workers by Langdon (1966) found that about three-fourths of participants were "completely satisfied" with their artificial lighting, including a larger fraction of those with fluorescent lights (83%). Most workers who were dissatisfied thought their lighting was too dim. On the other hand, a survey by Hedge (1982) found that one third of employees in a single building complained that their light was "too bright."

Field studies

Nemecek and Grandjean (1973) measured lighting in 15 open-plan offices in Switzerland and administered a survey to the occupants. Average lighting ranged from approximately 37 to 74 footcandles, but three offices had brighter lighting of 93 to 186 footcandles. Results of the survey showed an unusually large number of reports of eye problems in offices with lighting of 93 footcandles or more.

In a study designed to evaluate a new office building, Boyce (1974) asked workers to rate their lighting before and after moving to an open-plan office from conventional offices. Measurements in the new office indicated that the average illumination was about 74 footcandles, which was rated "very satisfactory" on average. This rating compared with an average of "satisfactory" in the previous offices, which had lighting of about 37 footcandles. In brief, doubling the intensity of the lighting brought a modest increase in the average satisfaction with lighting.

An earlier Dutch study involved ratings by about 2,000 workers in offices with varied intensities of lighting. By Boyce's (1975) account, the study found "a reasonable level of satisfaction with the lighting" at about 46 footcandles, with only a small increase in the proportion satisfied with increases in illumination up to about 93 to 139 footcandles (p. 101).

The BOSTI project (1981) found a connection between the intensity of lighting and satisfaction with the physical environment. Participants were asked to express agreement with the statement, "my work space often feels dark." Only about 10–20% agreed. Among those questioned both before and after changing offices, those whose response to this question indicated an improvement in lighting showed an increase in satisfaction with the environment. Those whose lighting worsened showed a very slight decrease in satisfaction (p. 125). The intensity of lighting was not measured in this study, so we do not know what levels of lighting were associated with perceptions that the workspace was dark.

The BOSTI project also associated reports of glare with dissatisfaction with the environment. Participants were asked about glare from written materials, equipment, and windows. The first two types of glare were associated with dissatisfaction with the environment (BOSTI, 1981, pp. 129–130).

In summary, three field studies in offices found satisfaction with lighting of an intensity of about 40 footcandles. Slightly higher levels of satisfaction occurred with brighter light, but so did reports of eye problems in one study. A fourth study indicated an association between intensity of lighting and satisfaction with the environment and between glare and dissatisfaction.

Laboratory experiments

One project assessed subjective reactions to a series of experimental variations of lighting (Saunders, 1969). The series began with a pilot study in an experimental room with light-colored walls, furnished with eight desks, illuminated at about 5 footcandles. Participants sat at one desk while the illumination gradually increased until they indicated that they were "just, but definitely satisfied with the lighting level." The

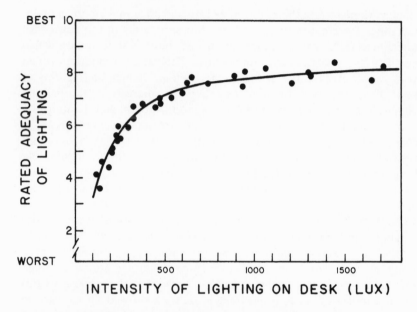

Figure 5.2. Rated adequacy of lighting as a function of intensity. *Source*: Redrawn from Saunders, J.E. (1969). The role of the level and diversity of horizontal illumination in an appraisal of a simple office task. *Lighting Research and Technology*, *1*(1), 39.

average illumination at this point was about 35 footcandles, near the British Illuminating Engineering Society standard, and far lower than the U.S. standard. As the lighting was intensified to about 140 footcandles, participants generally indicated seeing an improvement in the appearance of the desk and room.

In the main experiments, participants sat at one of two designated desks under lighting of one of several intensities. They rated the adequacy of the light for reading standardized text at the first desk, then sat at a second desk and made similar ratings. They left the room while the lighting was adjusted and returned for another set of two ratings. This procedure was repeated in four experiments, with participants mostly between 20 and 30 years of age, using levels of illumination ranging from about 12 to about 157 footcandles. A total of 33 participants took part in one or more of the four experiments, which differed in uniformity of light and arrangement of the room. (Thirteen people took part in all four variations; each variation involved five naive participants who were not involved in any other variation.) Ratings of the adequacy of the light increased with its intensity, but increases in the ratings became successively smaller at higher illuminations, as shown in Figure 5.2.

Ratings of adequacy increased sharply up to about 400 lux (37 footcandles), then rose more slowly up to about 800 lux (74 footcandles), and then essentially leveled off. Very bright lighting brought complaints about glare; one-half the participants complained under lighting of about 102 footcandles. (This approximates the level of illumination officially recommended for offices in the United States.)

The Saunders experiments included variation of the uniformity of the distribution of lighting but found no accompanying differences in ratings of the adequacy of lighting. ("Uniformity" was defined in terms of the ratio of the least intense to the most intense light in the room; experts often recommend ratios of 0.7 or higher.) Saunders varied the uniformity ratio from 0.5 to 1.0. Participants had no trouble in accurately judging the uniformity of the light; uniformity ratios above 0.5 were rated about equally satisfactory for reading.

Another laboratory study varied the uniformity of lighting, asked for evaluative judgements, and found a significant preference for nonuniform lighting at the periphery of the room (Flynn, Spencer, Martyniuk & Hendrick, 1973). A total of 95 adults of varying age and background sat in groups of eight around a rectangular table and indicated their impressions of the room in a questionnaire. The room was lighted in one of six ways at first; then the group rated the five other lighting arrangements in random order. The variations included high-intensity (100 footcandle), diffused-overhead lighting; low-intensity, diffused-overhead lighting; "downlighting" plus end-wall lighting; and downlighting plus peripheral lighting plus diffused overhead lighting (30 footcandles). A statistical technique (multidimensional scaling) showed the ratings contained three dimensions: bright versus dim, uniform versus nonuniform, and peripheral versus overhead. Evaluative ratings were unrelated to ratings on bright vs. dim, but were highest for nonuniform, peripheral lighting.

In summary, laboratory experiments suggest that people were satisfied with lighting of modest intensity – 30 to 35 footcandles in two studies. More light added slightly to satisfaction, but eventually brought some complaints of glare. Other findings suggested that the quality of lighting is important to satisfaction, and is rated highest and most satisfactory when nonuniform.

Lighting from windows

Sunlight from a window is highly variable; its angle changes with the position of the sun; its brightness changes with the time of day and the amount of cloud-cover. Sunlight also helps define textures and contours of surfaces, because it is partly horizontal (Wotton, 1976). Besides providing varied lighting, windows provide a view outside and sometimes ventilation as well. Even if occupants can see nothing but neighboring buildings or sky, they can at least find out about the weather. However, some experts have argued for windows purely because of variation in lighting:

People need a varied visual environment, and, if possible, continuous variation. Otherwise, the resulting privation of the senses will materialize as
boredom, fatigue, lack of concentration, and even a reduction of intellectual capacity. . . . The convenience of achieving a certain temporary variation in the lighting is a basic motivation for the installation of windows.
(Valciras, 1976, p. 37)

Another writer argued:

[W]e must guard against a uniform, standardized bath of white, glare-free
light, which can be a very boring environment in which to work. (S. Evans, 1968, p. 29)

These researchers implicitly claimed that people are stimulated by slight variations from conditions to which they have become accustomed – in other words, by small departures from adaptation level; see Chapter 4.

Windows may provide benefits besides variety in lighting and a view. They permit fine adjustment of light through curtains or venetian blinds. In some buildings they open to allow ventilation. They even provide distant points of visual focus, which in the opinion of some experts can relieve eye fatigue (e.g., Hall, 1966). And if windows overlook sidewalks or other centers of daily commerce, they may give a source of information and vicarious contact with other people. (On the other hand, they do bring added costs associated with construction, maintenance, heating, and cooling.)

Attempts have been made to reproduce the lighting from windows artificially, without much success. One such system involved slowly mov-
ing baffles near overhead lamps (Manasseh & Cunliffe, 1962). However, such projects are costly and uncommon (Wotton, 1976). For the most part, artificial light is relatively uniform and lacks the variety of daylight.

Research on windows comes primarily from Britain, and consists of both surveys and field studies. This section first reviews the studies of windows and satisfaction, then describes a very limited literature on windowless work places.

Windows and satisfaction

The study of London offices by Langdon (1966) included an open-ended question on "likes" and "dislikes" concerning the office environment.

The most frequent object of favorable comment was the illumination; nearly half of the participants spontaneously said "they liked the natural lighting of the room – that the room was light, bright, sunny, had plenty of windows" (Langdon, 1966, p. 6). In fact, 98% of the offices had windows in at least one wall. The employees also rated the adequacy of the lighting in their offices, and Langdon measured the percentage of wall of each office covered by windows. Results showed that

while an increase in fenestration reduces the percentage of occupants who find daylighting inadequate, this gain is offset by an increase in the percentage who find it too bright. Thus, with maximum fenestration, there remain 20% of occupants who find their offices too dim while a similar proportion find their offices too glaring. (Langdon, 1966, p. 10)

The wide variation in response is probably at least partly attributable to individual differences. For instance, older workers may have preferred brighter light.

A survey among office employees at a Manchester company revealed that they overestimated the contribution of daylight to their illumination (Wells, 1965a; see also Manning, 1965). Approximately 2,500 office employees completed a questionnaire as part of an evaluation of the new office building of the Cooperative Insurance Company. A majority (89%) considered it important to be able to see out, even if they had plenty of artificial light. Furthermore, two-thirds thought it was not "as good for their eyes to work by artificial light as by daylight" (Wells, 1965a, p. 57). Wells observed that the farther an employee was from a window, the more he or she seemed to overestimate the amount of daylight. He tested this idea in a sample of 156 employees from two floors of the office building. He measured the distance of each desk from the nearest window, and measured the artificial light on each desk at night (when there was no daylight). He remeasured in the daytime the total lighting from artificial sources and windows. Occupants of the desks estimated how much of the lighting on their desks was sunlight. Wells's prediction proved correct, as shown in Figure 5.3. Employees who sat relatively far from windows did tend to overrate the contribution of daylight to their lighting.

Another part of the research project at Manchester found a powerful preference for desks near windows. Clerical employees viewed pictures of a model office and indicated where they would prefer to have their desks. Most (81%) chose a position next to a window. When asked to explain their choices, 77% said the main reason concerned the window (Manning, 1965).

A study in Bristol, England also found a preference for natural light.

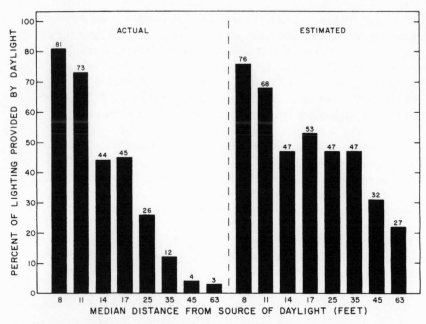

Figure 5.3. Actual and estimated contribution of daylight to total illumination as a function of distance from the nearest window. *Source*: Histogram adapted from Wells, B. (1965a). Subjective responses to the lighting installations in a modern office building and their design implications. *Building Science*, *1*(1), 57–68.

In a survey of 400 office employees, most said they liked to work by daylight (96%). Female employees expressed a stronger preference for sunshine than males did, but the average female worked farther from a window than the average male. With distance from windows held constant, the difference between genders disappeared. Results suggested that the preference for sunshine increased with the distance from a window (Markus, 1967).

Still another survey asked 263 English office workers whether they considered sunshine inside buildings a "pleasure or a nuisance." About three-fourths thought it a "pleasure." Asked to explain, they mentioned the light, the appearance of the room, the warmth, and the theraputic effects of sunlight. They were also asked about their preference for having a good view but no sunlight versus a poor view with sunlight; 61% chose the view (Longmore & Ne'eman, 1974; Ne'eman, 1974).

In summary, the surveys of English office workers suggest that lighting from windows represents a source of satisfaction with the physical working environment. Reasons for satisfaction include the view provided by the window and the belief that daylight is inherently better than artificial light.

Reactions to windowless work places

By one estimate, approximately 85% of U.S. factories existing in the mid-1960s had no windows. This occurred in spite of problems in the "blacked-out" factories of World War II:

In wartime blackout projects, workers scraped peepholes through the panes, and we had reports of their throwing wrenches through the opaqued windows to get a look at the weather outside. (Bowden, 1946, p. 101)

[A]part from the psychological effects due to the exclusion of daylight, there occurred in some blacked-out factories an increase of nervous irritability among workers and supervisory staff, with consequent friction. Part of this irritability seems to be associated with a feeling of being denied something that is one's right. (M. Smith, 1944, pp. 58–59)

[E]mployees broke so many wall panels that it became necessary to provide some visual contact with the outside world. Even when windows have been provided in the external wall there were numerous references to trouble with men breaking windows to get the "feel" of fresh air in artificially ventilated plants. (Collins, 1975, p. 21)

These anecdotes suggest that employees reacted negatively to windowless work places primarily because of the lack of a view outside (see Fig. 5.4).

One of the few systematic studies of windowless offices also suggested that workers want a window for the view. In a survey of 139 female employees in Seattle offices without windows, three-quarters said their offices were as good as or better than other offices they had seen. Most found their lighting adequate (88%). But an equally large majority expressed a preference for a window (91%), primarily because of their feelings in the windowless offices. They described their feelings this way: "cooped up, isolated, claustrophobia"; feelings of being "depressed, tense"; desire for a view or desire to "look in the distance"; and a desire to "know weather conditions." Preference for a window was unrelated to the size or color of the office, the level of illumination, or the distance to the nearest window. However, unlike British office workers, most of these employees did not think the lack of windows affected them physically (Ruys, 1970).

An informal series of interviews with occupants of windowless offices indicated similar reactions (Sommer, 1974):

It is more dull here. Time loses meaning. I have that basement feeling, burrowed in for the day. There is a lack of any buoyancy and change. The

"These windowless factories give me claustrophobia . . ."

Figure 5.4. Cartoon by Alan Dunn. *Source*: Reprinted from *Architectural Record*. (1945, Nov.). *98*(5), 7. © 1945, by McGraw-Hill, Inc. with all rights reserved.

work in this particular office is not stimulating, and so things here are depressing. One has to work at maintaining feelings in spite of grey walls and neon lights. I go upstairs to use the bathroom and then I get to look outside. (p. 116)

The lack of windows creates more tension. It is relaxing to look out a window for a few seconds. Artificial light, no matter how good, is less good than natural light. (p. 117)

I get claustrophobia, I need to get out to see sunshine. I am depressed and go out whenever possible. (p. 117)

I was bothered at first, but I am more used to it now. I have been here for six years. No idea of the weather, no idea of what is happening especially regarding light and dark. I feel isolated from the world. (p. 117)

The last reaction suggests that people can adapt to the lack of windows, an idea supported by a study of a Swedish factory. In an interesting study, a group of workers who were moved underground showed more absenteeism at first, but later were found to have rates of absenteeism approaching those of workers above ground (Collins, 1975).

On the other hand, adaptation may be difficult for some. One of Sommer's (1974) interviewees declared, "I am going to quit, partly due to the lack of windows" (p. 117). Adaptation may be especially difficult under certain conditions:

The small, restricted environments with little activity or personal interaction appear to be the ones in which the absence of windows is most noticeable. . . . the smaller and more restricted a windowless space is, the more repetitive and monotonous a task is, and the more reduced the freedom of movement and interaction its inhabitants have, the more unpleasant and oppressive it will be. (Collins, 1975, p. 35)

One explanation for dissatisfaction in windowless workspaces concerns inequity: Those who work without windows may feel they deserve the same amenities that other workers have, and may react negatively because of the apparent injustice of being deprived. If so, people in windowless areas might be satisfied with some compensating amenity. (If inequity is not the main factor in dissatisfaction, however, such compensation would not remedy it.)

In summary, windowless work places seem to create dissatisfaction because of the lack of variety in the lighting and the lack of a view, and perhaps because of inequity. People may be able to adapt somewhat to the lack of windows, but we have practically no evidence on this question.

Summary

When electric lights became available shortly before 1900, factories in the United States quickly incorporated them, and windowless factories became common. Offices only adopted electric lighting in the 1930s, after electrical air-conditioning made large interior office spaces usable throughout the year. After an "educational" campaign by power companies standards for lighting in offices in the United States rose, eventually to levels far above those of other industrialized countries. The basis of these standards was laboratory research. Early field studies had linked the intensity of illumination with output in factories, which was poor when workers could not discern critical details. Early laboratory research used the analytic approach to show that the visual difficulty of tasks depended on the size and contrast of details to be discriminated. The main finding was that brightness of illumination followed a principle of diminishing returns – each added increment in light brought smaller benefits in performance; for simple tasks, the benefits of extra light quickly became negligible. Research also showed the importance of age: older people need substantially more light than younger people to achieve the same level of performance. Later the more artificial "visibility" approach confirmed the findings on lighting and performance and provided the basis for controversial standards of lighting in offices and factories in the United States. Studies using actual office tasks leave doubts about the appropriateness of the standards. Researchers did not test the plausible hypothesis that lighting augments arousal and can influence performance in the laboratory for reasons other than the visibility of details. Studies of the quality of lighting suggest that *glare* (uncomfortably bright light from the task or surrounding area) may adversely affect performance, but it has more often been connected with dissatisfaction. Studies of lighting and satisfaction show findings consistent with a principle of diminishing returns, with bright light bringing complaints about glare. Research on the quality of light has sometimes suggested a preference for nonuniform lighting. Windows provide varied light, and office workers tend to overestimate its contribution to their lighting, but surveys suggest that workers also gain satisfaction from the views that windows provide.

Practical considerations

The problem confronting the designer of lighting for an office or factory is quite complex: to provide each worker with enough light to illuminate the details of all of his or her tasks, without creating glare or distracting contrasts, while at the same time providing a satisfying ambient environment.

The evidence indicates that lighting requirements depend on the worker's task and age. It may be tempting to adopt the simple expedient of supplying uniform overhead light bright enough for the oldest worker doing the most visually demanding task. Another even simpler solution is to follow the motto, "the brighter, the better." Unfortunately, brighter is not always better, and it may even cause glare and discomfort (not to mention high power bills). A more complex alternative, not always feasible, is to provide separately controlled lighting for each work-position, ideally allowing each occupant to select the intensity of the light for his or her work.

Some modern offices use *task-lighting*, or in other words, desk lamps. The engineer's drafting lamp is one common example; another is the modular work station with built-in light. Especially if adjustable, task lights have many advantages: (1) they direct light toward the task and make it brighter than the background; (2) they create nonuniform ambient lighting, which may be desirable; and (3) they can be positioned to minimize glare. Adjustable lamps can allow the intensity of the light to be altered to match the worker's needs. The presence of task lighting means that the ambient lighting throughout the building can be limited to the minimum necessary to create a pleasant appearance and safe movement about the building. On the other hand, some offices have had problems with task lighting, especially when provided by overhead lights (see Galitz, 1980).

Lighting in factories is complicated by the practically endless variety of tasks, many of which have unique requirements for lighting. Inspection frequently calls for special lighting, involving horizontal surface grazing, translucent surfaces, polarized light, spotlighting, edge lighting, stroboscopic lighting, and other arrangements (see Faulkner & Murphy, 1973).

Lighting from windows may be desirable to many employees in offices or factories, but people often outnumber windows, making windows into scarce resources and status symbols (see Chapter 11). One alternative to windows is the provision of an "internal view" (Manning, 1965), overlooking an open office or an enclosed courtyard, or even an indoor area such as a shopping mall. Such internal views can be found in several office complexes in the United States, including American Telephone & Telegraph's corporate headquarters in Basking Ridge, New Jersey.

6
TEMPERATURE AND AIR

Of the qualities of a work place that make up the ambient environment, temperature and ventilation were among the first to receive systematic study. This chapter traces the history of the treatment of temperature and ventilation in the work place, briefly discusses some of the problems in studying thermal comfort, and examines research on the effects of temperature on satisfaction and performance. Air quality is explored in a separate section.

The research evidence suggests that individuals vary in their responses to indoor climatic conditions. Small departures from the range of comfort can apparently create dissatisfaction. The effects of temperature on performance depend on the type of task and on other factors. Sparse research on air quality suggests that it is a problem in offices and factories.

Indoor climate in work places

During the early 1800s it was commonly believed that the discomfort and malaise that occurred in hot, crowded workshops was due to bad air. For awhile carbon dioxide was held to blame, as a French scientist had found unusual concentrations of it in occupied rooms. But in 1862 a new hypothesis emerged: toxic organic substances exhaled from the lungs and skin caused illness. The "anthropotoxin theory" provoked intense interest in the effects of ventilation, temperature, and humidity. By the time the theory was discredited around 1913, research evidence had begun to accumulate (Bedford, 1961).

By World War I, researchers recognized the primary factors that influenced thermal comfort: air temperature, humidity, air movement, and sources of radiant heat. Experiments had demonstrated that some of the uncomfortable effects of heat and humidity could be alleviated by ventilation (e.g., Hill, Flack, McIntosh, Rowlands & Walker, 1913).

Ventilation became a critical issue in factories during the 1800s. Until then, most factory buildings were narrow and had plentiful windows, so workers were never far from a source of fresh air. When the form of factory buildings shifted to huge single-story structures lit with skylights or electric lights, windows alone could no longer provide adequate ventilation. Furthermore, new industrial processes gave off more dust and fumes than before, making hot, contaminated air commonplace in factories of the 1800s.

Changing technology brought a solution for emerging problems of ventilation: the electric exhaust fan. As soon as it became available, factory managers became sensitive to its benefits:

There is no longer any excuse for subjecting the foundryman to the choking fumes of the pickle house, to the suffocating dust of the rattlers or to the debilitating effects of an overheated atmosphere. The emery grinder and polisher, the workers in the plumbago mill, the grist in the shoe shops and clothing factories, all have a right to demand protection from the dust and the overheated and vitiated air that so insidiously undermined their health. (Snow, 1891, p. 473)

Unfortunately, many factories still had poor ventilation, which represented one of the first issues to prompt public outcry in the United States around 1900 (see Chapter 2). In response to pressures from organized labor, many factories did incorporate mechanical ventilation systems. Other factory owners provided better ventilation in the belief that it would add to their profits. Office managers also saw improved ventilation as a stimulus to better performance. For instance, in a poorly ventilated drafting room employees had difficulty executing complex drawings:

No doubt the work in that ill-ventilated den cost 10 per cent more than it would have done in a comfortable well-ventilated office. (Allen, 1901, p. 76)

Soon after 1900, lobbying by labor unions had helped precipitate large-scale, publicly financed investigations both in the United States and Great Britain. In 1913 the New York State Commission on Ventilation began a program of experiments by scientists from several disciplines. The Commission published its findings 10 years later, and concluded, among other things, that even small departures from the range of comfort, 68° to 75°F (20° to 24°C), could impair physical labor (Leffingwell, 1925).

Meanwhile in 1913 the British House of Commons held hearings on ventilation, which eventually led to the formation of the Industrial Fatigue Research Board. The first report of the Board contained the results of a study of production in tinplate factories, which suggested that output declined at high temperatures (see Chapter 3). A later study found heat to be associated with decreased factory output (Weston, 1921). Such evidence helped convince factory owners of the value of adequate ventilation.

By World War I, architects had become quite knowledgeable about temperature and ventilation:

[T]he usual allowance of 30 cubic feet of air per occupant per minute, based on the amount of dilution to maintain a certain standard of chemical purity, is also the amount of air which is required to remove the heat and moisture given off by one person when introducing it into the room at a temperature 10 degrees less than the room temperature, which is about as low as is possible without causing drafts or chilling the occupants. (Hubbard, 1917, p. 55)

The 1930s saw the introduction of refrigerated air-conditioning, which permitted buildings to be kept at a comfortable temperature and humidity all year. Air-conditioning augmented ventilation systems in some industries, such as the manufacture of dairy goods and candy. In industries in which air-conditioning was less critical to manufacturing, it was adopted more slowly.

The refrigerated air-conditioner had a powerful impact on offices. Until the 1930s, offices had mostly been confined to narrow buildings where workers could be near windows for light and air. The electric light had solved only half the problem – interior spaces could be lighted, but they were hot and stuffy in the warm months of summer. The air-conditioner removed the last technical obstacle to the use of huge, windowless interiors as offices (see Shultz & Simmons, 1959). The "block" office building became feasible; it consisted of several stories of vast floors, with temperature and ventilation regulated by a central mechanical system.

Block office buildings have created special problems for maintaining comfortable temperatures. With large windows, the buildings can gain or lose heat much faster at the exterior than at the core. As a result, temperatures in work-stations may vary considerably within one building. In some ways, advancing technology has complicated the problem of maintaining comfortable temperatures and ventilation. When buildings were heated by radiators and cooled by open windows, employees were able to control their own environments. With central HVAC systems, the controls are centralized. Employees in glass-sheathed office towers and vast factories depend on central systems that may or may not meet their needs.

Problems in studying thermal comfort

A major goal of research on temperature has been the development of a single numerical index of thermal comfort. This has turned out to be a difficult task. The usefulness of even the best index is limited by the wide variation in thermal comfort experienced by different individuals.

In search of an index

Once researchers had identified the environmental factors that influence comfort in various climatic conditions, they sought to develop a numerical index that would reflect subjective responses to different combinations of temperature, air movement, humidity, and radiant sources of heat. Such an index would permit comparison of the comfort provided by environments that differed on several factors at once. (For instance, an ambient air temperature of 78°F [26°C] with 90% relative humidity may feel as warm as a temperature of 84°F [29°C] with only 10% relative humidity.)

The first widely accepted index of thermal comfort, called *effective temperature* (ET), was developed in 1923 (Houghten & Yagloglou, 1923). The researchers systematically varied air temperature, humidity, and air movement and asked volunteers to report on their comfort while at rest. The "normal scale" of ET gives a numerical value in degrees Fahrenheit for an average person's subjective comfort in various combinations of air speed (feet per minute) ambient air temperature and humidity (indicated by wet-bulb temperature). The index has frequently been employed in laboratory research on temperature and seems to provide the best basis for comparing the existing empirical studies (even though it is now seldom used).

Critics of the ET scale pointed out defects. These included the failure to take account of the production of body heat generated while working, the effects of radiant sources of heat, and the uncomfortable effect of high humidity in extreme heat. At least eight alternative indexes of thermal comfort or thermal stress have been proposed. All have been criticized (see Bedford, 1964; Givoni, 1976; Jones, 1970). No index has been widely enough accepted to provide a standard for the entire research community. The American Society of Heating, Refrigeration, and Air-Conditioning Engineers (ASHRAE) has endorsed an index called new effective temperature, (ET^x which corrects certain defects noted in the original ET scale (see McCormick, 1976).

Individual differences

The best indexes of thermal comfort correlate highly with reports of comfort by the occupants of rooms of various temperatures, humidities, air speeds, and wall temperatures. Even so, people reportedly show wide differences in thermal comfort under similar climatic conditions. When an average person is comfortable, a substantial fraction of people may experience the room as too warm or too cold (see Griffiths, 1969).

Individual differences in comfort apparently cannot be attributed to gender, age, or geographical origin (Griffiths, 1975). Thermal comfort does vary predictably with the level of physical activity and with the amount of clothing, both of which tend to lower the temperature at which a person is comfortable (see Fanger, 1972). But even in studies controlling for these factors, unaccountable individual differences still occur (see, e.g., Grivel & Barth, 1980).

One reason for wide individual differences in thermal comfort may be that comfort depends not only on the physical environment, but on suggestion. Two recent experiments showed that college students' reports of comfort were just as responsive to purported changes in the temperature as to actual changes in temperature in the range of 70° to 76°F (21° to 24°C) (Stramler, Kleiss & Howell, 1983).

Constant versus variable temperature

Most research on temperature and comfort has rested on the premise that people have an optimal range of temperature for comfort and performance. Researchers have attempted to discover the extremes of the optimal range – the points at which people begin to get uncomfortable or begin to perform poorly. They have assumed that a constant temperature within the optimal range would produce maximal comfort, and have proceeded to try to find the limits of the range.

Unfortunately, researchers have generally ignored the question of whether constancy in temperature is more comfortable than variation. According to Gerlach (1974), people prefer variation in temperature. If so, any constant temperature may become uncomfortable after awhile through "thermal boredom." Gerlach conducted an experiment in a keypunch room by introducing a fluctuation temperature on alternate days for 10 days. (Temperature varied from 72° to 76°F [22° to 24°C] every hour on variable days, compared with a relatively constant 74°F [23°C] maintained within 1 degree.) Workers reported greater comfort in variable temperatures.

If variation is preferable to constancy, research to date has overlooked some important questions. For instance, what rates of change are most comfortable? Within what ranges? Are gradual changes preferred over sudden ones? And so on. These issues seem to be largely unexplored.

Temperature and satisfaction

The temperature is apparently associated with much dissatisfaction in offices and factories. For example, in the 1977 *Quality of Employment Survey* about one-third of office workers and half of factory workers reported having unpleasant working conditions. The foremost complaint concerned the temperature (32% of all problems mentioned). Poor ventilation was also a common problem (Quinn & Staines, 1979). An earlier survey of office workers in London found that 25% complained of overheating, and 21% complained of being too cold (Langdon, 1966). Other surveys have shown similar results (Black & Milroy, 1967; Boyce, 1973; Hedge, 1982).

Complaints about temperature could partly reflect the wide range of individual preferences. The 1980 survey of U.S. office workers by Louis Harris and Associates included a question on the "perfect" temperature. For 81% of the sample it fell between 68° and 73°F (20° and 23°C). The other 19% preferred warmer or cooler temperatures. The hottest and coolest comfortable temperatures also varied, as shown in Table 6.1. The median preferred temperatures was within the range found in most laboratory studies (see Wilkinson, 1974). An earlier survey in 15 offices included measurements of ambient temperature at each of 519 workspaces, along with questions on the occupants' comfort. Results showed the largest fraction of workers comfortable at about 72°F (22°C). But even at this temperature about 20% of the workers said they were either too hot or too cold (Nemecek & Grandjean, 1973).

BOSTI (1981) is apparently the only empirical study to have linked thermal comfort and job satisfaction. More than half of all participants in the study indicated that the temperature in their workspaces went up and down too much, at least as often as "sometimes." A total of 389 people completed the questionnaire 1 to 2 months before changing offices and 7 to 9 months afterward. They were divided into three groups, for whom temperature fluctuations were more frequent, less frequent, or the same after changing offices. Those whose new offices brought more frequent fluctuations in temperature experienced a significant decline in job satisfaction (BOSTI, 1981, p. 118).

Table 6.1. *Preferred temperatures among 1,003 office workers*

	Percentage of office workers selecting		
Temperature (°F)	Perfect temperature	Hottest acceptable	Coolest acceptable
≤ 59	—	—	4
60–61	1	—	9
62–63	—	—	7
64–65	5	1	29
66–67	4	—	11
68–69	26	3	24
70–71	36	12	11
72–73	19	19	3
74–75	5	30	1
76–77	1	10	—
78–79	1	10	—
80–81	1	9	—
≥ 82	—	5	—
Median	71	75	66

Source: Louis Harris & Associates, Inc. (1980), p. 35.

In summary, the research evidence suggests that a substantial fraction of workers find their offices or factories too hot or too cold. Their complaints probably reflect the wide range of individual preferences regarding indoor climate.

Temperature and performance

This section reviews theory and research linking temperature with performance. After briefly outlining the main theory on the effects of temperature – an arousal hypothesis – it describes a few industrial studies and a large body of laboratory experiments on heat and cold.

Arousal and the impact of temperature

A well-accepted hypothesis holds that temperature influences performance through physiological and psychological arousal. Moderate departures from the range of comfort are thought to create arousal. (As environmental conditions approach the extremes of human tolerance, performance breaks down through other of physiological processes; see Bell, 1981.)

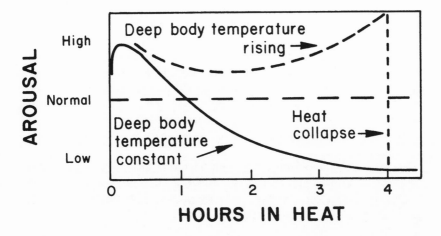

Figure 6.1. Arousal in heat after various periods of exposure, based on Poulton's hypothesis. *Source*: Poulton, E.C. (1980). *The Environment at Work*. Springfield, IL: Thomas, p. 78. Courtesy of Charles C Thomas, Publisher, Springfield, Illinois.

Within the range of tolerance, the psychological effects of temperature apparently develop over time. So, the impact of a particular environment probably depends to some extent on how long the individual has been exposed to it. The reaction to a departure from the climatic range of comfort begins with automatic, physiological responses directed toward maintaining a constant body temperature of 98.6°F or (37°C). In uncomfortable heat, homeostatic mechanisms cool the body: dilation of peripheral blood vessels to radiate heat at the skin, sweating for evaporative cooling, and faster breathing for air cooling. Heat may also produce arousal, at least for the first few minutes of exposure (Poulton, 1980). Cold environments induce constriction of peripheral blood vessels, increased metabolic rate (and accompanying arousal), shivering (which generates heat), and piloerection (goose bumps). All these reactions to cold lead to conservation or generation of heat.

After initial exposure, however, the effects of temperature depend on the effectiveness of homeostatic responses. If body temperature remains stable, the initial arousal may disappear. In heat, if the body temperature begins to rise, it is only a matter of time before the individual must find some means of cooling to prevent collapse. As body temperature rises, arousal remains high, or if it fell at first, it begins to rise again. If body temperature remains too high, the arousal level may fall below normal after awhile, as shown schematically in Figure 6.1. Continued exposure to cold may lead to a slowing of the metabolism and subnormal arousal.

If the effect of climatic conditions on arousal changes with time, then according to the arousal hypothesis, climatic conditions should affect performance in a complex way. The effects should depend on both the temperature and the duration of exposure. In brief exposures to heat, performance of relatively simple tasks should be better than in comfortable environments, because of temporary arousal. However, performance of complex tasks in brief exposures to heat should suffer. On the other hand, prolonged exposure to moderate heat should hurt the performance of even simple tasks, as arousal eventually falls to subnormal levels.

The effects of temperature are complicated by acclimatization. After living for several weeks or months in a hot climate, people begin to develop greater tolerance for heat. However, acclimatization hardly occurs at all in cold climates (Poulton, 1980).

Field research

As outlined in Chapter 3, the British Industrial Fatigue Research Board published its first report on seasonal variation in temperature and average output among tinplate workers (Vernon, 1919). As shown in Figure 6.2, output fell with the rise of temperatures in the summer. Seasonal variation in output was much less pronounced in plants with ventilation equipment. The low summer output in poorly ventilated buildings probably reflects the adverse effect of heat on the workers' capacities to perform heavy physical labor. A study done at about the same time at a munitions factory found accidents more frequent as temperatures departed from about 68°F (20°C) (Vernon, 1918). Another study of the seasonal variation of temperature in linen weaving sheds found performance optimized at 73°F (23°C) (wet bulb). Performance decreased at higher or lower temperatures (Weston, 1921). (Heat makes linen threads easier to weave, so performance should have been easier to maintain at higher temperatures, but output declined anyway.)

One of the more recent industrial studies yielded results consistent with the earlier findings of declining performance in heat. Research at a New Jersey garment factory incorporated measurements of individual output among 24 experienced workers, along with recordings of temperature and humidity for 96 days. Output declined as temperature rose from 75° to 90°F (24° to 32°C) but was unrelated to humidity (Link & Pepler, 1970). Pepler (1973) studied a Puerto Rican garment factory as it moved from an older building into an air-conditioned one and reported output unrelated to temperature (output was generally quite low, and the workers may have been less motivated than in the New Jersey factory). Another study of a factory found no correlation between daily

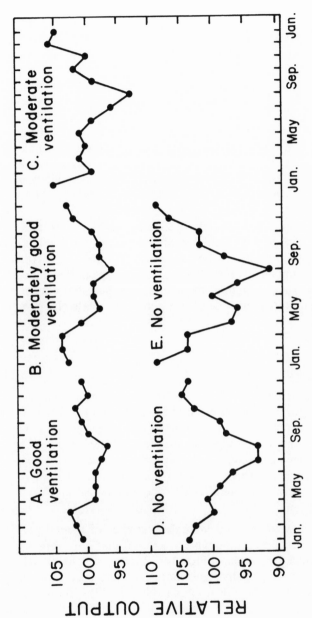

Figure 6.2. Monthly variation in the relative output of five tinplate factories with different levels of ventilation. *Source:* Redrawn from Vernon, H.M. (1919). *The Influence of Hours of Work and of Ventilation on Output in Tinplate Manufacture.* Industrial Fatigue Research Board, Report No. 1. London: H. Majesty's Stationery Office, p. 22.

ambient temperatures in a welding operation (up to 110°F or 43°C) and the daily deviation from the average cost of production per unit (Lifson, 1957). (The use of average daily costs as a measure of production may have rendered the study insensitive to variation in individual output, so the lack of a correlation with temperature is not very informative.) In all the field studies, the impact of temperature on output is difficult to assess in relationship to other factors that could have affected output.

One field study found uncomfortable heat associated with relatively poor performance in an office. Researchers analyzed data from an experiment by the New York State Commission on Ventilation done in 1914 on the effects of temperature on typewriting. The new analysis showed greater output by typists at 68°F (20°C) than at 75°F (24°C) (Wyon, 1974).

In summary, three of five studies on the connection between temperature and output in factories found declining output with rising temperatures. One study found heat to be associated with accidents. And a study in an office found an adverse effects of heat on the performance of a group of typists. Taken together, these studies suggest that uncomfortably high temperatures may be associated with relatively poor performance.

Laboratory studies of heat

Laboratory studies of performance under environmental stress from heat have generally incorporated one or more of the five types of tasks outlined in Chapter 3. Temperatures have ranged almost to the limits of tolerance, and exposures have ranged from a few minutes to nearly 8 hours. Results have been complicated. Sometimes heat produced a decrement in performance, sometimes it had no effect, sometimes it led to better performance. However, the effects varied among tasks.

Mental tasks. A review of selected laboratory studies of mental performance by a U.S. Air Force researcher suggested that only very extreme heat hurts mental performance. Figure 6.3 summarizes the "lowest temperature at which a statistically significant decrement occurred" for various durations of exposure to heat (Wing, 1965, p. 23). The review concluded that mental performance remains unaffected until the temperature approaches the limit of tolerance.

On the other hand, published laboratory studies listed in Table 6.2 suggest that heat does impair mental performance of some tasks at temperatures within the range of tolerance. Heat was associated with errors in highly demanding tasks that involved fine motor responses in

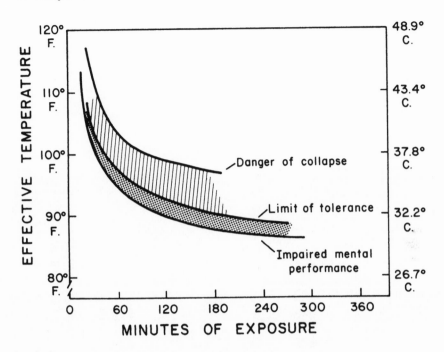

Figure 6.3. Effective temperatures and durations of exposure associated with impaired mental performance. *Source*: Adapted from Wing, J.F. (1965). *A Review of the Effects of High Ambient Temperature on Mental Performance.* Aerospace Medical Research Laboratories, Wright-Patterson Air Force Base. Report #AMRL-TR-65-102, p. 24.

four of six of the experiments in the table. The one study that found a decrement in a task with no requirement for fine motor coordination failed to replicate in the same laboratory (Allen & Fischer, 1978). Four others found decrements after an hour or more of sustained effort involving mental calculation, plus rapid, coordinated hand movements or eye movements. These include two of the classic studies by Mackworth (1950), which represent some of the best research on the topic. In one study, a difficult version of the task showed a decrement (Pepler, 1958), but a less demanding version of the same task was unaffected by heat in two studies in another laboratory (Chiles, 1958).

The longest study of heat and performance (Fine & Kobrick, 1978) exposed volunteers to heat for 7 hours while they listened through earphones for certain signals. Their job was to record and either decode the signals or use them as a basis for calculations. These tasks all called for quick handwriting; some required the use of a special slide rule or

Table 6.2. *Laboratory studies of the effects of heat on performance of mental tasks*

Study	Task	Duration (minutes)[a,b]	Reference temperature (°F)[b]	Temperature associated with effect on performance[b]		
				Decrement	No effect	Increment
Allen & Fischer (1978)	Paired-associate learning (#1)	15+	72[c]	82, 92	—	—
	Paired-associate learning (#2)	15+	72[c]	—	77, 82	—
Chiles (1958)	Paced symbol comparison (#1)	60 (30)	76	—	81, 86, 91	—
	Paced symbol comparison (#2)	60 (30)	75	—	81, 94, 98	—
Pepler (1958)	Paced symbol comparison (#5)	80 (60)	76	86, 91	—	—
Givoni & Rim (1962)[d]	Mental multiplication	120	70	—	80, 85, 90	75
Mackworth (1950)	Telegraph reception	180	79	88, 92, 97	—	—
	Coding task	180	79	88, 92, 97	—	—
Pepler & Warner (1968)	Programmed learning	180	74[c]	—	88, 86, 92	—
Fine et al. (1960)	Anagrams	425 (35)	69	—	81, 93	—
	Auditory discrimination	445 (20)	69	—	81, 93	—
Viteles & Smith (1946)	Coding	330 (30)	73	—	80, 87	—
	Mental multiplication	330 (30)	73	87	80	—
Fine & Kobrick (1978)	Decoding & calculation	420 (360)	70	92	—	—

[a] Figures in parentheses represent time spent performing the task, if shorter than exposure to heat.
[b] Effective temperature, normal scale, unless otherwise noted.
[c] Ambient temperature.
[d] Based on reanalysis by Wing (1965), differences $p < 0.065$ (most conservative test available).

code wheel, others called for the location of data in reference books. Participants received a week's training before the experiment, and each worked on different days under all experimental conditions. In heat they made significantly more errors, particularly during the last 3 hours of exposure. This result suggests that the adverse effects of heat became more severe with time.

Performance of tasks with no requirement for fine motor responses was generally unaffected by heat. An exception was a study that found better performance at 75°F (24°C) than at 70°F (21°C) (Givoni & Rim, 1962). Another exception was a decrement in mental multiplication in an exposure to heat lasting more than 5 hours (Viteles & Smith, 1946).

In summary, four experiments found that heat tended to produce errors in the performance of sustained mental tasks under certain conditions: (1) the task continued for 60 minutes; (2) the task called for rapid, coordinated, hand movements or quick visual scanning; and (3) the task was highly demanding and externally paced.

Motor tasks. Heat produced a decrement in performance in most published laboratory studies of motor tasks listed in Table 6.3. Most of the studies that found a decrement used tracking tasks. Eight studies reported poorer performance in heat while working more or less continuously for periods of 1/2 to 3 hours. In the best designed studies, the participants returned for several sessions (e.g., Mackworth, 1950). Exceptions to the trend toward poor performance in heat included faster reaction time in a brief exposure to heat (Bell, Loomis & Cervone, 1982) and better tracking in moderate heat than at a comfortable temperature (Pepler, 1958, study #3). Both could reflect temporary arousal in brief exposures to heat. Another study found no effects of extreme heat in a 15-minute tracking task after almost 2 hours at rest (Nunneley, Dowd, Myhre, Stribley & McNee, 1979); the brief performance test may not have been demanding enough to show a decrement. Similarly, studies by Russell (1957), Reilly and Parker (1968), and J.A. Vaughn, Higgins & Funkhouser (1968) found neither adverse nor positive effects of heat. However, all of them used brief performance tests interspersed with periods of rest. Decrements only emerged after sustained performance of the same task for about 30 minutes.

The adverse effect of heat on tracking performance probably at least partly reflects physiological effects of heat on muscular activity, along with psychological effects on arousal. Poorer performance after prolonged exposure to heat is consistent with the arousal hypothesis.

Clerical tasks. One published study concerned clerical tasks (Viteles & Smith, 1946). Volunteers were exposed for 5 1/2 hours to moderate heat

Table 6.3. Laboratory studies of the effects of heat on performance of motor tasks

Study	Task	Duration (minutes)[a,b]	Reference temperature (°F)	Temperature associated with effect on performance		
				Decrement	No effect	Increment
Bell et al. (1982)	Reaction time	10	72[c]	—	—	98
Teichner & Wehrcamp (1954)	Tracking	28	70[c]	85, 100	—	—
Pepler (1959)	Tracking	30	76	110	—	—
Pepler (1960)	Tracking (#1)	40	69	100	—	—
	Tracking (#2)	40	69	100	—	—
Russell (1957)	Tracking (two types)	58 (33)	68[c]	—	86; 104[c]	—
Nunneley et al. (1979)	Compensatory tracking	120 (15)	77[c]	—	95/77; 104/86[d]	—
Pepler (1958)	Tracking (#1)	120	76	84, 91	—	—
	Tracking (#2)	120	72	84, 92	—	—
	Tracking (#3)	120	76	86, 91	—	—
Vaughn et al. (1968)	Pegboard; written coordination test	120	80[c]	79	88, 92, 97	—
Mackworth (1950)	Tracking	180	79	88, 92, 97	—	—
Reilly & Parker (1968)	Tracking (four types);	360 (2–5)	74[c]	—	86	—
	mirror tracing;	360 (5)	74[c]	—	—	—
	dexterity tests	360 (5)	74[c]	—	86	—
Viteles & Smith (1946)	Simulated lathe	330 (30)	73	87	80	—
	Pursuit tracking	330 (30)	73	87	80	—

[a] Figures in parentheses represent time spent performing the task, if shorter than exposure to heat.
[b] Effective temperature, normal scale, unless otherwise noted.
[c] Ambient temperature.
[d] Dry/wet-bulb temperature.

(80° or 87°FET, 27° or 31°C) while performing several different tasks in 30–minute sessions. A task that called for number checking showed a decrement at the warmest temperature. Two other tasks showed no decrement; they involved number recognition and recording or location recording. Although only suggestive, these findings are consistent with the research on mental tasks.

Vigilance. Of six studies of vigilance shown in Table 6.4, three found decrements in relatively extreme heat. The three that found poorer vigilance in highly demanding tasks lasted for 2 hours. Some studies also found a facilitative effect of moderate heat on vigilance. Mackworth's (1950) clock test found heat associated with poorer vigilance in a very demanding task. Participants watched the hand of a dial as it revolved 360 degrees in 100 seconds in equal 1–second jumps, occasionally jumping twice the usual arc; the task was to detect the unusual jumps. This required constant attention, as even a 1–second lapse could bring an error. The studies by Pepler (1958) and Reilly and Parker (1968) also used demanding tasks. In contrast, C.R. Bell, Provins & Hiorns (1964) found no decrement due in extreme heat in a task that allowed up to 30 seconds to identify each unusual signal, which was heralded by an oscillating indicator on one of 20 dials. In some studies moderate heat even facilitated vigilance. These findings can be explained in terms of arousal, as either an initially stimulating effect of heat or as the result of an eventual decline of arousal to subnormal levels in heat. (Low levels of arousal may particularly hurt the performance of highly demanding tasks.) Only three of the studies examined temperatures around 79° to 82°F (ET) (26° to 28°C); vigilance seems to be optimum at about this temperature, at least for sessions of 2 hours or so.

Dual tasks. Most published studies of simultaneous tasks found that heat impaired the performance of the secondary task (see Table 6.5). The typical effect was an increase in the tendency to overlook peripheral signals or low-priority inputs. This resembles the narrowing of attention that sometimes accompanies other kinds of stress (see Chapter 4). In brief exposures to heat, the decrement in performance might reflect over-arousal. In the longer studies (Azer, McNall & Leung, 1972; Bursill, 1958; Griffiths & Boyce, 1971), the decrement might reflect subnormal arousal in continued heat. In one case, performance on the central task improved as peripheral cues were noticed less often (Poulton & Kerslake, 1965). In most cases, however, the secondary task suffered without benefit to the primary one.

Factors that modify the impact of heat. Besides the type of task, several

Table 6.4. *Laboratory studies of the effects of heat on performance of vigilance tasks*

| Study | Task | Duration (minutes)[a,b] | Reference temperature (°F) | Temperature associated with effect on performance | | |
				Decrement	No effect	Increment
Bell et al. (1964)	20 dials test (#1)	19–240	80	—	96; 97; 110; 145/117[a]	—
	Auditory vigilance (#2)	19–240	89	—	97; 103; 110; 133/109[a]	—
Colquhoun & Goldman (1972)	Single light (after exercise)	120 (60)		—	103/93[a]	—
Reilly & Parker (1968)	Two dials	120 (4)	74[c]	86	—	—
Mackworth (1950)	Clock test	120	70	88, 97	—	79
Pepler (1958)	Clock test (#6)	120	82	67, 92	—	—

[a] Figures in parentheses represent time spent performing the task, if shorter than exposure to heat.
[b] Effective temperature normal scale, unless otherwise noted.
[c] Ambient temperature.
[d] Dry-bulb/wet-bulb temperature.

Table 6.5. *Laboratory studies of the effects of heat on performance of dual (simultaneous) tasks*

Study	Task	Duration (minutes)[a,b]	Reference temperature (°F)	Temperature associated with effect on performance		
				Decrement	No effect	Increment
Bell (1978)	Pursuit + auditory vigilance	12	72[c]	85	—	—
Poulton & Kerslake (1965)	Five dials (vigilance) + listening for repeated letters	20	65	86 (2nd task)	—	86[d,e] (central task)
Griffiths & Boyce (1971)	Tracking + auditory vigilance	20	70[c]	75	80	—
Bursill (1958)	Tracking + peripheral lights (#1)	84 (40)	65	95	—	—
		144 (40)	65	95	—	—
	Tracking + peripheral lights (#2)	84 (40)	65	—	95	—
	Tracking (slow speed) + peripheral lights (#3)					
Azer et al. (1972)	Tracking + peripheral lights	95 (60)	76	89	85, 88	—
Provins & Bell (1970)	Five-choice (serial reaction time) + peripheral lights	175 (130)	68/59[d]	—	—	104/94[d] (temporary)

[a] Figures in parentheses represent time spent performing the tasks, if shorter than exposure to heat.
[b] Effective temperature, normal scale, unless otherwise noted.
[c] Ambient temperature.
[d] Dry-bulb/wet-bulb temperature.

other factors apparently help determine the impact of heat on performance:

1. *Body temperature* in a hot environment rises at different rates for different people (see McNall & Schlegel, 1968); as a consequence, the effect of heat on arousal should vary greatly.
2. *Metabolic cost of physical activity* varies (e.g., Grieve, 1960), and with it the psychological impact of heat.
3. *Acclimatization* apparently lessens the effect of heat (see Pepler, 1963).
4. *Skill* of the individual at the task may be important; one study found a relatively slight effect of heat on skilled performers (Mackworth, 1950).
5. *Motivation* may modify the level of performance (Jones, 1970), but the effects of incentives are limited (Mackworth, 1950).
6. *Stress* may vary among people exposed to an environment because some see it as more threatening than others do.

Relevance of laboratory findings to work places. The laboratory studies reveal adverse effects of heat on tasks that call for quick, small movements of eyes or hands, or simultaneous performance of two tasks. However, we cannot be sure as to how well the laboratory findings describe what happens in actual work places, particularly in long-term exposure to heat. The temperatures at which performance deteriorates are probably rather uncommon in offices. However, extreme heat and humidity are more common in factories, and the tasks that suffered in the laboratory have many of the same elements found in factory work.

Laboratory studies of cold

Research on the effects of temperatures below the range of comfort has been relatively uncommon, and the results inconsistent. Pepler and Warner (1968) found that military personnel completed a programmed learning course faster, but with more errors, in 3–hour exposures to a slightly cold environment (62°F, or 17°C, ambient temperature). Another study found poorer learning of paired words in only one of two experiments involving 15–minute exposures to a cool environment (Allen & Fischer, 1978). However, another experiment involving longer exposures to a cool setting (65°F, or 18°C, ET) found no effects on performance of an anagram task or auditory discrimination (Fine, Cohen & Crist, 1960). Two studies found a decrement in tracking below 50°F (19°C) (ET) than at a warmer temperature (Pepler, 1958). Another found no effect of cold (50°F, or 10°C) on manual performance (Vaughn et al., 1968).

Although more laboratory studies of cold environments found a decrement in performance than an improvement, there are too few studies of any one type of task to support strong conclusions. Furthermore, the laboratory research has the usual limitations of artificial settings and brief durations, both of which leave their generalizability to work places open to question.

Air quality

Empirical research on the psychological influences of air quality in work places seems to be practically nonexistent. The central issue is air pollution, or any gas, dust, mist, vapor, or fiber present in the air besides its natural constituents (e.g., nitrogen, oxygen, water vapor, carbon dioxide). Certain air pollutants do have well documented effects on health (see Evans & Jacobs, 1981).

Although its psychological effects are largely unknown, air pollution is apparently a significant problem in factories and offices. In the 1977 Quality of Employment Survey of a sample of U.S. workers, about one-half of those who worked in factory jobs and about one-third of those in office jobs reported unpleasant working conditions; more than 6% of the complaints concerned poor ventilation or specific noxious vapors (Quinn & Staines, 1979). The same survey included a question about exposure to health hazards, and 40% of all respondents said they were exposed to hazardous air pollution (this figure includes more than just factory and office workers). The BOSTI study of office employees reported that about one-fourth said their offices were "too smoky or smelly" at least "sometimes" (BOSTI, 1981).

Air pollution in the office or factory has the potential for creating annoyance and dissatisfaction. Laboratory studies have identified many odors (e.g., Dravnieks & O'Neill, 1979). BOSTI (1981) reported that people whose offices became more smoky or smelly after changing offices experienced a significant drop in satisfaction with their physical environments, in contrast with responses of workers who did not experience poorer air quality. On the other hand, a British study of workers in heavy manufacturing found that exposure to dust and fumes bore no association to absenteeism, which is generally regarded as an outgrowth of dissatisfaction with the job (Shepherd & Walker, 1957).

One type of air pollution that creates special problems is cigarette smoke. Many nonsmokers apparently find smoke aversive (Jones, 1978). One study even found that cigarette smoke led nonsmokers to feelings of aggression toward smokers (Jones & Bogat, 1978). Louis Harris and Associates (1980) found that cigarette smoke posed problems for a large fraction of office workers. About one-third said they smoked (35%).

Of the nonsmoking majority, about one-quarter (26%) said that when their co-workers smoke near them, it bothers them a great deal. (p. 27). About one-half the employees in the survey said they believed smoking should be limited to certain areas. However, 94% of executives surveyed said smoking was not limited in their companies. A minority of workers (smokers) seems to be unrestrained in polluting the atmosphere of their co-workers, thereby creating annoyance for many.

Air pollution, or the perception that it exists, can create stress among employees who believe that it poses a threat to their health. The stress may be particularly intense among people who believe they have no control over the pollution (Evans & Jacobs, 1981). However, adaptation might diminish the stressful impact of air pollution after continued exposure.

A few studies have shown that certain air pollutants, such as carbon monoxide, can adversely affect the performance of tasks. In some cases the effect has been attributed to decreased or increased levels of arousal (see Evans & Jacobs, 1981). However, laboratory studies have been rare and the tasks and air pollutants widely divergent, making the results difficult to compare.

In sum, the evidence suggests that air pollution presents a problem in offices and factories, but its psychological impact has only rarely been studied. Air pollution may bring about annoyance and dissatisfaction with the environment, and it can create stress if seen as a hazard. Some types of pollution may affect some types of performance. Smoking is a widespread source of air pollution.

Summary

Temperature and ventilation became an issue during the 1800s; by the turn of the century, the ill-ventilated factories of the United States led to public outcry. By World War I, mechanical ventilation systems were fairly common, and a good deal was known about climatic comfort. Researchers had shown that the ambient temperature, relative humidity, speed of air movement, and radiant sources of heat all contributed to thermal comfort. By 1923 researchers developed the first of several numerical indexes of thermal comfort, called effective temperature. The value of such indexes is limited by substantial differences in what individuals find comfortable; the differences appear to be independent of gender, age, and geographical origin. Survey research suggests that temperature represents a source of widespread dissatisfaction in factories and offices. Individuals vary greatly in conditions they find comfortable.

Field studies have associated uncomfortably warm temperatures in factories with decreased output. Laboratory studies showed that the effect of heat on performance varied with the type of task. Mental tasks were unaffected by heat (within the physical limits of tolerance), except when they involved quick, coordinated movements. Motor tasks showed a fairly consistent decline in heat when performance continued for 30 minutes or more. Heat had no consistent effect on vigilance, although the optimum temperature seems to be about 80°F (27°C) for brief watches. Simultaneous performance of two tasks showed a fairly consistent decrement in heat, largely attributable to errors of omission in the secondary task. Fewer studies of the effects of cold temperatures were done, supplying no basis for clear conclusions.

Air quality concerns the presence of air pollution, which survey research has shown to be a considerable problem in offices and factories. However, research on specific forms of pollution has been infrequent.

Practical considerations

Ideal climatic conditions for the average employee in an office or factory probably consist of an ambient temperature around 70°F (21°C), moderate humidity, moderate air movement, and air that is as free as possible from sources of pollution. (Ventilation requirements depend on the population density and other factors; see Woodson, 1981.)

As conditions depart from the range of comfort, people who work in offices or factories can be expected to experience annoyance and dissatisfaction long before their capacity to perform their jobs is affected. Problems with comfort are complicated by consistent and substantial differences among individuals in the thermal conditions they find acceptable. In fact, it seems unlikely that any office or factory can be entirely free of complaints about the temperature.

Perhaps the most ideal solution to problems related to thermal comfort is to give each individual maximum control over the temperature in his or her own work-station. This solution is easiest to apply in the design of a new building. Unfortunately, individual control over the temperature may be difficult to achieve in existing buildings served by central heating and cooling systems with centralized controls. As an alternative to providing control over the ambient temperature, managers can actively encourage employees to ensure their own comfort through the clothing they wear and the use of small space heaters or fans, windowshades or curtains, and so on.

Employees whose complaints about the temperature go unheeded may become dissatisfied not only with the physical environment, but with a management apparently unresponsive to their needs. If so, the physical environment could become the focal point of a wider problem if not given attention.

7
NOISE

Noise is an intensely studied aspect of the ambient environment, widely regarded as a source of dissatisfaction and impediment to performance. The first section of this chapter briefly traces the history of attempts at controlling noise; subsequent sections deal with the research literature. After exploring some of the problems involved in studying the effects of noise, research is reviewed on the relationship between noise and dissatisfaction. The next and longest section reviews the voluminous research on noise and performance.

The battle against noise

Office managers recognized noise as a problem long before they could effectively deal with it. An early text on office management pointed out that noisy machines create a "steady drain upon the nerve force" (Galloway, 1919, p. 177). Suggestions for minimizing the noise included the placement of felt padding beneath office machines and under floor coverings.

By the 1930s, many companies had initiated experimental measures to control noise. Managers began to publish reports of increased productivity and decreased errors, absenteeism, and turnover as a consequence of reduced noise. For example, Aetna Life Insurance Company in 1928 installed sound-absorbing materials in clerical offices, and reported a substantial reduction of ambient noise; a measure of efficiency collected a year after the change showed an increase of 98% (see Berrien, 1946). Optimistic reports following other efforts to reduce noise encouraged the use of acoustical ceilings, carpeting, and other measures. By the 1940s, acoustical ceilings were common in offices, and carpeting was widely used (Hardy, 1957).

Factories contained few of the measures applied in offices, but many industrial engineers and industrial hygienists insisted that manufacturing processes be as quiet as possible. Factory-workers wore ear protectors long before the U.S. Occupational Safety and Health Administration (OSHA) set stringent standards for exposure to noise in 1970 (see Allen et al., 1976).

The development of the open-plan office in the sixties and seventies brought old problems with noise into sharp relief and led to advances in office acoustics. Improved ceilings sometimes had vertical "baffles," or suspended pieces of absorbent material. (Criss-crossed baffles that looked like inverted egg cartons gave nearly complete absorption of sound; see Egan, 1972.) In many offices, electronic sound generators emitted a constant hiss or hum to mask other sounds. The same purpose was served by mechanical ventilation systems, when they were running. Manufacturers of office furniture developed cloth-covered, sound-absorbing panels to separate desks. Overhead light fixtures were designed in small sizes to minimize the amount of hard surface that reflects sound. Work places that incorporated such measures were supposed to have hushed atmospheres conducive to comfort and efficiency. Unfortunately, not all work places reached the ideal (see Fig. 7.1).

Studying the impact of noise

For purposes of research, noise is usually defined as unwanted sound (e.g., Kryter, 1970). Noise creates problems because, for one thing,

[D]isturbance or irritation may arise from the peculiar nature of the sound, such as the rasping, grinding, screeching sound of the friction of metal on metal, as . . . from an unoiled bearing; or it may be disturbing because of its repetition, or because of echoes or reverberation. (Leffingwell, 1925, p. 237)

Sounds not inherently irritating can also constitute noise:

Speech is (or should be) coherent sound. So is music . . . coherent sounds, just because they have meaning, are far more disturbing than incoherent ones. And a coherent sound is likely to be all the more disturbing when you are off your guard, it breaks in upon you; your mind instinctively turns to follow its meaning; but it is not completed . . . you are left baffled and irritated. (Copley, 1920, p. 61)

"Quiet!"

Figure 7.1. Cartoon by Alan Dunn. *Source*: Reprinted from *Architectural Record*. (1973, Nov.). *154*(6), 10. © 1973, by McGraw-Hill, Inc. with all rights reserved.

Although noise has generally been regarded as a source of annoyance and environmental stress, what makes it stressful is a matter of debate. The traditional view is that purely physical properties of noise, especially its loudness, are related to psychological arousal or stress. On the other hand, noise may create stress through its meaning – as a signal of a potentially threatening event, or through the perception that the noise itself is threatening (Cohen, 1980b). However, most research had focused on the physical properties of noise, particularly its loudness and regularity.

Research on the effects of noise dates back to the beginnings of experimental psychology. In 1874, German psychologist Wilhelm Wundt explored the influence of noise on reaction time in his Leipzig laboratory (Wundt, 1893). Like Wundt's work, much subsequent research on noise had occurred in laboratories, and has focused primarily on the effects of noise on performance. The typical experiment has exposed people to sounds as loud as 115 decibels during clerical, mechanical, vigilance, or mental tasks, for periods lasting a few minutes to a few hours. Several studies have assessed reactions to noise in actual work settings, primarily in offices.

By most accounts, the results of dozens of studies of noise have been complicated (see the reviews by Berrien, 1946; Broadbent, 1957a, 1979; Davies, 1968; Glass & Singer, 1972; Kryter, 1970; Murrell, 1965; Poulton, 1970, 1977). One reviewer called the research "confusing, contradictory, and inconsistent" (Grether, 1971, p. 35). However, a few findings emerge with some consistency, as outlined in the remainder of this chapter.

A theme that cuts across the research findings on noise is the variability of response: differences among individuals have typically been wide. One study exposed volunteers to noises of varying intensity, asked for ratings of annoyance, and found that people most sensitive to noise indicated much greater annoyance than the least sensitive people exposed to the same sounds (Moreira & Bryan, 1971). Wide differences in response to noise have appeared in many settings, and are apparently independent of age, gender, and education (Canter & Stringer, 1975). There is evidence of differences between extroverts and introverts on sensitivity to noise (e.g., Stephens & Anderson, 1971) and of differences associated with anxiety on sensitivity to noise (Moreira & Bryan, 1971). People who complain most about noise may tend to complain about other things as well (Broadbent, 1957a).

In summary, noise has been seen as a source of annoyance and stress, and has been studied in the laboratory and in the work place. Research findings are complicated by the wide variation in individual response.

Noise and dissatisfaction

Research on noise in offices has included surveys and field studies. This section reviews studies concerning the prevalence of noise as a problem for workers, its most disturbing sources, and its connection with dissatisfaction.

Noise in the office

There is a substantial literature on reactions to noise in the office. Research evidence includes studies of the prevalence of office noise, its most annoying sources, and its correlation with dissatisfaction with the environment and with the job.

Prevalence of disturbance by noise. Noise has often been a prevalent source of complaint about the physical environment in studies of offices. The survey of U.S. office workers by Louis Harris and Associates (1978) included a question in which participants chose from a list of 17 features of their physical environments the two or three most important for doing their jobs well. The item most frequently chosen was the "ability to concentrate without noise and other distractions" (p. 50). However, when participants rated the adequacy of their offices on the same 17 features, the ability to concentrate without noise and distraction ranked near the bottom of the list, fifteenth of seventeen. Noise emerged as a critical issue, and U.S. offices were apparently viewed by many as too noisy. Similarly, in the second survey (Louis Harris & Associates, 1980), 84% of participating office workers said that having quiet surroundings affected their personal comfort on the job "a great deal" or "somewhat" (p. 13), but 49% said that they did not have quiet in their offices (p. 18).

An earlier study of English offices found a similar result: Of several aspects of the physical environment rated by more than 2,000 office workers, noise was the most frequent source of complaint, with more than 20% indicating that noise made them "definitely uncomfortable" (Langdon, 1966). In another survey of English office workers, noise received lower ratings of "acceptability" than any other feature of the physical environment (Keighley, 1970, p. 84).

Offices seem to be plagued with noise, but open offices are particularly afflicted. Noise has represented a critical problem in surveys in open offices (e.g., Hedge, 1982; McCarrey, Peterson, Edwards & Von Kulmiz, 1974). Table 7.1 presents the results of 10 studies of employees who moved into *Burolandschaft* offices or open-plan offices (see Chapter 2). Noise was often a greater source of disturbance after changing to open offices, even in organizations where it was a serious problem before. Of nine studies that assessed change after moving from conventional to open offices, four found noise a greater problem after moving, four found no change, and only one reported an improvement. At least two of the offices where no change was found incorporated special features to combat noise, as did the one that registered an improvement. These included fabric-covered panels (e.g., Sundstrom, Herbert & Brown, 1982) or electronic background sound (e.g., Riland and Falk, 1972), as well as carpeting and acoustical ceilings (e.g., Brookes, 1972a).

Probably the best explanation for the prevalence of disturbance by noise in open offices is the lack of walls to contain the sounds. With few walls to the ceiling, sounds can travel freely from one workspace to another, unless absorbed or contained by acoustically treated ceilings, carpets, or partitions, or masked by ambient sound.

Some research has found noise in offices unrelated to the loudness of the ambient sound. In the study by Boyce (1974), employees moved from five buildings into one new facility, where more than half of them were still disturbed "often" by noises, despite the relatively low meas-

Table 7.1. *Summary of the findings concerning noise in 10 studies of open-plan offices*

Study	Change in ratings of noise after changing offices	Most disturbing sources of noise
Before-and-after studies[a]		
Boyce (1974)	No change	Phones (67%); people talking (55%); air conditioning (34%); typing (28%)
Brookes (1972a)[b]	No change	Conversations (43%)
Hanson (1978)	Increase	"Auditory intrusion"
Riland & Falk (1972)	Decrease	—
Sundstrom, Herbert & Brown (1982)	No change	—
Retrospective studies[c]		
Boje (1971)	Increase	Visitors; passers-by; conversations/phones
Hundert & Greenfield (1969)	Increase	Noise from people
Kraemer, Sieverts & Partners (1977)	Increase	Conversations (46%); phones (40%); typewriters (25%)
Nemecek & Grandjean (1973)	(79% disturbed)	Conversations (46%); office machines (25%); phones (19%)
Sloan (undated)	No change	—

[a] Included assessments before and after relocation to open offices.
[b] Apparently reports same data as Brookes (1972b) and Brookes & Kaplan (1972).
[c] Participants rated earlier, conventional offices from memory.

ured level of ambient sound, 54 decibels. Similarly, the study by Kraemer, Sieverts & Partners (1977) included measures of ambient sound at 19 offices, but reported no relationship between sound levels and disturbance by noise. Nemecek & Grandjean (1973) incorporated more precise measurement of sound. In 15 offices they took more than 8,000 readings of ambient sound with decibel meters but found no correlation between these readings and disturbance by noise among 519 employees.

Other researchers have reported a similar lack of correspondence between the measured intensity of ambient office sound and annoyance
among workers (e.g., Cavanaugh, Farrell, Hirtle & Watters, 1962).

Objective measures of the average level of ambient sound may not
correspond with employees' annoyance because the critical feature of
noise is intermittent sound heard above the background. A major study
by Keighley (1970) included multiple measurements of the ambient level
of sound, along with measurements of the "peak level" of sounds above
the background in 40 offices. Results indicated no relationship between
ambient sound and "acceptability" of the noise, as in the other research.
However, when a "peak index" was calculated separately from the
average sound level, Keighley found a strong and highly significant
association with reported acceptability of noise. (The ratings of acceptability predicted from noise indexes showed a correlation of 0.91 with
actual ratings of acceptability.)

In summary, surveys among office workers consistently identify noise
as a prevalent problem, particularly in open offices. Field research shows
disturbance by noise related to the loudness of sounds that can be heard
above the ambient background sound.

Sources of disturbing noise. The most disturbing sources of noise in the
office are apparently not necessarily the loudest. Surveys of office workers that included questions on disturbing sources of noise consistently
found conversations by co-workers a primary source of annoyance, along
with sounds made by office equipment and passing motor traffic. As
shown in Table 7.1, most studies of open offices that explored sources
of noise found conversations by co-workers a major annoyance.

Langdon's (1966) study of English offices also found co-workers the
most important source of noise in the office, and that complaints increased with the number of people who shared the same room. As shown
in Figure 7.2 nearly one-half the occupants of rooms containing more
than eight people complained of noise. This finding is consistent with
the tendency of workers who move into open offices to complain more
of noise than in conventional offices.

Sources of noise experienced as most disturbing are apparently the
ones that carry information or meaning. Noise from co-workers' conversations may demand attention because of the possibility that their
contents are important. The ringing of the telephones may be disturbing
because the sound signals a demand for a reaction. By contrast, the
sounds of office machinery are unlikely to have such meanings and are
apparently less disturbing.

Correlation of noise with dissatisfaction. Research in offices suggests

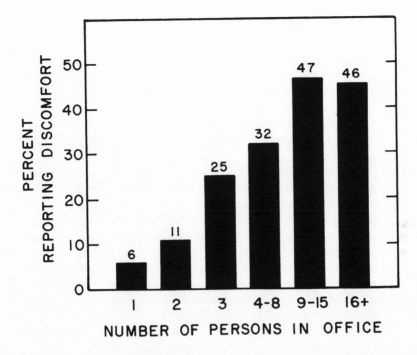

Figure 7.2. Percentage of office workers complaining of noise in relationship to the number of people in the office. *Source*: Adapted from Langdon, F.J. (1966). *Modern Offices: A User Survey.* National Buildings Research Paper No. 41. London: H. Majesty's Stationery Office, p. 26.

that noise represents an important source of dissatisfaction with the physical environment, and perhaps even with the job. The hypothesis has been directly addressed in two studies, and confirmed in both. Nemecek and Grandjean (1973) assessed correlations of ratings of qualities of the physical environment with general preferences for working in an open office, which may be taken as a measure of satisfaction with the physical environment. These investigators reported a significant, inverse correlation between disturbance by noise and preference ($r = -0.59$), indicating a strong association between noise and dissatisfaction with the office.

One study linked noise from co-workers with dissatisfaction with both the environment and job. It included assessments of eight types of noise, satisfaction with the physical environment, and job satisfaction among more than 2,000 office workers. As in other research, noise was a prevalent problem, with more than 75% of the participants reporting that they were bothered at least "sometimes" by people talking and by telephones ringing. Other types of noise bothered a substantial percentage of participants. Some of the participants completed the questionnaire both before and after moving to a new office; they were divided into groups for whom each type of noise increased, remained the same, or decreased. Those who reported an increase in disturbance from people talking showed decreased satisfaction with their environments; the no-change group showed no change in environmental satisfaction; those who experienced decreased noise from people talking showed an increase in satisfaction with the environment. These results suggest a direct link between noise from co-workers' conversations and dissatisfaction with the office environment. Similarly, noise from telephones and type-writers was linked with dissatisfaction with the work environment, but noise from ventilation systems and traffic was not. The project also found that people who experienced an increase in noise from co-workers' conversations after changing offices also experienced a significant decrease in job satisfaction, as shown in Figure 7.3. This finding suggests that noise from co-workers' conversations is a potent enough source of dissatisfaction to affect attitudes toward the job as a whole (Sundstrom, Town, Osborn et al., 1982b). Similar conclusions based on the same data are also reported in BOSTI (1981).

In summary, noise from co-workers' conversations, telephones, and typewriters has been directly associated with dissatisfaction with the physical environment. Noise from co-workers' conversations has even been associated with job dissatisfaction among office workers.

Noise in the factory

Research on the psychological effects of noise on factory workers has been much less common than research on office workers. One explanation may be the belief that people can adapt to noises that do not cause physical damage. An early industrial psychologist wrote,

[N]oise of the machines in many factories makes it impossible to communicate except by shouting . . . the laborers themselves usually feel convinced that they no longer notice it at all. (Munsterberg, 1913, pp. 210–211)

Instead of simply becoming accustomed to noise, perhaps factory workers overcome disturbance through their effort. If so, they may pay a psychological price.

The statement is commonly made that individuals can adjust themselves to noisy conditions and that they do not mind them. In point of fact they are obliged to use energy in combating such conditions and this energy is

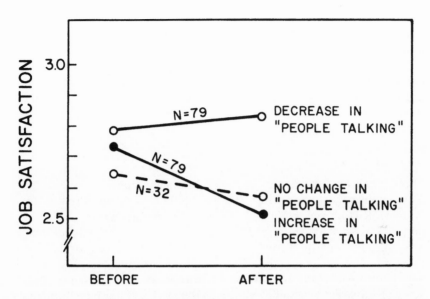

Figure 7.3. Changes in job satisfaction among office employees who reported an increase, a decrease, or no change in disturbance by people talking after changing offices. *Source*: Sundstrom, E., Town, J., Osborn, D., Rice, R., Konar, E., Mandel, D. & Brill, M. (1984). *Office Noise and Employees' Satisfaction and Performance*. Unpublished paper was presented at the 1982 Conference of the American Psychological Association, Washington, D.C.

therefore lost as far as its effective use for working purposes is concerned. (Hopf, 1931, p. 763)

One reason why factory workers might not be conscious of the noise is that they help make it themselves. Some evidence suggests that people find their own sounds or sounds from beneficial sources more tolerable than someone else's noises (Broadbent, 1957a; Poulton, 1970). This might stem from the workers' ability to control or a least predict when their own noises will occur. For example:

In three factories where there was considerable noise, namely chocolate-shaping, tin-stamping, and printing, the workers were asked about noise, and the opinion of the majority was that they got used to it. In each case, however, it was the manager who objected, and in one factory the manager was trying to get noiseless machines invented. The explanation was, I think, that the workers were helping to make it, while the manager was forced to hear it but was powerless to prevent it. (M. Smith, 1944, p. 73)

In factories, machinery not only makes a racket but provides a way to earn a living. Perhaps it is not so surprising that people who work at a factory say they can "get used to" the noise.

Whatever the role of noise in dissatisfaction among factory workers, researchers have apparently ignored it. This state of affairs unfortunately applies to most aspects of the physical environment and factory workers' satisfaction.

Noise and performance

The relationship between noise and performance represents one of the most intensively studied issues for the psychology of the physical environment. However, most studies come from the laboratory. This section reviews the findings on the influence of predictable and unpredictable noise on individual performance. The review is organized around the five types of tasks outlined earlier: clerical, mental, motor, vigilance, and dual (see Chapter 3). The extensive research on personality characteristics associated with differences in the effects of noise on performance is not covered here (e.g., Davies & Hockey, 1966; Davies, Hockey & Taylor, 1969; Hockey, 1972). The following section presents an account of studies on the average effects of noise.

Predictable noise

Predictable noise includes continuous sounds, such as those made by ventilation systems and motors, and repetitive or regular sounds, such as those made by stamping machines, presses, and many other types of equipment. If such noises affect performance on the job, the influences probably come from one of two processes: arousal or masking. If constant or regular noise creates arousal, it may augment the performance of simple tasks, but degrade the performance of complex ones (see the discussion of the "Yerkes-Dodson law" in Chapter 4). However, if people can become accustomed to regular noise, its effect may only be temporary. Noise can mask or obscure useful sounds that provide feedback, like the click that accompanies the depression of a key on a calculator. Masking of auditory cues might detract from performance if the auditory feedback is crucial for speed or accuracy. According to one expert, noise also can literally keep people from hearing themselves think, by masking "inner speech" (Poulton, 1977; see also Poulton, 1976b; Broadbent, 1976). If so, predictable noise may adversely affect mental performance through such masking. Following is a review of studies on predictable noise and performance.

Clerical tasks. Clerical tasks comprise probably the least demanding tasks studied in laboratory experiments on noise. As shown in Table 7.2, adverse effects of predictable noise appeared in only two of 11 experiments. The decrement occurred after an unannounced change in the loudness of the sound (Teichner et al., 1963) and in a 36–minute exposure to very loud noise (Harris, 1972). This finding involved a change in ambient sound, which could have resulted in distraction of attention. In three other studies, continuous or repetitive noise had no effects. Broad-band or "white" noise had beneficial effects in two studies in which work sessions were brief (16 minutes), and the noise was keyed to a machine-paced task (Warner, 1969; Warner & Heimstra, 1971).

In summary, the evidence suggests that predictable noise only affects clerical performance when it starts, changes, or serves as a signal. Unfortunately, the studies all involved work-sessions of an hour or less, so it is impossible to tell what effects, if any, occur with longer exposure.

Mental tasks. Table 7.3 lists studies of predictable noise and mental tasks. Seven of 10 experiments found no effects of noise during work-sessions of up to 4 hours. These experiments incorporated simple tasks that were only slightly more demanding than clerical tasks. One study found faster but less accurate performance of arithmetic problems during 30–minute sessions in 90–decibel noise (Viteles & Smith, 1946). This improvement in performance might reflect the stimulating effect of arousal brought about by the loud noise. However, none of the studies involved a task that could reasonably be described as complex.

Motor tasks. Evidence on the effects of predictable noise on motor tasks includes at least 16 studies, as shown in Table 7.4. One of the studies came from an extensive program of research conducted around the time of World War II (Stevens, 1972; the details are described in longer reports, mainly Stevens et al., 1941). Adverse effects emerged in 11 of the studies; positive effects appeared in two. Most of the studies involved work-sessions of less than 2 hours.

The adverse effects generally took two forms: more errors after the onset of the noise, or more errors after spending more than 30 minutes at an especially demanding task. One task that showed the decrement is the five-choice task (Broadbent, 1953, 1957b; Hartley, 1973, 1974). In this task the participant watches a display of five lights and notices which one lights up. Then, as quickly as possible, the participant touches the corresponding relay on the same display (or another display), using an 18–inch wand. The light goes off and another comes on. Continuous 90–decibel noise for periods of about 1/2 hour led to increased errors. Other tasks showed similar decrements (Eschenbrenner, 1971; Hack,

Table 7.2. *Summary of laboratory findings on the effects of predictable noise on the performance of clerical tasks*

Study[a]	Task	Noise	Duration (minutes)[b,c]	Decibel level in quiet[d]	Decibel-level associated with effect on performance[d]		
					Decrement	No effect	Increment
Glass & Singer (1972)	Finding A's	Regular bursts	23 (8)	No noise	—	56, 108	—
	Number comparison (#1)	Regular bursts	23 (8)	No noise	—	56, 108	—
	Finding A's	Regular bursts	24 (8)	No noise	—	56, 108	—
	Number comparison (#2)	Regular bursts	24 (8)	No noise	—	56, 108	—
	Finding A's	Regular bursts	25 (8)	No noise	—	56, 108	—
	Number comparison (#3)	Regular bursts	25 (8)	No noise	—	56, 108	—
Chatterjee & Khrishnamurty (1972)	Typing, transcription	Continuous recorded sounds	10 (10) 3 sessions	No noise	—	Varied	—
Warner (1969)	Letter recognition machine paced	Repetitive white bursts keyed to task	16 (16) 4 sessions	No noise	—	—	80, 90, 100 fewer errors
Warner & Heimstra (1971)	Letter recognition machine paced	Repetitive white bursts keyed to task	16 (16) 8 sessions	No noise	—	—	100 faster detection
Viteles & Smith (1946)	Number transcription	Continuous fan	330 (30) 42 sessions	72	—	80, 90	—
	Number checking	Continuous fan	330 (30) 42 sessions	72	—	80	90
	Location checking	Continuous fan	330 (30) 42 sessions	72	—	80, 90	faster detection
Harris (1972)	Number searching	Continuous broad band	36 (36) 4 sessions	60	105 fewer completions	—	—
Schoenberger & Harris (1965)	Tracing sequential numbers	Continuous broad band	45 (45)	No noise	—	85, 95, 110	—

| Teichner et al. (1963) | Letter recognition (#1) | Continuous white | 60 (60) | 57 | — | 69, 81, 93, 105 — |
| | Letter recognition (#2) | Continuous white with shift in from 81 dB | 60 (60) | None | 57, 69, 93, 105 less gain from practice | — |

[a] Studies listed in order of increasing task-performance session. Numbered studies are separate experiments.
[b] First number indicates exposure to the noise condition in one session. Number in parentheses indicates the amount of time spent doing one task during one session, excluding practice sessions and rest periods.
[c] When participants performed during two or more separate sessions, or under two or more conditions, the number of sessions is indicated.
[d] Decibels on the A scale unless otherwise noted.

Table 7.3. *Summary of laboratory findings on the effects of predictable noise on the performance of mental tasks*

Study[a]	Task	Noise	Duration (minutes)[b,c]	Decibel level in quiet[d]	Decibel-level associated with effect on performance		
					Decrement	No effect	Increment
Glass & Singer (1972)	Simple addition (#1)	Regular 9-second bursts of recorded sound	23 (8)	No noise	—	56, 108	—
	Simple addition (#2)	Regular 9-second bursts of recorded sound	24 (8)	No noise	—	56, 108	—
	Simple addition (#3)	Regular 9-second bursts of recorded sound	25 (8)	No noise	—	56, 108	—
Broadbent (1958)	Mental subtraction	Continuous broad-band sound	—	70	—	100	—
Hartley & Adams (1974)	Color-naming (card-sort) (#1)	Continuous broad-band sound	30 (varied) 2 sessions	70 dBC	100 dBC longer times	—	—
	Color naming (written test) (#2)	Continuous broad-band sound	10 or 30 (varied) 2 sessions	70 dBC	100 dBC more errors in 30-min session	—	—
Pollock & Bartlett (1932)	Word making (#7)	Continuous recorded sound	30 (30) 2 sessions	No noise	—	Unknown	—
Viteles & Smith (1946)	Mental multiplication	Continuous fan noise	330 (30) 42 sessions	72	90 more errors	80	90 faster
	Coding	Continuous fan noise	330 (30) 42 sessions	72	—	80, 90	—
Stevens (1972)	Letter coding	Continuous aircraft noise	420 (75) 16 sessions	90	—	115	—

| Vernon & Warner (1932) | Long division & multiplication | Metronome | 220 (220) multiple sessions | No noise — | Unknown — |

[a] Studies listed in order of increasing task-performance session. Numbered studies are separate experiments.

[b] First number indicates exposure to the noise condition in one session. Number in parentheses indicates the amount of time spent doing one task during one session, excluding practice sessions and rest periods.

[c] When participants performed during two or more separate sessions, or under two or more conditions, the number of sessions is indicated.

[d] Decibels on the A scale unless otherwise noted.

Table 7.4. *Summary of laboratory findings on the effects of predictable noise on the performance of motor tasks*

Study[a]	Task	Noise	Duration (minutes)[b,c]	Decibel level in quiet[d]	Decibel-level associated with effect on performance		
					Decrement	No effect	Increment
Zenhausern et al. (1974)	Reaction time	Continuous noise	200 trials	Hearing threshold	—	+10, +40 over threshold	+70 faster times
Hack et al. (1965)	Compensatory tracking	Repetitive noise	10 (10)	No noise	—	—	—
Doering (1977)	Pursuit rotor	Repetitive white bursts	20 (20)	50	60 more errors first 5 min	70, 90	—
Eschenbrenner (1971)	Complex image tracing	Continuous white noise	20 (20) 3 sessions	No noise	50, 70, 90 more errors	—	—
	Complex image tracing	Repetitive white noise	20 (20) 3 sessions	No noise	50, 70, 90 more errors	—	—
Weinstein & Mackenzie (1966)	Dexterity test (turning over blocks)	Continuous white noise	12 (25)	No noise	—	—	100 more blocks
Pollock & Bartlett (1932)	Timed assembly task (#5)	Continuous recorded noise	11 to 30 + (11 to 30 +)	No noise	Unknown; longer times	—	—
Theologus et al. (1974)	Reaction time	Patterned intermittent sound	30 (30) 2 sessions	No noise	—	85	—
	Compensatory tracking	Patterned intermittent sound	30 (30) 2 sessions	No noise	—	85	—
Viteles & Smith (1946)	Pursuit rotor	Continuous fan noise	330 (30) 42 sessions	72	—	80, 90	—
	Simulated lathe	Continuous fan noise	330 (30) 42 sessions	72	90 more errors	80	—
Poulton & Edwards (1974)	Five-choice task (serial reaction time)	Continuous low-frequency sound	90 (30) 4 sessions	80 dBC	—	—	102 dBC fewer errors, last 5 min

Study	Task	Noise type	Duration min (min)				
Broadbent (1957b)	Five-choice task (serial reaction time)	Continuous machinery noise, high or low frequency	25 (25)	80	100 more errors, especially high frequency	90	—
Broadbent (1953)	Five-choice task (serial reaction time)	Continuous broad-band sound	30 (60)	70	100 more errors	—	—
Hartley (1974)	Five-choice task (serial reaction time) (#1)	Continuous broad-band sound	40 (40) 3 sessions	70 dBC	95 dBC more errors	—	—
	Five-choice task (serial reaction-time) (#2)	Continuous broad-band sound	40 (40) 4 sessions	70 dBC	95 dBC more errors	—	—
Hartley (1973)	Five-choice task (serial reaction time)	Continuous broad-band sound	20 or 40 (20 or 40) 8 sessions	70	100 more errors	—	—
Hartley & Carpenter (1974)	Five-choice task with separate response panel	Continuous broad-band sound	40 (40) 4 sessions	70 dBC	95 dBC more errors	—	—
Stevens (1972)	Remote maze tracing	Continuous simulated aircraft	420 (50 to 75) 16 sessions	90	115 slower, more errors	—	—
	Serial pursuit	Continuous simulated aircraft	420 (50 to 75) 16 sessions	90	—	115	—
	Four-choice task	Continuous simulated aircraft	420 (50 to 75) 16 sessions	90	—	115	—
	Pursuit-rotor	Continuous simulated aircraft	420 (50 to 75) 16 sessions	90	—	115	—
Pollock & Bartlett (1932)	Peg-in-hole with 2 moving targets (#4)	Continuous recorded noise	480 (480) 2 sessions	No noise	—	Unknown	—

[a] Studies listed in order of increasing task-performance session. Numbered studies are separate experiments.

[b] First number indicates exposure to the noise condition in one session. Number in parentheses indicates the amount of time spent doing one task during one session, excluding practice sessions and rest periods.

[c] When participants performed during two or more separate sessions, or under two or more conditions, the number of sessions is indicated.

[d] Decibels on the A scale unless otherwise noted.

145

Robinson & Lathrop, 1965). An early decrement in accuracy could reflect overarousal created by the noise at onset. The decrements could also reflect the masking of auditory cues, such as the sound of the wand touching the relay in the five-choice task (Poulton, 1977).

The task that showed a decrement after a hour in loud, predictable noise (115dB), involved the use of a flight simulator that required corrections of pitch and roll. It was highly demanding (Stevens, 1972). It is possible that the noise produced overarousal. Less demanding tracking tasks showed neither the early decrement in accuracy nor the eventual decrement after an hour of work (Doering, 1977; Stevens, 1972). Perhaps in moderately demanding tasks the noise did not produce enough arousal to disrupt performance.

Beneficial effects of loud, continuous noise (above 100 decibels) appeared in the speed of performance of a manipulative task (Weinstein & Mackenzie, 1966). Low-frequency noise led to improved accuracy in a tracking task (Poulton & Edwards, 1974). Both of these positive effects involved work-sessions of 1/2 hour or less. As in some other relatively simple tasks, constant noise apparently had a stimulating effect on performance for a brief period. The positive effects may have been caused by arousal (there seems to be no other satisfactory explanation).

In summary, predictable noise generally led to a decrement in performance of difficult motor tasks. However, the decrement did not occur in all tasks, and in some circumstances constant noise during brief work-sessions was actually associated with improved performance.

Vigilance tasks. This demanding type of task involves "keeping lookout for brief signals which are difficult to discriminate" (Poulton, 1970, p. 321). Vigilance is usually machine paced. Performance can suffer from the slightest distraction, and it may begin to deteriorate after less than an hour under the best of conditions (Mackworth, 1948). Table 7.5 summarizes the results of 13 experiments on the influence of predictable noise on vigilance tasks.

Loud, predictable noise (100 decibels or louder) produced decrements in performance in four studies that involved very difficult vigilance. The decrement consisted of more frequent errors of omission (missing of signals). The tasks required the monitoring of either 20 sources of signals (Broadbent, 1954), three sources of signals at one per second (Broadbent & Gregory, 1963; Jerison, 1959), or one source of very rapid signals, 3 per second (Broadbent & Gregory, 1965). Other studies involved less demanding vigilance tasks and found no effects of continuous noise (Blackwell & Belt, 1971; Broadbent, 1954; Broadbent & Gregory, 1965; Jerison, 1957). Only two experiments found a positive effect of continuous noise on vigilance, one of which occurred when the noise was keyed to the task (Watkins, 1964).

A decrement in the performance of demanding vigilance tasks in continuous noise is difficult to explain. Arousal is usually regarded as favorable to vigilance, and continuous noise is usually seen as a stimulus to arousal. So noise should help, not hurt, performance. However, the decrement in performance could reflect an excessively high level of arousal for a complex task. It could also reflect a form of fatigue that eventually grows out of being aroused for a prolonged period. Arousal stimulated by the noise may have created an extra drain on the participants' capacities, which may have begun to take a toll after a while.

Another explanation of the decrement in performance is that the noise led to distortions in judgment, perhaps as a consequence of arousal. In two studies of vigilance, participants expressed confidence in more of their judgments under noisy conditions (Broadbent & Gregory, 1963, 1965). Perhaps noise led people to make faster or sloppier decisions out of overconfidence.

One of the few published examples of an experiment on noise in an industrial setting involved continuous noise and a vigilance task. In a Kodak Ltd. plant in England that produced film, researchers studied employees who ran film-perforating machines. These employees worked in two dimly lit bays, each tending several machines that had to be threaded like projectors; they were paid on a piece rate. The task was

sensitive to any momentary lapses of attention on the operator's part since, if he makes a mistake in threading the film he is likely to have a breakage of the film or other breakdown of the machine. (Broadbent & Little, 1960, p. 134)

Measurements demonstrated that the noise in the bays was about 98 to 99 decibels and was more or less continuous. The researchers persuaded the company to acoustically treat one of the two bays, reducing the sound level to about 90 decibels. Records of film breakage and breakdowns were kept for 6 weeks before and after the treatment. Errors became less frequent in the treated bay, in comparison with the untreated one. Work output remained approximately the same. Fewer errors in the treated bay could conceivably reflect increased motivation among the workers in response to outside attention. However, the lower error rate persisted in the treated bay for long enough to make this seem implausible. It is also conceivable that the noise in the untreated bays led to fatigue among the workers by keeping them chronically overaroused. With the noise reduced, perhaps they were less fatigued. However, this explanation overlooks the possibility of adaptation to the

Table 7.5. *Summary of laboratory findings on the effects of predictable noise on the performance of vigilance tasks*

Study[a]	Task	Noise	Duration (minutes)[b,c]	Decibel level in quiet[d]	Decibel-level associated with effect on performance		
					Decrement	No effect	Increment
Samuel (1964)	Machine-paced mental arithmetic, digits in 1 or 2 locations	Continuous white noise	21 (21)	80	—	—	100 fewer omissions with 2 locations
Poulton & Edwards (1974)	Monitoring one flashing light	Continuous low-frequency sound	90 (30) 4 sessions	80 dBC	—	102 dBC	—
Blackwell & Belt (1971)	Monitoring visual display	Continuous white noise	40 (40)	50	—	75, 90	—
Watkins (1964)	Monitoring one flashing light	Repetitive white noise keyed to trials	30 (30)	75	—	—	75 more detections
McCann (1969)	Auditory number checking	Continuous monotone	20 (60)	No noise	—	50	—
Broadbent & Gregory (1965)	Monitoring 3 flashing lights (#1)	Continuous valve noise	70 (70) 2 sessions	75	100 more extreme judgments	—	—
	Monitoring one flashing light (#2)	Continuous valve noise	70 (70) 2 sessions	75	—	100	—
Broadbent & Gregory (1963)	Monitoring 3 dials	Continuous valve noise	80 (80) 2 sessions	75	100 more extreme judgments	—	—
Broadbent (1954)	Monitoring 20 dials (#1)	Continuous broad band	90 (90) 5 sessions	70	100 more errors	—	—
	Monitoring 20 flashing lights (#2)	Continuous broad band	90 (90) 5 sessions	70	—	100	—

Jerison (1957)	Monitoring one dial	Continuous masking	105 (105)	79	—	112	—
Jerison (1959)	Monitoring 3 dials (#1)	Continuous masking	90 (120) 2 sessions	83	114 fewer detections	—	—
	Three flashing lights with counting (#2)	Continuous masking	90 (120) 2 sessions	78	—	112	—

[a] Studies listed in order of increasing task-performance session. Numbered studies are separate experiments.

[b] First number indicates exposure to the noise condition in one session. Number in parentheses indicates the amount of time spent doing one task during one session, excluding practice sessions and rest periods.

[c] When participants performed during two or more separate sessions, or under two or more conditions, the number of sessions is indicated.

[d] Decibels on the A scale unless otherwise noted.

loud noise. A more likely explanation is based on masking – that the less intense background sound in the treated bay allowed the operators to hear their machines and diagnose problems in time to prevent them.

In summary, very loud predictable noise in the laboratory led to a decrement in the most difficult vigilance tasks, but not in moderately difficult ones. One industrial study found a reduction of continuous noise associated with fewer errors in a job that demanded vigilance, probably because the loud noise had masked valuable auditory cues.

Dual tasks. Studies that used two simultaneous tasks often examined the idea that arousal from continuous noise produces "narrowing of attention" (see Chapter 4). Researchers reasoned that if predictable noise creates a narrowing of attention, the individual given two things to do at once may concentrate on one task to the detriment of the other.

Table 7.6 summarizes the results of 11 experiments, which found mixed results. Three of five studies with very loud noise (100 decibels) found that it degraded the performance of at least part of the secondary task (Hockey, 1970a,b; Hamilton & Copeman, 1970). One other study found performance of the primary task degraded in 105–decibel noise, but not the secondary one (Loeb & Jones, 1978). One study found that low-frequency intense noise improved vigilance (Poulton & Edwards, 1974). On the other hand, five studies that used less intense noise (80 to 92 decibels) failed to find any adverse effects (Forster & Grierson, 1978; experiments #1, 3, and 4; Finkelman & Glass, 1970; Theologus, Wheaton & Fleischman, 1974).

The studies by Hockey (1970a,b) clearly showed the "narrowing of attention." Participants performed a tracking task while at the same time watching lights around them in a semicircle for certain signals. In the first study, participants exposed to loud, continuous white noise apparently focused their attention on the lights directly in front of them. They made more errors of omission with the "peripheral" lights but actually did better with the "central" lights. The second experiment showed that when the likelihood of a signal was systematically varied, participants focused their attention on lights most likely to give a signal. (The focusing of attention on high-yield signals represents one of the methods for dealing with overload discussed in Chapter 4.) Three later attempts to replicate the finding in less intense noise failed to produce the effect (Forster & Grierson, 1978). The reasons for the failure to replicate are a matter of debate (Hockey, 1978; Forster, 1978).

In summary, studies of dual tasks found decrements in the performance of one task in very loud, regular noise (100 decibels or more) but not in less intense noise (92 decibels or less).

Summary of findings on predictable noise. Laboratory studies found that continuous or regular noise led to decreases in the accuracy of performance under four conditions: (1) during clerical tasks, when the noise changed; (2) during some highly demanding motor tasks; (3) during highly demanding vigilance tasks when the noise was very loud (100 decibels); and (4) during dual tasks when the noise was very loud (100 decibels). In contrast, continuous or regular noise occasionally led to improved speed or accuracy under four specific conditions: (1) during simple clerical tasks when the noise was keyed to the task; (2) during a simple mental task in a brief work-session; (3) during a simple, repetitive motor task; and (4) during a motor task when the noise was of very low frequency.

Unpredictable noise

This section deals with unpredictable noise – sounds that occur suddenly, without warning, or at irregular intervals. Describing one such sound, Schopenhauer wrote of tradesmen cracking their whips over horse-drawn carts:

The sudden, sharp crack which paralyses the brain, destroys all meditation and murders thought, must cause pain to anyone who has anything like an idea in his head. (Smith, 1944, p. 68)

Schopenhauer may have been right, but on the other hand there is ample evidence of the remarkable capacity of people to adapt. An older experiment gives a graphic illustration (J.J.B. Morgan, 1916). Participants sat at a table containing a keyboard. When a display showed a letter in the alphabet, they were asked to look on a code list for a corresponding number from 0 to 9 and to press the correct key. (The list was frequently changed, to prevent memorization.) The experiment included the following "disturbances":

A fire bell with an 8–inch gong . . . eight feet away. . . . A bell mechanism with the gong removed and the hammer striking against a resonance-box placed behind the subject and to the left. . . . Another bell mechanism with the hammer vibrating against a metal beam which ran the length of the room. . . . A bell hammer vibrating against the table where the subject sat. . . . A buzzer placed upon the subjects' table. . . . A bell to the left and in front of the subject. . . . A bell behind the subject to the right. . . . A buzzer on a tin box under the table. . . . A buzzer on the left wall on a resonance board. (J.J.B. Morgan, 1916, pp. 18–19)

Besides this, the experimenter played gramophone records of two vocal solos, two instrumental selections, and two humorous speeches.

Table 7.6. *Summary of laboratory findings on the effects of predictable noise on the performance of dual (simultaneous) tasks*

Study[a]	Task	Noise	Duration (minutes)[b,c]	Decibel level in quiet[d]	Decibel-level associated with effect on performance[d]		
					Decrement	No effect	Increment
Davies & Jones (1975)	Delayed recall of words & locations	Continuous white noise	1 (1)	55	95 more errors, 2nd task	—	—
Finkelman & Glass (1970)	Compensatory tracking + delayed digit recall	Regular white bursts	2 (2) 18 sessions	No noise	—	80	—
Loeb & Jones (1978)	Tracking + monitoring 6 peripheral lights	Continuous industrial noise	10 (10) 3 sessions	75	105 more tracking errors	—	—
Hamilton & Copeman (1970)	Pursuit tracking + monitoring 6 peripheral lights	Continuous noise	30 (30) 6 sessions	70	100 fewer peripheral detections	—	—
Theologus et al. (1974)	Compensatory tracking + reaction time	Patterned intermittent recorded sound	30 (30)	No noise	—	85	—
Poulton & Edwards (1974)	Tracking + 6 peripheral lights	Continuous low-frequency sound	90 (30) 4 sessions	80 dBC	—	—	102 dBC better tracking last 5 min
Hockey (1970a)	Tracking + monitoring 6 peripheral lights	Continuous broad band	40 (40) 2 sessions	70	100 fewer peripheral detections	—	100 better tracking, more central detections

Hockey (1970b)	Tracking + monitoring 6 peripheral lights	Continuous broad band	40 (40) 2 sessions	70	—	100 better tracking, faster central detection
Forster & Grierson (1978)	Tracking + monitoring 6 peripheral lights (#1)	Continuous broad band	40 (40) 2 sessions	70	92	—
	Tracking + monitoring 6 peripheral lights (#3)	Continuous broad band	40 (40) 2 sessions	70	92	—
	Tracking + monitoring 6 peripheral lights (#4)	Continuous broad band	40 (40) 2 sessions	70	92	—

[a] Studies listed in order of increasing task-performance session. Numbered studies are separate experiments.

[b] First number indicates exposure to the noise condition in one session. Number in parentheses indicates the amount of time spent doing one task during one session, excluding practice sessions and rest periods.

[c] When participants performed during two or more separate sessions, or under two or more conditions, the number of sessions is indicated.

[d] Decibels on the A scale unless otherwise noted.

Despite the cacophony (of unknown intensity), participants in the experiment showed only a momentary lapse in speed after the onset of noise. They worked with undiminished accuracy for several hours. After a few days they sometimes even worked slightly faster in noise than in relative quiet!

If the researcher's efforts succeeded in murdering any thoughts, how could these people maintain their efficiency? A partial answer comes from measurements of the depths of the impressions left when they struck the keyboard. They hit the keys much harder during the noise. They also made more movements of their lips. These data and records of breathing suggested that participants articulated each step of the task to overcome the distractions by the noise (Morgan, 1916). Another experiment showed similar results (J.J.B. Morgan, 1917). Apparently it took considerable effort to overcome the distractions created by unpredictable noise while performing even a simple clerical task.

Psychological processes through which unpredictable noise might affect performance include distraction and overload. Unpredictable sounds may distract attention, perhaps through "internal blinks" (Broadbent, 1957). These could lead to lapses and mistakes, especially in difficult tasks. Many distractions could create overload or excessive demands on the individual's capacities, which may in turn lead to poor performance. Research evidence comes almost entirely from laboratory experiments, reviewed in the remainder of this section.

Clerical tasks. Apart from the finding of a temporary slowing at the onset or offset of noise in Morgan's (1916) experiments and one other finding, research on clerical tasks has shown no effect of unpredictable noise. Findings of no effects occurred in four separate experiments on transcription of numbers, number checking, and other tasks, during irregular noise as loud as 100 decibels (Glass & Singer, 1972; Wohlwill, Nasar, DeJoy & Foruzani, 1976) (See Table 7.7) In two cases, noises were associated with improved performance during brief work-sessions, perhaps because of temporary arousal (Smith, 1951; McBain, 1961).

Mental tasks. Much of the earlier research on noise concerned mental tasks, and treated noise as a source of disturbance. Table 7.8 summarizes the results of 15 laboratory experiments that introduced intermittent noises.

Unlike the studies of clerical tasks, most of those on mental tasks found some kind of effect on performance in unpredictable noise. Nine experiments found adverse effects. One used a task that called for mental calculation, and found an increase in errors during the 30 seconds following loud bursts of noise (Woodhead, 1964a). This clearly reflects

Table 7.7. *Summary of laboratory findings on the effects of unpredictable noise on the performance of clerical tasks*

Study[a]	Task	Noise	Duration (minutes)[b,c]	Decibel level in quiet[d]	Decibel-level associated with effect on performance		
					Decrement	No effect	Increment
Glass & Singer (1972)	Finding A's	Intermittent bursts	23 (8)	No noise	—	56, 108	—
	Number comparison (#1)	Intermittent bursts	23 (8)		—	56, 108	—
	Finding A's	Intermittent bursts	24 (8)	No noise	—	56, 108	—
	Number comparison (#2)	Intermittent bursts	24 (8)		—	56, 108	—
	Finding A's	Intermittent bursts	25 (8)	No noise	—	56, 108	—
	Number comparison (#3)	Intermittent bursts	25 (8)		—	56, 108	—
Smith (1951)	Number checking	Irregular bursts	30 (7)	No noise	—	100	100 higher % correct
	Name-checking	Irregular bursts	30 (7)	No noise	—	—	100 more attempts
	Form-board	Irregular bursts	30 (14)	No noise	—	—	—
Chatterjee & Krishna-murty (1972)	Typing (transcription)	Intermittent sounds	10 (10) 3 sessions	No noise	Unknown; more errors	—	—
Wohlwill et al. (1976)	Dial transcription, machine paced	Intermittent bursts	30 (30)	No noise	—	80–85	—
McBain (1961)	Copying block letters, machine paced	Recorded sound fragments	42 (42) 4 sessions	No noise	—	—	Unknown; fewer errors
Morgan (1916)	Letter coding	Bells, buzzers, etc.	Varied, multiple sessions	No noise	Unknown; temporary slowing at onset	—	Unknown; sometimes faster

[a] Studies listed in order of increasing task-performance session. Numbered studies are separate experiments.
[b] First number indicates exposure to the noise condition in one session. Number in parentheses indicates the amount of time spent doing one task during one session, excluding practice sessions and rest periods.
[c] When participants performed during two or more separate sessions, or under two or more conditions, the number of sessions is indicated.
[d] Decibels on the A scale unless otherwise noted.

Table 7.8. *Summary of laboratory findings on the effects of unpredictable noise on the performance of mental tasks*

Study[a]	Task	Noise	Duration (minutes)[b,c]	Decibel level in quiet[d]	Decibel-level associated with effect on performance		
					Decrement	No effect	Increment
Rabbitt (1966)	Learning word lists (#1)	White noise of varying intensity	Varied	No noise	Unknown; more errors	—	—
Houston (1969)	Stroop color tests (color-naming & color-word)	Irregular sounds	Varied (avg. 1 min)	No noise	78 avg. slower color naming	—	78 avg. faster color word
O'Malley & Poplawsky (1971)	Stroop color tests (color naming & color-word) (#2)	Intermittent white bursts	Varied (avg. 1–2 min)	No noise	—	—	85 faster, both tests
	Word recognition & recall (#1)	Intermittent white bursts	Varied	No noise	85, 100 fewer peripheral words recalled	—	—
Houston & Jones (1967)	Stroop color tests	Irregular sounds	Varied (avg. 4 min)	No noise	—	—	Unknown; faster color word
Weinstein (1974)	Proofreading	Teletype machine operating intermittently	14 (14)	36	70 fewer contextual errors other errors detected	70	—
Tinker (1925)	Otis intelligence test	Intermittent bells	Unspecified 2 sessions	No noise	—	Unknown	—
Hovey (1925)	Alpha intelligence test	Bells, buzzers, gongs, etc.	19 (19) 2 sessions	No noise	—	Unknown	—

Study	Task	Noise type	Duration (sessions)		Effect	
Park & Payne (1963)	Long division	Air chimes	20 (20)	50–70	—	98–108
Pollock & Bartlett (1932)	Number setting task (#6)	Irregular recorded music	20 to 30 (20 to 30) 10 sessions	No noise	Unknown; temporary initial decrement	—
	Word making (#7)	Discontinuous recorded music	30 (30) 2 sessions	No noise	Unknown 3.4% fewer words	—
Woodhead (1964a)	Paced mental subtraction using memorized 6-digit numbers	Bursts of rocket noise	Varied (avg. about 36 min.)	No noise	100 more errors for 30 sec after bursts	—
Morgan (1917)	Learning word pairs	Gramophone, gong, buzzer	Varied; multiple sessions	No noise	Unknown; less incidental learning	—
Ford (1929)	Addition from series of mixed numbers & letters	Auto horn, recorded voice	Varied; multiple sessions	No noise	Unknown; temporary initial decrement	—
Harmon (1931)	Column addition	Recorded street & office noises	Varied; multiple sessions	No noise	50–65; 60–75; temporary initial decrement	—

[a] Studies listed in order of increasing task-performance session. Numbered studies are separate experiments.

[b] First number indicates exposure to the noise condition in one session. Number in parentheses indicates the amount of time spent doing one task during one session, excluding practice sessions and rest periods.

[c] When participants performed during two or more separate sessions, or under two or more conditions, the number of sessions is indicated.

[d] Decibels on the A scale unless otherwise noted.

distraction (if not the murder of thoughts). Other decrements involved slower learning of new material, especially at the beginning of work-sessions (J.J.B. Morgan, 1917); slower and less accurate calculation after the onset of noise (Harmon, 1933); poorer recall of material learned in noise (Rabbitt, 1966); and poorer recall of incidental material (J.J.B. Morgan, 1917; O'Malley & Poplawsky, 1971, experiment #1). Some of these disturbances in performance seem to reflect disruption of short-term recall or narrowing of attention during unpredictable noise.

A few studies found no effects of noise, generally during tasks that called for the retrieval of well-learned information or the use of highly practiced skills. Two early experiments found no effects of intermittent bells or buzzers on scores on tests of intelligence (Hovey, 1928; Tinker, 1925). A later study found no effects of irregular noise on long division (Park & Payne, 1963). (The effects of distractions in this study were probably minimal, as the calculations were written on paper and de-pended little on mental retention.)

Three experiments found a beneficial effect of noise on the perform-ance of the Stroop test. This task calls for the ability to ignore irrelevant information, which may be aided by stress and narrowing of attention (Houston, 1969; O'Malley & Poplawsky, 1971, experiment #2).

In summary, unpredictable noise was associated with errors in tasks involving mental calculation with short-term memorization and recall. Intermittent noise had no effect on tasks that called for long-term recall or well-practiced skills.

Motor tasks. Table 7.9 summarizes the results of 12 experiments on the effects of irregular noise on the performance of motor tasks. They were fairly consistent in showing adverse effects.

In 10 of the experiments, people performed more poorly on motor tasks during intermittent noise than during relative peace. Tasks ad-versely affected by noise included simulated lathe work (Grimaldi, 1958), the "five-choice" task (Hartley, 1974), tracking (Eschenbrenner, 1971; Thackray & Touchstone, 1970), and tasks resembling factory work (Laird, 1933; Pollock & Bartlett, 1932, experiment #3). The decrements in performance of motor tasks involved errors and slower output, usually in noise of 90 decibels or louder. One study found errors concentrated in the 10 seconds after loud bursts of noise (115 decibels), which seemed to reflect a "startle" reaction (Thackray & Touchstone, 1970). In the only study to find a positive effect of noise, the researchers found better tracking, which could be attributed to an orienting response following bursts of noise (Thackray, Touchstone & Jones, 1972).

Vigilance. As shown in Table 7.10, five of six experiments on vigilance showed adverse effects of irregular noise. The exception involved varied sounds of low intensity (72 decibels) and a simple task calling for monitoring only one light (McGrath, 1963). The other studies found noise associated with poorer performance of the monitoring of rapid audio signals (McCann, 1969) and searching moving displays (Woodhead, 1959, 1964b, 1969). Poorer performance consistently involved errors of omission. For example, Woodhead (1964b) asked participants to look at a display through which cards passed, each containing different symbols. The task was to find a matching card in another display, which also changed. When exposed to unpredictable sonic booms, participants made more errors during the 30 seconds after the noises, mostly errors of omission. This suggests that the noise distracted attention or temporarily diminished the individual's capacity to process information.

Dual tasks. In three of six experiments involving simultaneous tasks, unpredictable noise consistently produced poorer performance in the secondary task. The experiments are summarized in Table 7.11. The tasks included a four-choice (like the five-choice task) plus auditory monitoring (Boggs & Simon, 1968), tracking plus "delayed digit recall" (Finkelman & Glass, 1970), and pursuit rotor plus auditory vigilance (Bell, 1978). One experiment found the primary task degraded (Loeb & Jones, 1978). Two others with longer periods of performance found no effects, possibly reflecting adaptation.

Summary of findings on unpredictable noise. Laboratory experiments found irregular noise asssociated with errors or slower reactions in five conditions: (1) during clerical tasks, immediately after onset or change in noise; (2) during mental tasks involving mental calculation or short-term recall; (3) during highly or moderately demanding motor tasks; (4) during vigilance; and (5) during relatively brief dual tasks. In short, intermittent noise disrupted the performance of all but the simplest tasks. A plausible explanation in most cases involved distraction of attention.

Noise and performance in work places

Whether noise affects performance in offices and factories as it does in the laboratory is an open question. If the laboratory findings do generalize, people exposed to very loud noise while working may perform relatively poorly on highly demanding motor, vigilance, or dual tasks. If the noise is unpredictable, adverse effects may also occur on certain mental tasks, and on moderately demanding motor, vigilance, and dual

Table 7.9 *Summary of laboratory findings on the effects of unpredictable noise on the performance of motor tasks*

Study[a]	Task	Noise	Duration (minutes)[b,c]	Decibel level in quiet[d]	Decibel-level associated with effect on performance[d]		
					Decrement	No effect	Increment
Pollock & Bartlett (1932)	Peg-in-hole with moving target (#1)	Asynchronous clicks	2 (2) 6 sessions	(Synchronous clicks)	Unknown; more misses	—	—
	Peg-in-hole with moving target (#2)	Whistle, rattle, claxon horn	2 (2) 6 sessions	No noise	—	Unknown	—
Hack et al. (1965)	Compensatory tracking	Intermittent sounds	10 (10)	No noise	60 initial decrement	—	—
Plutchik (1961)	Mirror tracing	Intermittent tones	4–8 (8–16)	No noise	105–122 errors more variable	—	—
Eschenbrenner (1971)	Compensatory tracking	Intermittent tones	8 (16)	No noise	—	105–122	—
	Complex image tracing	Aperiodic white noise	20 (20)	No noise	50, 70, 90 more errors	—	—
Pollock & Bartlett (1932)	Peg-in-hole with 2 moving targets (#3)	Asynchronous clicks	20 (20) 10 sessions	No noise	Unknown; more misses	—	—
Thackray et al. (1972)	Compensatory tracking	Sonic booms	26	No noise	—	—	1–4 PSI; fewer errors after booms
Thackray & Touchstone (1970)	Compensatory tracking	White bursts at irregular intervals	30 (30)	No noise	115 more errors after bursts	—	—

Study	Task	Noise	Time (sessions)	Control	Effect	
Pepler (1960)	Pursuit tracking	Quiet speech	20 (40) 2 sessions	No noise	Unknown: more errors	—
Theologus et al. (1974)	Reaction time	Random intermittent sounds	30 (30) 2 sessions	No noise	85 slower	—
	Compensatory tracking	Random intermittent sounds	30 (30) 2 sessions	No noise	—	85
Hartley (1974)	Five-choice task (serial reaction time)	Intermittent broad-band sound	40 (40) 4 sessions	70 dBC	95 dBC more errors	—
Grimaldi (1958)	Simulated lathe (pattern tracing)	Intermittent tones, varied frequency	30 (60)	No noise	90, 100 slower & more errors	70, 80
Laird (1933)	Stylus-in-hole task	Various sounds	270	No noise	90 more errors	—

[a] Studies listed in order of increasing task-performance session. Numbered studies are separate experiments.

[b] First number indicates exposure to the noise condition in one session. Number in parentheses indicates the amount of time spent doing one task during one session, excluding practice sessions and rest periods.

[c] When participants performed during two or more separate sessions, or under two or more conditions, the number of sessions is indicated.

[d] Decibels on the A scale unless otherwise noted.

161

Table 7.10. *Summary of laboratory findings on the effects of unpredictable noise on the performance of vigilance tasks*

Study[a]	Task	Noise	Duration (minutes)[b,c]	Decibel level in quiet[d]	Decibel-level associated with effect on performance		
					Decrement	No effect	Increment
Woodhead (1959)	Searching a moving display (#1)	Bursts of rocket noise	12 (12)	70	110 more omissions for 30 sec after bursts	—	—
	Searching a moving display (#2)	Bursts of rocket noise of varied intensity	12 (16)	70	95, 115 more omissions for 30 sec after bursts	85	—
Woodhead (1964b)	Searching a moving display	Bursts of rocket noise	15 (15)	No noise	110 more omissions for 30 sec after bursts	70	—
Woodhead (1969)	Searching a moving display	Sonic bangs of varied intensity	8 (8)	No noise	1.42 or 2.53 1b/ft² more omissions for 30 sec after bangs	—	—
McCann (1969)	Auditory number checking	Intermittent monotone	20 (20) 3 sessions	No noise	50 more omissions	—	—
McGrath (1963)	Monitoring one flashing light	Recorded sounds (variety audio program)	60 (60) 8 sessions	72	—	—	72 more detections

[a] Studies listed in order of increasing task-performance session. Numbered studies are separate experiments.

[b] First number indicates exposure to the noise condition in one session. Number in parentheses indicates the amount of time spent doing one task during one session, excluding practice sessions and rest periods.

[c] When participants performed during two or more separate sessions, or under two or more conditions, the number of sessions is indicated.

[d] Decibels on the A scale unless otherwise noted.

Table 7.11. *Summary of laboratory findings on the effects of unpredictable noise on the performance of dual (simultaneous) tasks*

Study[a]	Task	Noise	Duration (minutes)[b,c]	Decibel level in quiet[d]	Decibel-level associated with effect on performance		
					Decrement	No effect	Increment
Finkelman & Glass (1970)	Compensatory tracking & delayed digit recall	Irregular white burst	2 (2) 18 sessions	No noise	80 more errors, 2nd task	—	—
Boggs & Simon (1968)	Four-choice task (serial reaction) & auditory vigilance	Random bursts (saw cutting metal)	10 (10) 4 sessions	No noise	92 more errors, 2nd task	—	—
Loeb & Jones (1978)	Tracking & monitoring 6 peripheral lights	Periodic impulse noise	10 (10) 3 sessions	75	105 more errors, tracking	—	—
Bell (1978)	Pursuit rotor & auditory vigilance	Random white bursts	12 (12)	55	95 more errors, 2nd task	—	—
Theologus et al. (1974)	Reaction time	Random intermittent sound	30 (30) 2 sessions	No noise	85 slower	—	—
	Compensatory tracking	Random intermittent sound	30 (30) 2 sessions	No noise	—	85	—
Forster & Grierson (1978)	Pursuit tracking & monitoring 6 peripheral lights (#2)	Intermittent broad-band bursts	40 (40) 2 sessions	70	—	92	—

[a] Studies listed in order of increasing task-performance session. Numbered studies are separate experiments.

[b] First number indicates exposure to the noise condition in one session. Number in parentheses indicates the amount of time spent doing one task during one session, excluding practice sessions and rest periods.

[c] When participants performed during two or more separate sessions, or under two or more conditions, the number of sessions is indicated.

[d] Decibels on the A scale unless otherwise noted.

tasks. In other words, laboratory findings suggest that only the simplest clerical and factory tasks are immune to disruption by noise.

Three key questions on the generalizability of the laboratory findings concern adaptation. First, can people adapt to noise? The answer may be "yes," at least under some conditions. For instance, Glass and Singer, (1972) showed that physiological reactions to repeated, loud, unpredictable noises diminished in a matter of minutes. Second, does adaptation carry costs to the individuals? At the very least, people may have to exert extra effort to concentrate on their work in noisy conditions, as in the studies by Morgan (1916) and Ford (1929). If so, people may be able to maintain their performance in noisy conditions only for awhile without beginning to pay the price for extra exertion. In other words, noise may add to the difficulty of a job. Third, does noise have delayed or cumulative effects? There is evidence from the laboratory that loud, unpredictable, uncontrollable noise has adverse aftereffects on performance (Glass & Singer, 1972; Glass, Singer & Friedman, 1969; see the review by Cohen, 1980a). Whether such effects accumulate or dissipate over time is an unanswered question.

If people in offices and factories can adapt to noise without suffering more than temporary costs, disruptive effects on performance may occur relatively seldom in work places. On the other hand, if adaptation takes continued effort, or if it carries cumulative costs, the disruptive effects of noise in offices and factories could even be more pronounced than in the laboratory.

At least one source of disruption of performance by noise may be unaffected by adaptation: sound masking. Noise can mask auditory feedback, as it may have done in the study of the film factory cited earlier (Broadbent & Little, 1960). In effect, a task may become more difficult when auditory feedback is obscured by noise. The worker may be able to compensate through extra visual vigilance, but the task still takes more effort.

Sound masking can also disrupt performance by interfering with conversation (Chapter 12). On the other hand, background noise in an office may mask the sounds of conversation and prevent distraction (Chapter 13).

In brief, the applicability of laboratory findings on noise and performance to factories and offices is debatable.

Summary

This chapter discusses the psychological influences of noise, or unwanted sound. Noise has long been recognized as a problem in offices and factories. Measures to combat noise introduced into offices have included padding under machines, carpeting on the floors, and acoustical tiles on the ceilings. In open-plan offices noise was a particular problem, and was combatted with advanced ceilings, sound-absorbing partitions, and electronic background sound. Measures to deal with noise in factories have been less elaborate, but have been stimulated by government regulations that dictate maximum exposures to noise in work places.

Studying the psychological impact of noise is complicated by two issues. First, noise can be annoying not only because of its physical qualities, but also because of its meaning to the listener. Second, people differ widely in what they define as noise and in the way they respond to it.

Research suggests that noise in offices is associated with dissatisfaction with the environment, and in some cases with dissatisfaction with the job. In offices noise represents a prevalent problem, affecting a large fraction of workers. Noise is a special problem in open offices. Particularly annoying sources of office noise include conversations by co-workers and ringing of telephones. Annoyance by office noise has been unrelated to its general intensity but strongly related to the intensity of sounds audible above the background. (Similar research on noise in factories was not available.)

Research on noise and performance comes mainly from the laboratory. Studies of predictable noise – either constant or repetitive – found it to be associated with decreases in accuracy under four conditions: (1) during clerical tasks when the noise started or changed; (2) during certain highly demanding motor tasks; (3) during highly demanding vigilance with very loud noise (100 decibels); and (4) during dual tasks with very loud noise (100 decibels). Predictable noise was sometimes associated with improved performance: (1) during brief work-sessions with simple clerical tasks, with the noise keyed to the task; (2) during brief sessions with relatively simple mental tasks; (3) during a simple, repetitive motor task; and (4) during a motor task when the noise was of very low frequency. Almost all the effects of predictable noise on performance could be explained in terms of the increased arousal created by noise, by distortions in judgment created by increased arousal, or by the masking of useful auditory cues by the noise.

Laboratory studies of unpredictable noise – intermittent or irregular sound – found it to be associated with decreases in performance under five circumstances: (1) during clerical tasks after onset or offset of noise; (2) during mental tasks involving mental calculation or short-term recall; (3) during highly or moderately demanding motor tasks; (4) during all but the simplest forms of vigilance; and (5) during dual tasks. In certain, highly specific circumstances, unpredictable noise was associated with improved performance. Most of the adverse effects of unpredictable noise could be explained in terms of temporary distraction of attention; in some studies the effects were pronounced during the few seconds immediately after bursts of noise.

Whether the adverse effects of noise on performance found in the laboratory occur as well in offices and factories is an open question. People may be able to adapt to noise after awhile, but adaptation may require extra effort. Adaptation may be associated with delayed or cumulative effects.

Practical considerations

As with many qualities of the ambient environment, the practical issues concerning noise may be reduced to a question of balance. If noise is too loud or erratic, workers are likely to experience annoyance, dissatisfaction, and perhaps disturbance of their work. On the other hand, if background sound is too subdued, any moderately loud sound may be audible above it, including conversations by co-workers. (Conversations by co-workers represent some of the most annoying noise, and their audibility also compromises the privacy of confidential conferences.) Moderate background noise may mask unwanted sounds. However, if the background sound is too loud it can also mask wanted sounds, such as auditory feedback from machines and desirable talking by co-workers within conversation distance of each other (see Chapters 12 and 13).

Resources for controlling noise are many. Unwanted sounds can sometimes be eliminated at the source, for instance, by redesigning a noisy machine or by padding a hard or resonant surface. Inevitable noises can be contained through the use of walls or partitions. Noises can be dampened by sound-absorbent surfaces, including acoustical ceilings, carpeting, fabric-covered panels, and draperies. Or noises can be masked by ventilation systems (when they are operating) or by music, or by electronic systems that emit masking sounds.

Unfortunately, applied acoustics is a complicated business in which it is easy to make mistakes. For example, the effect of a sound-absorbing ceiling may be eliminated by paint, or substantially reduced by large light fixtures. The sound-absorbing qualities of drapes are lost when they are open; windows reflect sounds back into the room. A private office can be rendered non-private by sounds traveling through ventilation ducts.

According to some experts, the acoustics of any work environment depend upon its weakest link. For instance, Kring Herbert of Ostergaard Associates used the analogy of a leaky bucket – the water level is only as high as the lowest leak. Similarly, an office or factory is only as quiet as allowed by the feature that creates or transmits the loudest sounds.

8
MUSIC

The ambient environment of some offices and factories includes music, which, unlike noise, is sound introduced for pleasure. This chapter discusses the role of music in offices and factories, as well as its relationships with satisfaction and performance.

The changing role of music

Music is probably as old as work itself, but its role in the work place has changed. In times past, workers sang while they worked. Sailors sang at sea; weavers sang at their looms; railroad workers sang as they laid track. During the past century, however, the tradition of singing during work has been replaced. Many people in today's offices and factories work to the soft strains of recorded instrumental music, designed to create a relaxed and cheerful atmosphere through "music conditioning."

In Europe, apprentices in early factories sang songs while they worked (Uhrbrock, 1961). But the Industrial Revolution soon brought noisy machines, which drowned out the song and introduced their own rhythms. A visitor to an early New England weaving mill reported that textile workers made themselves hoarse trying to sing over the racket of the looms (Throstle, 1847). Later, in another factory, singing ceased, as workers "could not hear their voices above the roar of the machinery" ("The Value of Music in Factories," 1913).

During the late 1800s and early 1900s, factories incorporated music to boost morale. Some of the quieter industries encouraged singing during work. For instance, at a tobacco factory in 1886, the management hired women with good voices to sing among the workers; they too, soon began to sing. Other tobacco factories followed the example (Meakin, 1905). However, factories in other industries were far from quiet, and singing remained uncommon during work. In the era of "welfare work" around 1900, many companies sponsored glee clubs and choruses, in which the workers participated on their own time. Other companies hired orchestras to play during work, not only to lift employee morale but to discourage unnecessary conversation. Company orchestras or glee clubs were regarded as good for publicity (Clark, 1929).

Soon after 1900 several things happened to encourage the idea that music motivated people to work faster. In 1911 a bicycle race took place in Madison Square Garden, during which a band played part of the time. A statistician recorded the speeds of the cyclists and reported that they went about 10% faster while the music was being played (Ayres, 1911). In 1916, a laundry introduced phonographs to play continuous ragtime music and popular ballads, with widely publicized results. The workers speeded up and ironed in time to the music. In the "ragtime laundry," the music had "solved better than any shop foreman or superintendent the problem of voluntary 'speeding up' among employees" ("The Ragtime Laundry," 1916).

Soon it was widely believed that the rhythm of music induced people involuntarily to work in time with it. One psychologist thought that rhythmical movement reduced fatigue (Munsterberg, 1915). Others thought music acted to "stimulate effort" and "efficiently organize work" (Hollingworth & Poffenberger, 1926, p. 266).

Music became a tool for boosting productivity. For instance, in 1922 the Minneapolis Post Office introduced recorded music for the mail clerks of the night shift; a popular article reported that sorting errors decreased on the "music nights," compared with quiet ones. Such projects answered Frederick Taylor's call a few years earlier for "psychological experiments" in factories to increase production (Uhrbrock, 1961).

The impetus for music also came from workers. At a Westinghouse plant in Newark, New Jersey, in 1925, employees who tested sound equipment listened to phonograph records all day as part of their job. Employees in other departments sent delegates to complain to management that they, too, deserved music.

By 1930 the use of music was widespread in industry, although it was still usually live rather than recorded. A survey of 679 industrial plants found that most had introduced music or had sponsored employee participation in bands or choruses (Clark, 1929).

During the intensified industrial activity of World War II in the United States, many companies introduced music by bringing in military bands or playing phonograph records over public address systems. In Europe, music often came from the sound systems used to announce air raids (Burris-Meyer, 1943).

A survey of factories toward the end of World War II found that nearly half used recorded music, which had largely replaced the live music of a few years earlier (see Uhrbrock, 1961). In another project a researcher visited 100 industrial plants and reported that 76 played recorded music, and officials in more than half of them believed that music increased production (Uhrbrock, 1961). However, certain music did create problems. British plants during World War II had to quit playing "Deep in the Heart of Texas" because workers stopped to clap their hands to it (Kirkpatrick, 1943, p. 93).

The popularity of recorded music in wartime factories encouraged the development of companies that distributed recorded music. Perhaps the largest, Muzak, gained success through the distribution of "special work music" over telephone lines. Muzak had begun selling its programs to hotels and restaurants before World War II, and enjoyed great popularity among wartime subscribers. After the war, Muzak marketed its product in offices as well as in factories.

Through World War II the idea prevailed that music aided productivity through rhythm–that people could be made to work at a prescribed speed by playing music of the proper tempo. But the importance of rhythm waned with the growing realization that many industrial processes could not easily be keyed to music. Sometimes the machinery was too noisy. Sometimes managers had trouble finding "a variety of pieces having just the right tempo and rhythm for a given operation" (*Music in Industry*, 1944, p. 22). Also, managers discovered that employees sometimes resisted the implicit suggestion that they speed up to meet the pace of the music.

As the emphasis shifted away from rhythm, music gained importance as a source of influence on mood. The Industrial Recreation Association claimed that music is best considered a means of "creating a spirit of cheerfulness" (*Music in Industry*, 1944, p. 29). Another reason given for the use of music was relief from monotony (Benson, 1945).

Music finally found its way into offices after it had been in factories for some time. The delay may have reflected a belief among managers that music might disturb "mental work" (Burtt, 1948). So music entered as unobtrusive background:

Music in the office does not and should not serve as a timing device for
work speed, nor should it distract attention. To be successful it must have

a background effect almost as a subconscious experience to the listener.
... [O]ffice music is intended to create a more pleasant atmosphere and
relieve nervous tensions as well as produce a relaxing effect. (Wylie, 1958,
p. 371)

Recorded music appeared widely in offices of the late 1940s, and by
the late 1950s a single company – Muzak – claimed that its music reached
the ears of 50 million people each day in the United States ("Muzak
Theory and Practice," 1959, p. 689). Subscribers included Prentice-Hall,
which introduced music to 24 clerical employees who stuffed envelopes
in a direct mailing operation. Productivity reportedly increased nearly
7% during the 6 months after the Muzak began, as compared with the
previous 5 months. This and similar cases helped gain a place for "piped-
in" music in many clerical offices.

Muzak tried to do more than create a cheerful backdrop with its
instrumental music. The selections represented attempts to subtly stimulate employees during times when they otherwise worked slowly:

Work tempo starts off at high levels, falls gradually to a low level at mid-
morning, and rises again as lunch time approaches. Muzak attempts to
stimulate work tempo when it is at its lowest. ("Muzak Theory and Practice," 1959, p. 689)

Muzak of the late 1950s usually played for 10 to 15 minutes each half
hour, with selections chosen for their "stimulatory value," based on
tempo, rhythm, instrumentation, and orchestra size. Tempo varied up
to 130 beats per minute. Rhythms came from dance music: foxtrot,
waltz, samba, quickstep. Instrumentation for the least stimulating music
consisted of stringed instruments. To increase stimulation, Muzak added
woodwinds, then brass instruments, then subtracted the strings, and,
for greatest stimulation, used only brass. Orchestras varied from 6 to
30 instruments. The use of music by Muzak to stimulate employees was
more subtle than the earlier use of rhythm to increase the pace of work.
However, the idea was essentially the same: music was a tool for increasing productivity. At the same time, the emphasis on music to keep
up morale also continued.

Muzak and its competitors gained popularity in the 1960s and 1970s
despite occasional criticism. For instance, one critic labeled Muzak "pal-
lid pap that will cause all our music teeth to fall out" ("Background
Music: But It's Good for You," 1963, p. 35). However, among management, at least, opinions of musical programs were often favorable.
The Administrative Management Society surveyed 336 member companies in 1971, and found that 254 provided music for their employees.
In response to the questionnaire, 92% of company representatives re-

Table 8.1. *Opinions of 281 company representatives on the effects of music*

Proposed effect of music	"Yes" responses (%)
Help reduce turnover?	76
Help "cool down" temperamental workers?	55
Help "level out" noise peaks?	85
Help in recruiting new employees?	58
Appreciably relieve job monotony?	87
Improve employee morale?	87

Source: "Piped in Music is Money to Employers" (1971).

plied "yes" when asked whether they would invest in music again if they had to do it over ("Piped-in Music Is Money to Employers," 1971). The survey also asked for opinions about the effects of music, as shown in Table 8.1. Apparently the company representatives believed that music relieved monotony and improved morale, but the role of music had expanded to include more functions.

The use of music in factories and offices may still reflect the belief that music brings many favorable consequences, or at worst does little harm. A 1975 handbook of office management includes a section on *music conditioning*:

Music serves as an environmental aid because the physiological and psychological power of music may be used to produce and improve the behavior patterns. Music can make you alert or relaxed, happy or blue. 'Music while you work' programs are designed to . . . relieve mental and visual fatigue, reduce nervous tension, and make employees feel better in general. (Terry, 1975, p. 451)

Current practice seems consistent with this rationale, as recorded music plays in many offices and factories.

Research on music in factories

Despite widespread use of recorded instrumental music in industry since World War II, surprisingly little research has been published concerning its effects on employees. Most of what has been published came from the 1940s.

Probably the first controlled experiment on the effects of music on

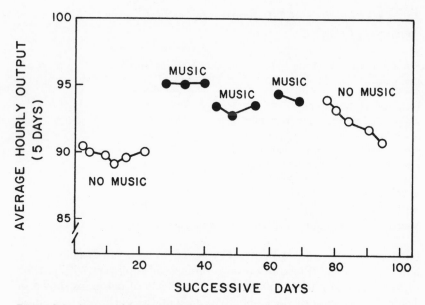

Figure 8.1. Average hourly output in a factory under conditions of music and no music. *Source*: Wyatt, S. & Langdon, J.N. (1937). *Fatigue and Boredom in Repetitive Work*. Industrial Health Research Board, Report No. 77. London: H. Majesty's Stationery Office, p. 33.

factory output took place in the late 1930s, as part of a series of British studies on boredom and fatigue in factory work (Wyatt & Langdon, 1937). Recorded music was introduced at a single factory to relieve boredom among 68 employees who assembled firecrackers. (The job called for a 30-second procedure to be done repetitively.) Output was measured routinely every 15 minutes, and employees were paid on a piece rate. The researchers observed the output under existing conditions for 6 weeks, then introduced recordings of miscellaneous dance tunes for the next 6 weeks. They used three different schedules of music, involving sessions in the mornings, and sometimes the afternoons, that lasted 75 to 180 minutes. Results showed that output increased by an average of 6% during the first 3 weeks of music, remained about 3 – 6% higher throughout the 6 weeks of music, and fell back to earlier levels after the music ended. Figure 8.1 shows the results. These findings encouraged the view that music aids productivity.

Other experiments followed during the 1940s, primarily in radio assembly operations. These studies all employed "no-music" conditions for comparison with periods of music. The researchers generally followed the lead of the early British experiment and played music during only part of the work shift. This practice was based at least partly on the idea that people would become accustomed to continuous music, and it might lose its capacity to relieve boredom or create stimulation. Intermittent music became the accepted practice.

An early experiment that had introduced 64 minutes of recorded music per shift in a group of female radio-tube assemblers reported a significant decline in defective work. The experiment had to be discontinued, however, because during a "no-music" period after music had been played for 9 weeks, more than two-thirds of the employees petitioned to have the music resumed (Humes, 1941).

A series of four controlled experiments at RCA factories involved more than 600 people. None of the four experiments showed statistically significant changes in output or error rate during sessions of music that lasted up to 2 hours per shift. However, all four experiments found marginal increases in output. (Taken one at a time, these increases are within the range expected by chance, but taken together they are highly suggestive of a small increase in output.) One study found a slight increase in errors during music; another found a slight decrease (Kerr, 1944, 1945).

Another study of radio assemblers involved music sessions up to 5 hours per shift, and found significant gains in production. Errors also increased in some groups. Employee attitudes were assessed and were almost unanimously favorable (H. C. Smith, 1947). An experiment at around the same time in a rug factory found no significant change in output with the introduction of 80 minutes of music per shift, but 89% of employees expressed favorable attitudes toward the music (McGehee & Gardner, 1949).

One of the few experiments reported since the 1940s found no effects of music. Researcher played recordings for 4 hours per shift in a small group of skateboard assemblers; output was not different during the music. However, 88% expressed favorable attitudes toward the music (Newman, Hunt & Rhodes, 1966). The other two experiments published since the 1940s involved small groups of parts inspectors and found significant increases in detections of designated parts during brief work sessions with "lively" music (Fox & Embrey, 1972).

In summary, results have been fairly consistent in 11 published experiments on music in factories. As shown in Table 8.2, three experiments found music associated with statistically significant increases in output. Five other experiments found small (nonsignificant) increases. This leaves just two of 10 experiments in which output was measured and found unchanged; in no case did it decrease. The consistent pattern of marginal increases in output suggests that the music may have had a

Table 8.2. *Summary of the results of 11 experiments on music in factories*

		Reported effect of music		
Study	Task	Output (%)	Errors (%)	Favorable attitude (%)
Fox & Embrey (1972), Expt. #1	Inspection	+18*	—	—
Fox & Embrey (1972), Expt. #2	Inspection	+ 7*	—	—
Humes (1941)	Assembly	—	– 2*	—
Kerr (1944, 1945), Expt. #1	Assembly	+ 0–1	+10–14	—
Kerr (1944, 1945), Expt. #2	Finishing	+ 5–7	– 2–8	—
Kerr (1944, 1945), Expt. #3	Assembly	+ 1–2	—	—
Kerr (1944, 1945), Expt. #4	Finishing	+ 1–11	—	—
McGhee & Gardner (1949)	Rug setting	No change	No change	89
Newman et al. (1966)	Assembly	No change	No change	88
Smith (1947)	Assembly	+ 4–25*	+0–33	98
Wyatt & Langdon (1937)	Assembly	+ 3–6	—	—

Note: Asterisk (*) indicates statistically significant change; — indicates that the item was not assessed.

slight stimulating effect. (However, this is a tenuous conclusion.) The effect of music on errors was less uniform, although the only increases in errors accompanied increased output and could reflect faster work. The findings are consistent with the idea that music creates a slight increase in psychological arousal, which could account for increased output in these simple tasks. However, none of the studies addressed the arousal hypothesis.

The most consistent result of the experiments on music in factories is that a large majority of employees said they liked it. (This finding was only reported in three studies.) Such positive attitudes among employees could help account for the widespread use of recorded background music in industry.

Research on music in offices

Empirical evidence on the effects of music in offices is practically nonexistent. Brochures circulated by Muzak and its competitors describe a few case studies, but these quasiscientific reports lack information needed to determine whether the results were due to chance or artifact (Uhrbrock, 1961). Apart from these, we found only three published experiments on the effects of music on office work – one in a drafting room and two in computer data-processing operations.

The experiment in the drafting room involved an early Edison "laboratory model" phonograph. After hearing two hours of music of various types, a group of 56 male draftsmen completed a questionnaire. No objective measures of output were taken. The draftsmen expressed generally favorable opinions, with more than 80% saying that music made their work easier and about half saying they worked more quickly. They expressed a clear preference for familiar pieces and preferred instrumental over vocal music (Gatewood, 1921). These preferences are consistent with the later practice of playing only instrumental music in offices.

Apparently, the next published experiment came 40 years later in the keypunch room of a data-processing company in New Mexico. Twenty-two operators were responsible for receiving data, scheduling work, and punching data cards using IBM keypunch machines. The study was designed to find out whether music would aid the performance of a relatively complex task (compared with factory work). The researcher played recordings of dance music and other instrumental pieces prepared by a commercial distributor. Music was played on alternate days for 2 hours per shift, in five brief sessions distributed throughout the shift. Measurements taken on 20 music days and 20 nonmusic days revealed 4% more cards punched with 11% fewer errors on music days. However, these differences were not statistically significant (W. A. Smith, 1961).

Another experiment in a keypunch operation showed no effects of music on output but found a temporary increase in errors after the music began. The study involved commercial music programs played intermittently during the majority of the work shift. Output was measured by keystrokes per hour. While the music had no effect, the operators believed it made them more efficient, and nearly all of them said it made their work more pleasant (Gladstones, 1969).

In summary, for two types of office work – drafting and keypunching –

employee satisfaction seemed to improve somewhat with the introduction of music. Output did not appreciably improve, although it did not decline either. Evidence is lacking for other types of office work, but perhaps as office work becomes more complex, music becomes more disruptive.

Laboratory studies of music

Researchers have examined the effects of music on many of the same tasks used in studies of noise. A common hypothesis has been that music improves performance by creating subtle stimulation and arousal. The music has not been nearly as loud as the irregular noise that disrupted the performance of some of these tasks in other experiments.

Clerical tasks. One experiment using a card-filing task (Santamaria, 1970) found no effects of music on performance.

Mental tasks. Pollock and Barlett (1932) found poorer performance of a word-making task with gramophone recordings than without them. Freeburne and Fleischer (1952) found no effects of music on a mental task that involved comprehension of Russian history.

Motor tasks. Results on motor tasks have been mixed. One experiment that used a tracking task found better performance with paced rhythm (Conte, 1966), whereas another found no effects (Mikol & Denny, 1955). One early researcher even reported that music led to poorer visual discrimination (Dannenbaum, 1945). (The inconsistencies may be attributable to differences in the tasks, the types of music, or the particular populations involved.)

Vigilance. In six of seven published experiments, music has led to better vigilance. Three experiments found more correct detections in brief work-sessions with recorded music than without (Davenport, 1974; Fox & Embrey, 1972, experiments #3 and #4). Other experiments used relatively demanding vigilance tasks and found that music delayed the usual decline in performance that occurs with continued vigilance (Davies, Lang & Shackleton, 1973; McGrath, 1963). The music in these studies was deliberately designed to increase arousal, using unpredictable onset of music or stimulating programs. It apparently succeeded. One experiment on vigilance used a simple dial-monitoring task and reported no effects of music (Poock & Wiener, 1966).

The general tendency of music to improve vigilance suggests that it can lead to slightly increased arousal. This has been shown directly in the laboratory with at least one index of physiological arousal: galvanic skin response (GSR). Santamaria (1970) asked graduate students to work on a card-filing task as music played during 10%, 25% or 50% of the time and found GSR higher the longer the music played. Other research suggested that certain types of music can raise GSR (e.g., Zimny & Weidenfeller, 1963). However, evidence on other indexes of arousal is inconsistent, especially for heart rate (see the review by Santamaria, 1970).

The clearest conclusion from the laboratory studies is that music can increase performance of vigilance tasks in the short term, probably because it can slightly augment arousal. This is consistent with slight improvements in factory work associated with the introduction of music.

Summary

The role of music in the work place has shifted from singing by workers, to live music played during work, to recorded music designed to create "music conditioning." Managers have expressed the belief that music can boost morale and relieve monotony.

Research on the effects of music has been infrequent; much of it came from the 1940s. Of 11 experiments on the effects of music on output in factories, eight showed small increases (although only three were statistically significant). In three studies that included an assessment of attitudes, more than 85% of participants expressed favorable attitudes. Of three studies of music in small offices, none found a significant improvement in output. However, most of the office employees liked working to music.

Laboratory studies of the effects of music on performance have involved four types of tasks. Studies involving motor tasks found mixed results; the few studies involving clerical or mental tasks generally found no effects. Only vigilance showed a consistent improvement with the introduction of music, in six of seven studies. The apparent reason for the beneficial effects of music on vigilance is its capacity to increase arousal, which has been shown in some laboratory research.

Practical considerations

A manager might consider introducing music into an office or factory for any of several reasons: to boost production by stimulating individual performance, to improve morale through greater satisfaction among individual employees, or to provide an appropriate level of background sound. Evidence is scant but can be seen as consistent with all three of these applications of music.

The introduction of music as a stimulant to performance is probably best supported for vigilance tasks, such as inspection. (The most effective music for this purpose is specifically designed to create arousal.) For other relatively simple tasks, such as clerical work or assembly, research suggests that music may lead to slight improvement under some conditions, and probably does not hurt in most cases. For complex tasks there is practically no direct evidence, but there is strong theoretical reason to suspect that music can create distraction and overload.

The introduction of music for employee satisfaction appears likely to succeed, provided that the employees are engaged in work that demands little concentration or attention, and that the music suits most employees' preferences. One caution seems to be the possibility that a small minority could find it annoying. However, this problem might be solved by arrangements that allow some people to work in quiet while others hear music. Another caution is that even the most desirable music may lose its appeal and become monotonous if played for too long. (Companies that provide background music usually intersperse periods of silence and changes of pace.) A third caution is that some musical programs contain intermittent speech, which may be more distracting than music by itself. (For this reason, radio broadcasts may be less desirable than programs provided by vendors of background music, even though radios are probably less expensive.)

Background music, like constant background sound, can serve as sound masking. However, if it is played intermittently, no-music periods would need to be filled with "white" noise to maintain a constant sound-masking effect.

9
COLOR

The effect of color on workers represents one of the least understood topics in the psychology of the work place, but remains the subject of extravagant claims regarding efficiency and morale. This chapter briefly examines the use of color in the work place, then reviews the limited research that attempts to link color with satisfaction, perceptions, or performance. Most of the evidence comes from the laboratory. It suggests that people prefer blues, greens, and lighter colors and that they tend to associate blue and green with cool temperatures; also, people perceive light-colored rooms as relatively large or open. There is no evidence that color stimulates performance.

The use of color in work places

Color has been a concern in factories since the late 1800s, when managers used it to highlight the machines:

The engines in Jewell's Mills, Brooklyn, are painted with coach black, and striped with real gold leaf. Seems reckless extravagance don't it? Well, it isn't. The engineer feels that he has charge of two noble machines, and gets their best out of them. (Loquial, 1891, p. 542)

When artificial lighting came into widespread use in factories around 1890, managers began to paint the interiors in bright colors, generally because they believed it boosted morale or productivity. (At the time, morale and productivity were thought to be closely connected with each other and with the environment.) Many factories were "gloomy, depressing, half-cleaned barns," but the McCormick Harvester Works in Chicago had a colorful environment:

The iron work is painted in colors differing from room to room, but all bright – red, blue, yellow, and green. Who will question the certainty not only of greater accuracy, but also of better work all round under such improved conditions? (Meakin, 1905, p. 99)

Another impetus for introducing color into the factory came from the stereotypical belief that female workers needed special treatment because "the temperament of woman makes her acutely sensitive to color." Furthermore, women were supposed to be intuitively "opposed to surroundings that satisfy the average man" (Lord, 1917, pp. 1141–1148). This archaic view did prompt some improvements in working conditions.

Psychologists around 1900 began to point out the energizing or "dynamogenic" influence of exciting colors such as red, in contrast to the supposedly calming effect of blue or green (e.g., Munsterberg, 1915). Some believed that warm colors such as orange could actually influence perceptions of temperature; others thought color schemes could influence perceptions of the size of a room.

By the 1950s the belief that color could influence workers enjoyed considerable popularity. A textbook of office management gives an impressive list of benefits to companies that effectively use colors:

Increased institutional prestige, increased employee cooperation and loyalty, reduction in worker nervous tension through remedying of eye fatigue, and improved office morale. (Wylie, 1958)

Such claims were only supported by anecdotes, if they were supported at all, but nevertheless seem to have gained wide acceptance. Later, another writer claimed even more expansively that

color in industry can help improve production, workmanship, and care of equipment, as well as raise morale and enthusiasm. It can reduce fatigue, accidents and absenteeism. (Draeger, 1977, p. 61)

Similar claims, using almost the same phrases, appeared elsewhere (e.g., Most, 1981; "Using Color and Design to Increase Efficiency," 1979).

Some factories used color for very specific purposes. For instance, at the General Motors plant in Oklahoma City,

To make the complex seem less overwhelming, GM divided the sprawling facility into eight color-coded areas. "We want to bring the plant down to a human scale." ("Using Color and Design to Increase Efficiency," 1979 p. 1124).

Other factories used colors to identify various production areas and provide directions to visitors through "environmental graphics."

Subjective responses to color

Probably the principal way in which color can contribute to workers' satisfaction with their physical working environments is by creating favorable attitudes. This section reviews research on evaluative judgments of colors, or preferences, and beliefs about the meanings of colors.

Preferences concerning colors

Early research on the psychology of color focused on the "affective value of colors," which translates roughly as liking for different hues such as red, green, or blue (see McCormick's 1976 discussion of "hue"). In one study, more than 1,000 university students viewed pairs of small squares of cardboard of different hues, and indicated which they preferred. Results of many comparisons for each person revealed a clear pattern of preference that held for both men and women: they liked blue and red best, followed by green and violet; they liked orange and yellow least (Walton, Guilford & Guilford, 1933). These results agreed on the whole with practically all earlier findings on preferences regarding hue (see reviews by Guilford, 1934; Norman & Scott, 1952).

Early research focused on hue to the exclusion of other features of color. However, in 1934 a laboratory study involved variation not only of hue, but also of saturation (or purity of hue) and of value (or lightness – the amount of light reflected). With saturation and value held constant, the same ordering of preferences for hues observed in earlier studies appeared: blue, red, green, violet, orange, and yellow. Results also revealed a preference for lighter values and pure colors (for instance, a light, pure tint of red received higher rating than a dark shade or a grayish "mixed" shade of red). However, hue was more important to preference than value or saturation (Guilford, 1934, p. 369).

Later research supported the early findings. Eysenck (1941) analyzed earlier published studies of color preference and combined the data from more than 21,000 people. The combined results showed the same rank ordering that Guilford had reported: blue, red, green, violet, orange, and yellow. The research included a test for racial differences, and found none.

Regarding the influence of lightness and saturation of colors, a later

Table 9.1. *Preferences for color schemes among 1,097 office workers*

Color scheme	Preference (%)
Cool colors (blues and greens)	72
Pastel colors (e.g., light blue or pale yellow)	67
Warm colors (yellows and reds)	59
Subdued colors with intense color accents	53
Neutral colors (e.g., beige, putty, or tan)	50
White	26
Intense colors (e.g., fire engine red or Kelly green)	20
Grays	10

Source: BOSTI (1980a), p. 25.

study of ratings of more than 300 different colors from the *Munsell Book of Color* found essentially the same results as before: increasing preference with increasing lightness, and increasing preference with increasing saturation of color. The researchers even constructed elaborate charts to indicate average "affective values" for each of 316 colors (Guilford & Smith, 1959). Another study suggested that liking for a color combination was highly predictable from the "affective values" of the colors that made up the combination (E. C. Allen & Guilford, 1936).

In sum, the findings from the laboratory studies of color preference have been consistent, at least for western cultures (see Choungourian, 1968, for cultural differences). However almost all of them involved judgments of small patches of color viewed for brief periods, so it is doubtful that the findings apply directly to offices or factories.

The scanty evidence from actual work environments only partly agrees with the laboratory findings. The BOSTI survey, in a preliminary report on 1,097 office workers from 21 locations, showed that they preferred some of the hues ranked highest in the laboratory: blues and greens (BOSTI, 1980a). Most color schemes listed in the questionnaire were acceptable to the majority, as shown in Table 9.1. However, unlike the participants in the laboratory studies, most office workers disliked saturated colors like "fire engine red" or "Kelly green."

One reason for a dislike of saturated colors may come from the belief that pure colors reflect little light. Lighter colors are apparently preferable over dark ones because light-colored walls, floors, and ceiling tend to reflect more light from the surfaces.

In sum, the BOSTI study suggests that in offices, the most widely

Table 9.2. *Results of three studies on the meanings of colors*

Color (hue)	Representative associations		
	Aaronson (1970)	Schaie (1961)	Wexner (1954)
Red	Adventurous	Protective	Exciting
	Sociable	Powerful	Protective
Orange	Impulsive	Exciting	Disturbed
	Quarrelsome	Stimulating	Upset
Yellow	Affectionate	Exciting	Cheerful
	Impulsive	Cheerful	Jovial
Green	—	—	Calm
	—	—	Peaceful
Blue	Affectionate	Pleasant	Calm
	Cautious	Soothing	Peaceful
Violet	Gloomy	Dignified	Dignified
	Impulsive	Stately	Stately
Black	Gloomy	Distressed	Powerful
	Sullen	Disturbed	Despondent
Gray	Cautious	Despondent	—
	Gloomy	Melancholy	—
White	Shy	Tender	—
	Sociable	Soothing	—

preferred hues are blues and greens and lighter colors are generally preferred.

Meanings of colors

Psychologists have tested the idea that particular colors excite particular feelings, by showing people various hues and asking for associations. Results have generally supported the idea that different colors do elicit different responses – but the responses have been inconsistent. Even so, experts still contend that colors have specific meanings (e.g., Sharpe, 1974).

One investigator asked for associations with red and blue and concluded that red connoted happiness, whereas blue meant serenity and dignity (Hevner, 1935). Another study involved 44 raters, who each judged ten hues on eleven "mood tones" (Schaie, 1961). Results appear in Table 9.2, which gives two illustrative associations for each hue. The table also presents results from rating studies by Aaronson (1970) and Wexner (1954). Results are uneven, perhaps because each involved a different list of alternative associations. Other researchers have tried, with limited success, to identify the underlying dimensions of color perception through statistical procedures (see, e.g., Kuller, 1970; Wright & Rainwater, 1962).

The meanings associated with different hues varied, but one commonality stands out: associations with red, orange, and yellow tend to be energetic, whereas associations with blue and green are relatively calm (Sharpe, 1974, p. 2). This distinction parallels perhaps the most consistent association with hue: "warm" versus "cold" (see Birren, 1968). "Warm" hues include red, orange, and sometimes yellow; "cold" hues are blue and sometimes green.

Color and perceived temperature

Researchers have also tested the association between color and temperature, by showing people cards of various hues and asking for ratings of apparent warmth or coolness. One early study found warm ratings for red, and cool ratings for a range of hues from yellow through green and blue to purple. In explaining their responses, participants typically mentioned conditions that create thermal sensations: "like red coals, like the cold blue of steel, cool of the gray-green sea" (Newhall, 1941, p. 204; see also Wright, 1962). The "warm-cold" association is apparently learned, as suggested by a study in the United States in which the association only occurred reliably in subjects older than 18 years (G. A. Morgan, Goodson & Jones, 1975).

Anecdotes from offices and factories suggest that warm and cool colors can actually induce differences in perceptions of the temperature. At a New England insurance company

the office manager changed their drab office color scheme to a cool, relaxing plan featuring blue. The office was painted in August. When winter came, [employees] complained of feeling too cool. The normal temperature maintained in these offices was 70 degrees. When the complaints continued, it was raised to 75 degrees – but [employees] were still uncomfortable.

After much discussion and study the color scheme was changed to warm yellows and restful greens. The temperature was left at 75 degrees. Soon [employees] protested that it was too warm. When the heat was reduced to the normal 70 degrees, the complaints ceased. (Wylie, 1958, p. 7–13).

Similarly, "a bank found it had fewer complaints about summer heat when its office was painted light blue" (Robichaud, 1958, p. 256). And in another case, when the lunchroom of a big midwestern office building was redecorated a light blue, employees began to complain that it was chilly; women employees began wearing their coats to lunch.

Actually, there was no temperature difference in the lunch room. The heating engineer of the office building kept the room temperature at a steady 72 degrees, the same as before. Then the walls were repainted orange, and orange slip covers were placed on the chairs. There were no more complaints about the chilly room – until summer came. (Wylie, 1958, p. 7–13).

Anecdotes go hand in had with practical advice:

Trouble arises psychologically if an environmental color scheme in a factory is too cold or too warm. If it is too cold and the area large, excessive demands will arise for more heat during autumn, winter, spring. Such a lack of balance will also lead to monotony and contempt for the environment and equipment. A scheme that is too warm will produce discomfort, irritation. (McCullough, 1969, p. 31)

In a factory where

intense heat is produced by some of the processes in a space, the walls should be painted a cool color, regardless of the size of the space, to psychologically assist the workers to bear the heat. Similarly, in areas that are extremely cold, warm tones should be used in the walls. (Halse, 1968, p. 50)

If hue is associated with thermal comfort, the connection is probably weak, and probably due to psychological processes rather than thermal sensations. One explanation is that colors sensitize people to the ambient temperature, so they pay more attention to the cold in blue surroundings and to heat in red or orange surroundings. Another possibility is that colors suggest temperatures through their associations (red–hot, blue–cool), and people experience the temperatures through suggestion.

Whatever the explanation of the anecdotal link between color and thermal comfort, three out of four attempts to reproduce it in the laboratory have failed. One research team placed 21 students in an environmental test chamber; asked for ratings of comfort while they wore red, blue, or clear goggles; and systematically varied the temperature during the three 20-minute sessions from about 73° to 80°F (23° to 27°C). The goggles produced no differences in thermal comfort (Bennett & Rey, 1972). Another experiment with 25 participants involved the performance of a task under each of five different-colored lights during a 90-minute experiment. Ambient temperature also varied; participants indicated when they were too warm by closing a switch. The colored lights produced no difference in "heat tolerance" (Berry, 1961). In a third experiment, 144 students filled out questionnaires and did a task in a carrel with red, blue, or white walls in an environmental chamber kept at one of four ambient temperatures. Temperature influenced comfort, but the color of the carrel had no effect (Greene & Bell, 1980). A fourth laboratory study exposed men and women to either blue or red light for 150 minutes while physiological measurements were taken. Participants indicated every 10 minutes whether they would like the ambient temperature kept the same or to be made warmer or cooler, and it was adjusted. Results indicated a preference for temperatures about one-half degree warmer in the blue light, which was statistically significant (Fanger, Breum & Jerking, 1977). (However, the difference of one-half degree Fahrenheit is probably not practically significant.)

The generally disappointing results of the laboratory tests seem to contradict the anecdotes from work environments. However, the three laboratory tests that failed may have been too brief; none involved exposure to a single color for longer than 29 minutes. The effect on thermal comfort, if any, may take much longer to develop. The one positive effect lasted 150 minutes. The participants knew they were taking part in experiments on the effects of color or temperature and may have suppressed any tendency to allow their responses to be influenced by associations of color with temperature. In light of these possibilities, the hypothesis may not be seriously compromised by the three negative laboratory findings. Even so, it is best regarded as no more than an hypothesis.

Perceived size or openness of rooms

One of the few influences of color on perception that has been demonstrated with any consistency concerns the perceived "openness" of a room. Light colors apparently induce a room to seem more open, and perhaps larger, than it would in dark colors. One study found this effect in ratings of a three identical full-size rooms painted dark green, intense medium green, and white. The white room was rated most open, the dark room most closed. The same researchers found similar results in ratings of miniature rooms (Acking & Kuller, 1972). Associations between lightness and apparent openness also appeared in study of miniature rooms (Baum & Davis, 1976) and in a study of dormitory rooms (Schiffenbauer, Brown, Perry, Schulack & Zanzola, 1977). Whether this applies in work environments, however, remains an open question.

Another effect of color on the perception of a room concerns "advancing" and "receding" colors. Warm colors are supposed to appear to move toward the perceiver, whereas cold colors appear to move away. Consequently a blue surface is supposed to seem farther from the viewer than it actually is, whereas a red surface appears closer (Birren, 1968).

[A] long narrow room may be visually shortened so that the distance from work-bench to locker rooms seems less than it really is by painting the end walls in a dark value of an advancing color like burnt orange or maroon. Conversely, small rooms may be given greater apparent dimensions, so that personnel will not feel crowded by the use of a light tint of a cool color. (Garnsey, 1948, p. 120)

The advancing character of warm colors has apparently not been demonstrated in published research. However, current practice in interior design commonly does incorporate dark end-wall treatments for an appearance of distance, and light colors for "openness."

Color and performance

If color aids performance, as some experts claim it does, perhaps the most likely hypothesis is that certain colors create arousal, which in turn stimulates faster work. As one early psychologist wrote:

[O]ur will-impulse is much more effective when our surrounding is red than when it is blue. The red color stirs up the mind and brain to more forceful will-action. The technical term is "dynamogenic influence." The owner of a large cotton mill who has a number of centrifugal dyeing machines reports that the work is mostly with red and black color and expresses his surprise that his workmen are always behindhand when they deal with the black material and never when they deal with the red. Any psychologist would have foreseen that. (Munsterberg, 1915, pp. 191–192)

Researchers have twice tested the stimulating effect of red in the laboratory and twice confirmed it. In one study students saw red and green color slides while a physiological index of arousal was measured (galvanic skin response, or GSR, is a common index of arousal). Red brought significantly higher GSR (Wilson, 1966). A later study involved the showing of color slides of red, yellow, blue, and green; GSR was highest with red and lowest with blue. Green gave a GSR only marginally lower than that of red (Jacobs & Hustmeyer, 1974).

The results from the laboratory may reflect a short-lived effect that disappears with adaptation. If so, red would only stimulate people for a short time. However, one color expert thinks the effects are lasting (Birren, 1968). Another wrote:

Orange has a stimulating effect and should usually be used in relatively small amounts. The occupant of an orange office, for instance, will become ill at ease after a short time and will leave it at every opportunity. (Halse, 1968, pp. 45–46)

An early writer told of two presidents of large companies who could not "work with any repose of mind at home or in the office if not surrounded by blue" (Davison, 1918, p. 278). Similarly a color expert advises, for "sedentary tasks requiring greater than normal visual and mental concentration," cool colors are best (Birren, 1968, p. 168).

In summary, the evidence that color can create arousal is limited, comes from the laboratory, and could reflect a short-lived effect. Perhaps the claims that color can augment performance cannot be completely dismissed, but we found no evidence for them.

Summary

This chapter reviews the evidence related to the influence of color upon workers' satisfaction and performance. Despite a long history of experts' claims about the many influences of color, there seems to be little evidence of any.

Responses to color potentially related to individual satisfaction include attitudes toward colors, or preferences. Research on hue in the laboratory suggested that people prefer blue, red, green, violet, orange, and yellow, in that order. Research also suggested a preference for light colors and saturated colors. However, other evidence suggested that preferences depend upon many factors, including background colors and cultural differences. These results may or may not apply in the work place, but one study of offices found a preference of blues and greens over some other color schemes.

Research on the meanings of colors has found them quite inconsistent, except for an association with temperatures. "Warm" colors have generally included red and orange; "cold" colors have included blue and sometimes green. Anecdotes have suggested that "cold" or "warm" colors induce people to perceive the temperature as cold or warm. However, three of four laboratory studies failed to confirm this idea.

Research on the influence of color on perception suggested that light colors may be associated with the appearance of a relatively large room size. Similarly, experts have suggested that certain colors make surfaces appear closer ("advancing" colors) and others make surfaces appear farther ("receding" colors).

As for the effect of color on performance, there is evidence from the laboratory that some colors can enhance arousal. However, there seems to be no direct evidence of an effect on performance in an office or factory.

Practical considerations

With so few reliably demonstrated effects of color on employees, there are correspondingly few practical constraints on the use of color in offices and factories. The primary limitations concern employee preferences, the light, and safety codes.

As for employee preferences about color schemes, we found no reason not to allow at least some latitude by employees in choosing colors they like best. This may be a relatively painless form of participation by workers in the design of their environment (see Chapter 11). However, employees' choices may have to be limited by considerations regarding lighting.

Color is important to lighting because it plays a major role in the reflectance of surfaces (the proportion of light reflected), which in turn is critical to the arrangement of lighting. For instance, a wall with too little or too much reflectance creates a background of too much or too little contrast with an employee's work (see, e.g., Bowles, 1962). Also, the type of lighting can affect the appearance of colors through a phenomenon called "color rendering" (Boyce, 1981).

As for safety, color can play a major role in calling attention to potential hazards. Some colors have widely recognized meanings in industrial applications. However, any organization can introduce local color codes for its own purposes. The key is to render certain objects visible against their background and for the hazard to be immediately recognizable to anyone familiar with the local code.

10

WORK-STATIONS AND SUPPORTING FACILITIES

Besides the ambient environment, perhaps the most important part of the work place for the individual comprises his or her work-station. This chapter explores some common elements of work-stations in offices and factories – floorspace, equipment, and chairs – along with supporting facilities, such as restrooms and cafeterias. First, some of the complexities involved in the relationship between people and their work-stations are examined.

The individual and the work-station

An understanding of the relationship between a worker and his or her work-station is complicated by the variety of work-stations and their many possibilities for influence, and the variety of workers and jobs. One way of viewing the relationship is as a *man–machine system*. For individual satisfaction and performance, one key process seems to be fatigue.

Variety in work-stations and workers

Perhaps the only safe generalization about work-stations is that most office workers, and some factory workers, spend most of their time seated before horizontal work surfaces or machines. For these people the work-station usually includes a chair and a table or desk or machine stand. However, many factory workers and some office workers work from standing positions, and their work-stations include neither chairs nor work surfaces. Furthermore, the equipment with which people do their jobs varies as widely as the technology behind it. In a certain food-processing factory, for example, one work-station comprises a floormat from which a worker uses a long stick to dislodge pieces of baked dough from moving metal surfaces. Another worker in the same factory stands before a machine that would fill several rooms and controls it through a computer console as tall as its operator. Figure 10.1 shows still another work-station in a factory. Even in offices, where most people sit at desks, the equipment installed in work-stations ranges from typewriters to telephones to microcomputers.

Not only do the components of work-stations vary, but each component has many details of potential importance to the individual who occupies the work-station. For instance, the comfort of a chair may depend on the height, contour, padding, and material of the seat; the height, tilt, tension, and shape of the backrest; the height, size, position, and contour of the armrests; the size of the base; the presence of rollers and their operation; and so on. Comfort in a chair also depends on factors besides the chair itself, including the way the individual sits in it, adjusts it, and positions it, and the tasks he or she does while sitting in it.

The relative importance of each component of a work-station depends to a great extent on the individual's job and habits of work. For instance, the comfort of a chair is critical to the operator of a video display terminal, since the job calls for constant hand movements, and the worker spends most of the day in approximately the same posture. On the other hand, for a factory shift supervisor who spends most of the day circulating among work-stations or attending meetings elsewhere, a comfortable chair at his or her work-station may be a relatively minor concern.

For many aspects of a work-station, the individual's comfort and efficiency depend on the fit of the work-station with the dimensions of the worker's body. For instance, at a position on a production line where metal parts pass for inspection along a conveyor belt 3 feet wide and 4 feet above the floor, the operator occasionally has to reach the far side of the belt for defective parts. For an average-sized man (about 5 feet, 10 inches), this would be fairly easy; for a small woman, it would be difficult at best, even while standing on a stool.

Assuming that a work-station adequately fits the worker's bodily dimensions, comfort and efficiency depend on other characteristics of the worker. For instance, the use of certain programmable controllers for industrial machines calls for rudimentary skills at computer programming, interpretation of visual displays, and using a typewriterlike key-

Figure 10.1. A work-station in a factory. *Source:* Photograph courtesy of Kaiser Aluminum Company, Oakland, CA.

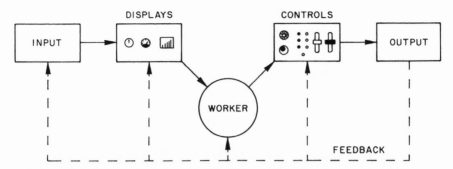

Figure 10.2. Components of the man–machine system.

board. Whether a worker has these skills depends on his or her training, experience, and ability. Even with training, some workers may be unable to carry out the necessary operations quickly enough to meet the demands of the job. Others who have special aptitudes may perform the same job with celerity.

In brief, the relationship between the person and the work-station depends on a long list of concerns: the variety of components of work-stations; the many important details of each component; the differences among jobs in the importance of the components; the way the individual actually uses the work-station; the fit between the dimensions of the work-station and the dimensions and capacities of the worker's body; and the worker's training and ability.

The man–machine system

One useful way of thinking about the relationship between the individual and the work-station treats it as a system. Human factors psychologists have traditionally referred to the man–machine system (e.g., Mc-Cormick, 1976), which consists of people in concert with technology. Usually the system consists of a machine and an individual operator. The worker receives inputs from displays of information, which can be visual, auditory, tactile, thermal, or some combination. The worker considers the information, makes decisions, and manipulates the controls accordingly. The machine produces output, which is usually subject to the worker's scrutiny. The machine and its output provide information (feedback), which allows the worker to adjust the controls to achieve or maintain a desired effect.

Figure 10.2 provides a diagram of the key components of the man–machine system. One illustration is a typist transcribing recorded dictation. Input comes from the earphones of the dictating machine, controlled by footpedals. The display is auditory (recorded speech delivered through earphones). The typist listens to the speech and operates a typewriter through its controls (the keys). The output consists of typed manuscript. The typist proofreads, perhaps while typing; errors are detected (using feedback) and are corrected by retyping. If the input comes too quickly. the typist can temporarily stop the recording through the control pedal (another form of feedback).

The man–machine system emphasizes the dynamic quality of the relationship between worker and work-station. From this perspective, the psychological impact of the work-station grows out of the constant interchange between the individual and the technology involved in the job.

The concept of a man–machine system applies most clearly to the relationship between workers and their equipment or machines. In particular, it suggests that the worker's comfort and efficiency depend on the design of controls and displays, including the display of output in a way that provides feedback. For example, the worker's satisfaction with a work-station at a garment factory may depend on the location, configuration, and ease of operation of the controls of the sewing machine, and the design of the table onto which the garments are placed for inspection and transfer to the next operation. In some cases the garments may require a special display (such as the translucent, backlighted tables used for the inspection of nylon hose).

The worker's performance and satisfaction with a work-station may also depend on his or her attitudes, which in turn may hinge on the degree to which its discomforts seem inevitable. For example, an office worker whose video-display unit lacks adequate contrast for visibility may experience neck pain, eyestrain, and fatigue. If the worker sees the discomfort as avoidable, because a manager has failed to have a defective unit repaired or replaced, the dissatisfaction may be magnified.

In brief, the man–machine system emphasizes the dynamic interplay between operator and machine. It suggests that the worker's satisfaction may depend on the design of controls and displays and on associated comfort or fatigue.

Support for the person and the task

The individual's relationship with the work-station is a function not only of machinery and equipment, but of the support the work-station gives the person's body and work. Specifically, the work-station provides places to stand, sit, or lean; it often includes work-surfaces on which to support

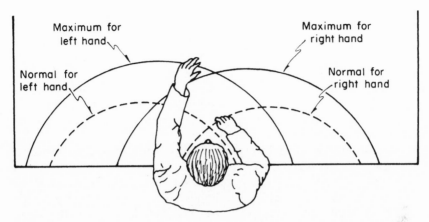

Figure 10.3. Usable work-area on a horizontal surface. *Source:* Redrawn from Donald, W.J. (Ed.). (1931). *Handbook of Business Administration.* New York: McGraw-Hill, p. 641. © 1931, by McGraw-Hill, Inc. with all rights reserved.

the things involved in the job and provides places to store and gain access to materials, supplies, tools, and references. All these supportive elements of the work-station have the potential to influence the worker's satisfaction and performance.

Supportive elements of the work-station. The work-station literally supports the worker's body. For those who spend most of their time seated at a desk or a machine, a key component of the workstation is the chair. For those who stand, a floormat, footrest, or footstool may make the difference between comfort and discomfort. Some jobs call for small hand movements done most easily when the arms are supported. For any work-station, an important element is the amount of floorspace in which the worker can move freely without interfering with co-workers.

Many office and factory workers use horizontal work-surfaces. They sit at desks or tables or stand at workbenches or counters. These surfaces vary in size, shape, and height from the floor. The work-surface supports the individual in his or her task by providing a place to put things while working on them. The most easily usable work-surface is within the worker's reach, as shown in Figure 10.3.

The work-station also provides accessible storage for things the individual uses often, particularly tools, supplies, materials, and references. Ideally, the things used most often are closest at hand.

Potential influences of work-stations on satisfaction and
performance

The individual's satisfaction with a work-station probably depends on
the absence of discomfort created by it. A work-station that necessitates
tiring postures, awkward body positions, or long reaches may create
discomfort. Similarly, a work-station that fails to support the task or its
materials or that requires needless effort to retrieve tools and supplies
may cause discomfort. All of this may contribute to the worker's
dissatisfaction.

Because of its potential to create dissatisfaction through discomfort,
the work-station seems to qualify as a "dissatisfier." This term was
introduced in Herzberg's theory on job satisfaction (see Chapter 4). In
the theory, physical working conditions fell into the category of job
factors that can contribute to dissatisfaction by failing to meet the worker's needs. However, they only lead to indifference when adequate.
(The "satisfiers" can move a worker's attitude from indifferent to positive, adding to job satisfaction.)

The possibility for a work-station to contribute to dissatisfaction is
limited by adaptation. After working for awhile even in an ill-suited
work-station, an individual may change habits to accommodate the work-
station. Heavily burdened muscles may strengthen with use; unaccus-
tomed postures may become commonplace; long reaches may become
practiced and habitual. Such adaptation may represent a conscious attempt to make the best of the situation, or an unconscious adjustment.
Either way, an uncomfortable work-station may create less and less
discomfort and dissatisfaction as time passes. (Such adaptation may carry
psychological costs, but they apparently have yet to be demonstrated.)

The work-station may be important for the individual's performance
because of its relevance to economy of effort. To the extent that the
work-station minimizes the necessity of efforts peripheral to the job and
economizes on effort required for the central tasks, the worker can work
at maximum efficiency.

In brief, the work-station supports the person through places to sit,
stand, or lean. It supports the task through work-surfaces, and through
storage of supplies, tools, materials, and references. These elements
may contribute to dissatisfaction by creating discomfort, although workers may adapt over time. They can aid performance by economizing on
effort.

Research on work-stations

This section provides a selective review of research concerning the connection between work-stations and the satisfaction or performance of

the occupants. Such research necessarily focuses on specific components of the work-station. Under ideal circumstances it also assesses the contribution of each component to the individual's satisfaction with the work-station as a whole, or to job satisfaction, or to job performance. Unfortunately we found very little research concerning the work-station as a whole.

Research concerning the components of work-stations has usually approached them from the perspective of the designer or engineer. As a primary goal, it has sought to develop practical guidelines (see, e.g., McCormick, 1976). Consequently, understanding the psychological impact of work-stations has often represented a secondary objective. Furthermore, some research deals with highly specialized work-stations, which appear in very few offices or factories.

This section first describes what little research we could find on the work-station as a whole. Then for three common elements of work-stations – floorspace, equipment, and chairs – it summarizes some historical issues and evidence related to satisfaction and performance.

The work-station as a whole

The two surveys of office employees by Harris and Associates (1978, 1980) examined the adequacy and relative importance of elements of office work-stations. In the 1978 survey, participants were asked, "Which 2 or 3 of these characteristics do you feel are most important in helping you get your job done well?" (p. 50). The list of possibilities included 17 features of the office environment. As shown in Table 10.1, seven of the items concerned work-stations.

The feature of the work-station chosen most frequently as one of the two or three most important was access to tools and equipment, selected by 25% of participants. Four other elements of the work-station were selected by more than 10% of the participants: the capacity to adjust the work-station to the occupant's job; work-related storage; a comfortable chair; and working surfaces. (These all represent what we have called supportive elements of the work-station.)

Results of the survey indicated that the average office employee in the 1978 survey found many aspects of his or her work-station adequate. As shown in Table 10.1, the average ratings of seven features were all above the midpoint on a scale of 0 to 100, where 67 translated as "pretty good." (Harris and Associates did not analyze the relationship between these ratings of elements of the work-station to any measure of general satisfaction. However, they did ask participants to name two or three job factors "important to them" from a list that included two items on the physical environment; see Chapter 4.)

Table 10.1. *Aspects of the work-station selected as important for the job by 1,047 office workers*

Feature of the workspace	Percent select-ing as important	Average rating of workspace[a] (Score)
Access to the tools, equip-ment, and materials you work with	25	72
Ability to adjust your work surface, chair, and storage space to suit your work requirements	15	58
Storage space for working materials	11	55
Comfort of your chair	11	70
Working surfaces	11	66
Back support of your chair	4	68
Storage space for personal things	1	54

[a] 100 = excellent; 67 = pretty good; 33 = only fair; 0 = poor.
Source: Louis Harris & Associates (1978), pp. 50, 52.

The average ratings of the elements of work-stations are difficult to interpret for two reasons. First, the variability of response is not reported. Perhaps it was small, and most people rated the adequacy of components of their work-stations close to the average of "pretty good." On the other hand, perhaps responses varied greatly, with a substantial fraction at "excellent" and a substantial fraction at "poor." Second, the employees' standard of reference – "pretty good" compared with what? Physical descriptions were not included in the research.

The 1978 survey also included a series of questions on problems employees have in their work. One was "feeling that your work-surface, chair, storage space and other office furniture are out of date or not suitable for your job," which the average participant said happened "occasionally" (average of 19 on a scale that ran from 0 = never to 100 = always). A similar response greeted another problem: "Feeling that the tools, equipment, and materials you have to work with are out of date or not suitable for the job." Perhaps more to the point, participants considered whether they might be more productive if certain changes were made, such as the company's making sure "that their work surfaces, chairs, lighting, and storage space are what they need to do their jobs."

Table 10.2. *Ratings of elements of work-stations on importance and comfort by 1,004 office workers*

Feature of the work-station	Influences personal comfort "a great deal" (%)	"Very important" to have (%)	Have this item (%)
A comfortable chair	73	73	84
Machines and reference materials within easy reach	67	69	83
Enough space to move at your desk	57	57	77
The ability to change your office furniture as your job changes	24	24	40

Source: Louis Harris & Associates (1980), pp. 13, 14, 18.

Almost two-thirds of participants (62%) said that they would be more productive, and only about one-third said "about the same" (Louis Harris & Associates, 1978, p. 23).

The 1980 survey by Louis Harris and Associates assessed the importance of four elements of the work-station to individual comfort. Participants were asked whether each of a total of 12 aspects of the environment affected their comfort, including the four shown in Table 10.2. Almost three-quarters of participants indicated that a comfortable chair greatly influenced their comfort. Two-thirds said the same of accessible machines and references. More than one-half indicated that sufficient floorspace affected their comfort; only one in four believed that adjustable furniture affected their comfort "a great deal."

A large majority of participants said their work-stations contained the things that mattered most to their comfort. As shown in Table 10.2, more than 80% said they had comfortable chairs and accessible materials. Almost as many said they had enough space to move at their desks.

We found no study of factory workers analogous to the two surveys of office workers by Harris & Associates. Other research on work-stations deals with their specific facets, to which we turn next.

Floorspace

The amount of floorspace available in a work-station matters for several reasons. First, floorspace can affect physical comfort. Without enough

Table 10.3. *Standards for minimum floorspace for work-stations in offices*

Source	Minimum work-station (square feet)
Barnaby (1924)	50
Wylie (1958)	40–60
Manesseh & Cunliffe (1962)	45–65
Fetridge & Minor (1965)	40
Ripnen (1974)	65
Pile (1978)	50

space an individual may not be able to change posture, change positions, extend his or her legs, stretch or walk around. The result may be prolonged periods in one posture, with accompanying discomfort. Second, a shortage of space may cause people to bump into each other or get in each other's way as they move. This may be annoying and inconvenient in an office, perhaps unsafe in a factory. Third, floorspace helps determine the density of people in an area, which can in turn affect the experience of crowding among the occupants, a form of stress due to overstimulation by other people or their interference with activities (see Chapter 13). Fourth, when people have assigned workspaces, floorspace may be important to individual satisfaction because of its value as a symbol of status (see Chapter 11).

For decades, office managers have used specific guidelines concerning floorspace. In 1983 one source recommended that a "standard office" contain about 135 square feet, for greatest flexibility in renting the office to business tenants (Hill, 1893, p. 448). In 1924 another source suggested an average of 100 square feet per employee, to be allocated according to rank, with a minimum of 225 square feet for a private office (Barnaby, 1924).

Although standards for floorspace have varied over the years, the minimum work-station has remained about the same size. As shown in Table 10.3, the space recommended for a minimal work-station in an office was around 50 square feet in six fairly representative sources dating from 1924 to 1978.

Research on the connection of floorspace in the office with employee satisfaction has been rare. The present review uncovered only two empirical studies on the subject. The first was the Langdon (1966) survey of British office workers, which included measurement of the "net area" of each of 1,661 offices. (Floorspace occupied by furniture was not part of net area.) Not surprisingly, floorspace was directly related to status. Senior professional and management personnel had an average of about 115 square feet, excluding their furniture, compared with about 90 square feet for junior professionals and about 60 square feet for copy typists (see Chapter 11 on status). Independent of status, the amount of floorspace allocated to each person fell as the number of people in the room increased. Most people in private offices (86%) had more than 80 square feet of net floorspace (the equivalent of an area 8 by 10 feet plus enough room for furniture). On the other hand, more than one-half of those who shared a room with one other person had less than 80 square feet. In rooms with three or more occupants, most workers had less than 60 square feet of floorspace. The tendency for floorspace to decrease with the number of people in the room was pronounced up to about four people, after which "there seems to be no further economy in the use of space" (Langdon, 1966, p. 20).

The Langdon survey also considered occupants' satisfaction with their floorspace. As shown in Figure 10.4, economy of floorspace was associated with dissatisfaction, which occurred primarily among those who worked in areas with less than 60 square feet of space per person. (Most of these people occupied rooms with others.)

A more recent study involved direct measurements of the workspaces of 154 office workers, including the floorspace allocated to each individual. When job categories were analyzed separately, floorspace was a significant predictor of satisfaction with the workspace (Sundstrom et al., 1982a).

The size of work-stations in factories is perhaps more variable than in offices, because requirements are oriented as much to the machinery as to the personnel. Guidelines depend on the manufacturing process and technology. However, there seems to have been very little research on psychological responses to floorspace in factories.

Equipment

The machines used in offices and factories vary tremendously, and have evolved with changing technology. There is probably no such thing as a typical piece of equipment. However, the man–machine system suggests that the critical elements of any piece of equipment for the worker consist of displays, controls, and provisions for monitoring the operation and output of the machine.

Factory machinery. In early factories, before the days of human factors engineering, workers had to adapt to machines. Indeed, around 1900,

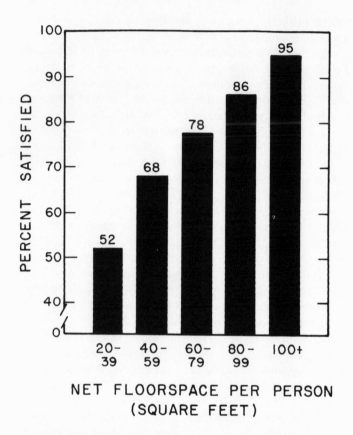

Figure 10.4. Percentage of office workers satisfied with their floorspace as a function of net floorspace per person. *Source*: Adapted from Langdon, F.J. (1966). *Modern Offices: A User Survey.* National Building Research Paper No. 41. London: H. Majesty's Stationery Office.

workers were regarded as little more than replaceable parts for the equipment they operated (see Chapter 2; see also Brown, 1954; Cahn, 1972). In an early automobile factory, the workers were literally chained to the machines:

In front of each machine stands a worker, feeding it pieces of steel by hand. A lever is geared to the mechanism, and to this lever a man is chained by a handcuff locked to his wrist. As the punch comes down, the lever moves back, taking the hand with it. If for any reason a man wishes to leave the room, all the machinery must be stopped and his handcuffs unlocked by the foreman. To look down the long room is to see machines,

levers and men in unison – feed, punch, jerk back, feed, punch, jerk
back. (S. Chase, 1929, pp. 142–143)

Workers often had to find creative ways of operating their machines.
In an extreme case in France, the worker had "to adapt his human
machine to the mechanical one; workmen incapable of making all the
necessary movements with their hands within the measured time aided
themselves by using their heads as a third arm" (Friedmann, 1955, p.
42).

The principle of letting the worker adapt to the machine eventually
gave way to the principle of designing the machine to fit the worker.
There is no telling how well or how widely the principle has been applied,
but even relatively modern factories fall short of ideal. For example, a
worker at a textile mill described his job of operating a group of knitting
machines. Each machine drew thread from a series of spools ("cones").
While running properly it produced finished fabric. The operator replaced empty spools, watched for stray threads, checked for correct
feed, stopped a machine when something went wrong, and fixed minor
mechanical problems:

Watching the cones, checking the fabric, attending the machines which
constantly break down, you're on the go all the time . . . putting up ends,
changing cones, starting machines and trying to watch the fabric. The machines aren't designed for the operator. You bend low to see the fabric,
and climb up on the machine to reach the arms holding the thread. To see
all the cones you have to walk twenty-five feet round. Usually an opera-
tive has three machines with a total of 150 cones, many of which you can't
see immediately because they're on the other side of the machines; you
have to memorize which cones are going to run out . . . Hey, a machine's
stopped. A top red light? Find a stick, disentangle the thread, break off
the balled-up yarn, put the end up, check the thread is not caught, press
the button, throw the handle. (Fraser, 1969, pp. 88–89)

This equipment demanded much walking, bending, climbing, and
reaching, which might have been eliminated by relatively minor changes
in the machines. This worker adapted to the machines, perhaps enduring
backaches and headaches as a consequence. It is impossible to tell how
typical his situation is, because of the dearth of published research on
employees' views of working conditions in factories.

Under ideal circumstances, the machines of a factory embody a series
of well-accepted principles of design that have evolved over time. Practitioners suggest that their application produces work-stations that min-

imize fatigue and maximize efficiency. For example, L. Gilbreth (1931) articulated principles of "motion and fatigue economy" (pp. 640–641), based on earlier time-and-motion studies (see Chapter 2). More recently, Konz (1979) offered these principles for the design of work-stations:

[A]void static loads and fixed work postures; set the work height 50 mm below the elbow; furnish every employee with an adjustable chair; support limbs; use the feet as well as the hands; use gravity, don't oppose it; conserve momentum; use two-hand motions; pivot movements around the elbow; use the preferred hand; keep arms motions in the normal work area. (Konz, 1979, pp. 253–298)

Another source recommends some different principles: "minimize the number of motions . . . minimize the length of motions . . . minimize the number of eye-fixations required" (Blair & Winston, 1971, p. 245).

Unfortunately, it is difficult to find published research describing either the properties of actual machines in factories or employees' psychological reactions to them. (Such studies would be analogous to "post-occupancy evaluations" of buildings.) Similarly, evidence is rare on the connection between the properties of factory equipment and employee satisfaction or performance.

Office equipment. In contrast with factories, offices contain a relatively homogeneous collection of machinery. Even so, the equipment used in offices varies considerably. Office workers use items from a list that includes typewriters, punches, staplers, binders, paper-cutters, shredders, telephones, calculators, teletypes, facsimile senders, microfiche readers, microfilm readers, dictation recorders, tape players, photocopiers, mimeographs, collaters, word-processors, computers, and other machines.

A relatively new and controversial item of office equipment, the video display terminal (or VDT), illustrates some of the issues created by office machines for workers. This TV-like adjunct to computers and word-processors is also known as a video display unit (VDU) or cathode ray tube (CRT). Figure 10.5 shows an example. (See Chapters 2 and 16 for discussions of history and prospects.)

As VDTs began to spread through offices in the 1970s, reports of complaints by employees also started to spread. For instance, a review of the sources of stress in the office pointed to VDTs as one source, and cited research that found such problems as fatigue and eye strain in VDT operators (Wineman, 1982).

The VDT is essentially a television screen with a keyboard, so it comes

Figure 10.5. Work-stations with video display terminals (VDTs) in an open-plan office. *Source:* Photograph courtesy of Steelcase, Inc., Grand Rapids, Michigan.

as no surprise that operators complain of eye problems. VDTs permit wide variation in the details of the display, with corresponding possibilities of visual difficulty. For instance, the visibility of text displayed on the screen depends on the size, contrast, and spacing of the characters; their discriminability; the brightness of the characters and the background; the illumination in the room and possibility of glare; the presence of flicker; the angle of vision; and other factors (see the manual by Cakir et al., 1980).

Research on VDT operators has found widespread visual fatigue among this group. A review of research concluded that

despite a lack of understanding concerning the locus of specific psycho-physical/psychophysiological mechanisms, visual fatigue is an important problem for VDT operators. (Dainoff, Happ & Crane, 1981, p. 423)

These researchers conducted a study among 121 office employees who used VDTs. They found that 45% of workers reported symptoms of visual fatigue, a finding similar to the results of earlier research. Furthermore, visual fatigue was correlated with the amount of time spent looking at the VDT screen (average in their study was 47% of working time). The literature contains many other such findings (see the bibliography by Matula, 1981).

A laboratory study found measurable deterioration in visual functioning during work-sessions at VDTs that lasted only two or three hours. Participants performed a letter-finding task presented on a VDT or printed on standard white paper. Researchers measured, among other things, the amount of time taken for shifts of eye focus from the VDT screen or "hard copy" to other elements of the task. Results showed greater deterioration of "outfocus" times in the VDT version of the task, as well as higher rates of blinking at the VDT (Mourant, Lakshmanan & Chantadisai, 1981).

Other research has shown that VDT operators, particularly in clerical jobs, experience not only visual fatigue but other signs of job-related stress. For example, Smith, Cohen, Stammerjohn & Happ (1981) surveyed approximately 250 VDT operators, along with about 150 office workers who did not use VDTs. About one-half the VDT operators held professional jobs, and one-half held clerical jobs. As in earlier research, VDT operators generally reported symptoms of visual fatigure, including eye strain and "burning eyes." These symptoms were significantly more prevalent among VDT users than among non-VDT users. In the VDT-clerical group, 91% complained of eye-strain and 80% reported "burning eyes." Furthermore, the clerical VDT group complained of significantly more health problems than the other groups.

Their scores on job characteristics that usually contribute to stress were also much higher; they reported greater work pressure, closer supervisory control, greater work-load, more dissatisfaction with their work load, and greater boredom than the other groups. In brief, the clerical VDT operators showed many of the classical signs of job stress (see Cooper & Payne, 1978).

Job stress among VDT operators with clerical jobs may stem, at least in part, from characteristics of the job created indirectly by the VDT. Before the advent of VDTs, clerical workers used typewriter and paper; their jobs included the activities required to obtain work (such as getting rough drafts, insurance forms, dictation tapes, and so on). They also had to deliver finished work, if only to an out box. Their performance could be monitored in person by a supervisor, or through an examination of finished work.

The VDT created new possibilities for supervision and allocation of work. For one thing, VDTs connected to central computers potentially allowed remote, unannounced supervision of every keystroke, from other terminals, without the operator's knowledge. Supervisors could find out exactly how much time each worker spent on each piece of work. Furthermore, the VDT permitted efficient delivery of work to and from the workers via electronic transfer. In brief, the VDT made it possible for office managers to assign work and supervise its execution much more closely. For the workers, this probably translated into greater workloads, fewer breaks, and less autonomy.

The case of the VDT illustrates a general hypothesis concerning both office and factory equipment: that new machines call for new job activities. The changes may be subtle, but even slight shifts in activities may have a powerful impact on the individual's satisfaction. Furthermore, changes in jobs not only represent psychological effects, but social-psychological and organizational ones as well. For instance, clerical VDT operations may require fewer supervisors for a given number of clerical workers (see Chapter 16 on the future of offices).

In summary, the VDT illustrates some of the possibilities for office equipment to create fatigue and discomfort. Furthermore, it illustrates the implications of equipment for changes in job activities, job satisfaction, and even the organization.

Chairs

For workers in offices and factories who spend even part of their day sitting, the chair represents an important, supportive element of the work-station. It also seems to represent one of the more satisfactory aspects of today's working environment.

As early as the 1920s, chairs were at least partly adjustable. For instance, typists' chairs were available with seats of adjustable height and adjustable backrests (see Galloway, 1919). Early factory managers also saw the value of comfortable seating for workers. For instance, at one factory the operators formerly stood at workbenches but were supplied with chairs that allowed them to sit or stand alternately (Mullee, 1933). The same arrangement has been recommended for office workers, apparently without much acceptance (see Fucigna, 1967; Galloway, 1919).

Research on chairs has generally addressed the practical problem of how to design a comfortable one. It is a complex problem, because the optimal design of a chair needs to take account of the occupant's body dimensions, body mechanics, task demands, and posture while sitting. A major study by Burandt and Grandjean (1963) incorporated systematic observations of the way people sat in chairs, along with their preferences regarding seating arrangements (e.g. height of seat, height of work surface, depth of seat) and their ratings of comfort in the chairs. Results indicated that participants used the chairs differently, and in each posture their comfort depended on different features of the chair. (For instance, people who sat at the back of their chairs – 33% of the participants – made little use of their backrests.) Later research uncovered wide individual differences in habits of sitting, and regular changes over time in the posture of the occupant of a chair (e.g., Branton, 1969). Other researchers found marked and significant differences among chairs, with some rated much more comfortable than others (e.g., Shackel, Chidsey & Shipley, 1969; see Kleeman, 1981, for a review of unpublished U.S. government research). Taken together, the research suggested some detailed guidelines for the design of chairs (e.g., see Ayoub, 1973; Kleeman, 1981; Woodson, 1981).

Modern chairs seem to incorporate many of the guidelines suggested by researchers. These include not only adjustable seat height, backrest, and tilt, but other refinements, such as a resilient padding for the seat and back, padded armrests, and a gently rounded front edge on the seat (to prevent the pressure of the edge against the undersides of the thighs). Manufacturers of office furniture, such as Herman Miller and Steelcase, have designed a new generation of chairs in which it is difficult to imagine anyone being uncomfortable. Examples are shown in Figs. 10.6 and 10.7. (However, the present review located no published research on the comfort of these chairs.)

The 1980 survey of office workers conducted by Louis Harris and Associates included a detailed assessment of their chairs. In all, 84% of participants said they had comfortable chairs (p. 18). They were asked about several specific features of their chairs, as listed in Table 10.4. More than three-fourths of the participants said their chairs gave good

Figure 10.6. A modern office chair: the Ergon® chair made by Herman Miller.
Source: Photograph courtesy of Herman Miller, Inc., Zeeland, MI.

Figure 10.7. A modern office chair: the ConCentrx Professional® chair made by Steelcase, Inc. *Source*: Photograph courtesy of Steelcase, Inc., Grand Rapids, Michigan.

Table 10.4. *Features of office chairs reported by 1,001 workers*

Feature of chair	Percentage of sample
Wheels for moving around	94
Swivels on its base	93
Seat height correct for desk and work	93
Adjustable seat height	83
Balanced (for leaning forward or backward)	82
Covered in fabric	78
Supports the lower back	77
Attractive color	62
Arm rests	50
Adjustable back height	48
Adjustable tilt tension	47
Adjustable tilt	46
Seat adjustable forward or backward	24

Source: Louis Harris & Associates (1980), pp. 56–57.

back support, had proper height and balance, and had swivel base, wheels, adjustable height, and fabric covering. About one-half of subjects had chairs with adjustable back height, arm rests, adjustable tilt, or adjustable tilt tension; only about one-quarter had chairs with seats adjustable forward or backward. The survey also asked whether participants believed they could be more productive under certain conditions. About one-quarter (26%) said they could be "a great deal" more productive if they had a more comfortable chair.

Whether the office employees actually could be more productive in more comfortable chairs is largely an academic question, but there is some evidence. A laboratory experiment was done on the effects of chair comfort on the performance of a proofreading task at the University of Connecticut. The researchers deliberately misadjusted two of four chairs and asked groups of four undergraduates to work in them. Results showed that those who sat in the misadjusted chairs and rated the chairs as uncomfortable performed more poorly on the task (Mandel, McLeod & Malven, 1980).

In summary, research on chairs has suggested guidelines for design. Many of these guidelines have apparently been incorporated in modern office chairs. One national study of office workers found that a large majority said they had comfortable chairs.

Supportive facilities

Although the work-station comprises the immediate physical environment for most office or factory workers, these employees use other parts of the building as well. Specifically, most people use at least some of the following areas:

Hallways, corridors, walkways, foyers, entry halls
Staircases, elevators, escalators
Restrooms, washrooms, lavatories
Locker rooms, dressing rooms, showers
Storerooms, warehouses, supply rooms, stockrooms
Special work areas (e.g., copy rooms, laboratories, machine shops, computer centers)
Lounges
Conferences rooms, video-conference centers, auditoriums, classrooms
Cafeterias, lunchrooms, vending rooms
Libraries, reference rooms
Recreation facilities (e.g., exercise rooms, gymnasiums)
Parking garages

Unfortunately, the psychological impact of these supportive facilities remains essentially unexamined, at least within the context of offices and factories. (Manning, 1965, reported on a survey of office workers concerning their restrooms in which 40% found them inadequate in some way.) One possible explanation for the lack of psychological research is that specialized supportive facilities are seen as the province of technical experts, such as architects and industrial engineers. Another possibility is that such areas are largely taken for granted and ignored, or treated as incidental. For whatever reason, supportive facilities constitute a blind spot in research on offices and factories.

Summary

This chapter examines work-stations and supportive facilities in offices and factories. The relationship between worker and work-station depends on many factors, including the variety of different types of work-stations, the many important components of each work-station, the job activities, and characteristics of the individual. One view of the relationship is based on the *man–machine system*, which applies mainly to machinery and equipment, and points to the importance of displays and controls. Other important elements of the work-station include places to sit, stand, or lean; work surfaces; and storage of tools, supplies, materials, and references. These components of the work-station have the capacity to create discomfort through fatigue or through attitudes. Discomfort may lead to dissatisfaction with the environment or job. However, workers may adapt over time to an uncomfortable work-station.

Research on work-stations has generally dealt with their components, not the work-station as a whole, and has usually sought to establish guidelines for design. The survey of office workers conducted by Louis Harris and Associates did consider the whole work-station and found that workers identified a few components as important for their performance: accessible tools, equipment and materials, adjustable work-station, storage, chair, and work-surfaces. Similarly, components of the office work-station important to comfort included chair, storage, and floorspace.

A selective review of research on specific elements of work-stations focused on floorspace, equipment, and chairs. A few studies linked floorspace with workers' satisfaction with the environment in offices and factories. Studies of equipment in the factory have been rare. Research on a specific piece of equipment – the video-display terminal (VDT) – illustrates the possibilities for a machine to create discomfort, to promote changes in job activities, and to influence job satisfaction. Studies of chairs suggested guidelines for design, which apparently led to a new generation of comfortable office chairs.

The psychological impact of supportive environments outside the work-station has seldom been studied. Nevertheless, workers routinely use such areas as restrooms, hallways, stairs, locker rooms, and other special facilities.

Practical considerations

The design of work-stations represents a topic of long-standing interest in several professions. These include engineering psychology, ergonomics, human factors psychology, industrial engineering, and others. Practitioners have developed extensive and detailed guidelines for a seemingly endless list of highly specific situations.

The abstract questions concerning the impact of the work-station may not be as well understood as they might be, but many concrete questions concerning particular types of work-stations have been studied, and the results have been published. Consequently, a variety of excellent practical resources is available. These include general treatments of engineering psychology (e.g., Chapanis, 1976) and human factors psychology (e.g., McCormick, 1976), as well as handbooks of guidelines for design (e.g., Konz, 1979; Woodson, 1981).

PART III

INTERPERSONAL RELATIONS

This part of the book deals with the second unit of analysis – interpersonal relationships – and shifts from a psychological to a social-psychological perspective. It focuses on the role of the physical environment in the way people perceive one another, communicate, regulate their interaction, and form groups.

An analysis of interpersonal relationships cannot deal with the environment in terms of unitary dimensions, such as the brightness of light. At this level of analysis, many different features of the work place can serve the same function. For example, the size of a person's workstation, the amount of furniture, and the presence of a window can all signal a person's position in the local status hierarchy. Similarly, a single aspect of the environment can serve many functions. For instance, an enclosed office can signal status, permit comfortable conversation, and provide privacy.

So in exploring interpersonal relationships we no longer emphasize the description of the physical environment itself. Instead, we try to characterize the social-psychological processes that incorporate the environment. Consequently, the four chapters of this section emphasize social-psychological processes more than specific elements of the physical environment.

This part of the book begins with a chapter on some of the symbolic functions of the workspace, the expression of self-identity and the demarcation of status. The next two chapters concern communication (Chapter 12) and privacy (Chapter 13) and deal with two sides of the same issue: interpersonal accessibility. The chapter on communication explores the role of the physical environment in face-to-face conversation, including features of the layout of buildings and the arrangement of workspaces that promote accessibility and make conversations convenient. The chapter on privacy examines facets of the environment that allow people to limit their accessibility, particularly the physical enclosure of workspaces. Finally, Chapter 14 discusses small groups and examines the importance of physical proximity and separation of workspaces in the formation of groups and the development of cohesion.

11
SYMBOLIC WORKSPACE: SELF-IDENTITY AND STATUS

This chapter explores aspects of the workspace that convey information about the occupant to other people. Here the workspace (or individually assigned work-station) represents a symbolic medium for the expression of the worker's self-identity and the individual's status in the organization's hierarchy. To the extent that the workspace permits satisfactory self-expression and appropriately displays the occupant's status, it may contribute to individual satisfaction with the physical environment. Much of the research evidence related to self-expression and status demarcation concerns their connection with satisfaction.

This chapter first discusses self-identity by addressing the concepts of personalization, territoriality, and participative design. It then discusses the demarcation of status, identifies some common status markers, and examines evidence on their relationship with employee satisfaction.

Expression of self-identity

This section examines how the use of workspaces in offices and factories expresses workers' self-identities, and the implications for satisfaction and interpersonal relations. (The term *self-identity* means an individual's own vision of his or her lasting characteristics and habits, particularly those that differentiate that person from other people.) Self-expression in a workspace presupposes two things. First, a work-station is assigned to a specific person and recognized by others as that person's (in other words, it fits the present definition of "workspace"). Second, the occupant of the workspace has at least some freedom to decorate or arrange it to suit his or her preferences.

The section includes no empirical research concerning the prevalence of the practice of assigning work-stations to individuals, although the practice seems much more common in offices than factories. In offices, even the lowest-ranking employees usually seem to have assigned workspaces. However, exceptions to this general rule appear in typing pools, word-processing centers, and data-entry operations, where machines are sometimes assigned to nobody in particular.

In factories, assigned work-stations are often impractical. The technology generally dictates whether a worker even stays in one area; if so, he or she may circulate among several work-stations. In factories where people work a whole shift at one work-station, production may continue for two or three shifts each day, 7 days each week. In such factories, any one work-station might have three or more operators. It may be unusual for a work-station at a factory to have only one operator, but just how unusual it is impossible to tell.

In offices and factories where people work in assigned workspaces, *personalization* describes the display of personal or work-related items or the arrangement of the workspace to distinguish the occupant from others (see Sommer, 1974). This section first discusses personalization, then addresses the possibility that workspaces represent personal territories or zones of control for individual workers. The last part of the section discusses worker participation in the design of their workspaces.

Personalization

The term *personalization* comes from environmental psychology. For example, Robert Sommer (1974, p. 111) used it to refer to the deliberate adornment, decoration, modification, or rearrangement of an environment by its occupants to reflect their individual identities. Personalization in workspaces is complicated by the fact that in most offices and factories, people besides the user of a workspace have some control over it. In effect, personalization expresses not only the individual's self-identity, but also the amount of freedom and control the organization allows the individual to exert over the workspace.

Personalization seems to represent an important issue for both office and factory workers. According to one description,

For artisans of the out-box, millions of us, the office is [a] highly personal tool shop, often the home of the soul. Unless it fits our habits and bears at least a faint mark of the user's personal stamp, it is a strange and hostile ground. (Harris, 1977, p. 15)

Similarly,

> Identity is established with place. . . . Thus women operatives working at
> identical tasks on identical machines will insist on a machine being theirs
> and will adorn it with photographs or by other means, perhaps a name, to
> distinguish it and themselves. (Chapman, 1967, p. 156)

Examples of personalization. In one factory, a visitor related this story:

> I was recently invited to visit a machine factory in the midwest and when I
> walked in I was assaulted with a kaleidoscope of orange, blue, pink, yel-
> low, red and multi-colored machines. My host laughed at the expression
> on my face and then went on to tell me that the management of the com-
> pany had told the workers they could paint the machines any color they
> wanted and the company would furnish the paint if they furnished the
> manpower. The result was a very unusual looking factory to me, although
> it was a pleasing work environment to those who worked there every day.
> (Korman, 1977, p. 181)

Similarly, workers in offices have personalized their workspaces, sometimes in a very distinctive manner:

> For 10 years Dr. Ben Barkow hung a giant inflatable banana from the
> ceiling of whatever office he was occupying in the Ontario government,
> Bell Telephone laboratories, or York University. . . . He argues that by al-
> lowing the employee the freedom to personalize his or her workspace the
> company gets a happier worker. (Witten, 1978, p. 61)

In another office, Elaine, an insurance claims adjustor, worked in a
"cavernous and impersonal room":

> [S]he'd created a home. She'd set up family photographs and, for hating, a
> poster of glum Nixon. There were four carnations on her desk, crocheted
> containers for her pencils and paper clips, a bright red cozy around her
> teapot. She'd refused to let that workspace – unpromising as it was – stay
> the company's. (Coombs, 1977, p. 69)

Limits on personalization. For most workers, the freedom to personalize their workspaces depends on the policies of the organization, the
decisions made by local executives, and the physical capacities of the
workspace. In effect, the limits on personalization are set by forces
within the organization that favor a particular appearance or arrangement. In the most extreme case, policies may dictate uniformity. For
example, an insurance investigator in a large office of Blue Cross/Blue

Shield was "confined to a nine-foot-by-four-foot glass and metal working space."

I'm a fish in a glass container, and there's no way I can make this fishbowl mine. The authorities request that every desk be cleared. Everyone must use the same sort of filing cabinets, the same waste-paper baskets. No posters are allowed. No photographs. Plants have to be a certain height (Coombs, 1977, p. 69)

Similar stories came from CBS headquarters in New York City:

[Y]ou can't hang anything on the walls, you can't have any live flowers or plants on your desk, etc. You can't rearrange your furniture without getting written permission. One man got ready for a conference at which he was to exhibit kinescopes of television shows. He got the viewer ready and called, 'lights out!' That's when he discovered there was no light switch in his office. When he asked for a chair to stand on, so he could unscrew the bulb, he was told it would require two inter-office memos, one to move the chair and another for permission to touch the bulb. (Beatty, 1965, p. 12)

The limitation of personalization seems to reflect a preference for an orderly, business-like appearance by architects, planners, and managers. By one account some exhibit "a mania for uniformity, in space as in furniture, and a horror over how the messy side of human nature clutters up an office landscape" (T. G. Harris, 1977, p. 51). The pressure for an orderly appearance may allow employees very little latitude. One source of institutionalized pressure against personalization is the long-standing assumption that an orderly-appearing environment promotes efficiency. An early psychologist wrote, "much better work is produced by employees whose senses are not maltreated by dirt and disorder" (Munsterberg, 1915, p. 192). On the other hand, "clerks in a disorderly office tend to become as their surroundings" (Leffingwell, 1919, p. 331). Another early writer claimed that orderliness exerts a "moral influence" on workers by giving an example for them to follow in their work (Meakin, 1905).

Today's office planners still stress orderliness. For instance, one planner mocks the "scene of horrendous clutter" in the average office (Pile, 1978, p.22). Even the *Business Etiquette Handbook* admonishes:

Avoid over-decorating your desk or area. When your desk, shelves, and wall space are covered with mementoes, photographs, trophies, humorous mottoes, and other decorative effects, you are probably not beautifying the office; rather you may be giving it a jumbled, untidy look. You may also be violating regulations against using nails in the walls, and so on. The proper atmosphere for a business office is one of neatness and efficiency, not hominess. (1965, p.17)

The advent of the open plan office has created another source of pressure against personalization: with the whole office more or less visible at a glance, planners want the office to look the way they designed it to look. (And if the occupants personalize the workspaces, they might spoil the "esthetic environment" intended in the plan.) A recent office-planning book points out:

While individuals can be permitted to furnish their own conventional office spaces with the *damnedest things*, it is another story when many individuals are asked to accept and live with these oddments in an open area. (Palmer & Lewis, 1977, p. 105)

In an article entitled "Keeping Blight from the Open Office," an engineer from the U.S. Internal Revenue Service recounted some highlights of his struggle to prevent the appearance of open offices from "going downhill." Employees had reportedly created blight in many subtle ways, by making "indiscriminate changes" in work-stations or layouts. For instance:

[E]mployees who were originally assigned a single pedestal desk with a side chair somehow hatched a little typing table (with typewriter), a desk-top organizer, a two-drawer lateral file, a plant or two, or another screen. (Schumann, 1974, p. 2)

In other words, employees had altered their environment to suit their purposes. However, they had also created a disparity between the appearance of the office and the designer's concept. The recommended course of action for managers was to notify the employees that "no changes are to be made without the approval of the designer."

Managers may tolerate a certain amount of personalization and "disorder," perhaps to the point of overlooking minor infractions in the interest of morale. Such tolerance reveals a tacit acceptance of the importance of self-expression through personalization of workspaces.

Despite its long history and apparently widespread acceptance, the assumed link between superficial orderliness and efficiency seems to have no basis in empirical evidence. Furthermore, the assumption has been criticized. For instance:

[W]e all have this desire for formal order. The only problem is that it con-
flicts severely with the more organic kind of spatial order human interchange uses best (Propst, 1968, p. 27)

Even so, the desire for formal order seems to remain powerful.

Prevalence of personalization. Limited evidence suggests that personalization may be quite common among office workers. BOSTI's (1981)
survey of office workers included the question, "[H]ave you included
any *work related* things such as charts, phone numbers, pencil holders,
awards, etc. to your work space?" A total of 79% of the participants
said they did. Asked whether they had added "such *personal* thing as
pictures or paintings, clocks, plants, rugs, or cushions," a total of 61%
replied yes. (Although these results are based on workers' own reports,
not on direct observation of their workspaces, the self-reports are probably fairly reliable.)

If the BOSTI findings are representative, perhaps three out of four
office workers personalize their workspaces. Whether the remaining
workers fail to do so by choice, or because of restrictive policies in their
organization, or because their workspaces are physically unsuited to
personalization, we do not know. (The prevalence of personalization in
factories also remains unknown.)

Personalization and satisfaction. A physical environment that accom-
odates self-expression (in an organization that allows it) may contribute
to the individual's satisfaction with the physical environment or with the
job. For one thing, freedom to personalize the environment probably
conveys the uniqueness of each person and shows that individuality is
recognized and appreciated in the organization.

The recognition of a worker's individuality may be associated with
job satisfaction. For instance, office workers who participated in the
1978 Steelcase survey rated the importance of 19 characteristics of their
jobs, including "I feel like an individual on the job, not just a cog in a
machine." Results showed that 77% rated it "very important." This
item ranked fifth in the list of job factors mentioned most frequently.
It was chosen by more people than good pay or pleasant physical surroundings. (Other research on job satisfaction suggests that recognition
in an organization represents an important component of job satisfaction; see Locke, 1983.) So, if personalization promotes recognition of
individuality, it may also contribute to job satisfaction. On the other
hand, a work environment that discourages self-expression may make
people feel like cogs in machines, and may even suggest that they are
regarded in the organization as interchangeable and replaceable.

We found little research concerned directly with the relationship between personalization and satisfaction. The survey by Harris and Associates (1978) did include a question on the characteristics of a workspace important to its appearance (not to its general adequacy). Participants were asked to choose two or three from a list of eleven characteristics of workspaces, and 20% chose "the way it reflects the personality of the person working there" (p. 5). (The project did not include a direct test of whether this item was statistically related to satisfaction with the working environment.)

BOSTI (1981) found a connection between the amount of room available for displaying personal items and office workers' satisfaction with the physical environment. Among employees who changed offices, those who had more room for display of personal items after the change reported greater satisfaction with the environment. Those with less space for display in their new offices reported lower satisfaction. However, office employees with supervisory responsibility reported having more room for display than nonsupervisors. Also, having space for personal display was directly associated with the size of the workspace, which suggests that display space was a perquisite of rank.

There is some evidence from non-work settings that personalization may be correlated with commitment by the occupants to the place. In a study of a dormitory at the University of Utah, Hansen and Altman (1976) selected a sample of rooms and recorded the numbers and types of personal things there, such as posters, rugs, stereos, pictures, and so on. School records showed which students later dropped out of school for nonacademic reasons. The dropouts had fewer personal items in their rooms than the students who remained. A later study in the same dormitories found that dropouts had more personal objects. However, in contrast to other students, these dropouts' objects of personalization concerned localities outside the university, such as their former residences (Vinsel et al., 1980). Through the lack of personalization, or through its reference to other places, the students who eventually dropped out had apparently failed to show a commitment to their current environments.

If personalization of a workspace is associated with commitment to the organization, it is not clear which is the cause and which the effect. The display of personal objects may result from satisfaction with the job and the associated commitment to the organization. On the other hand, personalization may give people a sense of control over their workspace, which might eventually lead them to feel attached to their organization, and the display of personal objects could actually contribute to commitment. (However, we found no evidence that personalization is associated with commitment.)

In summary, personalization of workspaces may contribute to employees' satisfaction in part because personalization may lead people to feel that their individuality is recognized. Limited evidence suggests that office workers regard personalization as important, and that they are relatively satisfied in workspaces that have room to display personal and work-related items.

Implications for interpersonal relationships. Personalization of workspaces seems to have the capacity for sending several messages to co-workers and visitors. Some are purely self-expressive, and concern the occupant's tastes, preferences, attitudes, opinions, history, nonwork roles, hobbies, or personality. For example, a former U.S. army officer displays in his office his military medals, photos of his platoon, and a bayonet. A mother displays photos of her husband and children along with selections from the children's artwork.

How such messages affect interpersonal relationships is largely unknown. One possibility is that visitors feel relatively comfortable with occupants of highly personalized workspaces because they feel familiar with them. This idea is analogous to a preference for face-to-face meetings over telephone calls because of the peripheral cues available in the meeting (see Chapter 12).

The personalized workspace may symbolically indicate to visitors or co-workers the occupant's desires regarding psychological distance. For instance, the placement of the desk in an office may lead a visitor to address the occupant from the opposite side of the desk, creating a psychological barrier. (This is discussed further in Chapters 12 and 13.)

Personalization of a workspace may also convey messages concerning the worker's dominion over a particular area. For instance, one implicit message might proclaim, "This is *my* space, and I'm in control here." Similarly, personalization may delineate boundaries: "My workspace extends to the edges of my Scandinavian rug." In effect, additions to the workspace or its arrangement may symbolically define the workspace as a territory, discussed next.

In summary, personalization refers to the adornment, decoration, modification, or rearrangement of a workspace by the occupant. It may represent a form of self-expression; anecdotes suggest that workers see it as an important issue. However, organizational policies that favor uniformity or an orderly appearance may limit workers' freedom to personalize their workspaces. Available evidence suggests that personalization is common in offices, involving perhaps three out of four workers, and that it is associated to some extent with satisfaction with the physical environment. Its implications for interpersonal relations remain largely unexplored.

Workspace as territory

Does a workspace constitute a territory for the occupant? If so, then according to the theory of Irwin Altman (1975), the workspace represents a zone of control that helps the individual regulate his or her contacts with others. However, the extent to which people are territorial is a matter of debate.

The concept of territory originated with ethologists studying nonhuman animals. Among species that exhibit territorial behavior, a territory is a fixed piece of geography with specific boundaries. An individual or family uses it for nesting, mating, foraging, and other activities necessary for survival and propagation. Some nonhuman species physically mark the boundaries of their territories; the members of many species actively defend their territories against intruders (see, e.g., Ardrey, 1966; Carpenter, 1958; Lorenz, 1966).

Some ethologists, notably Konrad Lorenz (1966), contend that humans are territorial. Environmental psychologists point out that people do tend to frequent specific places and try to control others' access to them. These are at least superficial indications of territoriality (see Altman, 1975; Edney, 1974; Sundstrom & Altman, 1974, Sundstrom, 1984).

For environmental psychologist Irwin Altman (1975), a key feature of human territoriality is the individual's (or group's) control over a space. Altman distinguishes three types of territories. The type most relevant to work environments is the primary territory, a place that an individual uses frequently for personally important activities. In such a place the occupant has relatively permanent, recognized rights to control the access of others to the place. Examples in work organizations include private offices and personally assigned machines.

According to Altman, an individual uses a primary territory to establish psychological boundaries between self and others. By virtue of having a physical territory in which the individual's influence is recognized, the occupant can use the control to regulate contact with others. This permits maintenance of the appropriate psychological distance – not too close and not too far – which is in Altman's view prerequisite to healthy interpersonal relationships.

Altman's theory implies that people treat places as territories only when they have a sense of control there. In offices and factories, the amount of freedom allowed for personalization of a workspace establishes the limits of the individual's control. Personalization may represent a demonstration to co-workers and visitors (and the occupant) that the workspace is, in fact, that person's zone of control. If so, personalization is a central component of territoriality in the work place.

To the extent that workspaces represent territories, workers may be able to use them to regulate interpersonal interactions. When a person feels overloaded or overstimulated, he or she can use the territory to retreat and temporarily minimize contacts. When a worker desires more social contact, he or she can seek others out, by finding them or inviting them to the workspace. According to the theory, as long as the workspace constitutes a territory – a recognized zone of control – co-workers and visitors respect its use for setting or dissolving social-psychological boundaries. (This process is part of privacy regulation, which we discuss further in Chapter 13.)

An important implication of a territorial work environment concerns occupants' feelings of responsibility for "their" workspaces. Workers who feel psychological (if not legal) ownership of their workspaces are likely to take initiative in their care and maintenance. This could help account for the observation by some factory managers that machines assigned to specific individuals tend to receive better care than machines assigned to nobody in particular (Friedmann, 1955). However, we found no direct evidence for the plausible hypothesis that the encouragement of territoriality leads workers to exercise personal responsibility for their environment.

In summary, an individual workspace may become a territory or zone of control, but this probably only occurs if the occupant has the freedom to personalize it. Territorial workspaces may help regulate interaction and encourage individual responsibility for the environment, but we have no evidence that they do.

A nonterritorial office. One of the few published research projects concerning territoriality in the office involved the conversion of individually assigned workspaces to shared work-stations. Allen and Gerstberger (1973) conducted a year-long study of a group of 13 to 19 product engineers whose conventional one- or two-person offices were converted to an open office. Most internal walls were removed, and with them went almost all permanent assignments to specific work-stations (a central receptionist's position was retained). The new work-stations consisted simply of chairs at circular tables or at laboratory benches in a large, open area. A special "quiet area" was located behind curtains in one corner of the open office; a private conference room also remained. Employees took home all personal items such as pictures and books; the company provided all necessary books, which remained "departmental property."

The job of product engineer was well suited to the nonterritorial office, because the work called for a good deal of mobility. The engineers needed frequent contact with people in other departments, especially in the product testing laboratory, and with people in other buildings.

Only about two-thirds of the engineers were usually in the building at a given time; rarely were as many as 80% present. The work was apparently quite portable, and the nonterritorial arrangement posed few practical problems.

Having read *The Territorial Imperative* (Ardrey, 1966), the investigators envisioned "a distinct possibility that the nonterritorial concept would fail because occupants might 'stake a claim' to their own territories" within the office area (Allen & Gerstberger, 1973, p. 489). This is just what the concept of territory implies.

To find out whether the engineers did stake out territories, the researchers recorded their seating positions three times each week on a randomly selected day, for eight months after the change. Results contradicted predictions based on the concept of territory:

[R]ather than laying claims to any specific position, the occupants seem[ed] to prefer to move about considerably over the course of a day. No one spent more than 50% of his [table] time at a single table. (Allen & Gerstberger, 1973, p. 493)

Even after several months, the product engineers apparently preferred variety over territory.

The workers reported a high level of satisfaction with their new work environment. They were questioned on their feelings about the nonterritorial office both before and after the change and gave significantly more favorable ratings afterward. Perhaps the initially low ratings of the nonterritorial office reflected apprehensions about it before it was introduced. Later increases in ratings may have reflected relief that initial fears were not justified. However, the engineers gave the nonterritorial office high marks – an average of approximately 4.2 on a five-point scale.

It is perhaps not so surprising that the engineers refrained from staking out individual territories. With explicit policies that favored shared workstations and prohibited leaving personal objects, the engineers probably could not have claimed specific places even if they had tried. Furthermore, their need to work away from the building ensured that no individual could occupy a work-station more than the few days each week he spent in the building.

Had the engineers felt territorial about their workspaces before the change, the new arrangement might have shifted their territorial orientation to a group territory. The group did share the same area on an equal basis, but it was for their use as a group. (No other workers used the work-stations.) If so, the nonterritorial office might be more accurately called a group territorial office. One possibility not examined in the study is that some workers felt more territorial about their work-spaces than others did. If so, territoriality represents a personality trait.

Territoriality as a trait. If the need to claim a workspace as a territory varies from one person to another, territoriality may be viewed as trait. Psychologists have rarely approached it this way, but at least one architect has. Sam Sloan was retained by an Australian insurance company to design an office. He systematically observed the occupants and categorized them as either territorial or nonterritorial. (Sloan also categorized them on sociability and aggressiveness.) He then designed a different workspace for each personality classification. For instance, a workspace with defined limits was specified for individuals categorized as territorial. (The limits of workspaces were to be defined by suspended fabric panels.) The company redesigned the office according to Sloan's suggestions. Data from a questionnaire administered before and after the changes suggested that employees were much more satisfied with the new arrangement in which workspaces were tailored to their territorial inclinations (Sloan, 1972).

In summary, according to one theory, people treat places as territories if they use them frequently for important activities and have control over them. If workspaces constitute territories, they may help organize interpersonal interactions. However, a study of a nonterritorial office found a group of engineers satisfied with shared work-stations. (The arrangement might be viewed as a group territory.) An architect conceived territoriality as a trait and found that when workspaces were tailored to employees' territorial inclinations, they were satisfied.

Participation in the design of the workspace

One way an individual can leave a personal imprint on a workspace is to participate in its design. In doing so, the individual can express his or her self-identity through the types of equipment chosen, the kinds and arrangement of furniture, the colors and finishes, decorative items, and so on.

Participation in the design of a workspace potentially involves greater control over a workspace than personalization, which is limited by the physical possibilities for rearrangement, addition, and display. In contrast, participative design is limited only by the budget allocated to the workspace. In principle a workspace can be completely personalized, in every sense of the word. For example, an artist and art dealer filled his office with things that were a comfort to him: a seventeenth century carved and canopied Flemish bed ("one needs to lie down once in a while"); Persian rugs on the floor; an eighteenth century crucifix above the bed; a New Guinean sculpture; a collection of Persian and Roman glass; furniture of exotic appearance; and other items (Slesin, 1977, p. 59).

Such examples are rare. For most employees who work in offices and factories, participation in the design of workspaces is closely circumscribed, if allowed at all. In the words of one expert,

From the dingiest, greasiest, noisiest, and most ill-lit factory in New Jersey's industrial outback to the clean, bright, quiet, Muzak-sweetened atmosphere of a firm manufacturing scientific instruments in Palo Alto, *most offices and factories have one thing in common. They are designed and tended by others.* It is up to the person who comes there to work to fit in, not the reverse. [italics added] (Dickson, 1975, p. 281)

According to environmental psychologist Franklin Becker (1981), workers are commonly excluded from decisions about their work environments because of professionalization. Becker suggested that professionals who are recognized as experts, such as architects and office planners, traditionally have the responsibility of designing offices and factories, and they jealously guard their prerogative.

A notable exception to Dickson's and Becker's observations occurred in an office of the Federal Aviation Administration in Seattle, where employees had a substantial role in planning their workspaces. After describing this rare example, we review the limited research evidence on the prevalence of participation in the design of offices and factories, and its connection with worker satisfaction.

The Federal Aviation Administration office project. In 1972 the U.S. General Services Administration sponsored an experiment in participative design that represented a significant departure from existing practice. The site of the project was the northwest regional office of the Federal Aviation Administration (FAA) in Seattle, which housed approximately 360 employees. The project called for a design team to work with employees and enlist their participation in planning a new building. The team included architects and behavioral scientists.

Instead of designing the work-stations themselves, as is traditional, the team allowed the workers to make many of the decisions. In a vacant airplane hangar near the office building, each worker

designed his or her own work-station with a member of the design team. Each piece of furniture offered was available so that a work-station could be arranged in its actual pattern. . . . The floor was carpeted and a ceiling installed to stimulate that in the new building. . . .

With thirteen desks, fifteen chairs, six credenzas, sixteen colors of fab-

ric, a full range of telephone colors, and even six different in and out baskets available for each person's choice, the power of selection was real,
and was exercised. (Kleeman, 1981, pp. 299–300)

According to an interview with Dennis Green, a member of the design
team, the resulting office had the following appearance:

very heterogeneous, something like coming into a party and seeing a
bunch of people dressed in different clothes in different styles and colors.
The only real trend in the place is that there are a large number of desks
with teak tops because this was by far the most popular choice when people picked out their equipment. (Dickson, 1975, p. 302)

The project included a postoccupancy evaluation. One year after the
new building was occupied, the design team administered a questionnaire, which was completed by 250 employees. For comparison, the
questionnaire was also completed by 436 FAA employees at the new
western regional office at Hawthorne (Los Angeles), one year after they
occupied their building. The Los Angeles facility had been designed in
the traditional way, with minimal participation by the employees.

The questionnaire assessed satisfaction with 14 aspects of the building.
These included "building aesthetics, sound/noise, climatic comfort, light
adequacy, space quality, equipment, color/texture, space arrangement,
communication, privacy, personalization, management policy, job performance, and building safety." There were also questions on employees' degree of participation in the project (Sloan, undated).

Responses to the questionnaire indicated that the Seattle employees
participated more in the design of their offices and were more satisfied
with the building they worked in. Only 21% of the Los Angeles group
said they took part in the design of their building. By contrast, 55% of
those at Seattle said they "very actively" or "moderately actively" participated. For 12 of the 14 issues listed in the questionnaire, a larger
fraction of the Seattle employees expressed satisfaction than at Los
Angeles. (The two features that satisfied larger fractions of the Los
Angeles employees were "color/texture" and "communication," for which
the differences in the proportion of people satisfied at the two locations
were 1% and 3%.)

Although the Seattle building was generally more satisfying to its
occupants than the Los Angeles building, only a minority of the workers
at both sites were satisfied on the issue of personalization. (It was defined
as "the ability to express oneself in the total fabric of the environment.")
Overall, only 34% expressed satisfaction at Seattle, compared with 23%
in Los Angeles. However, those who most actively participated in the
project were most satisfied. For instance, of the 60 people who said they

"very actively" took part at Seattle, 48% were satisfied on the issue of personalization (Sloan, undated).

It is puzzling that such a small fraction of the people at Seattle expressed satisfaction on the issue of personalization. Perhaps the managers of the FAA offices allowed very little display of personal items. Even the ability to choose furniture and equipment may not have allowed sufficient self-expression for workers whose freedom to display personal items was curtailed.

In summary, the Seattle FAA project allowed a group of office workers to participate in the design of their workspaces, and gave them a wide range of choices in furniture and equipment. After 1 year the employees were better satisfied with their building than were the occupants of another building where participation was minimal. However, only a minority of the workers were satisfied on the issue of personalization.

Prevalence of participative design in offices. Available evidence suggests that office employees usually participate very little, if at all, in decisions about their offices. The survey by Louis Harris and Associates (1978) included a question asking office workers to indicate who has "some say in planning new offices in your organization." Only 19% of the office workers answered "employees." (However, 37% of executives answered that employees had a say.) On the other hand, two-thirds of the office workers indicated that architects, interior designers, or office planners had a say in the design of their offices (p. 90). Office workers in the survey were also asked whether their management would favor or oppose "letting employees have a say in planning office space and selecting equipment." Exactly half answered "oppose."

Similar results were found by the BOSTI (1981) study. Participants were asked, "were you allowed to participate in the planning or design of your workspace?" A total of 77% answered "no." Only 23% said "yes," which is quite close to the corresponding fraction in the Harris survey. However, more office workers with supervisory responsibility said they participated than nonsupervisors (41% versus 17%).

The BOSTI study examined the details of office workers' participation in decisions about their workspaces, and found that even when employees did participate in the design of their offices, their influence was limited. For six specific aspects of the office, participants were asked to indicate whether they gave an opinion or information, or actually made the decision. Results appear in Table 11.1, which shows that for all six issues, more people gave opinions than made decisions. One of the issues involving least participation concerned esthetics (color schemes, graphics, plants), the traditional province of the office designer. Overall,

Table 11.1. *Types of participation among office employees who participated in the design of their workspaces*

Aspect of workspace	Percentage of employees[a]	
	Gave opinion or information	Made decision
Location of workspace	46	16
Size of workspace	39	6
Selection of furniture, storage, partitions	38	14
Choice of color schemes, graphics, plants	23	9
Location of equipment	36	30
Planning of workflow	37	19

[a] Based only on the people who participated in the design of some aspect of their workspaces, who comprised about 24% of the whole sample.
Source: BOSTI (1981), p. 225.

slightly more than half the people who participated in the design of their workspaces said they made decisions on one or more issues (56%). The average worker was only involved in three of the issues. However, those with supervisory responsibilities were more likely to make decisions and were involved in more issues than nonsupervisors.

In summary, surveys of two large samples of office employees found that only about one out of five of them had participated in the design of his or her office. These findings corroborate Dickson's (1975) claim that most employees work in environments designed by somebody else. Furthermore, the findings are consistent with Becker's (1981) assertion that the design of offices is regarded as the province of experts. However, people with supervisory responsibilities were more likely than nonsupervisors to participate in the design of their workspaces, which suggests that participative design is a perquisite of rank.

Participation and satisfaction. Perhaps the most frequently offered hypothesis concerning the involvement of employees in decisions about the design of their offices is that it leads to greater satisfaction with the environment, greater efficiency on the job, or both. This is plausible for several reasons. First, participative design allows a form of self-expression, which may lead occupants to feel committed to their environments or to their organizations. (Control over the environment could even create some form of psychological attachment to it.) Second, participative design may lead to better environments, by promoting better decisions. (At the very least, employee participation in design ensures that decisions are based on more information than if employees do not take part.) Third, participative design may be intrinsically satisfying. Fourth, it provides an opportunity for cooperation among workers.

Unfortunately, we found very little research evidence that links participative design with satisfaction among office workers or factory workers. We also found little evidence on participative design of environments other than offices and factories. However, there is substantial literature on participative decision-making in general.

The strongest evidence of an association between participation by office employees in the design of their workspace and satisfaction comes from BOSTI (1981). Those who participated in the design of their offices expressed significantly greater satisfaction with the physical environment, greater job satisfaction, and better self-rated job performance. A doctoral dissertation based on the BOSTI data incorporated a multivariate statistical test of whether the association between participation and satisfaction held after taking account of other factors that might explain it. Control variables included gender, age, job-type (managerial, professional-technical, or clerical), and government versus private sector. Even after taking account of the control variables, participation in the design of the workspace was still significantly associated with environmental satisfaction, job satisfaction, and self-rated job performance (Town, 1982).

The Steelcase study found that workers generally believe their participation in office design would produce a more satisfactory environment. The survey included the question,

If you and your work group had a lot of say in planning the office spaces and equipment with which you work, all in all, do you feel this would have a good effect on your office environment, a bad effect, or not much of an effect at all? (Louis Harris & Associates, 1978, p. 87)

Almost three-fourths of the sample of office workers answered "good effect" (72%); most of the others said "not much of an effect" (21%). Practically none said it would hurt. This finding shows that most of the office workers believed that participative design leads to a better and presumably more satisfying environment. By contrast, the BOSTI (1981) study found a correlation between participation and satisfaction when both variables were independently assessed.

Research on the participative design of settings other than offices has also been infrequent. However, what there is suggests that people who helped design their environments were more satisfied than those who did not participate (see the reviews by Wandersman, 1979a,b).

Evidence on participative decision-making concerning issues besides design of environments suggests that participation is often, but not consistently, associated with employee satisfaction. A thorough review of the empirical research by Locke and Schweiger (1979) uncovered 22 field studies that measured satisfaction among employees who were involved in some form of participative decision-making. Of these, 13 studies reported that participative decision making was associated with greater satisfaction; only one study found lower satisfaction. The review considered other studies, and concluded that the evidence for a connection of a participative decision-making with satisfaction was equivocal, and depended on contextual factors (p. 325). In particular, programs for participative decision-making seem to have failed when people were given responsibility for making decisions but lacked necessary knowledge.

Summary. Participation by workers in the design of their workspaces potentially allows considerable self-expression. In practice, however, it is limited, despite successful examples of participative design like the FAA offices in Seattle. There, individual workers made many of the decisions regarding the design of their own workspaces. The resulting office building was rated more satisfactory than a comparable building planned in the traditional way (with minimal participation). Limited evidence suggests that perhaps one out of five office workers participates in the design of his or her workspace, and participation is more likely among higher-ranking people with supervisory responsibility. However, when workers do participate, their influence is usually restricted to a few issues, and often involves nothing more than giving information or opinions. Even so, available evidence suggests that participative design is associated with satisfaction with the physical environment.

Demarcation of status

This section discusses the use of the physical environment to display *status*, or the relative standing of an individual in the organization's hierarchy of authority and influence. Status is important to the organization for many reasons (see Barnard, 1946; Katz & Kahn, 1978). For the individual, the symbols of status represent concrete and visible evidence of rank in the organization, and the power that accompanies it.

Workspaces apparently symbolize status in many offices. For instance, when an executive at the offices of CBS in New York City receives a promotion, he or she moves to a larger office with more seating for visitors and a larger desk. If the individual's rank is high enough, he or

"They're widening his office by one modular unit—I think it's a promotion—"

Figure 11.1. Cartoon by Alan Dunn. *Source*: Reprinted from *Architectural Record*. (1960). *128*(1), 9. © 1960, by McGraw-Hill, Inc. with all rights reserved.

she may have a wood-veneered desk top instead of formica, and perhaps a potted plant (Harris, 1977). Similarly, in the Civil Service,

> the practice of having external badges of status has become institutionalized, and elaborate regulations prescribe at what level in the hierarchy one may have a desk lamp, a padded armchair, and finally a strip of carpet in one's office. (Brown, 1954, p. 139, quoting Gordon R. Taylor)

In the Canadian Ministry, the deputy minister receives a minimum of seven windows, assistant deputy ministers get six, directors have four, and the luckier of the less senior officers make do with a three-window bay (Wotton, 1976, p. 35).

The use of the work place to symbolize status seems to evoke ambivalent reactions. On one hand, anecdotes suggest that office workers desire distinctions based on their own rank, and are upset when someone of equal or lower rank has something they lack. On the other hand, workers may not admit any more than a slight interest in status symbols, as if recognizing that they contradict the values of democracy. In one study, office workers were reluctant to admit that features of their workspaces symbolized their ranks; instead they explained the differences in terms of utility and necessity for their jobs (Lipman, Cooper, Harris & Tranter, 1978). In effect, people may publicly down-play the importance of status symbols while privately harboring strong feelings about them. This could account for the observation that status symbols sometimes evoke emotional reactions far out of proportion with their apparent significance (Steele, 1973b).

The term *status markers* denotes characteristics of workspaces that signify the occupants' status (see Konar & Sundstrom, 1985). There is little empirical research on this subject, but many anecdotes. This section first outlines the functions served by status markers in organizations, then discusses the theory of status congruency, which suggests that people want status markers for social-psychological reasons. The section continues by identifying some traditional status markers and reviewing empirical research on the use and recognition of status markers and their connection with workers' satisfaction.

Functions of status markers

The principal function served by status markers seems to be communication. However, some writers suggest that distinctions among workspaces based on rank can also serve as incentives for performance, as compensation, or as props for use in carrying out the duties associated with specific jobs.

Communication. Workspaces that differentiate people on the basis of rank serve to communicate efficiently the hierarchy of influence in the organization:

> [I]mmediately upon entering a work organization a stranger can readily
> place most of its members in their status position. He has countless cues
> by which he can judge their status. (Dubin, 1958, p. 38)

This is especially important for visitors from other organizations, who may need reassurance that they are dealing with the appropriate person.

> [N]on-verbal clues help the workers in a corporate structure know clearly
> who wields the power and who does not. Such signposts keep things run-
> ning smoothly. (Holtzman, 1978, p. 76)

On the other hand, without signs of status, employees in an organization

> would either be a confused rabble or would spend most of their time
> trying to figure out how to relate to others in the system. (K. Davis, 1977,
> p. 32)

As with any signs, status markers can be misused or misinterpreted. This could happen particularly in the case of someone who was "kicked upstairs" to do a job with the trappings of authority but no real power (Duffy, 1969). On the other hand, some people in powerful positions may shun visible signs of status in order to appear equal to lower-ranking employees. However, in organizations like CBS and the Civil Service, workspaces can be read as literally as military insignia.

The importance of status markers as signposts in an organization becomes particularly salient where offices attempt to operate without them. The best illustrations come from cases of *Burolandschaft*, or office landscape. Proponents claimed that physical distinctions among office workspaces placed undue emphasis on rank (see Chapter 2). Morale is better, they argued, in an egalitarian environment that contains no distinctions based on status (see Pile, 1978). Accordingly, German versions of *Burolandschaft* placed workspaces in huge, undivided areas. Such arrangements also occurred in the United States, including the offices of McDonald's Corporation in Chicago and the M & M/Mars office in Cleveland, Tennessee. At both locations, even the top executive in the office sits at the same type of desk as everyone else, right out in the open.

Employees may react to egalitarian offices by improvising their own unique status markers. In one office, where the furniture provided no means of distinguishing people, the employees developed a code:

The man with the red ashtray is a senior analyst. The man with the green ashtray is one of our programmers. The ones with two plants next to their desks are supervisors. (Zenardelli, 1967, p. 32)

In brief, status markers apparently represent an important vehicle for communicating the status hierarchy in an organization. Where traditional markers are unavailable, people may improvise their own.

Incentives. According to some writers, status markers serve as incentives to those who strive for advancement (e.g., Holtzman, 1978). If so, status markers may be valued more for what they indicate than for what they are. For instance, the CBS employee who "moved up" to a large desk with a wooden top had the equivalent of a printed sign proclaiming the higher rank.

For workspaces to serve as incentives for advancement, they probably need to be closely tied to rank and probably operate most strongly where people have little other information about their standing in the organization. Where status symbols are scarce, even the smallest difference may be given significance:

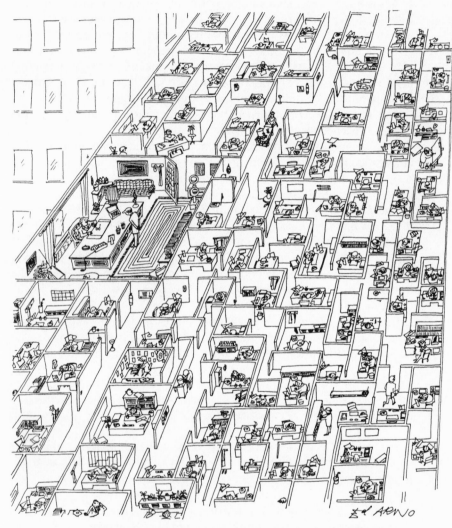

"I'm afraid a raise is out of the question, Benton, but in view of your sixteen years of service we are advancing you two spaces."

Figure 11.2. Drawing by Ed Arno. *Source: The New Yorker* (1977, April 18), p. 33. © 1977 The New Yorker Magazine, Inc.

I'm one of a large group of young lawyers who came into the firm at the same time. A few weeks ago I was told by the director to move to another office. It was purely because I need to be near another man for a long-term project we are developing, but nobody believed that. We get practically no information on how we're dong in the firm, so all the other guys at my level were trying to figure out what the move meant for them, and whether they should start looking for another job because I now have the "inside track." (Steele, 1973b, p. 53)

Workspaces seem to serve as incentives when people in the organization treat them as a medium of communication about an issue of central importance. At CBS, the messages were orderly, consistent, and deliberate. In the law office, an unintended message was received by information-hungry lawyers. In both organizations, status and promotion were apparently very important; advancement probably represented a critical benchmark of success. So in both organizations status markers only seemed to serve as incentives; instead, the incentives were the highly valued promotions that the status markers signified. The status markers were primarily symbols.

Props for job duties. A fourth purpose served by relatively lavish workspaces for high-ranking members of an organization is to give them props necessary for their jobs. For instance, a deputy secretary in the British Civil Service must deal with superiors from the Ministry, visitors, delegations, subordinates, and others. So, compared with lower-ranked employees,

the Deputy Secretary needs more support from the setting. He needs the pedestal table in front of the window to browbeat a clerk, the side table to serve sherry to visitors, the interview chair to hint around a delicate matter for the benefit of an inquisitive journalist, the curtains to make the room feel warmer, the tiles in the glass-fronted bookcase to remind his critics of certain claims to culture. Each routine, each role facet, requires an adjustment of the setting. (Duffy, 1969, p. 11)

However, low-ranking employees may have difficulty in obtaining the necessary props for their own jobs. For example, an insurance underwriter related an incident in which her manager had refused her request for an enlarged work surface "even though there [were] a lot of spare desks around." She had previously occupied a large desk – one that suited her needs beautifully. She now worked at a smaller, standard desk, she explained, "because they all have to be the same; though I pleaded to be allowed to keep it I was told most definitely no" (Lipman, Cooper, Harris & Tranter, 1978, p. 34). In such cases, where status seems to take precedence over efficiency, one explanation is based on the theory of status congruency.

Status congruency

The theory of "status congruency," put forth by sociologist Stuart Adams (1953), suggests that people strive for consistency in their status relationships. In any social system the members can be ranked on several different hierarchies, such as formal authority, education, and salary. The theory holds that people strive for agreement among the various rankings. Ideally, the highest-ranking individual on one dimension is also ranked highest on other dimensions, and each member shows agreement among ranks. Disagreement among the different rankings creates status incongruency, which is associated with "discontent" among individuals and division within the social system. According to Adams, incongruency can motivate people to try to redress the inconsistency or compensate for it.

The theory implies that office workers are most satisfied when workspaces are congruent with formal rankings in the hierarchy of power. People experience congruency if their workspaces are more desirable or better appointed than the workspaces of lower-ranking people but not as nice as those of higher-ranking people. However, if workers lack something that someone of lower or equal rank has, the theory predicts dissatisfaction and attempts to correct the situation. (This could account for the manager's refusal to allow a lower-ranking insurance underwriter to have a larger desk than his own.)

When a workspace seems to violate the status hierarchy, people sometimes react quite strongly. For example, a consultant tells of an incident in which a lower-level manager in a corporation moved into a small office that had carpeting. People at his rank were not entitled to carpet, so his boss had it taken up and discarded (Steele, 1973b). In another incident, an architect reported showing plans for an office to an official of the company:

The office assigned to the man in question showed 296 sq. ft. whereas his equal-ranking neighbor has an office marked 300 sq. ft. In all seriousness he called me up and asked me why he had been discriminated against in the matter of the size of his office. (Douglass, 1947, p. 122)

In another case, AT&T was planning its corporate headquarters facility at Basking Ridge, New Jersey, including open offices for executives. When they found out about the plans, the executives refused to cooperate.

They came from companies where many of them had been supervising five hundred to seven hundred people with a nice private office. When a man has worked fifteen to twenty years for a company he doesn't want to give up any of the prestige items. (Shoshkes, 1976, p. 24)

The company acceded to their demands for private offices.

In summary, the theory of status congruency and related examples suggest that any worker experiences satisfaction when status markers agree with rank. On the other hand, a workspace that seems inappropriate for the rank in the hierarchy may create dissatisfaction and discontent.

Traditional status markers

The tradition of using the work place to signify status is quite consistent with the importance of status markers for both individuals and organizations. In fact, several features of workspaces in offices have apparently become more or less traditional signs of status. These include location, accessibility, floorspace, furnishings, and personalization (see Konar & Sundstrom, 1985; Konar, Sundstrom, Brady, Mandel & Rice, 1982; Steele, 1973a,b).

Location. A workspace near a window is often a sign of status. In one of AT&T's offices in Basking Ridge, New Jersey, those next to a window hold the rank of district manager or higher. The choice corner locations are reserved for division managers and vice presidents. Similarly,

In a typical organization, the head of the hierarchy assigned to a floor gets the corner office with the nicest view, and the offices of his subordinates branch out from his corner in descending order of rank. Physical closeness to the center of power is considered evidence of status. (Packard, 1959, p. 102)

A sign of status in some tall office buildings is the distance between a workspace and the bottom floor – the higher the rank, the higher the floor (Steele, 1973). Some buildings have a special wing of offices designated for high-ranking executives, which may have a name like "mahogany row."

Accessibility. One of the most widely recognized (and emotionally loaded) perquisites of rank is the private office, which apparently symbolizes inaccessibility (see also Chapter 13). Physical enclosure seems to correspond closely with rank, even in open-plan offices. At Provincial

Table 11.2. *Standard floorspace alloca-*
tions by the U.S. General Services
Administration by G.S. rating

G.S. rating	Floorspace (sq ft)
GS–18A or above	500
GS–18B	400
GS–16 to GS–18	300
GS–14 & 15 (1)	250
GS–14 & 15	150
GS–12 & 13 (1)	150
GS–7 to 11 (1)	75–100
GS–7 to 11	75
GS–1 to 6	60

Property & Casualty Insurance Company, for instance, an employee with the job of manager is enclosed on two sides by 72-inch panels. An associate director has three panels; a director has four. Only the vice-presidents have walled offices with doors ("The Higher the Rank," 1977).

Where private offices are more common, a door is a standard sign of status. At the Sears Tower in Chicago, for instance, doors "hinge on rank: no one below the title of manager has the means to close his or her office" (Geran, 1976, p. 115). Besides having a door, high-ranking executives may further limit their accessibility by having an anteroom occupied by a private secretary who schedules appointments and screens visitors.

Research on offices has generally corroborated the link between status and enclosure. Langdon's survey of British office employees (1966) found that about 60% of senior management and professional personnel had their own offices. Research in the United States yielded similar finding (Sundstrom, Burt & Kamp, 1980; Sundstrom et al., 1982a).

Floorspace. Like the private office, floorspace is a well-accepted symbol of status. Many organizations have explicit standards for the floorspace allocated to people at each rank. For U.S. federal employees, the General Services Administration (GSA) provides the guidelines presented in Table 11.2.

Private-sector organizations have similar guidelines (Harris, 1977). At the CBS building in New York City a secretary has 60 sq ft of open space and another 15 sq ft for files and equipment. A manager receives

100 sq ft, easily calculated by looking at the ceiling and counting the lighting modules, each 5 ft by 5 ft. A director has six ceiling modules (150 sq ft), and a vice-president can obtain an office with 9 to 11 modules (225 to 275 sq ft). These allocations closely approximate recommendations of some office planners (see, e.g., Fetridge & Minor, 1975).

With the spread of open offices, workspaces have perhaps become smaller, while the cost of office space has risen. One government planner said, "We're beyond the point where we can use space to express somebody's rank. We can't afford it anymore" (Sawyer, 1979, p. C1). As distinctions based on floorspace disappear, other status symbols gain importance.

What then will separate the boss from the flock? A chrome strip, a higher quality wood veneer maybe, a chair with a higher back and a swivel mechanism that the others don't have. (Sawyer, 1979, p.C1)

Furnishings. Practically any element of the furnishings of a workspace can operate as a status marker. Rank may be reflected by carpeting, draperies, artworks, extra work-surfaces, a coat rack, or even a sofa and coffee table. However, perhaps the most common source of distinction appears in the two pieces of furniture most essential to office work: the desk and chair.

You realize, of course, that your status in the corporate hierarchy is silently affirmed by the size, shape, contour, tilt, and swivel of your office chair. It's as if managers and, say, secretaries were entirely different species. (Fitzgibbons, 1977, p. 65)

Furniture manufacturers even market their office chairs with names like "secretary," "manager," and "executive."

A desk gives user distinction through its materials. A utilitarian metal desk of the type often seen in government offices has perhaps the lowest status. Next may be "wood-grain" formica, and then wood veneer. And veneers are graded, with walnut or mahogany ranked above the sturdier oak (Duffy, 1969).

The size of the desk is also significant. Standard sizes given by one source are shown in Table 11.3. In an open-plan office, the differences among desks and chairs may be fewer than in a conventional office, but still noticeable ("More Controversy over Office Landscaping," 1968).

Personalization. Usually it is at least implicit that high-ranking personnel have more say about the appearance and arrangement of their workspaces than do people in the lower echelons. In some organizations the ability to personalize a workspace is an explicit sign of rank preserved

Table 11.3. *Standard desk sizes for employees of different ranks*

Rank	Standard desk size (inches)	Sq ft of desk area
Top executive	76 × 36	18.0
Executive	66 × 36	16.5
Junior executive	60 × 34	14.2
Clerical	52 × 34	12.3
Junior clerical	42 × 30	8.8

Source: Wylie (1958).

through regulations. For instance, at one of the AT&T offices in Basking Ridge, New Jersey, each promotion in rank brings more space for personal items. At the level of district manager three alternative furniture arrangements are possible. Division managers have more furniture and more choices about its arrangement. Only vice presidents can order their own furniture.

In summary, anecdotes suggest that many features of workspaces in offices serve as traditional status markers. The high-status employee may have a privileged location, a private office, a large area of floorspace, distinctive furniture, or the ability to personalize his or her workspace.

The use of status markers

How widely are the traditional status markers used in offices? Only two studies provide data relevant to this question: Louis Harris & Associates (1978) and BOSTI (1981). Both suggest that the traditional status markers are recognized in many offices.

Harris and Associates investigated existing practices regarding status markers, and found that several traditional status markers differentiated high-ranking people. The survey included the item: "which 2 or 3 characteristics do you feel usually make the working areas of senior executives seem different from other areas of an office?" (1978, p. 59). Only six items were mentioned by more than 20% of participants, as shown in Table 11.4. The most prevalent signs of rank seem to be the style and material of desks, tables, and chairs, but floorspace and accessibility were also relatively common sources of distinction. Results were essentially the same for conventional and open offices.

The main finding of the Steelcase study was that no single aspect of

Table 11.4. *Features of offices that differentiate executives from other workers*

Aspect of workspace that differentiates executives	Percentage of sample
Style of desks, tables, and chairs	34
Amount of privacy	33
Overall amount of personal space	29
Paintings, posters, or other wall decorations	27
Materials used for desks, tables, and chairs	26
Type of floor covering	21
Neat and well-organized appearance	15
Color of walls and partitions	12
The way it reflects the personality of the person working there	12
How up to date it is	9
Use of plants	9

Source: Louis Harris & Associates (1978), p. 59.

workspaces even came close to representing a universal status marker.
Instead, many aspects of workspaces were reported as status markers.
Apparently different status markers prevailed in different offices. This
is not surprising in light of the many possibilities available for differ-
entiating people of high status.

BOSTI (1981) examined office workers' preferences regarding status
markers. Instead of asking what actually differentiated status in their
office, the BOSTI survey asked people to indicate what they would like
to distinguish their own status. The survey asked, "If you got a promotion, would you want to change your workspace in any way to express
your new status or support your new role?" (BOSTI, 1981, Appendix
D, item L-14). Of the office workers who responded, 56% said "yes."
These people were asked to name three specific changes they would like
in their workspaces (from a list quite different from the one used in the
Steelcase study). As shown in Table 11.5 there were some definite fa-
vorites among preferred status markers.

Table 11.5. *Status markers desired by office workers*

Feature of workspace desired if promoted	Percentage of sample
More office space	65
Privileged location (such as a corner office, near a window, near the boss)	50
More office furnishings (e.g., a sofa, extra table)	30
High-quality furnishings and finishes	28
Controlled access (someone to screen calls/visitors)	24
Communications devices (e.g., micro-computer, dictating machine, telex)	14
More opportunity for displaying personal materials	12

Source: BOSTI (1981).

The most preferred status markers were floorspace and privileged locations, which clearly represent the scarcest and most valuable resources in an office. The workers in the BOSTI project expressed the implicit belief that status markers need to be uncommon to be effective – the rarer, the better.

Results of both studies suggest that what we called "traditional" status markers are widely recognized as such (See Figure 11.3). Workers may not always get what they want, but they seem to share a common understanding of the things that signify status.

Status markers and satisfaction

The theory of status congruency suggests that office workers experience greatest satisfaction in workspaces they regard as appropriate to their status. Two empirical studies dealt with the relationship between status markers and satisfaction.

One study found a correlation between "status support" in the workspace and employees' satisfaction with the environment. A total of 529 office workers were asked whether they agreed or disagreed with the statement, "my work space accurately reflects my status in this organization." Agreement was defined as indicating "status support" and it was significantly associated with satisfaction with the work environment. The association was stronger among those who probably needed status

"Do you know who you're talking to, Buster? You're talking to the guy with the biggest desk, biggest chair, longest drapes, and highest ceiling in the business!"

Figure 11.3. Drawing by Dana Fradon. *Source*: *The New Yorker* (1981, Sept. 21), p. 50. © 1981 The New Yorker Magazine, Inc.

symbols the most – those with supervisory responsibilities (Konar, Sundstrom, Brady, Mandel & Rice, 1982).

Many traditional status markers were associated with status support by the workspace. The survey used by Konar et al. (1982) included questions on features of participants' workspaces such as the size of the desk, the number of work surfaces, the number of people in the room, whether the room had a door, and so on. The researchers assessed the correlation between the presence of each item and the individual's perceptions of "status support." Items associated with greatest status support included desk size; quality of furniture; number of chairs; capacity to personalize; sufficient floorspace that a neighbor is not "too close"; amount of storage space; ability to work across a surface with a visitor; having a private office and the ability to screen calls and visitors; and having a door. The association of most of these items with status support was stronger among those who had supervisory responsibilities than among those who did not. The items associated with status support included many of the ones identified as traditional status markers.

BOSTI (1981) included an analysis of people whose workspaces had changed and reported a strong connection between status support and satisfaction with the environment. For those whose status support decreased, satisfaction with the environment showed a slight decline.

In summary, the available evidence supports the hypothesis that people whose workspaces appropriately reflect their status are relatively satisfied with their work environments. However, the evidence comes from only a few studies.

Summary

This chapter discusses the symbolic capacities of the workspace, focusing upon the expression of self-identity and status. Self-identity refers to an individual's perception of his or her own lasting characteristics and habits, especially those that differentiate that individual from others. Status refers to the individual's rank in the organization's hierarchy of authority.

Expression of self-identity through the physical environment presupposes that individuals have assigned work-stations, or workspaces. One means of self-expression is personalization, or the adornment, decoration, modification, or rearrangement of a workspace by the occupant. A study of office employees found that most said they personalized their workspaces; satisfaction with the workspace was correlated with the amount of space available for display of work-related and personal items. Other research points to the potential importance of personalization for job satisfaction. Its implications for interpersonal relations are largely unexplored, but personalization may contribute to an individual's definition of the workspace as a territory, or zone of control. According to a theory by Altman, territoriality can help an individual to regulate his or her interactions with co-workers. However, an experimental, non-territorial office – having no personally assigned workspaces – showed a high level of satisfaction with an environment that did not allow individual territories. Other research suggests that territoriality may be a personality trait that some people exhibit more strongly than others.

Expression of self-identity through the workspace can occur through participation by the individual in the design of his or her workspace.

An example occurred at the FAA office in Seattle, where employees each chose many of their own office furnishings. They later expressed greater satisfaction with their environment than did other employees of the same organization who participated much less in the design of their workspaces. However, research on two large samples of office employees found that only about 20% of them said they were involved in the design of their workspaces, although participation was more prevalent among higher-ranking employees. Other evidence suggests a link between participation and satisfaction with the environment and the job.

The use of the physical environment to express status serves several functions in an organization; physical status markers provide a means of communication, compensation, and props for performance of job duties. Adams's theory of status congruency implies that people are most satisfied in arrangements in which their workspaces are congruent with their formal ranks.

Anecdotes suggest that a variety of features of workspaces serve as traditional status markers, including privileged location, physical enclosure, floorspace, furnishings, and personalization. Research on office employees suggests that traditional status markers are widely recognized as such, and many different features of workspaces serve as status markers.

Research on the connection between status markers and satisfaction suggests that people who believe their workspaces accurately reflect their status are relatively satisfied with their work environments.

Practical considerations

The first decision concerning the symbolic character of the workspace is whether to assign work-stations to individuals. Only then can the environment convey information about individuals. We uncovered no evidence that greater satisfaction or better performance is found in assigned workspaces than shared work-stations. However, workers may feel responsible for their assigned workspaces and may maintain them better than nonassigned ones. Furthermore, assigned workspaces potentially permit personalization and demarcation of status, which in turn may contribute to satisfaction.

There are at least two circumstances in which a manager might reject the use of assigned workspaces. First, the physical limitations of a factory may require that each work-station have more than one operator. Second, a manager may want to de-emphasize individuals in favor of groups or teams. If so, work areas may be identified with groups, and work-stations shared within each group.

Where workspaces are assigned to individuals, a key decision concerns the amount of control and influence exercised by the workers over the physical environment. This control can take at least two forms: participation in the design of workspaces, and personalization of existing workspaces. Both involve workers in decisions that may be regarded as the province of professional designers, planners, or managers. (The result may be an opportunity for either conflict or cooperation, depending upon how the designer, planner, or manager approaches the matter.)

Personalization of workspaces represents a relatively limited form of self-expression, which may be desirable for several reasons. First, it allows workers to express their individuality and perhaps to avoid feeling like cogs in a machine. Limited evidence suggests that physical provisions for personalization contribute to a worker's satisfaction with the physical environment. On the other hand, there is reason to suspect that attempts to prohibit personalization may create dissatisfaction and resistance; individuals may try to leave an imprint whether or not the organization or environment encourages it.

Personalization need not conflict with a designer's plan for an office or factory. Instead, the plan can incorporate means of displaying personal objects, such as bulletin boards, hooks, tackboards, or shelves. Such physical accommodation of personalization can easily be designed into workspaces, and can probably be made compatible with the desired appearance of the work area. (Many commercially available work-stations have built-in bulletin boards and display areas.)

Personalization may be more important to some workers than others. For those who want to treat their workspaces as territories, personalization might represent a form of influence over the environment necessary to perceive it as a personal zone of control. For people with strong territorial inclinations, the ability to maintain a zone of control could make a substantial difference to their satisfaction. However, territories probably serve to regulate and organize interaction to some extent for all workers in an office or factory. (Some experts have advocated arrangements with defined territories for individuals and groups; see Davis & Altman, 1976.)

Participation by workers in the design of their workspaces is apparently far from common. One reason for its rarity concerns the time and effort required for involvement of workers in decisions about their workspaces. Another obstacle is "professionalization," or the practice of leaving decisions to professionals (see Becker, 1981).

On the other hand, research evidence suggests that participation by workers in the design of workspaces can lead to greater satisfaction with their workspaces. Participation itself may create satisfaction, and may lead to workspaces better suited to the workers. It at least creates the potential for a work environment tailored to the needs and habits of its occupants. (In participative design, the designer's task is to develop a range of alternatives that allows each worker to select a configuration that satisfies his or her habits of work and desires for self-expression.)

As for the display of status, the practitioner is unlikely to encounter indifference. Workspaces allow the expression of status in many ways, some of which are traditional and widely recognized. Individuals seem to want workspaces that accurately reflect their status, and they react strongly to any apparent discrepancy between rank in the hierarchy and distinctions among workspaces.

A facilities planner may be asking for trouble by trying to change the existing status markers in an organization. Status markers represent part of the local language of symbols. At best, a new set of status symbols would create confusion for awhile. At worst, it could foster conflict and dissension.

The display of status represents one area in which participative design may occur with or without the blessing of the facilities planner. Power in an organization includes the ability to influence decisions about its offices and factories. The more power an individual has, the more he or she can participate in such decisions. This point is probably not lost on planners who make an effort to find out just how (or whether) the members of an organization would prefer to have their status expressed in their workspaces.

12
COMMUNICATION

This chapter explores the role of the physical environment in communication, focusing particularly on exchanges between two people. The key issue here is the influence of the work place in face-to-face meetings. (Chapter 14 considers the role of the work place in small groups.)

The chapter begins by exploring historical trends in the planning of work places for communication, then advances some hypotheses on the relevance of the work place to choices in communication. The next two sections consider inter-workspace proximity and the properties of gathering places. Then the analysis shifts to a smaller scale, exploring the relationship between the arrangement of rooms and the quality of encounters.

In brief, the limited evidence associates physical proximity of workspaces with the frequency of informal, face-to-face conversation, but not with the frequency of job-related exchanges. Central places that permit convenient conversation away from workspaces (gathering places) have seldom been studied. Research on the arrangement of rooms suggests that people seated within comfortable conversation distance in positions that allow eye-contact are relatively likely to converse. Office workers apparently increase their chances of dominating an encounter by holding it in their own offices. Office workers can influence the psychological distance of an interaction through the positions of their chairs and desks.

Planning work places for communication

Offices were being specifically planned for efficient communication soon after 1900, when organizations grew and allocated larger and larger

252

proportions of their personnel to offices (see Chapter 2). Early planners acted on the pragmatic assumption that people whose jobs call for communication with each other should be located as close together as possible:

In order that the managers and others . . . should be properly housed, each with his logical neighbor, and with efficient ease of communication and association, the architects spent several months in consultation, asking advice, and studying the needs of every department and of every individual. (Dempsey, 1914, p. 472)

Such practice was unusual in 1914, but soon became standard. One writer described a case in which a company's new building was under construction when officials discovered that two groups of executives would be separated by 240 feet, even though their activities called for "constant personal contacts." An engineer suggested moving one group to the floor immediately above the other and installing a staircase, which transformed the 240–foot walk into a 15–foot climb:

[T]he result of the change was to facilitate extremely important contacts of constant occurrence . . . and thus to save a substantial expenditure of time, money, and energy. (Hopf, 1931, p. 753)

The implicit premise was that people who need to see each other do so, and the best arrangement minimizes the time they spend doing it.

The 1950s and 1960s brought a change of perspective: architecture came to be seen as a determinant of social interaction instead of a context for it. Social psychologists had found physical proximity associated with conversation and friendship, and had concluded that architecture could mold patterns of social interaction (e.g., Festinger, Schachter & Back, 1950; see also Gutman, 1966; Rosow, 1961). The concept of architectural determinism of social relations rapidly gained a following among architects, despite criticisms of the concept and weaknesses in its empirical support (Broady, 1966; Lipman, 1969).

Some office planners not only accepted architectural determinism, but tried to put it into practice. For instance, the Quickborner firm, promoter of *Burolandschaft* (see Chapter 2), argued that the arrangement of a building has a "decisive influence" on social interaction among employees:

To ease and facilitate communications, all departments and work groups with frequent contact should be located on as few floors as possible, *without being separated by fixed walls.* [italics added] (Lorenzen & Jaeger, 1968, p. 171)

The assumed link between physical accessibility and ease of communication was interpreted to mean not only minimal walking distance, but an absence of intervening barriers (see also Grobman, 1970, p. 14; Lieberman, 1969, p. 12; Shuttleworth, 1972, p. 12). The realization of these ideas was the open-plan office (see Pile, 1978).

Enthusiasm for architectural determinism apparently waned in the 1970s. Even its advocates saw that buildings cannot determine social interaction, but at most can provide convenient opportunities for it (see Lang, Burnette, Moleski, Vachon, 1974)

Whether office planners have regarded the environment as context or determinant of job-related conversation, they have tried to make it convenient. Standard practice in office planning calls for the systematic location or workers as near as possible to counterparts. Usually a matrix is constructed to indicate the frequency of necessary contact for all possible pairs of co-workers. The matrix is used to plan an arrangement that minimizes walking distances of the most frequent or important communication (see Shoshkes, 1976). The premise behind most office layouts is that face-to-face conversation is preferable to other means of communication and that convenience is important for its occurrence:

Very small amounts of effort, such as climbing a single flight of stairs, may become the threshold over which a person will not go visit rather than telephone a colleague. (Chapman, 1967, p. 156)

In summary, early planners arranged offices to minimize walking distances between the workspaces of people who needed frequent contact. Later, applications of architectural determinism led planners to maximize visual accessibility through open offices. Office planners have continued to design offices for the convenience of face-to-face conversation between counterparts.

Choices in communication

This section reviews some elements of communication relevant to an analysis of the role of the work place in choices in communication. It advances some propositions about the influences of the physical environment that serve as a backdrop for later discussion.

Elements of communication

Theorists envision communication as involving several key components (e.g., McGuire, 1969). These include a sender (the person who has something to communicate) and a recipient. The sender transmits a message, using a particular medium, such as a face-to-face conversation, telephone call, or written letter (see also Shannon & Weaver, 1949).

(If the medium is face-to-face conversation, important elements of the situation include the location of the encounter and the psychological distance between parties, which are discussed later in this chapter.)

For a person about to initiate a communication, his or her choices concern the message, the medium, and the recipient. The physical environment can enter into all these choices.

Medium. Means of communication can include a face-to-face conversation, a telephone call or video-conference, a letter or note, and others. Media differ in the kinds of information transmitted, the speed of response, and the presence of a record of the exchange. Face-to-face meetings permit instant response and carry the widest range of information, including vocal cues (intonation of voice, pauses, errors), visual cues (appearance, facial expression, gaze, posture, gestures), and peripheral cues (tactile information – as from a handshake – odors, clothing). Video-conferences carry less information (see Galitz, 1980) but still contain some visual cues and most vocal cues; the advantage is that the participants can be in different buildings, or even in different cities. Telephone calls are more convenient, as telephones are ubiquitous in most offices, but provide only vocal cues. Written media often provide restricted information and a slow response, but dependably leave a permanent record.

The role of the physical environment in the choice of a medium of communication probably hinges on the time and effort required for a face-to-face meeting. Time and effort depend at least partly on physical accessibility. Accessibility may not be important in the choice of a medium, if a face-to-face meeting is considered imperative (and time and effort secondary), or if partners are so accessible that a face-to-face meeting is the easiest choice. Other times an individual has to decide whether the purposes of communication warrant the time and effort required for a personal meeting. Other things being equal, a person is probably more likely to select a medium of communication other than a face-to-face conversation as a meeting becomes less convenient.

Research concerning the use of face-to-face meetings for communication suggests that people prefer them for certain purposes. A review of six recent studies concluded that the purposes include person-oriented discussion, dealing with strangers, short travel time/journey, prolonged discussion, negotiation, and persuasion (Galitz, 1980, p. 51) On the other hand, the review found a preference for "teleconferencing" for routine exchanges of information, dealings with acquaintances, impersonal exchanges, brief discussions, and conversations involving prolonged travel. (Telephone calls and a video-conference were equally desirable.) An English study of actual business conferences found that people used face-to-face meetings for negotiations, dealings with strangers, and sensitive discussions, while they used the telephone for brief exchanges of information and dealings with acquaintances (Goddard, 1973).

In summary, a face-to-face meeting is the medium of communication involving the greatest range of information. Research suggests that people prefer face-to-face meetings over other media for certain purposes, such as negotiation and personal discussions. However, telecommunications or written messages may be adequate or even preferable for some purposes, such as routine exchanges of information. The work place can enter the choice of a medium through the physical accessibility of the parties to communication.

Message. Probably the most important distinction among messages in organizations is whether they are formal or informal. *Formal* communication includes job-related messages between people, dictated by their roles in the organization. *Informal* communication includes all other messages, especially between people whose jobs do not call for contact. Informal communication includes friendly exchanges, which are usually oral, often face-to-face (Wofford et al., 1977).

The physical environment probably enters into an individual's decisions about communication of informal messages or discretionary formal ones. Physical accessibility and convenience may dictate whether or not a worker decides to seek out a co-worker for an informal chat. Similarly, convenience may be a decisive factor in whether a supervisor goes to visit a subordinate to discuss a low-priority issue. However, if a formal message has high priority, the work place probably has little bearing on whether it is sent (however, the environment may influence the choice of a medium). In brief, the work place may influence decisions on whether to communicate informal messages, or discretionary, formal ones.

Recipient. A worker can direct a formal communication to a recipient at a higher rank in the heirarchy of authority, the same rank, or a lower rank. Organizational psychologists refer to these as upward, horizontal, and downward communications. Downward, or directive, communication to subordinates includes instructions, rationales for tasks, company policies, company goals, evaluations of performance, and similar information (Katz and Kahn, 1966). It can take many forms, including face-to-face meetings, but may tend to be written (Wofford et al., 1977, p. 348). Upward communication, directed toward superiors, contains such information as suggestions for new procedures, problems with personnel, and issues concerning production. Upward communication has been found less common than downward communication (e.g., Likert, 1961), although modern organizations seem to emphasize upward communication more than before (e.g., Peters & Waterman, 1982). Horizontal communication parallels the flow of work, as in a note attached to an insurance claim that circulates from the sales agent to the claims agent.

The work place may be important to downward and upward communication when they concern sensitive topics that participants want to keep confidential. The physical environment can provide the privacy necessary for a confidential exchange, but may make such exchanges difficult and infrequent if privacy is inadequate (see Chapter 13 on privacy).

For horizontal communication, physical accessibility may be important when there is a choice regarding the recipient. Studies of communications among scientists and engineers suggest a preference for people who are easily accessible over more reliable sources of information who can only be reached with greater effort (Gerstberger & Allen, 1968).

People may rely on informal contacts for job-related purposes, using the grapevine that seems to develop in an organization (Wofford et al., 1977). Reliance on informal contacts may add to the importance of physical accessibility. Some research on the grapevine suggests a preference for informal contacts over formal ones for solving problems. In a sales organization in which a quality-control problem had developed, 14 people ultimately learned of it. However, only three messages followed the chain of command, and only six were within the group in question. Others went via the grapevine (K. Davis, 1953).

In summary, communication in organizations can flow vertically (toward recipients of higher or lower rank) or horizontally (toward recipients of the same rank). The work place may influence choices regarding vertical communication through the provision of privacy for confidential exchange. For horizontal communication, physical accessibility may influence the choice of a recipient or the choice of whether to use the informal network instead of the formal one.

Hypotheses on the role of the work place

When the physical environment has a role in choices regarding the recipient, medium, or message of a communication, it probably depends on convenience and expediency. To the extent that the work place makes a particular co-worker accessible, an individual may be more likely to select that co-worker as a partner in face-to-face conversation. In other words, choices in communication may follow a principle of least effort (Gerstberger & Allen, 1968).

If people tend to make the easiest choices, they probably do so in situations where expedient choices at least minimally satisfy their purposes. For a necessary, formal communication, such as a performance review, the satisfactory choices may be restricted to a face-to-face meeting with a specific person with a specific agenda. For other types of formal communication, a wide range of choices may give satisfactory results. A routine directive, for instance, could be communicated by a meeting, a telephone call, or a letter. For informal, friendly exchanges, the choice of a recipient is practically unlimited, except by the convenience of proximity.

In brief, the role of the work place in choices concerning communication based on the principle of least effort suggests two hypotheses:

1. For formal communication, in which an individual can exercise discretion as to the medium through which to communicate, the likelihood of face-to-face conversation increases with the accessibility and proximity of individual workspaces.
2. For informal communication, the preferred medium is face-to-face conversation. The chances of selecting a particular co-worker as a partner in conversation increase with the accessibility and proximity of his or her workspace.

Accessibility among workspaces

This section examines research evidence on the connection between inter-workspace proximity and formal and informal communication. It also explores the connection between physical enclosure of workspaces and communication.

Communication and proximity

Field studies have examined the relationship between proximity of work spaces and face-to-face conversation in both offices and factories. Consistent with the hypotheses outlined earlier, the findings differ for formal and informal communication.

Formal communication. Four field studies focused on job-related communication. Of these, two found proximity unrelated to formal contact. In two others, results were equivocal. One of the studies that reported no correlation of formal communication and proximity of workspaces involved 16 small office organizations. Each employed about 30 people.

A total of 361 employees at these organizations received a survey with a list of co-workers in the same building. They were asked to indicate the frequency of work-related, face-to-face contact with each person on the list. This provided a basis for indexes of the average frequency of communication, the average number of daily contacts, and the average number of weekly contacts. An index of accessibility of participants' workspaces was based on the proximity and visibility of the nearest four neighbors. Results showed that none of the composite indexes of communication was correlated with the average physical accessibility in more than a handful of the offices (Duffy, 1974b). (Unfortunately, Duffy did not assess the correlation between the proximity of each pair of employees and the amount of contact between that specific pair of people.)

In the second study to report no connection between proximity and formal contact, Farbstein (1975) surveyed 185 employees of three small London organizations. The employees kept "activity diaries" of face-to-face conversations (but not telephone calls). The researcher also measured the average distance between pairs of workspaces and calculated the average distance covered by each individual in trips between workspaces in the same building. Results showed no correlation of average distance between co-workers, workspaces, and the average amount of time spent in contact. However, the average distance an employee traveled was correlated with the average "distance to be moved." This finding implied that people walked as far as necessary for a formal conference within the same building.

Farbstein (1975) also reported "a clear pattern of allocating individuals who are very similar in rank and task to the same room but "little tolerance for mixing of different ranks or task levels" (p. 365). Apparently most people were located near co-workers of similar job and rank, the very people with whom they would probably be most likely to talk. (The study did not assess correlations between the distance separating each pair of people and the amount of contact in that specific pair, although the practice of locating workers near logical neighbors would probably have made the correlation quite high.)

A study of a corporate office indirectly suggested an association between inter-workspace proximity and the amount of contact between supervisor and supervisee. In an evaluation of the effects of a relocation, 96 professional employees of a divisional headquarters of an oil company moved from conventional offices to an open-plan office in a plush new office building. Before and after relocation, researchers counted the number of co-workers within a 50–foot walking distance of each employee's desk. The employees were divided for analysis into groups for whom the number of neighbors within 50 feet increased, decreased, or remained the same. The researchers also assessed the employees' perceptions of jobs before and after relocation. Results showed that those whose average proximity had increased also reported more feedback and less autonomy. This finding implies more contact with supervisors when average proximity increased. Those whose physical proximity with co-workers decreased reported less feedback and more autonomy, suggesting that they saw less of their supervisors (Szilagyi & Holland, 1980). Greater walking distance seems to have been associated with less frequent visits by supervisors to supervisees.

A fourth study by Conrath (1973) found a clear association between proximity and face-to-face contact, including both formal and informal conversation. Thirty employees in two departments at a single facility of Northern Electric Co., Ltd., in Canada recorded all contacts and messages they received for 5 days. Records included all face-to-face conversations (except greetings), all telephone calls, and all personally addressed written messages. The hypothesis was that physical proximity between two specific people would be associated with the amount of face-to-face contact between those two people. Telephone calls were expected to occur frequently between peers whose jobs called for contact (the "task structure"). Messages that followed the chain of command were expected to be primarily written.

Results generally confirmed the predictions. Written communication paralleled the chain of command; the "task structure" tended to involve telephone calls and face-to-face meetings more than written messages. Face-to-face contact between two people was very strongly correlated with the proximity of their desks (distance correlated -0.93 with occurrence of contact), as shown in Figure 12.1. Similarly, the number of contacts between any two people was strongly correlated with their inter-workspace proximity. Apparently, the farther two people were from each other, the less frequently they talked face to face. The frequency of telephone calls was also correlated with physical proximity, although not quite as strongly as face-to-face meetings were. (Occurrence of phone calls showed a correlation of -0.76 with the distance separating a pair of individuals. The number of calls correlated -0.59 with distance.)

The close association of face-to-face communication with physical proximity could reflect the company's policy of locating people close to each other when their jobs called for contact. It could also reflect the tendency of neighbors to initiate informal conversation. The association of telephone with physical proximity suggests that people were located near their counterparts, or that people maintained more frequent communication with their neighbors, or both. Apparently, communication between two specific people was more frequent if their workspaces were close together.

In summary, research evidence suggests that for people in the same

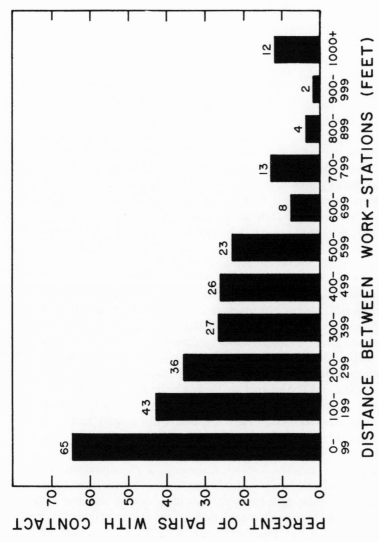

Figure 12.1. Percentage of pairs of office workers with contact as a function of distance between work-stations. *Source:* Adapted from Conrath, C. (1973). Communication patterns, organization structure, and man: Some relationships. *Human Factors, 15*(5), 459–470.

building, the average inter-workspace proximity has little to do with the amount of time spent in formal, face-to-face communication. On the other hand, physical proximity of workspaces of two specific people, especially supervisor and subordinate, may be associated with relatively frequent meetings, although evidence on this point is indirect.

Informal conversation. Evidence on the association of proximity with informal, face-to-face conversation is also limited, but it consistently suggests that people in factories and offices choose to converse with their closest neighbors and often make friends with them.

At factories, physical proximity may be critical for conversation, because many factory jobs require staying in one place most of the day. Conversation among people with limited mobility may also depend on the absence of loud noise, which can mask conversation (see Chapter 7), and on the distance or barriers separating the closest adjacent workstations.

Factory work may make informal conversation highly desirable to employees to "break the monotony" (Jasinski, 1956, p. 26). For example, an industrial engineer reported a case in which he had been called to help increase the efficiency of a commercial printing plant. He recommended drastic changes in the layout of the building to organize the routing of work, including rearrangement of work tables from a cluster in the center of the room to separate positions around its edges. As a result, "complaints mushroomed; production dropped" (Wagner, 1954, p. 3). The old layout had to be partly reinstated. The new arrangement had separated a group of women who were used to chatting while working. They could not move around while at work and bitterly resented what amounted to isolation imposed by the new floor plan.

Two studies by sociologists at factories found that employees talked informally with nearby neighbors when they could. At automobile Plant X, almost one-half of a sample of 179 employees said they talked with their neighbors at least once every five minutes, despite the loud background noise; only about 10% said they talked with neighbors fewer than three times per day (Walker & Guest, 1952). At another automobile factory, a group of workers moved from an outmoded facility into a newly automated one. In the old factory, work-stations were about 10 feet apart, and more than 60% of the workers reported social contact with neighbors at least once or twice an hour. In the new plant the work stations were about 20 feet apart and the work allowed little mobility. Social contact with neighbors became less frequent in the new factory; only 31% reported talking with a neighbor as often as once or twice an hour. Almost one-half the employees said they had made more friends at the old plant with its closer work-stations (Faunce, 1958).

Research in offices has also associated proximity with informal conversation. A case study focused on 10 young female employees who
worked as cash posters – clerks who recorded and processed payments
received from customers. They had formed cliques:

[The] most important determinant of clique formation was the position of
a poster's table during their first year on the job. [Those] who sat near
each other then had many chances to interact and tended to become
friends. (Homans, 1954, p. 729)

In another office, where 37 employees worked primarily in clerical
jobs, a sociologist observed and recorded who conversed with whom
for more than 4 months. Results showed that the closer two workers'
desks were, the more they conversed. This was especially true in a group
of 12 female clerical employees whose desks were arranged in three
rows of four, separated by file cabinets. With only one exception, all of
them talked more with immediate neighbors than with anyone else.
Friendships followed lines of conversation, although not all conversation
partners were friends. Correlations among proximity, informal conversation, and friendship were strongest among the younger employees
(Gullahorn, 1952). A study of university professors found that members
of different departments located on the same floor were better acquainted than the members of departments on different floors (Estabrook & Sommer, 1972).

Probably the largest published study on inter-workspace proximity
and informal interaction in the office occurred in an insurance company
were 297 clerks, supervisors, and managers occupied one floor of a
multistory building. Most worked in large open areas, but two groups
of about 30 people each worked in smaller, enclosed areas. Wells (1965b)
asked employees about their friendships. Results showed that friendships decreased steadily with distance between workspaces. The correlation is shown in Figure 12.2. Participants usually chose friends of
about their own age, consistent with the idea that personal compatibility
is critical to friendship (see Deaux & Wrightsman, 1984, on factors
related to friendship).

Similarly, in the study described earlier by Szilagyi and Holland (1980),
after moving into an open plan office some employees had more neighbors within fifty feet and some had fewer. Those with more neighbors
nearby reported greater "friendship opportunity."

In summary, case studies and field studies consistently found close
proximity among workspaces associated with informal conversation.
People tended to make friends with some of their nearby partners in

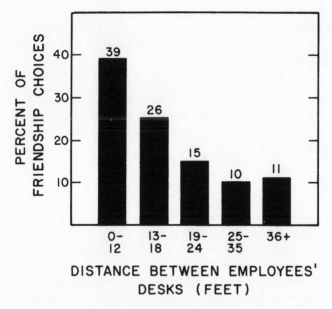

Figure 12.2. Percentage of office employees chosen as friends as a function of distance between the employees' desks. *Source*: Adapted from Wells, B.W.P. (1965b). The psycho-social influence of building environments: Sociometric findings in large and small office spaces. *Building Science, 1,* 153–165.

conversation, presumably those with whom they were personally compatible.

Physical enclosure of workspaces

A central premise of the *Burolandschaft*, and later the open-plan office, was that people who have unobstructed views of one another's workspaces can communicate more conveniently than those who cannot see each other. Environmental psychologist Albert Mehrabian illustrated this idea in what he called the "cabbage patch" (an undivided roomful of desks):

If someone comes across something on an invoice that looks a bit strange, he might look across the open pit at someone and ask, "Hey, Joni, we got a rep in Bangor, Maryland?" But if he has to stand up, leave his cubicle, and walk ten paces, or shout over two or three intervening modules, he may just shrug and pass it on . . . [I]n a cabbage patch you can see if someone you need to talk to is at his desk, on the phone, or has a visitor. (1976, p. 142)

An anecdote recounted in several articles on office planning provides another illustration, sometimes offered as evidence of more frequent communication with fewer barriers. As the story goes, interested parties had

set up a test situation in an oblong room with the door off-center in one of the long walls. The room was of ample proportions for two men. The two desk arrangements were identical and separated by a partition extending from the wall opposite the door. Into this situation were put two junior executives who were as equal as possible in their gregariousness and need for contact with other workers. In a short time . . . the one subject out of sight of the door began losing contacts . . . even the number of his phone calls dropped. The other subject experienced an increase in contact with others. When the subjects were reversed, so was their intercommunication. ("The Neglected Network," 1965, p. 20)

Details of this experiment are missing, but the obvious conclusion is drawn – that visual accessibility promotes communication, presumably both formal and informal.

Research evidence related to the hypothesis that conversation is associated with visual accessibility comes mainly from field studies. However, only a few studies separately examined formal and informal communication. These are reviewed first, followed by studies done in open offices.

Enclosure and informal contact. A field study associated physical barriers between workspaces and decreased likelihood of informal face-to-face contacts. In the study by Gullahorn (1952) cited earlier, in which clerical employees who occupied three rows of desks were separated by filing cabinets, interaction took place mostly within the rows. Only rarely did those separated by filing cabinets engage in conversation with each other. The clerks apparently chose partners in informal conversation at least partly on the basis of visual accessibility during work.

Enclosure and formal contact. Evidence on formal communication suggests that barriers between people in the same building do little to discourage face-to-face contact. In the study by Duffy (1974a–c) workspaces in small organizations were scored on the numbers and types of partitions around each. An index of enclosure was not correlated with average frequency of communication within the organization, with the frequency of visitors, or with the average percentage of the staff who were contacted daily or weekly by employees. (The study did not examine the possibility that the presence of barriers between specific pairs of people influenced formal communication between those people.)

The BOSTI (1981) project on office environments included an assessment of physical enclosure before and after participants changed offices, based on the number and height of partitions that surrounded the workspaces. Those whose physical enclosure decreased after the change reported no greater "ease of communication" with coworkers than those whose physical enclosure increased or remained the same. ("Ease of communication" referred primarily to work-related contact). However, physical enclosure of workspaces was associated with the ability to hold confidential conversations among managers, whose need for such conversation was greatest (see Chapter 13).

In summary, two field studies found physical enclosure of workspaces was unrelated to the amount of formal communication. However, it was associated with the ability to hold confidential conferences.

Communication in open offices. The largest number of studies relevant to the relationship between enclosure and communication consist of *post-occupancy evaluations* of open offices. The purpose of these studies was to assess the general adequacy of new offices, not to investigate communication. All involved relocations to offices with fewer walls. They involved general surveys of office workers' perceptions and attitudes and included only one or two items on communication. In some studies a survey given after employees had occupied new buildings asked them to compare the new offices with memories of former offices. (These are called *retrospective* studies.) Others involved surveys both before and after relocation and compared the two sets of ratings called before- and after-studies (see Chapter 3).

The usefulness of postoccupancy studies of open offices as evidence on enclosure and communication is limited. Most of the studies compared average ratings of communication in conventional versus open offices. Few included a direct assessment of the enclosure of individual workspaces, nor even the number of walls or partitions in the office. In consequence, the studies can only be used to support the conclusion that a relocation to a relatively open office is associated on average with higher or lower ratings of communication.

Table 12.1 summarizes the results related to communication from 10 postoccupancy evaluations of open offices. The findings were mixed. Of the studies that reported ratings of communication in general, two reported no change, and two reported an improvement. One other found the open office more "sociable." Another found more face-to-face conversation and more time communicating, but fewer phone calls and meetings in the open office. As for ratings of specific aspects of communication, contact among departments improved in one study, but

Table 12.1. *Ratings of communication after changing to open-plan offices*

Study	Change in ratings	Types of communication
Before-and-after studies		
Boyce (1974)	Mixed	Interdepartmental (increase)
		Supervisory (decrease)
Brookes (1972)[a]	Increase	Sociability
Clearwater (1979)	Decrease	Face-to-face talking
Hanson (1978)	Decrease	Confidential conversation
Oldham & Brass (1979)	Decrease	"Feedback"; "friendship opportunity"
Sundstrom et al. (1982)	Mixed	Communication (no change)
		Speech privacy (decrease)
Restrospective studies[b]		
Boje (1971)[c]	No change	Communication
Hundert & Greenfield (1969)	Mixed	Time communicating, face-to-face conversation (increase)
		Phone calls, meetings (decrease)
Ives & Ferdinands (1974)	Mixed	Communication (increase)
		Confidential conversation (decrease for managers)
Sloan (undated)[d]	No change	Communication

[a] Apparently the same data as reported in Brookes & Kaplan (1972) and Brookes (1972b).
[b] Workers rated or compared earlier offices from memory.
[c] Most saw no change in 7 of 9 locations; most saw improvement at one location.
[d] Ratings were higher for 9% of employees at one of two locations; interpreted as no change.

friendship and feedback declined in another. Privacy for confidential conversation declined in three studies.

One interpretation of the results of the studies of open offices in that visual accessibility added to the chances of discretionary, work-related conversations, or formal contacts that the initiator considered desirable but not necessary. This could account for the finding that interdepartment contacts increased in more open offices; it could also account for the perception that communication in general improved in some open offices. However, open offices consistently were associated with difficulties in holding confidential conversations.

In summary, research from open offices suggests that visual accessibility of workspaces is not consistently associated with communication. It was associated in some cases with informal conversation or discretionary formal contacts. However, a lack of enclosure often made confidential exchange difficult.

Communication in an open, nonterritorial office. Nonassigned work stations (see Chapter 11) brought an increase in communication in one office, perhaps through a combination of accessibility and mobility. In the Allen & Gerstberger (1973) study cited earlier, a group of product engineers had occupied conventional offices with one or two people in each. Their renovated office was almost entirely open, and the engineers could work wherever they chose; however, they were not permitted to leave behind any personal belongings. They kept diaries of all interpersonal contacts on one randomly chosen day each week for a few months before and after the change. With one or two people per office in the earlier arrangement, they had focused their communications on office-mates and neighbors, reporting an average of 8.0 communications per day with 3.6 different people. In the new arrangement, they reported an average of 11.8 communications per day with 6.3 different people, almost doubling the average number of people contacted. Contacts outside the department increased briefly, apparently out of curiosity about the new office, but soon fell to former levels. The greater communication within the office could reflect the absence of barriers, the new mobility allowed by nonassigned workspaces, or both. (There is no way to tell how much of the communication was formal and how much was informal.) The best explanation for this finding probably is that each employee's neighbors changed from time to time, and employees tended to talk to their more numerous neighbors, especially those with whom they were relatively unacquainted. This could account for the observed increase in communication. If so, much of it was probably informal.

In summary, research on physical accessibility and communication suggests that inter-workspace proximity, and a lack of barriers between workspaces, increase the chances of informal conversation among neighbors. However, proximity and accessibility of workspaces seem to have little relevance to formal communication, except perhaps to make discretionary exchanges more likely. On the other hand, a lack of physical enclosure may make confidential exchanges difficult.

Gathering places

People in offices and factories often converse in locations outside their workspaces, such as corridors, photocopying rooms, cafeterias, mailrooms, supply rooms, locker rooms, and areas around water fountains, bulletin-boards, coffee pots, computer terminals, or vending machines. We refer here to such spots as gathering places, or any habitual or frequent location for conferences, visits, impromptu meetings, or other conversation. Many buildings contain areas specifically intended as gathering places. However, in the absence of designated places for gathering, employees seem to improvise.

The ideal characteristics of a gathering place apparently include convenient accessibility to workspaces and a comfortable setting for conversation. Ecological psychologist Robert Bechtel (1976) proposed a similar concept, the *activity node*, a place where people's paths cross during their regular, daily activities. This suggests a third important feature of a gathering place: That it is integral to people's daily routines, such as collecting mail, getting coffee, making photocopies, and so on. Management consultant Fred Steele (1973a) gave his summary of the physical ingredients of a gathering place:

One is that it be central – that is, that people would naturally pass through it on their way to other places. A second is that there be places to sit or come to rest comfortably. Third, people need to be able to stop there, and converse or watch others, without blocking the flow of vehicular or foot traffic by their stopping. As I recently observed, a bulletin board in a busy narrow hallway is almost useless, since no one can stop there long enough to read it or chat with others about the notices without clogging up the whole hallway. (p. 444)

One of the few empirical studies on gathering places was done by the Building Performance Research Unit in Britain as part of an evaluation of a school building at St. Michael's Academy (Markus, 1970). The staff included 20 teachers whose opinions were surveyed and whose habits of space use were observed. All the teachers took coffee breaks at regular locations. Despite the existence of a central "staff room" the teachers frequented six different places, and many of them went for a whole year without seeing each other. Apparently the main staff room failed to function as a gathering place because teachers thought it was too small and too far from classrooms: "most teachers do not wish to walk far to where they spend their mid morning break. The break is short and they like to spend as little time as possible getting from classroom to coffee" (Markus 1970, p. 39). The longest walk was slightly more than 340 feet, but two-thirds of the teachers walked less than 200 feet to their preferred gathering place. They adapted smaller rooms to their purposes, including storerooms and supply rooms.

Another example of a gathering place occurred in a small company, as related by environmental psychologist Albert Mehrabian:

I recall a particular lounge, situated in executive wing of a small corporation. . . . It was almost never used for two reasons. First, employees had to go out of their way to get there and understandably felt reluctant to be seen relaxing or socializing by company officers. . . . Second, the area was furnished like a formal living room . . . All the employees, including the executives, socialized in the lunchroom, which . . . had vending machines, posters on the walls, many moveable small tables and chairs, and a view of the lawn. (Mehrabian, 1976, pp. 146–147)

The formal lounge intended for the executives ended up as an expensive waiting room. But the effect was beneficial, in that executives used the same gathering place as other employees.

Work environments often contain places like the lunchroom in which people "mix" from different sections of the organization that might not otherwise have any contact. Another example occurred among office employees in a hospital business office.

[They now] share a smoking room with other personnel. This resulted in a fortuitous accident, their old smoking room being (after remodeling) taken for a waiting room. . . . [T]echnicians and nurses aids relax with the business staff now and exchange hospital gossip. The office workers have commented on this, saying that they feel more a part of the hospital now since they get to know the story behind the patients with whom they deal. It makes their work more meaningful. (Lentz, 1950, p. 21)

The morale of these office workers improved noticeably after they began to gather in the room frequented by other employees.

Administrators sometimes even deliberately try to encourage or discourage informal contact by the location and design of common spaces. For instance, the faculty of the department of psychology at the University of Tennessee had offices in three buildings, and those in different buildings rarely saw each other. When the department prepared to move into one office building, administrators decided to use the building to encourage interaction. All of the faculty mailboxes were located in a single large room, along with a coffee pot, a refrigerator, comfortable chairs, a couch, and tables. No systematic observations were made, but contact seemed to increase among the professors. They often sat in the lounge to chat over coffee as they collected their mail. The lounge also became a gathering place for graduate students and secretaries, whose mailboxes were also located there, which apparently encouraged contacts among people from different parts of the organization.

In summary, the existence of convenient and comfortable places for conversation near individual workspaces may lead to the emergence of gathering places, especially in areas used for everyday activities such as eating lunch or receiving mail. The number, size, and relative locations of such spaces may determine how many people actually use them. At one extreme people may collect in small cliques in many isolated gathering places; at the other extreme a single space may serve as a collecting point for virtually the whole organization.

Arrangement of the room

This section examines the role of the physical environment within a single room in the quality of interpersonal encounters among the occupants. It explores features that can constrain physical or psychological distance, augment the ability to exert influence, or create discomfort or stress. Limited evidence suggests that people can adapt to a wide range of seating arrangements. However, a conversation across a desk is seen as psychologically more distant that one with nothing between conversants. Offices can be arranged to provide opportunities to exert influence, but the occupant may be dominant anyway, through a process analogous to a "home-field advantage." People in comfortable conditions may respond favorably to others; those in uncomfortable settings may prefer brief exchanges; noise can mask conversation and lead people to ignore certain social cues.

Interpersonal distance

Social psychologists suggest that the physical distance that separates two people usually serves as a sign of their psychological distance – physical closeness implies psychological closeness. Edward Hall (1966) noted that people in the United States seem to select different interpersonal distances for different types of encounters; Hall summarized his observations in a series of hypothetical "distance zones," outlined in Table 12.2, for conversations while standing. He suggested that people adopt close physical proximity only for intimate or emotional exchanges, but choose moderate distances for casual exchanges and larger distances for more formal occasions. Research evidence generally has supported the premise behind the distance zones – that physical and psychological closeness are associated when people can control their distance – but Hall may have slightly overestimated the distances selected for personal or formal exchanges (see the review by Altman & Vinsel, 1978).

An implication of the distance zones for offices and factories is that when an environment brings people into conversation distance, they may feel induced to talk with each other. Hall wrote that if a

receptionist is less than ten feet from another person, even a stranger, she will be sufficiently involved to be virtually compelled to converse. (1966, p. 123)

Table 12.2. *"Distance zones" for conversations in the United States*

Distance zone	Interpersonal distance (feet)	Type of encounter
Intimate	0–1½	Intimate exchanges in low voice; emotional encounters; usually with close friends or intimates
Personal	1½–4	Conversation at moderate voice, usually with friends, often concerning personal topics
Social	4–12	Conversations at "normal" voice (can be overheard at 20 feet) concerning "impersonal business" or formal matters
Public	12–25	Formal speech in raised voice, often to group of people or to important public figure

Source: Hall (1966).

Other researchers have found that an environment facilitates conversation among the occupants when the seating arrangements place them within comfortable conversation distance, but only when they face directly enough to allow eye contact (Sommer & Ross, 1958; see also Mehrabian and Diamond, 1971a,b). Rooms that provide opportunities for eye contact among people within conversation distance have been called *sociopetal spaces* (Osmond, 1957). Such arrangements are found in offices designed for interviews, in reception rooms, and in rooms intended for meetings. In factories where people do repetitive work, managers may encourage conversation by arranging work-stations within conversation distance facing toward each other enough to permit eye contact, but not so directly as to create unnecessary distraction.

Workers whose environments allow eye contact with nearby neighbors or passersby when they look up from their work may be distracted or involved in unwanted conversation. An example appears in Figure 12.3, in which the man at the desk faced his boss's office from a position within conversation distance of the door. The remedy may be a *sociofugal* arrangement (Osmond, 1957), which discourages unwanted conversation through seating that makes eye contact difficult for people who are within conversation distance, by facing them away from each other. One example is the waiting room of a personnel office, where chairs line the wall in a row, all faced the same direction. Another is the clerical pool with several workers in one room, their desks in rows,

"Bronson, would you mind sitting somewhere else? You're always the first thing I see when I open my door."

Figure 12.3. Drawing by Ed Arno. *Source*: *The New Yorker* (1980, May 12), p. 54. © 1980 The New Yorker Magazine, Inc.

facing the same way, so that each worker faces either somebody's back or a wall.

An environment can bring people too close for comfort, especially when a room is too small to conveniently accommodate the occupants. Such situations may involve violations of the individual's *personal space*, analogous to an invisible bubble surrounding the body that defines the limits of comfortable proximity with others (see Altman, 1975; Sommer, 1969; Sundstrom & Altman, 1976).

People typically cope with excessive proximity by avoiding signs of involvement under their control, such as eye contact (see Argyle & Dean, 1965; Patterson, 1973). Such reactions, called "compensatory responses" can be observed on a crowded elevator, where people who are forced to stand nearly touching avoid indications of involvement. For instance, people try not to face anyone else directly. Eyes that happen to meet are instantly averted; passers-by try to take up as little space as possible (see Hall, 1966).

Behaviors that permit people to adapt to close interpersonal proximity also allow them to adapt to a variety of arrangements for conversation. If available seating places people too close for their comfort, and the chairs are not easily moved, conversants can give themselves added psychological distance by facing only indirectly toward each other, or by making minimal eye contact. Research on preferences concerning arrangements for conversation suggests that people often choose to sit at a 90° orientation (as at adjacent sides of a square table), which permits the option of making eye contact or of avoiding it (Sommer, 1959, 1962; see review by Sundstrom, 1984).

When people try to hold conversations at uncomfortably large distances, adaptation may be difficult. Participants in one laboratory experiment conversed face-to-face in chairs that left them either 5 or 11 feet apart. They experienced discomfort at the larger distance, found their partners "cold," and held their partners responsible for their own discomfort (Aiello & Thompson, 1980).

In summary, the seating arrangement in a room can encourage conversation by allowing eye contact between people and by allowing an interpersonal distance comfortable for conversation. At the same time, people can adapt to a variety of seating arrangements by regulating their involvement through distance, eye contact, directness of facing, and other behaviors. However, these behaviors may not permit adaptation to excessive distances, which in one experiment led to the perception of conversation partners as cold.

Psychological barriers

For people holding a conversation in an office, having a desk or table between them may create formality or psychological distance. If so, the desk serves as a psychological barrier. Limited evidence supports this idea.

By one account, it is quite natural to receive visitors to an office from behind a desk, because the occupant resembles a "cave-man":

The cave man was undoubtedly very pleased to find a good cave but he also undoubtedly positioned himself at the entrance looking out. . . . For those lucky enough to be granted a cave, i.e., a private office, the most automatic thing to do is to place the desk so that the user faces the door. (Propst, 1968, pp. 24–25)

The effect of this "automatic" arrangement is usually to put a desk between occupant and visitor.

One study found the "cave man" arrangement more prevalent in the offices of people in government and business than in universities, perhaps because academics wanted to create an informal atmosphere for conversation. Joiner (1976) examined 132 offices and classified them in

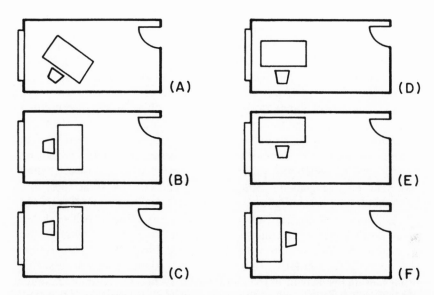

Figure 12.4. Six office arrangements. *Source*: Adapted from Joiner, D. (1976). Social ritual and architectural space. In Proshansky, H. Ittelson, W. & Rivlin, L. (Eds.), *Environmental Psychology*, 2nd ed. New York: Holt, Rinehart & Winston, p. 231.

terms of the six arrangements shown in Figure 12.4. Layouts A, B, C, and D all leave the occupant and visitors seated more or less face to face, within conversation distance, with the desk between them. Arrangements E and F, on the other hand, leave no part of the desk between occupant and visitor, and are typically seen as more "open," less formal. Joiner found a strong preference for the "desk-between" arrangements (A, B, C, and D) in government and commercial organizations, which contained most of these arrangements. (Favorite arrangements were A and D, which allowed the occupants a view out the windows in the rear walls as well as a view of the door.) On the other hand, professors tended to use arrangements E and F. Joiner (1976) concluded:

Academic occupants who spend a lot of their time in their rooms talking with groups of students organize their rooms in such a way as to minimize their social distance. (p. 232)

Another study found a similar preference among professors (D. Campbell, 1980).

Research generally confirms that "desk-between" arrangements are seen as formal and less open than arrangements with nothing between occupant and visitor. One researcher looked for a relationship between the layout of professors' offices and accessibility to students, and found professors with desk-between arrangements rated as less "easy to find outside of class" and less likely to provide individual attention to students (Zweigenhaft, 1976, p. 530). (The less accessible professors were also older and had higher rank. Perhaps the physical distance created in their offices matched the psychological distance created by their age and rank.) In another study, students rated color slides of offices in various arrangements. "Open" arrangements received higher ratings on the "degree to which the professor welcomed student visitors" than desk-between arrangements. Students also believed they would feel more comfortable and welcome in the "open" arrangements (D. Campbell, 1979). Another study used photographic slides. Offices with desk-between arrangements were rated lower on comfort and welcomeness, and the occupants lower on interest in students and friendliness (Morrow & McElroy, 1981). Similarly, a physician met patients in his office sitting either behind his desk or in front of it and classified the patient's manner as "at ease" or "ill at ease." More were ill at ease in the desk-between arrangement (White, 1953). However, one study failed to repeat these findings. A professor had students interview him once with a desk in between and once without. Interviews lasted 2 minutes longer in the open arrangement, although the difference was not statistically significant, and ratings of the professor were equivalent in both arrangements. He tried to seem equally friendly in all cases and apparently succeeded (D. Campbell, 1979). (The lack of differences could reflect the prearranged schedule of topics, which may have seemed stiffly formal even in the informal arrangement.)

Some visitors to offices may prefer the psychological distance created by a relatively formal arrangement. In one study a research team found that people anxious at the prospect of an interview actually saw that the interviewer was more friendly and pleasant when he sat behind a desk. Those who reported little anxiety gave the expected rating of more pleasantness and agreeability in the desk-not-between arrangement (Widgery & Stackpole, 1972).

If anxious visitors do find comfort in the psychological distance created by an intervening desk, sensitive hosts can put them at ease by sitting behind the desk. A lawyer wrote:

[M]any a law case has gone unstated because courage or determination or whim failed during the wordy preamble over politics, the weather, the crops; or the lawyer has made the interview so pleasant that the client forgets what was troubling him. (McCarty, 1946, p. 224)

The lawyer saw the seating arrangement as a tool for setting the tone of an encounter, and included in his office enough different chairs to permit flexibility in the choice of an arrangement to suit his purposes.

In summary, office arrangements that place occupants and visitors on opposite sides of a desk are consistently seen as less open than those with no barriers between conversants. However, some visitors may actually prefer the psychological distance created by a desk between themselves and their hosts.

Setting the stage for influence. Office workers sometimes consciously or unconsciously treat their workspaces as staging areas for attempts to influence visitors. Perhaps the simplest strategy is to place the desk and chair so that the occupant directly faces the door, as in some "cave man" arrangements (A–C in Figure 12.4).

Being able to see the door from one's working position implies a readiness for interaction . . . to be able to see who is coming into the room, and to be instantly prepared for them – that is, to have one's *front* correctly displayed. (Joiner, 1976, p. 232)

When occupants face away from their doors, perhaps toward windows, visitors can surprise them. Perhaps this explains why in Joiner's (1976) study, 83% of the office workers had their desks arranged so that they could see the door as they worked (arrangements A–E in Fig. 12.4).

Perhaps the people most likely to use their offices as resources for interpersonal influence are managers and executives, who spend large shares of their time dealing with others. By virtue of their high rank, they may have relatively large offices with a variety of furnishings, such as conference tables, sofas, coffee tables, bars, and so on (see Chapter 11).

In an office that permits a variety of seating arrangements for visitors, the occupant can influence the encounter by establishing the psychological distance. An example of an office arranged consciously for such purposes belonged to environmental psychologist Irwin Altman while he was chairman of the Department of Psychology at the University of Utah. As shown in the floor plan (Fig. 12.5), he had placed his desk in one of the popular "cave man" positions. In front of the desk was a circular coffee table surrounded by lightweight chairs, which could easily be moved. Altman received visitors from behind his desk for formal encounters or chose a chair at the coffee table for informal meetings. Adjacent chairs at the coffee table gave enough proximity for personal conversations, and the indirect orientation allowed the choice of whether or not to make eye contact. This position also allowed cooperative work

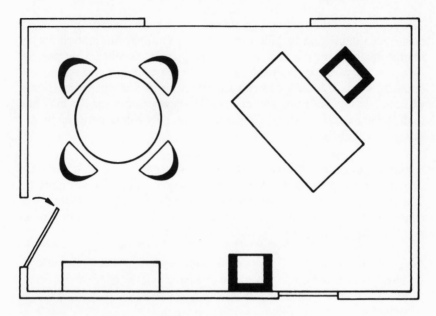

Figure 12.5. Schematic diagram of Irwin Altman's office.

on the same papers. The slightly more distant position across the coffee table left Altman and visitor about 4 to 6 feet apart, face-to-face, in a less personal arrangement than in adjacent chairs. Another choice he sometimes made was to receive visitors standing up. According to office managers, conversation while standing sets the stage for a truncated meeting:

[S]ome of the smartest young executives do not even have a chair to offer
a caller, but receive him standing up. . . . [W]hile this standing up reception can be made both courteous and cordial, there is nothing like it for
inducing a caller to cut his interview short. (Copley, 1920, pp. 61 & 176)

Other executives have gone so far as to choose specific furniture or arrangements for essentially manipulative purposes. For instance, according to one executive, it is best to choose a conference table with closed ends, forcing visitors to sit opposite the executive. He also employed another tactic:

The desk is placed against the wall and the table nearer the center of the
room, with chairs for visitors so located that their faces will be toward the
light so that it will be easy to study them. (Barnaby, 1924, p. 393)

Another executive had even more sophisticated uses for daylight:

In case a salesman calls I motion him to a seat opposite the window. The light by striking him full in the face enables me to read many subtle meanings in his eyes and facial expression which are not revealed by his voice, or his argument. On the other hand, if I am trying to sell a visitor something the chair near the radiator is selected. The visitor is permitted to look into my face which is in the full light and hence I add to my other powers of persuasion, the influence of my facial expression. (Galloway, 1919, p. 96)

More elaborate schemes have been devised to give the occupant of an office the advantage over a visitor. Loan officers have been known to order adjustable chairs for themselves, to literally elevate their positions. Their callers sit in couches chosen deliberately to put them close to the floor. As a result, the applicant for a loan literally looks up to the official, a position from which it may be difficult to be assertive.

According to an anecdote, a Russian bureaucrat carried the same principle – that of making visitors feel small – one step further. He had a small anteroom just outside the entrance to his office, designed so that visitors had to open the first door and enter, then open a second door. The anteroom was unlit, so visitors stood for a moment in complete darkness as the first door closed behind them. Then they emerged into the light to face the bureaucrat.

Occupants of offices can probably find many ingenious ways of arranging the environment to their advantage, but their efforts only set the stage. Whether the actors follow the script is another question. For instance, one writer advocates tactics of intimidation for visitors to offices, such as deliberately sitting on or behind the host's desk to make him or her uncomfortable.

Office workers who receive visitors in their offices may have a psychological advantage regardless of the arrangement of the room, because they are on home ground. Psychologists have sometimes observed a phenomenon called *territorial dominance*, in which an individual tends to dominate others when in his or her own territory (Esser, 1970). This is analogous to the "home field advantage" in sports (see Hirt & Kimble, 1981), and seems to apply in workspaces. For example, managers may feel more confident and assertive in their own offices; subordinates are "called onto the carpet" there. Evidence for territorial dominance comes from experiments in dormitories, where residents in their own rooms typically dominate encounters with visitors (Martindale, 1971; Taylor & Lanni, 1981), except perhaps when the resident defers to a cooperative visitor out of hospitality (Conroy & Sundstrom, 1977).

In summary, office workers can arrange their furniture to allow them to influence others, particularly through the arrangement of seating. Visitors may not act according to plan, but the occupant may be dominant anyway, by virtue of being on home turf.

A comfortable environment

Observers of offices and factories have for some time expressed the belief that pleasant surroundings lead people to be sociable, while unpleasant or stressful environments contribute to interpersonal friction. For instance:

The gloom and unpleasantness of the surroundings lowers vitality, and makes men and officials irascible and displeased with conditions. Little annoyances in the work which would be passed over without any comment whatever, are just sufficient to cause loss of temper. (Duncan 1915, p. 159)

Evidence that pleasant settings create a favorable climate for conversation is scarce and comes from laboratory and classroom. In an early laboratory experiment, researchers invited college students to view and rate 10 photographs of faces in one of three equal-sized rooms. The "beautiful" room was carpeted, nicely furnished, well lit, and decorated with works of art. The "average" room was a well-used professor's office, tidy but clearly a place of work. The "ugly" room resembled a janitor's store room, with a dirty, bare floor, windows with tattered shades, and drab walls lined with buckets, mops, and brooms. Lighting came from a bare, overhead bulb. As predicted, participants gave most favorable ratings of the faces in the beautiful room, least favorable in the ugly room (Maslow & Mintz, 1956). Unknown to the interviewer, one researcher recorded the durations of sessions and found them to be longest in the beautiful room, briefest in the ugly one (Mintz, 1956). Similar findings have emerged in classrooms, where pleasant surroundings have been associated with greater participation by students in class discussions (see the review by Sundstrom, 1984).

The laboratory findings suggest that an uncomfortable physical environment may lead to rushed or truncated encounters, as people minimize the time they spend there. One potential source of discomfort is the chair:

There is a saying that . . . "The mind can absorb only as much as the seat can take. . . ." I think in terms of the hardness of the chair. How long can I sit without feeling uncomfortable? A real hard chair, just plain wood or steel, is a 20-minute chair. People sitting in such chairs longer than 20

minutes begin to squirm. They feel an urge to stand up and stretch. A
chair with a little padding on it is a 30–minute chair. . . . A chair that is
reasonably well padded is a 40–minute chair. (Matthies, 1959, pp. 14–15)

Environmental stress. Sources of stress may influence an interpersonal
exchange in several ways: by making people insensitive to social cues,
by leading them to respond negatively, or, paradoxically, by drawing
them together.

One source of environmental stress is noise. Some research suggests
that noise can lead people to overlook subtle interpersonal cues. If so,
the best explanation is probably based on overload: Loud noise distracts
attention and adds a demand on a person's capacities, leaving less capacity available for attending to people. Laboratory research found
people who were exposed to loud, intermittent noise to be relatively
insensitive to details of social exchanges pictured in slides (Cohen &
Lezak, 1977) and to be less responsive to visible characteristics of people
in staged incidents (Mathews & Canon, 1975; Korte, Ypma & Toppen,
1975). If noise does lead to social insensitivity, the consequences could
be serious. A manager of a noisy office pool might overlook a new
employee's difficulties with a task, a worker in a noisy factory might fail
to notice an accident about to happen, and an overloaded foreman might
not detect a worker too fatigued to handle a dangerous job.

Another possible effect of environmental stress is that it irritates people or puts them in a bad mood and leads them to react negatively
toward others. In line with their prediction, a group of researchers found
that loud noise led people in a management simulation to assign relatively low salaries to fictitious job applicants on the basis of their résumés
(Sauser, Arauz & Chambers, 1978). Other researchers found that uncomfortable heat has a similar effect. Participants in a laboratory experiment sat in an environmental chamber where the temperature was
a comfortable 70° or 100°F (21° or 37.7°C) with 60% humidity, and
examined a dossier of a person whose picture and biographical data
were included. Asked to rate the person described in the file, people in
the "hot" room gave lower ratings (Griffitt, 1970; also Griffitt & Veitch,
1971).

An important experiment suggests that the capacity of environmental
stress to create negative responses to other people may be limited to
situations like examining resumes, where the person being evaluated is
not in the room. When people actually occupy an environment together,
the "shared stress" may draw them together, and create a relatively
more positive response. Kenrick and Johnson (1979) found that loud
noise led people to express less liking for an absent stranger described
in a dossier, but more liking for the person when in the same room.

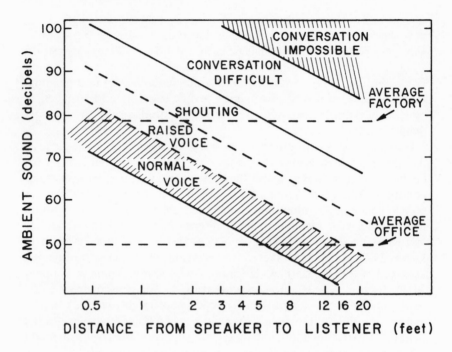

Figure 12.6. Intensity of ambient sound associated with interference with speech. *Source*: Adapted from Hawley and Kryter (1950) and Morgan et al. (1963).

These findings supported the widely accepted hypothesis that shared environmental stress creates a social bond.

Background noise. Besides creating stress, noise can interfere with conversation by masking the sounds of peoples' voices. For example, at one noisy automobile assembly line

the average exchange between operators lasted about *fifteen seconds*. . . . A considerable amount of interaction was by signal and sign language. Most of it was in shouts and phrases. (italics added) (Jasinski, 1956, p. 26)

According to acousticians, people can converse easily at face-to-face distances of up to 5 feet without raising their voices, provided the background sound is fairly quiet, around 50 to 60 decibels. As background sound becomes louder, people must usually raise their voices or move closer to understand each other. Figure 12.6 shows levels of ambient sound in which people are supposed to experience difficulty in talking at various distances. Figure 12.6 combines criteria from Hawley & Kryter

(1950) and Morgan et al. (1963). In the average factory, which has a background sound of 78 decibels by one estimate (Dreyfuss, 1966), workers must raise their voices to talk at distances greater than 1 foot, and they probably cannot converse at all at distances approaching 20 feet.

Noise that interferes with speech may lead to annoyance, errors in communication, or to the expenditure of extra effort to avoid errors. It may also discourage conversation or prompt people to communicate in other ways, for instance through sign language.

In offices a certain amount of interference with speech is desirable, both to mask distracting sounds and to keep conversations from being heard. Experts on acoustics in offices typically recommend background sounds of about 45 to 55 decibels (e.g., Hansen, 1974). Louder background sound can interfere with normal conversation, but against quieter background conversations are easily understood at considerable distances.

Background sound is critical in open-plan offices with no walls to contain the conversations. The first *Burolandschaft* in the United States at DuPont's offices in Wilmington, Delaware, was too quiet. The background sound was only 40 decibels, and people could understand each other from too far away. The solution was to add more sound by installing electronic sound makers. The planners apparently did not anticipate the fairly common tendency of workers to hush their voices in open offices, which could account for the unwelcome quiet. (This issue is discussed further in Chapter 13.)

Summary

This chapter reviews research and theory concerning the role of the physical environment in communications involving two people. It emphasizes face-to-face meetings. After a brief sketch of practices in the planning of work places, the choices involved in communication are reviewed and evidence connecting communication with accessibility among workspaces and properties of gathering places examined. The last section considers the environment at a smaller scale: the arrangement and conditions within rooms.

Planners of offices and factories have traditionally arranged them to minimize walking distances between the workspaces of people who require frequent contact. The goal was efficiency. More recently, office planners have acted on the premise that visual accessibility promotes conversation; the result was the open-plan office.

An analysis of communication suggests that its major elements include sender, message, medium, and recipient. The physical environment may enter into choices regarding the medium (face-to-face conversation vs.

written letter or telephone call) or the recipient. In organizations, communication is classified as formal (job related) or informal. It is hypothesized that for formal communications that allow a choice of medium, the likelihood of a face-to-face meeting increases with the physical accessibility of the recipient. For informal communication, it is hypothesized that people prefer face-to-face conversation as the medium and tend to select partners on the basis of physical accessibility.

Research on the relationship between physical accessibility and communication focuses mainly on inter-workspace proximity and physical enclosure of workspaces. Studies of formal communication in offices generally found no relationship between the average distance between workspaces and the average amount of time spent in face-to-face conversation with coworkers. (However, some evidence indirectly suggests that, for two specific people, proximity may be associated with the amount of time in face-to-face meetings). Studies of informal communication consistently found proximity associated with informal conversation, and in some cases with friendships. Most studies of physical enclosure of workspaces and communication consist of postoccupancy evaluations of open offices. A review of 10 such studies suggests that when people switched to open-plan offices, changes in communication were inconsistent. However, there was a tendency toward increased discretionary, formal contact (such as interdepartmental communication) and decreased confidential communication.

Face-to-face communication can occur outside of individual workspaces in gathering places – habitual locations for conversation among co-workers. Such places are thought to be centrally located, near pathways, used for daily activities, and comfortable for conversation. One empirical study in a school found that people tended to use gathering places within easy walking distances of their own workspaces.

Research on the connection between communication and arrangements and conditions within a room has focused on interpersonal distance, psychological barriers, arrangements that promote influence, and sources of comfort vs. environmental stress. Studies of interpersonal distance have found that people prefer certain ranges of distance for various kinds of encounters but can adapt to a variety of arrangements. However, when distances are uncomfortably great, adaptation may be difficult. Studies of offices suggest that the desk may serve as a psychological barrier and that arrangements in which people converse across a desk are less open than those without a desk between the conversants. However, for some purposes the barrier may be preferred. Anecdotes suggest a variety of ways in which people can arrange their offices to gain a position of influence over visitors. However, studies of territorial dominance suggest that the resident may be dominant anyway, by virtue of being on home turf. Studies of non-work settings have found comfortable or pleasant environments associated with relatively favorable reactions to people. Other research has associated sources of environmental stress, such as noise or heat, with insensitivity or negative reactions. On the other hand, there is some evidence that shared stress leads to positive reactions. Background noise, if loud enough, can interfere with conversation; the louder the sound, the closer two people must be in order to converse in a normal tone of voice.

Practical considerations

Where the physical environment has a role in communications between two people it seems to involve mainly face-to-face conversations or personal meetings. Physical accessibility can make meetings convenient; the arrangements and conditions in the room can make them comfortable. However, the manager or planner who wants to facilitate face-to-face communication needs to ask, what kind of communication – formal or informal – among which specific people?

If the goal is to facilitate formal communication, one alternative is to follow traditional practice: locate workers closest to those whom they need to meet most frequently in their work. This practice has the advantage of expediency: job-related meetings considered most necessary can be held with the minimal investment of time and effort. And because face-to-face conversation between counterparts is convenient, it is more likely to be the medium of choice, instead of the telephone or the office memo.

There are arguments against the traditional practice of locating people in workspaces adjacent to those of their counterparts. If (as the evidence suggests) formal meetings occur regardless of physical distance within a building, distance could some have benefits. One is the need for an occasional walk, which may be particularly welcome in jobs that give few opportunities for people to leave their chairs or work-stations (see Jockusch, 1981). A second benefit is that frivolous meetings may be less likely if they take at least some effort to arrange.

However, the decision about whether to locate people near counterparts also needs to take account of informal communication. The evidence suggests that people choose partners in informal conversation at least partly on the basis of convenience. (Proximity or accessibility provides an opportunity to talk.) If so, co-workers whose workspaces are close together, and whose jobs call for frequent contact, may develop close informal ties. These could form the basis of cohesive work-groups.

The case against grouping people according to formal job relationships depends on the desirability of interdepartmental contact. If people tend to talk informally with their neighbors, a consequence of not being near formal counterparts is the chance to become acquainted with co-workers in other specialties. Workers would still have to maintain their formal contacts, so the result would probably be a wider circle of contacts, perhaps at the expense of cohesive work groups within specialties.

A planner or manager can probably do a great deal to facilitate informal contact through the provision of convenient gathering places. Ideally, such places are located just off of the major pathways that people use in their daily work. Gathering places may contain items that give people work-related reasons to be there: mail boxes, copying machines, reference materials, bulletin boards, special computer terminals, or such. They also may provide facilities for work breaks: coffee pots, water coolers, vending machines, and other sources of food or drink. A gathering place also needs to provide a comfortable setting for conversation outside the traffic pattern, where people are not in one another's way.

The provision of gathering places is complicated by an occasional tendency to regard them as expendable. Since floorspace is costly, and potential gathering places do not house work-stations, cost cutting may begin with such areas as copying rooms, mail rooms, wide corridors, lounges, or libraries. Unfortunately, the result may be an "efficient" building with no comfortable places for informal conversation. The consequences may include a relative lack of informal communication.

Managers and planners can facilitate face-to-face conversation through the arrangements and conditions within rooms. Comfortable conversation calls for comfortable seating at reasonable interpersonal distances. It calls for ambient conditions within the range of comfort, especially the temperature. It calls for moderate levels of background sound that do not obscure normal speech, but mask more distant noises. For some types of conversation, the setting may also need to provide privacy, the subject of the next chapter.

13
PRIVACY

As in the previous chapter, this one explores some connections between physical accessibility and interpersonal relationships. The focus here is privacy, or control of the flow of information or regulation of interaction between people. The work environment has a potential role in privacy through its capacity to limit interpersonal accessibility by way of barriers between workspaces, walls, partitions, and other forms of enclosure.

This chapter begins with a brief discussion of the private office and the controversy that has surrounded it. The private office crystallizes key issues concerning privacy, which concern communication, motivation, and status. Next, the concept of privacy and related ideas from environmental psychology are examined. This analysis is followed by a discussion of resources for privacy in offices and factories as well as research findings on the connections between physical environments and privacy and between privacy and satisfaction and performance.

The controversial private office

The term *private office* refers to a workspace in an office that consists of an entire room with walls to the ceiling and one or more closable doors. Private offices apparently became common during the late 1800s and early 1900s, when organizations were expanding and beginning to incorporate large, highly differentiated office staffs. The principal occupants of private offices have usually been executives and other high-ranking personnel; private offices have generally been symbols of status.

The traditional view has held that executives and certain professional people need private offices in order to concentrate on complex tasks without interruption, or to receive visitors. Most advocates of this view have argued that only a small proportion of office workers need private offices and that people in clerical jobs are best accommodated in open areas accessible to supervision (e.g., Leffingwell, 1925).

Practice in large organizations has paralleled the traditional view. For example, a survey of 278 companies found that all used private offices to some extent; 43% placed all their executives and department heads in private offices; another 34% gave them only to executives. The remainder allocated private offices only to top executives (Fetridge & Minor, 1975, p. 850).

Controversy has surrounded the private offices primarily because critics have argued that they are overused, unnecessary, or counterproductive. The most vocal critics have advocated their abolition (in favor of open-plan offices) and have argued strongly against too much privacy:

In the end, most demands for privacy really cover a desire to hide from contacts and from work. (Pile, 1978, p. 27)

Overconcern for privacy may indicate retreat from responsibility and sagging motivation. (Propst, 1968, p. 2)

Specifically, criticism of private offices has focused on the issues of communication, motivation, and status.

Communication

Advocates of *Burolandschaft* and open-plan offices claimed that visual accessibility promotes face-to-face communication and that the enclosure of a private office discourages it (e.g., Lorenzen & Jaeger, 1968, see Chapter 12). However, research on open-plan offices generally failed to support the idea (see Table 12.1). Studies of open offices found widespread difficulties in trying to hold confidential conversations. Whereas a well-designed private office contains the sounds of conversation, a workspace in an open office may not. For example, in duPont's open-plan office, while discussing trading developments,

several manufacturers expressed fear that a competitor might be sitting in the next office behind a partition and that important competitive plans would inadvertently be revealed ("Mixed Reactions to the First U.S. Office Landscape," 1968, p. 77).

A private office does not always insure the containment of confidential conversations (e.g., Goodrich, 1982). However, conversational privacy may be attainable in open offices only with special acoustical treatments (see Hansen, 1974; Lewis & O'Sullivan, 1974).

Motivation

Critics of private offices have suggested that they isolate people from an important source of motivation: the sight of busy co-workers. For example, an early management consultant described the fate of a young executive given a private office:

Although his intentions remain good, the private office extends to him a subtle invitation to take things a little easier . . . It is not just because he is where no one can see him. He is in a little eddy, apart from the main current of the office. He no longer has the stimulus he unconsciously received from those activities when he was right among them. Gradually, while hardly being aware of it, he loses his edge. (Copley, 1920, p. 61)

More recently, the same premise appeared in allusions to "team spitit" and "group morale" (e.g., Palmer & Lewis, 1977), in which the sight of co-workers busy at work was thought to motivate the individual through identification with the efforts of the larger group. This was supposed to occur in open areas, not in private offices.

On the other hand, the sight of people at work may be distracting during a complex task. The traditional view of the private office has held that some types of work call for privacy:

Most men intent on one pursuit or problem are at their best in solitude, and this solitude should not be broken except when the individual's attention is demanded – and certainly not by the passage through individual territory of those seeking some other objective point. (Arnold, 1896a, p. 263)

Offices that provide for the sight of co-workers may allow distraction. A private office seems to represent an exchange of a source of motivation for insulation from distractions.

Status

Critics of private offices have implied that distinctions based on status are inimical to values of democracy. For instance:

The manager thinks that his is a position aloof or apart from the rank and file. He considers himself a little tin god having all sorts of special privileges. But modern management. at its best, does not tolerate this state of mind . . . so it takes him out of his private office into the open; places him right among his workers; requires him to work with them. (Copley, 1920, p. 179)

Advocates of the open-plan office have advanced similar arguments. For example,

if private offices were introduced for managers or executives, this symbol of class distinction would make other workers dissatisfied with open situations and would reintroduce a struggle to gain a private cubicle as an outward sign of importance. (Pile, 1978, p. 27)

However, despite the undemocratic character of status symbols, they serve important purposes in organizations (see Chapter 11).

Not only have executives often occupied private offices, but lower-ranking employees have usually been located in areas open to surveillance:

In all cases of day-wage every man should be consistently under the eye of many others, and should be perfectly aware that every act of his working hours may be seen by his paymaster. Hence every part of the workfloors of the shop should be exposed to view. (Arnold, 1896a, p. 264)

Similarly, the headquarters building of Fidelity Mutual Life Insurance Company was designed so that the offices of each department permitted visual supervision by the executive in charge:

This condition can be secured if the desks of the executive and his lieutenants are placed throughout the general workroom at points of ready accessibility where a convenient oversight of operations may also be maintained. (Solon & Hopf, 1929, p. 16)

In effect, a private office provides executives with freedom from the surveillance that accompanies many low-ranking jobs. With freedom from surveillance comes an ability to conduct conferences without unwanted audiences. This may be important for some jobs, such as personnel director, comptroller, or patent officer. While private offices may be unwelcome signals of differences in status, those differences may be associated with responsibilities that call for privacy.

In summary, the private office has usually been the province of executives and other high-status members of organizations. Critics have argued that communication is more convenient in open offices, although available evidence does not support this claim. In contrast, people in open offices have often complained about the lack of conversational privacy. Critics have also pointed out that private offices interfere with the motivating sight of busy co-workers (although they may also insulate against distraction). A private office has generally been a mark of status, and critics have claimed that such distinctions are unnecessary, even though they are customary.

Privacy and related concepts

This section first discusses three general definitions of privacy, then outlines specific uses of the term in work environments. Related concepts are also introduced: isolation, crowding, and social facilitation.

The concept of privacy

Psychologists have advanced several definitions of privacy, which in some cases reflect theories of social behavior (see the reviews by Altman, 1974, 1976, 1977; Margulis, 1977; Pennock & Chapman, 1971). Concepts of privacy have emphasized one of three central ideas: retreat from people, control over information, and regulation of interaction.

Retreat from people. Early definitions of privacy pictured it as a deliberate withdrawal by an individual or group from contact with other people (e.g., Bates, 1964; see review by Altman, 1976). Under this definition, privacy represents a situation in which the person has achieved solitude, for instance, to work uninterruptedly on a project or to hold a personal conversation. The conditions under which people seek privacy were sometimes left unspecified.

Control over information. A widely cited definition of privacy advanced by Westin (1967), is "the claim of individuals, groups, or institutions to determine for themselves when, how, and to what extent information about them is communicated to others" (p. 7). Similarly, Margulis (1979) defined privacy in terms of the individual's control over the flow of information to specifiable audiences. Information considered private may concern such issues as a person's health, sexuality, social deviance, protected contracts, and other data about the self.

Perhaps the most important implication of control over the flow of information concerns the *autonomy* of an individual or group. One theorist even defined privacy in terms of autonomy of action and selective disclosure of information (Beardsley, 1971). A theory by Kelvin (1973) suggested that privacy involves the ability of an individual to restrict others' knowledge about his or her actions, which provides a "positive limitation of the power of others" (p. 260).

According to Kelvin's theory, privacy permits a person to avoid unwanted influence by avoiding comparison of his or her activities against some standard of acceptable behavior. This in turn deprives others of a primary basis for influence: the implied threat of sanction for deviation from norms or role expectations. It is this sort of influence that a supervisor can exert through surveillance of employees.

The theory of *self-presentation* also emphasizes the importance of audiences to a person's activities. Sociologist Erving Goffman's theory (1959) identified "regions" for the presentation of self, including "front" areas in which the individual is "on stage" before an audience and tries to exhibit a satisfactory performance. In "backstage" areas less accessible to observation, the individual is relieved of the necessity of paying attention to the audience's reactions. In effect, such "back regions" provide privacy. Goffman wrote of an office:

The fact that a small private office can be transformed into a back region by the manageable method of being the only one in it provides one reason why stenographers sometimes prefer to work in a private office as opposed to a large office floor. On a large open floor someone is always likely to be present before whom an impression of industriousness must be maintained; in a small office all pretence of work and decorous behavior can be dropped when the boss is out. (Goffman, 1959, p. 26)

In summary, viewing privacy as a form of information management or of self-presentation suggests that an individual seeks privacy to gain autonomy from the unwanted influence of others.

Regulation of interaction. Another widely accepted definition of privacy comes from the theory by environmental psychologist Irwin Altman (1975): the "selective control of access to the self or one's group" by other people (see also Marshall, 1970, 1972). Altman's definition reflects a general theory of the regulation of social exchange, based on the premise that an individual tries to maintain an *optimal level of social interaction*:

If a person desires a lot of interaction and gets only a little then he feels lonely, isolated, or cut off. And he if actually receives more interaction than he originally desired, he feels intruded upon, crowded, or overloaded. However, what is too much, too little, or ideal shifts with time and circumstances. If I want to be alone a colleague who comes into my office and talks for fifteen minutes is intruding and staying too long. If I want to interact with others, the same fifteen minute conversation may be far too brief. (Altman, 1975, p. 25)

The theory emphasizes not only the flow of information about the self to others, but also the regulation of incoming stimulation.

The central proposition of Altman's theory is that when a person experiences too much or too little interaction with other people, he or she uses privacy-regulation mechanisms to withdraw from interaction or to seek it out. These mechanisms include territoriality (the use of places where the individual or group has control); personal space (the adjustment of interpersonal distance and other signals of closeness); and a variety of verbal and nonverbal behaviors. The privacy-regulation mechanisms are said to be operating properly when the individual's actual level of interaction approximates his or her desired level of interaction.

When an individual experiences more social stimulation or interaction than desired, one possible result is *crowding*. Crowding is a form of stress that sometimes accompanies the concentration of people into insufficient space. On the other hand, if a person obtains less interaction than desired, he or she may experience isolation or deprivation of social contract. (The concepts of crowding and isolation are discussed later in this chapter.) In Altman's theory, privacy occurs when an individual achieves an optimum level of interaction, which may be low, moderate, or high.

In brief, viewing privacy in terms of regulation of interaction suggests that an individual tries to control both outgoing information and incoming stimulation. When these are not at the desired level, the individual is thought to take action to promote a more ideal state of affairs.

Privacy in work environments

Uses of the term "privacy" in work environments correspond with all three of the conceptual definitions: retreat, information management, and regulation of interaction. One empirical study uncovered a variety of meanings of privacy among office workers. Justa and Golan (1977) questioned 40 business executives who had administrative responsibilities and asked them to describe what privacy meant within the context of the office. Many listed more than one situation, including being able to work without distractions (60%); controlling access to information (35%); having freedom to do what they want to do (35%); controlling access to space (35%); and being alone (25%).

Office planners and designers have distinguished some specific types of privacy. *Speech privacy* refers to an individual's ability to hold a conversation inside the workspace without being overheard and understood by people outside it (Cavanaugh, Farrell, Hirtle & Watters, 1962; Sundstrom, Herbert & Brown, 1982). The term *conversational privacy* is synonomous. (Technically, a workspace is said to have some degree of conversational privacy if not more than 5 to 30% of words spoken in the normal voice can be understood outside it. The proportion of speech that can be understood is used as a measure of speech privacy and is called the articulation index, see Herbert, 1978.) *Acoustical privacy* includes speech privacy plus isolation from noise. *Visual privacy* means isolation from unwanted observation. Visual privacy is available in a work environment that obstructs direct visibility and renders unlikely the sudden appearance of a potential observer. A private office with a closeable door may provide complete visual privacy, but with less enclosure an individual may be seen or approached, and may be accessible to surprise audiences. See Archea (1977) on the relationship between visibility and privacy.

Definitions of privacy used in work places generally imply a form of limitation of accessibility to other people. In particular, privacy connotes an intentional retreat from observation or audition, or from unwanted interruption, distraction, or interaction. Uses of the term "privacy" in offices or factories suggest that people use their control over information or their ability to regulate interaction, to achieve deliberate, calculated, and temporary limitation of exchanges with other people.

Concepts related to privacy

This section explores several concepts related to privacy. By definition, privacy is related to *communication* in that it represents a form of control over interactions between people. Efforts to attain an optimal level of interaction with co-workers can fail at least in two ways. When an individual experiences too little interaction, the result may be *isolation*; too much may result in *crowding* (Altman, 1975). However, the effect of crowding may not always be detrimental; in some cases it may actually enhance performance through a phenomenon called *social facilitation*. This section discusses the concepts of isolation, crowding, and social facilitation.

Communication. The definition of privacy as a form of control over information suggests that it represents a restriction of communication. However, privacy is not simply the opposite of communication. Certain forms of privacy may allow confidential or protected conversations that might not otherwise occur. According to Westin (1967), one type of privacy, called intimacy, involves the seclusion of a small group, permitting intimate exchanges without an audience. In effect, privacy is prerequisite to confidential communication.

Privacy can represent the opposite of communication under some circumstances. When an individual experiences unwanted surveillance or wants to restrict the circulation of personal information, communication can be an invasion of privacy. In offices and factories such invasions can occur through the physical environment. In one case, closed-circuit television cameras were installed on an assembly line to facilitate electronic surveillance of workers. In another company, the doors to restrooms were removed to "insure that no one is wasting time" (Lublin, 1980). Employees of both companies were understandably annoyed.

Isolation. The term "isolation" refers to an unwanted limitation of interpersonal contact. It may occur in work places where people must stay at their work-stations for long periods of time, where the environment precludes interaction while at work-stations. For example, at a Western Electric plant,

> talking helped many people make the day go by. Our work spaces being as close as they were, it was easy to talk. . . . However, at times it became obvious that the talk was little more than a device to pass the time. Arlene told me, "When I get bored, and believe me that is quite often, I like to talk to someone. . . . I don't even care what we talk about. I just want to hear another voice." Ellen Smith said she didn't mind the work, but she did wish that she wasn't working in a row by herself. . . . "When I have to work in a row by myself for several days I feel like screaming." (Balzer, 1976, pp. 31–32)

These workers' jobs provided little stimulation, so contact with co-workers was particularly important. Social contact may be less an issue in complex jobs:

> When a worker does a job which requires concentration and skill, he may (other things being equal) perform it as a craft, and he is not bored. . . . When a worker does a job which is almost entirely automatic, boredom will not arise provided the situation permits daydreaming, conversation, and social distractions to take place. . . . What is frustrating is to have work which does not make sense whilst separated by noise or space from other workers. (Brown, 1954, p. 207)

As outlined in Chapter 12, an environment can limit or preclude informal conversation among workers through distance, barriers between work-stations, or loud noise. These may create feelings of isolation. However, isolation and its effects have apparently not been systematically studied in work places.

Crowding. Crowding may be defined as a form of stress that sometimes occurs in a densely populated environment (Baum and Epstein, 1978; Stokols, 1972; Sundstrom, 1975a,b). Research in the laboratory has shown that people experience crowding when high population density is introduced through a relatively large group size in a small room, or through small room size in a constant-sized group, or through close seating arrangements (see the review by Sundstrom, 1978). Crowding has been consistently associated with discomfort, and in some cases with signs of physiological arousal (e.g., Aiello, Epstein & Karlin, 1975; Evans, 1979).

Perceptions of crowding in the laboratory are highly predictable from the number of people in an environment and their distance from the perceiver (Knowles, 1983). However, according to one theory, crowding also depends on the perceiver's attribution of discomfort to the other people in the situation (Patterson, 1976). According to another theory, crowding is relatively intense in settings where an individual "spends much time, relates to others on a personal basis, and engages in a wide range of personally important activities" (Stokols, 1976, p. 73).

As a form of stress, crowding should affect performance. Specifically, the arousal hypothesis suggests that crowding should adversely affect the performance of complex tasks, but not simple ones. Early laboratory experiments generally failed to find any effect of high density on the performance of routine clerical tasks and some mental tasks (e.g., Freedman, Klevansky & Ehrlich, 1971; see the reviews by Sundstrom, 1978, 1984). Some laboratory studies found adverse effects of high population density on the performance of a complex motor task (three-dimensional maze tracing; Paulus et al., 1976). Another study found this effect limited to the first few minutes of exposure to high density (Paulus & Matthews, 1980). One laboratory study found a decrement in the performance of a dual task in high population density (Evans, 1979). Others found crowding associated with decrements in the performance of tasks sensitive to physical obstruction by other people (e.g., Heller, Groff & Solomon, 1977; McCallum, Rusbult, Hong, Walden & Schopler, 1979). In brief, crowding has been associated with adverse effects on performance in the laboratory during the performance of highly demanding motor tasks and tasks sensitive to physical interference.

There is some evidence that living in high-density environments is associated with symptoms of prolonged stress. For instance some studies found crowded dormitory rooms associated with poor grades and health problems (see the summary by Sundstrom, 1984). Studies of crowding in prisons found it associated with physical symptoms (Paulus, McCain & Cox, 1978). Like other forms of stress, crowding has also been associated with adverse aftereffects in the laboratory (Sherrod & Downs, 1974; see also Spacapan & Cohen, 1983).

Few studies of crowding have been done in offices or factories. The prevalence of crowding, the conditions for its occurrence, and its consequences in work environments are largely unknown. One field study in an office found workers' perceptions of crowding to be associated with the numbers and distance of neighboring co-workers (Sundstrom et al., 1980). As expected, crowding was associated with dissatisfaction with the physical environment. However, it was not significantly associated with supervisors' global ratings of employee performance.

Beyond the association of crowding with dissatisfaction with the work environment, it is difficult to extrapolate existing research findings regarding crowding to work places. At least two problems exist. First, the preconditions for crowding in offices and factories remain to be specified and second, most of the existing evidence on crowding derives from short-term laboratory studies, which cannot take account of long-term *adaptation* by people in densely populated settings. Although a few studies of dormitories and prisons suggest that prolonged crowding can create serious problems, the findings may not be generalizable. In work places other forms of adaptation may be possible. In brief, the importance of crowding in work places is largely unknown.

Social facilitation. Laboratory research by social psychologists suggests that people perform simple or well-learned tasks faster and/or more accurately in the presence of others then when alone. For example, an early laboratory experiment showed that people performed simple clerical chores better in a room with co-workers than in private cubicles. However, the presence of co-workers actually hurt the performance of a highly complex task (Allport, 1924). Later research also found facilitating effects of co-workers or onlookers on the performance of simple tasks (see reviews by Cottrell, 1972; Zajonc, 1965). The best explanation seems to be that the presence of other people creates *arousal*. (It is not only due to competition among co-workers, because a passive audience also produces social facilitation.) The arousing effect of an audience also seems to grow out of the possibility of being evaluated (Geen & Gange, 1977). However, it may also be attributable to the close proximity of others (Knowles, 1983). Either way, the facilitating effect of an audience may occur in settings that minimize privacy.

If social facilitation does occur in offices and factories, people in work-spaces that render them easily visible to others may perform routine tasks faster or more accurately than in more secluded quarters. On the other hand, social facilitation may be a brief phenomenon that disappears after a period of adaptation. (The laboratory studies generally lasted only a few hours.) Whether social facilitation does occur in offices or factories is an empirical question.

In brief, privacy can represent a retreat from communication or a precondition for intimate or personal communication. A person can have too much privacy – in an environment that creates isolation through excessive physical separation of people. Too little privacy may result in crowding, a form of stress that sometimes occurs in densely populated settings. Crowding may have adverse effects on satisfaction and performance but has seldom been studied in offices or factories. Social facilitation, the beneficial effect of the presence of others on performance of simple tasks, has been demonstrated in the laboratory, but not in offices or factories.

Resources for privacy

This section reviews the resources available to people in offices and factories for achieving or maintaining privacy. These resources include physical enclosure of workspaces; special facilities such as conference rooms; norms and customs; and verbal and nonverbal signs and signals.

Physical enclosure of workspaces. A conventional private office with sound-insulated walls and a closeable door provides practically complete separation from other workspaces. The occupant has visual seclusion, speech privacy, and about as much control over accessibility as can be obtained in an organization. However, even a private office does not guarantee privacy. Consultant Ronald Goodrich (1982) recounted cases in which people in private offices complained of sound "leaking" through walls and ductwork. In other offices, hard-surfaced walls in a hallway funneled sounds from one office to others.

Variations of the private office provide less seclusion. Some offices have one or more glass walls, perhaps with curtains that can be left open for visibility or closed for privacy. Without curtains, however, the glass panel might create a "fishbowl" that almost invites people to look in (Goodrich, 1982). Another variation incorporates a one-way mirror that permits the occupant to see out, but nobody to see in. Such offices can be found in factories overlooking work-areas in which managers can maintain surveillance without having their own activities seen.

Work-spaces that provide still less seclusion are only partly enclosed by barriers, such as movable panels, blackboards, file cabinets, storage cabinets, counters, potted plants, and other objects. Many such barriers provide some visual seclusion, but still permit sound to pass over, under, around, or through them. (See, for example, Fig. 13.1.) The shoulder-high panels used in "office landscapes" (see Chapter 2) permitted sounds to travel freely above; they also allowed passers-by to peer over into workspaces. Tall panels may prevent most passers-by from looking in, but still may not block sound. Executives at Chrysler's corporate head-quarters solved this problem by installing clear plastic panels in the gaps

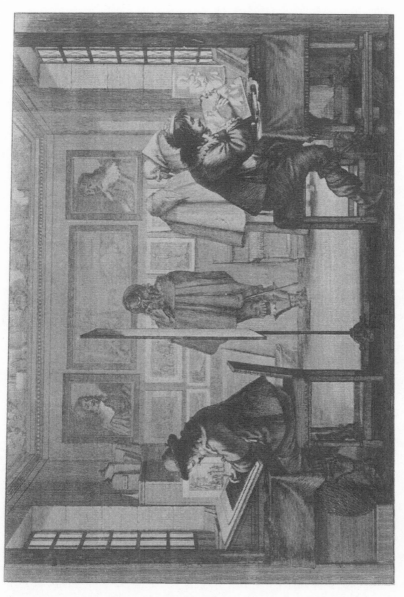

Figure 13.1. Etching by Abraham Bosse: Graveurs en taille-douce au Burin et à l'eaue forte, Philadelphia Museum of Art, given by Staunton B. Peck. *Source:* Photo provided by the Philadelphia Museum of Art, and reproduced with permission.

between 7–foot partitions and ceilings. The result was almost equivalent to conventional walls with "borrowed light" panels at the top, common at the turn of the century (see Chapter 5).

Special facilities. Outside an individual's workspace, physical separation from other people can be found in places specifically designated for retreat. An example is the "think tank" at the corporate offices of McDonald's Restaurants. It consists of a cluster of rooms in an otherwise open office, surrounded by floor-to-ceiling walls. The think tank contains facilities for solitary work and for conferences. Its rooms have fabric-covered walls, plush carpets, and rounded corners. Being inside is probably somewhat like being inside a flying saucer. One section even has a water-filled mattress for a floor. The door is lockable, and users take the key with them when they go inside ("McDonald's Think Tank," 1976).

Other organizations have more traditional conference rooms available for employees whose workspaces do not provide enough privacy. In many open offices, small "pause rooms" provide a temporary substitute for the physical isolation of a conventional private office. In some companies, however, the conference rooms have glass panels in doors or walls, so they provide acoustical isolation without visual seclusion.

Norms and customs. The use of the physical environment to achieve privacy depends to a large extent on the norms of the organization. In one company, employees regarded the "pause rooms" as the exclusive province of upper management, who had private offices and seldom used them. Norms also dictate the use of workspaces. For example, the executives interviewed by Justa and Golan (1977) said they often closed the doors of their offices when they wanted to work alone but seldom refused visitors or calls. According to their norms, "being available" to other people took precedence over solitary tasks. Other organizations may have unwritten rules, or even written policies, that office doors are always open.

When workspaces are not separated by distance or barriers, office workers may rely on norms for privacy. In one open office, employees

developed the habit of calling out to coworkers for solutions to problems or short, on-the-spot business discussions that broke down individual work patterns and were annoying. The men saw this as a natural outcome of the plan, and realized that they would have to discipline themselves to compensate for the [lack of] visible barriers of cubicle-offices. They are making a conscious effort to *not* interrupt each other, and hope it will become a habit. ("Office Landscape Gives Olsten Future Flexibility," 1970, p. 62)

A norm that developed in some open-plan offices was hushed voices. One result may have been fewer distractions for co-workers. However, where quiet voices are the norm, the resulting low level of background sound could actually work against privacy; it may not be loud enough to mask the sounds of even hushed conversations. And visitors to the building unaware of the norm may be particularly intrusive.

Signs and signals. In environments with little physical separation among workspaces, people may develop ways of advertising the times when they want to avoid interaction. In the 1920s, for instance, a Boston executive who worked in an open office handled it this way:

[He] obtained a slender vertical standard and to it attached a card one side of which bore the legend

NOT BUSY

When engaged in tasks which permit interruption without serious loss of time and energy this side of the sign welcomes callers. But when the pressure of work requires that he shall not stop to speak except on the most imperative occasions, he reverses the sign so that the following notice, in red letters, can be seen halfway across the room:

DO NOT DISTURB. VERY BUSY.
DON'T TALK TO ME NOW.

(C. T. Hubbard, 1921, p. 287)

More recently, another executive said that when things get too hectic, she hangs outside her door a needlepoint sign that reads, "Leave Me Alone – I'm Having a Crisis" ("Managers Use a Variety of Tactics against Time-Wasters," 1983, p. 33). In another company, the occupants of semienclosed work-spaces at the offices of Smith-Kline in Philadelphia used another type of sign to convey the same message: they hung small doors across the entries of their work-stations. The doors had no practical value, but were "closed" to let others know that the occupant wanted to be left alone ("The Trouble with Open Offices," 1978, p. 85). In still another office, people without doors learned to "knock" by clearing their throats near the desk of someone they wanted to visit. The visitor was either greeted or ignored, and if ignored left quietly. Of course, the effectiveness of such signals depends on the cooperation of would-be callers or visitors.

A small observational study of an open office revealed another type of signal – objects arranged on desktops as barriers to communication. Some people placed things such as files or books along the fronts or sides of their desks, occasionally to the point of obscuring their faces. Interactions were recorded for a group of 21 workers, along with the

"Damn it, Palmer, you don't have to greet me every time you pass by!"

Figure 13.2. Drawing by Modell. *The New Yorker.* (1980, Dec. 15), p. 148.
© 1980 The New Yorker Magazine, Inc.

number and types of barriers on their desks. The barriers apparently had the intended effect. The more of them were present on a desk, the fewer interactions were initiated by other workers with the occupant (Burger, 1983).

In summary, the physical environment can provide a resource for privacy through physical enclosure of workspaces or in special facilities such as conference rooms. However, the use of such facilities depends on local norms. In the absence of physical separation, people may develop norms or individual signals regarding desires to avoid interruption.

Physical enclosure and privacy

This section reviews empirical evidence on the link between physical enclosure of workspaces and privacy. Relevant research includes studies of the number of people per room in offices; surveys and evaluation studies in open offices; and field studies on the enclosure of individual workspaces.

Number of people per room

Two surveys of office employees investigated preferences regarding the number of people per room in offices and found them highly varied. A survey of 1,180 English workers included a question on the "size of room" in which they preferred to work, meaning the number of people in an area defined by barriers above eye level while seated. Choices ranged from "one to four people" up to "more than eighty people." Preference declined as numbers increased. Nearly half (44%) preferred the smallest category (Canter, 1968). The study did not assess preferences for offices containing fewer than three office-mates.

BOSTI (1980a) reported the results of a survey of 1,097 office workers (this was a subset of the workers in BOSTI, 1981). Participants were asked to indicate how many people were in the same room with them, and how many they would prefer. Results appear in Figure 13.3. Only about 12% of the participants had rooms to themselves. About three-fourths of the participants said they worked in rooms with eight or more people. However, only about one-fourth preferred these arrangements. About three times as many people wanted private offices as had them. The arrangement preferred by most participants was a room shared with two to seven people.

The findings from the two surveys suggest that a majority of office employees may not want the seclusion of a private office. Instead, a room with a handful of other workers apparently provides the desired balance between physical separation and accessibility for most. However, the wide variation in preferences points to the potential importance of congruence between an individual's workspace and his or her desires for privacy.

Privacy in open offices

Offices that incorporated either *Burolandschaft* or open plan prompted considerable research. Investigators looked for, and generally found, complaints about the lack of privacy. Two types of studies addressed employees' responses: surveys and postoccupancy evaluations.

Surveys. Several surveys of workers in open offices found privacy a central concern. An English study used a statistical technique (factor analysis) to analyze responses to a survey and identify the major dimensions of perceptions of an open office. The most important dimen-

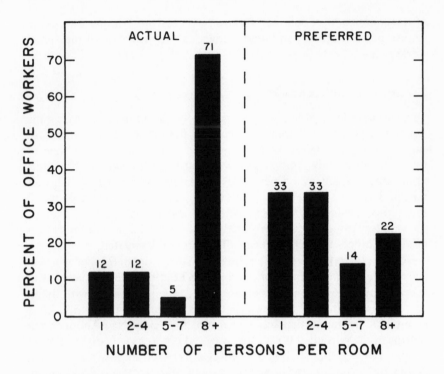

Figure 13.3. Actual and preferred numbers of people per room in offices. *Source*: Adapted from BOSTI. (1980a). *The Impact of Office Environment on Productivity and Quality of Working Life: First Interim Report.* Buffalo, NY: Buffalo Organization for Social and Technical Innovation, p. 15.

sion comprised privacy and disturbances (Hedge, 1982). An earlier study used the same technique and reported similar results (McCarrey et al., 1974). A survey in a new open office asked for evaluations of several aspects of the environment, and found strikingly low ratings on visual and conversational privacy (Marans & Spreckelmeyer, 1982a). Similar findings were reported by Wolgers (1973). In brief, privacy was a salient issue in four surveys of occupants of open offices.

Postoccupancy evaluations. Several studies evaluated employees' responses to open offices after renovation or relocation from conventional offices. They compared employees' reactions to new offices with their reactions to, or recollections of, earlier accommodations. The open offices generally had fewer walls and fewer fully enclosed workspaces than existed in earlier, conventional arrangements. (However, a few of the workspaces in open offices were more enclosed afterward than before; some clerical employees shifted from unenclosed desks to work-spaces partly segregated by partitions.) Most of the evaluation studies were designed to assess the office as a whole, not to investigate the connection between enclosure and privacy. They generally included only sketchy information on the enclosure of individual workspaces.

Most of the evaluation studies found ratings of privacy lower after changing to open-plan offices. Four studies included employees' ratings or comments on privacy in general, and reported an increase in the proportion of complaints or a decline in ratings after moving into open offices (Boyce, 1974; Hanson, 1978; Hundert & Greenfield, 1969; see also the reports by Brookes, 1972b, and Brookes & Kaplan, 1972, on the last study.) Riland and Falk (1972) reported that privacy for tele-phone conversations declined, but privacy for business conversations remained unchanged (it had been low before). Sloan (undated) reported a decline in privacy at one open-plan office but an increase at another location where partitions were introduced to separate workspaces. Ne-mecek and Grandjean (1973) reported that 6% of employees named the lack of privacy as a disadvantage of their open offices; they also complained about disturbances and interruptions (69%) and a lack of conversational privacy (11%). Ives and Ferdinands (1974) reported that managers experienced problems with the lack of conversational privacy in an open-plan office. Oldham and Brass (1979) found that employees who moved to open-plan offices experienced a decline in "concentra-tion" as a job characteristic.

One study of an open-plan office specifically designed to look at the issue of privacy included data on individual workspaces. Sundstrom, Herbert and Brown (1982) assessed perceptions of privacy in a group of office employees at four job levels, before and after they relocated from conventional offices to an open-plan office. Before relocation, workspaces were identical within job levels, though the four levels had different types of workspaces. Afterward, workspaces changed for the four groups but were again identical within job levels. Managers (levels III and IV) left private offices for individual doorless enclosures of 60–inch or 78–inch partitions. Staff (level II) left two-person offices for small, doorless individual enclosures of high partitions. Clerical em-ployees (level I) left unenclosed desks for partial enclosures with par-titions on two sides. In effect, only the managers lost enclosure; clerical employees gained some.

Ratings of privacy declined significantly after relocation. The general decline in privacy reflected a drop in ratings of speech privacy, partic-ularly among the managers who left private offices, shown in Figure 13.4. Acoustical measurements of speech privacy, based on the Artic-ulation Index, declined with ratings of speech privacy.

These findings suggest that the change to an open-plan office affected

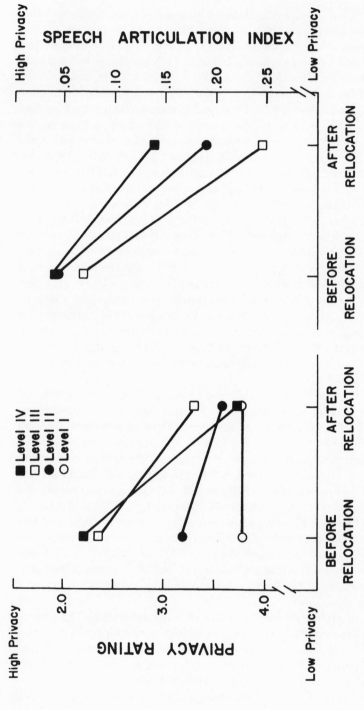

Figure 13.4. Privacy as rated by office employees at four job levels and values of the articulation index both before and after changing offices. *Source:* Sundstrom, E., Herbert, R.K. & Brown, D. (1982). Privacy and communication in an open plan office: A case study. *Environment and Behavior, 14*(3), 387. Reprinted by permission of Sage Publications, Inc., Beverly Hills, CA.

people differently, depending on their jobs and ranks. Managers were most affected; they lost conversational privacy in the change to open offices, and it was probably important to their jobs. Other workers did not have private offices to start with and apparently did not experience the same decline in privacy. In some earlier studies of open-plan offices, managers were also the most strongly affected, both in terms of decreased physical enclosure and lower privacy (e.g., Ives & Ferdinands, 1974). In some open-plan offices, executives found their workspaces so inadequate that they soon had them converted into private offices (e.g., Corlin, 1977).

In summary, most of the evaluation studies found a decline in privacy, on average, among employees whose new workspaces were in open offices. The only exceptions involved cases in which privacy was already low or in which partitions were introduced. The general decline in privacy sometimes involved an increase in disturbances or interruptions, and often involved a decline in conversational privacy, particularly among managers.

Field studies of enclosure of workspaces

Several studies of offices included assessments of the enclosure of individual workspaces in offices, and investigated the connection between enclosure and privacy. Privacy has generally been associated with enclosure, but the relationship between enclosure and privacy has sometimes varied among job categories.

In the first of a series of three field studies, 85 administrators indicated how many of the four sides of their workspaces were enclosed by partitions and whether or not they had a closeable door. The number of partitions and the presence of a door were both associated with ratings of privacy. A second study of 30 clerical workers incorporated observations of the number of co-workers visible while working. Ratings of privacy decreased as the number of people in the room increased. A third study included 98 employees from a variety of jobs and office arrangements. It incorporated observations of the number of walls or partitions at least 6 feet high enclosing each workspace (up to a maximum of four sides). Other measurements included the distance to the nearest neighbor and the number of neighbors in the vicinity. Ratings of privacy were correlated with the number of walls or high partitions around the workspace; privacy declined as the number of people in proximity in the vicinity increased (Sundstrom, Burt & Kamp, 1980).

A later study using the same methods included people in only three jobs – secretary, bookkeeper-accountant, and office manager. As before, the number of sides of the workspace enclosed by a wall or partition

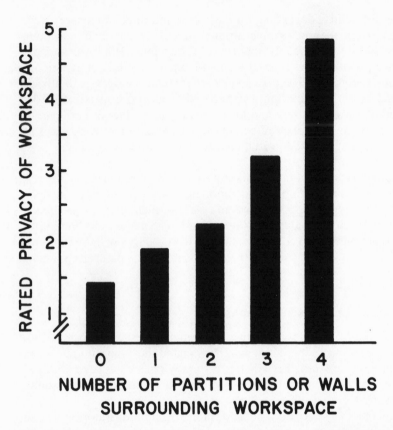

Figure 13.5. Privacy as rated by office employees as a function of the number of sides of the workspace enclosed by walls or high partitions. *Source*: Sundstrom, E., Town, J., Brown, D., Forman, A. & McGee, C. (1982b). Physical enclosure, type of job, and privacy in the office. *Environment and Behavior*, *14*(5), 550. Reprinted by permission of Sage Publications, Inc., Beverly Hills, CA.

at least 6 feet tall was correlated with ratings of privacy (Sundstrom, Town, Brown, Forman & McGee, 1982a). The relationship is shown in Figure 13.5.

The same study found differences in enclosure and privacy among three job categories. Secretaries had workspaces with less enclosure and fewer private offices than bookkeepers or managers. Furthermore, people in the three jobs gave different ratings of privacy in workspaces of equivalent enclosure – private offices. As shown in Figure 13.6, ratings of privacy in private offices were lowest among secretaries and highest

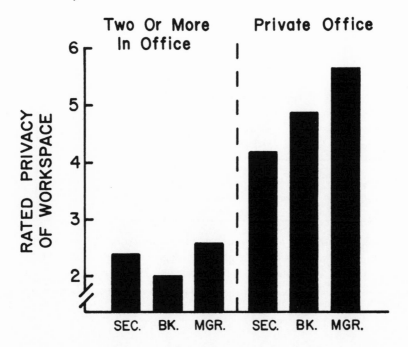

Figure 13.6. Privacy as rated by office employees in three job categories in private offices or with two or more persons per office. *Source*: Sundstrom, E., Town, J., Brown, D., Forman, A. & McGee, C. (1982b). Physical enclosure, type of job, and privacy in the office. *Environment and Behavior*, *14*(5), 551. Reprinted by permission of Sage Publications, Inc., Beverly Hills, CA.

among managers. The differences could reflect differences among the jobs – it is part of a secretary's job to take calls and receive visitors. It could also reflect a difference in the norms associated with the jobs – people may have felt freer to interrupt a secretary than a manager. However, other results of the study showed that the correlates of privacy differed for the three job groups.

The explanation proposed for the differences among the three job groups was that their needs for privacy differed, and they perceived privacy in terms of those needs. Specifically, Sundstrom and colleagues suggested that the most basic need is control over personal accessibility, which applies to some extent in all jobs. It can be met by a workspace that allows the individual to avoid crowding but that maintains enough social stimulation to avoid isolation. For clerical employees, this was seen as sufficient for privacy. However, people in professional and technical occupations may have the added need to avoid distraction and

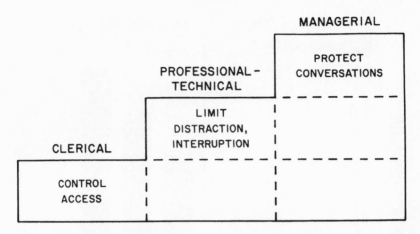

Figure 13.7. Hypothetical needs for privacy in three job categories. *Source*: Sundstrom, E., Town, J., Rice, R., Konar, E., Mandel, D. & Brill, M. (1982d). Privacy in the office, satisfaction, and performance. Paper presented at the annual conference of the American Psychological Association, 1982, Washington, D.C.

interruption in order to concentrate on their more complex work. And for people with managerial responsibility another need is added: conversational privacy for confidential meetings. This hypothesis regarding different needs for privacy is schematized in Figure 13.7.

A later study examined the relationship between different types of privacy and physical enclosure among office workers in clerical, professional-technical, and managerial jobs (Sundstrom et al., 1982c; the study used the same data base as in BOSTI, 1981.) The office workers rated their workspaces on control over accessibility, freedom from intrusions (interruption or distraction by people), and speech privacy. Workspaces were classified in terms of the number of sides enclosed by walls or "high" partitions (which could not be seen over while standing). Results suggest that the three kinds of privacy increased with the number of sides of the workspace enclosed by walls or high partitions. However, the correlations were stronger for control over access and speech privacy than for intrusions. Fully enclosed workspaces with doors were associated with much greater privacy than were other types of workspaces. Differences among partially enclosed workspaces were relatively small. (Similar findings were reported by BOSTI, 1981, using a different index of enclosure.)

To assess the connection between enclosure and privacy, workers who had completed the questionnaire before and after changing offices were divided into three groups: those whose physical enclosure had increased, had stayed the same, or had decreased. (Enclosure was defined as the number of sides of the workspace bounded by walls or high partitions.) Managers, professional-technical employees, and clerical employees were then compared in terms of their ratings of three types of privacy before and after moving. These comprised control over accessibility, intrusions, and speech privacy. Results showed that decreased enclosure was associated with fewer intrusions, especially among professional-technical employees. Decreased enclosure was also associated with lower speech privacy, especially among managers. The findings were consistent with the idea that managers are particularly sensitive to speech privacy, and that professional-technical employees are sensitive to intrusions. However, for clerical employees, physical enclosure was unrelated to privacy, suggesting that their needs for privacy were lower or were not satisfied through physical enclosure of workspaces.

Another field study assessed perceptions of privacy and physical enclosure of workspaces among 288 office workers at eight organizations. Privacy decreased as an index of physical "openness" increased (Ferguson, 1983). The index of openness was also associated with "aural distractions." The openness of workspaces was greatest at lowest job levels, and decreased with increasing job levels. Similarly, privacy increased with job-level.

In summary, field studies found enclosure of workspaces associated with privacy, although there were differences among job categories. Managers, professional-technical employees, and high-ranking employees had more enclosure and more privacy than workers in clerical jobs or lower ranks. One interpretation is that jobs create different needs for privacy: managers need conversational privacy, professional-technical employees need isolation from interruption, and clerical workers need a modicum of control over accessibility. However, the research suggested that people in clerical jobs obtain relatively little privacy from physical enclosure.

Privacy, satisfaction, and performance

This section explores the connections between privacy and the key psychological outcomes identified earlier: satisfaction and performance. After outlining some ideas on the potential effects of privacy, empirical evidence is summarized.

Potential impact of privacy

Privacy may contribute to satisfaction with the physical environment to the extent that it helps an individual maintain adequate control over information or regulation of interaction. Speech privacy may be particularly important to satisfaction among managers; isolation from distraction may be especially important for satisfaction in professional-technical jobs.

Privacy may aid an individual's performance of his or her job by contributing to the ability to limit interruptions during complex work. On the other hand, privacy may detract from performance by allowing the individual to avoid the motivating influence of visibility or surveillance. To the extent that privacy contributes to a person's ability to conduct necessary, confidential conferences, it may enhance performance. On the other hand, if relatively private workspaces make people inconvenient partners in informal conversation and if informal conversation contributes to performance or satisfaction, privacy could indirectly hurt performance or satisfaction.

Research on privacy, satisfaction, and performance

One study of office workers assessed their satisfaction with the environment and with the job, their job performance, and privacy. Office workers completed a survey in which they rated their control over accessibility, isolation from intrusions, and speech privacy. A total of 389 employees in clerical, professional-technical and managerial jobs completed a questionnaire before and after changing offices. For each type of privacy, they were divided into groups whose privacy had increased, had stayed the same, or had decreased. Results linked all three types of privacy with satisfaction with the physical environment but not with job satisfaction or performance. The association of the three types of privacy with satisfaction with the physical environment held for all three job categories, but the strength of the connections varied with the job category. The differences were consistent with the idea that jobs create different needs for privacy. Speech privacy was particularly strongly related to environmental satisfaction among managers; freedom from instrusions was particularly strongly related to satisfaction among professional-technical employees. On the other hand, control over access was only weakly related to satisfaction among clerical employees. The findings suggest that needs for privacy that derive from the job played a role in the relationship between privacy and environmental satisfaction (Sundstrom et al., 1982d; findings based on the same data are reported by BOSTI, 1981). A later study of 288 office workers also found privacy associated with satisfaction with the workspace (Ferguson, 1983).

In summary, available evidence suggests that privacy is associated with satisfaction with the physical environment. However, in one study the relationship depended to some extent on the job. Among professional-technical employees, isolation from interruptions was strongly related to environmental satisfaction; among managers speech privacy was strongly related to satisfaction.

Summary

This chapter discusses privacy in the work place, beginning with the controversy surrounding private offices. (A private office is completely enclosed by walls and has a door.) Private offices have traditionally been associated with high-ranking jobs. Critics have suggested that they isolate people from communication (although available evidence suggests that they aid confidential conversation). Critics have also pointed out that private offices interfere with the motivating sight of co-workers, and unnecessarily emphasize differences in status. Nevertheless, private offices are traditional for executives and for employees in certain other positions.

The concept of privacy may be defined in terms of retreat from people, management of information, or regulation of interaction. Privacy in work environments involves all three definitions but generally refers to the limitation of interaction or communication. Speech privacy (or conversational privacy) refers to the ability to conduct conversations without being overheard outside the workspace. Visual privacy means inaccessibility to view by other people.

Privacy is related to several social-psychological concepts. Privacy can contribute to communication by allowing confidential conversation. In an environment that provides too much seclusion from others, a person may experience isolation. When an individual experiences too much contact with others, the result may be crowding, a form of stress that sometimes occurs in densely populated settings. Crowding in offices has been associated with dissatisfaction with the environment. Crowding in the laboratory has adversely affected the performance of certain complex tasks. However, the relevance of crowding to performance in work settings is largely unexplored. Laboratory research has also demonstrated social facilitation, whereby people perform simple or routine tasks better with an audience than when alone. However, it is unknown whether social facilitation occurs in work places.

Research on the relationship between physical enclosure of workspaces and privacy includes several types of studies. Surveys on preferences regarding the number of people per office suggest that office workers' preferences vary greatly. (Only a minority prefer private offices.) Evaluation studies of open offices suggest that, on average, open offices are associated with lower privacy than are conventional offices. Field studies that assessed the physical enclosure of individual workspaces found enclosure associated with privacy. Furthermore, the association differed among job categories, with enclosure particularly associated with speech privacy among managers, and with isolation from interruption among those in professional-technical jobs.

Field studies have also shown a link between privacy and satisfaction with the environment. However, there was some evidence of differences among job categories, with managers particularly attuned to speech privacy.

Practical considerations

The key problem concerning privacy in offices and factories is the achievement of an appropriate balance between accessibility and physical separation among individuals. Physical enclosure of workspaces is generally associated with privacy. However, the appropriate degree of enclosure for a workspace depends on the individual's preferences and job. (However, a given degree of enclosure may not even provide the same level of privacy for people in different jobs.)

Office planners have sometimes made the mistake of assuming that one type of workspace is appropriate for people doing many different jobs, as in the case of *Burolandschaft*. However, different jobs may create different needs for privacy. In particular, managers have special needs for conversational privacy.

An office in which workspaces are tailored to individuals and their jobs may contain workspaces with different degrees of enclosure. And, in keeping with traditional practices, higher-status administrative jobs may be associated with relatively enclosed workspaces, perhaps private offices.

The range of variation in the physical enclosure of workspaces is surprisingly great. A workspace may be seen as a rectangular area that can be enclosed on each of four sides by a wall to the ceiling, or a high partition (say, 6 feet tall), or a low partition (say, 4 feet tall), or nothing at all. This yields at least 35 combinations. The option of having a closeable door in the four-sided enclosures with high partitions and/or walls increases the number of combinations to at least 40. A few more heights or kinds of partitions brings the number of possibilities into the hundreds.

As far as privacy is concerned, many of the possible configurations of partitions and walls may be interchangeable. Available evidence suggests that low partitions, over which people can look while standing, provide very little privacy, regardless of how many of them surround a workspace. (However, low partitions are useful for delineating boundaries of workspaces or for supporting office equipment.) For tall partitions to provide appreciable privacy, a workspace apparently has to be enclosed on at least three or four sides with tall partitions or walls. (However, even one or two tall, sound-absorbent partitions around a workspace may help minimize noise.)

Practically, there may be only three or four categories of physical enclosure as it relates to privacy. At one extreme, an unenclosed workspace contributes nothing to the occupant's privacy. At the other extreme, a fully enclosed office with a door gives as much privacy as a workspace can give. However, partially enclosed workspaces seem to provide substantially less privacy, and the differences among them may be small. So a decision on whether a particular workspace should have two versus three tall partitions may be made on grounds other than privacy. For instance, the decision may hinge on such factors as status, acoustics, esthetics, individual preferences, or space for bulletin boards or shelves.

In light of the expense associated with enclosure of workspaces, the practical ideal is to provide the minimum enclosure adequate for the occupant's satisfaction and performance. The critical decision seems to be whether or not an individual belongs in a private office (or in the nearly equivalent enclosure of four high partitions with a door). One basis for the decision is the job. Obvious candidates for private offices are managers, because of their need for conversational privacy, and professionals, because of their need for insulation from distraction. Another basis for the decision is status, but the result would probably be similar. A third basis is individual preference. However, more people may want a private office than can have one.

In partially enclosed workspaces, satisfaction is probably maximized by allowing individuals to choose their own configurations of partitions, within reasonable limits. This might work against the use of partitions as a status symbols (although other symbols are available).

For factories, issues surrounding privacy concern surveillance. In an organization that emphasizes surveillance, employees may be given little privacy, and workspaces may be designed accordingly. (On the other hand, provisions for surveillance may be minimal, reflecting an orientation toward autonomy for factory jobs.) If a work place is designed for surveillance, it may contain such features as raised "lookout galleries," supervision platforms, or electronic surveillance. However, even where such measures are ethically defensible, they still might create a sense of being spied on among employees. Resentment over surveillance could create not only dissatisfaction, but conflict between employees and their managers.

14
Small Groups

This chapter explores the role of the physical environment in the formation of small groups, as well as their development of cohesion. It extends some of the ideas introduced earlier in the chapters on communication and privacy. After briefly discussing the nature of small groups, this chapter examines the importance of physical proximity among workspaces in the formation of groups and the importance of physical enclosure for group cohesion. The focus is then shifted from the layout of buildings to the arrangement of rooms. The role of seating arrangements in group discussions and the effects of restricted communications in groups are explored.

The concept of a small group

This section briefly describes the study of small groups, the concept of a group, and its properties. A few types of groups are distinguished.

The study of small groups

Until the 1930s, when the Hawthorne studies drew attention to the importance of groups, psychologists had only studied them in a limited way. The 1930s began three decades of intensive research in both the laboratory and natural settings. By the mid-1960s, a substantial research literature had developed (see Cartwright & Zander, 1968; McGrath &

316

Altman, 1966). Since then, research has continued, but at a slower pace (see Shaw, 1981).

While psychologists studied groups, managers incorporated them into the planning of organizations. Groups were central to the human relations movement in management (e.g., McGregor, 1960). They gained even more importance in the design of organizations in the seventies and eighties, as they became integral to decision-making, problem solving, and other activities (see Nadler, Hackman & Lawler, 1979; Zager & Rosow, 1982).

Definition of a group

Social psychologists disagree about the definition of the term *group*. To some, a group is a social entity that represents more than the collection of individuals who make it up. To others, a group is a set of perceptions held in common among several individuals that exists only in their minds. One social psychologist used to say, "You can't stumble over a group" (Deaux & Wrightsman, 1984, p. 360).

A simple working definition of a group is two or more people who interact in such a way as to mutually influence one another (Shaw, 1981, p. 8). Other definitions emphasize certain properties that transform a collection of people into a group. These include a common goal or purpose, interdependence for the accomplishment of a shared activity or goal, mutual perception of the existence of a group, individual perception of membership in the group, regular or continued interaction among the members, and other commonalities (see Cartwright & Zander, 1968).

The term "small group" means a group with fewer than an arbitrary maximum number of members, typically about 20 or 30 (see Shaw, 1981). Probably the most important quality of a small group is the opportunity of each member to have a personal relationship with each other member.

Types of small groups

Psychologists have distinguished two main types of groups in work organizations: voluntary, or informal, groups – associations formed by choice – and organized, or formal, groups – assembled within an organization to do specific tasks (see Dubin, 1958). Voluntary groups have limited support from the organization and exist only as long as members can maintain communications during work, during breaks, or during off-hours. One type of voluntary group is the primary group, in which the individuals develop satisfying personal relationships that may even extend beyond the work environment. Another is a clique (or coalition) that forms within an organization to further the aspirations of individuals.

Organized or formal groups usually have the support of the host organization, and the members participate as part of their jobs. A rudimentary organized group is the technological group, whose members are tied together by a rigid technology, as in a production line. Other types include the task group, whose members have some choice in the way they do their jobs, and the team, with autonomy in work assignments as well as the details of the work (more recently called an "autonomous work group"; see Hackman & Oldham, 1981).

Properties of groups

The properties of groups can be divided into two categories; structure and process. The structure of a group refers to characteristics that remain relatively stable over its life, including norms, cohesion, and leadership. Norms are beliefs or habits shared by the members of a group. Cohesion refers to the strengh of the social ties that hold a group together, or to its attractiveness to its members. Leadership usually refers to the exercise of influence by one group-member. Process refers to the varied and complex interchanges among the members of a group. These can include patterns in participation, conflict, decision-making, and so on (see Shaw, 1981). The physical environment is important for both the structure and process of a group.

Proximity of workspaces and formation of small groups

Probably the most common hypothesis on the role of the physical environment in small groups is that physical proximity among people facilitates their development. If so, it is probably because of the convenience of conversation among people whose workspaces are close together, and a tendency to choose partners for conversation on the basis of convenience (as suggested in Chapter 12). People whose workspaces are close enough for them to talk with each other while working may do so, provided that noise, demanding work, or company policy do not prohibit conversation. Once they begin to talk, they may form mutual ties, which in turn may develop into an informal group. This probably applies only to people compatible in background and outlook.

This section reviews a handful of research projects that found an association between the development of informal groups and proximity of members' workspaces. All were conducted in offices or factories and involved direct observation of workers.

Technological groups in an automobile factory

Blue-collar workers at an automobile assembly plant perceived group membership in terms of the physical proximity of work-stations. In a case study done at Plant X, 179 workers were interviewed. A typical worker described his group as having 10 members: the person directly across the line, the two people in positions immediately preceding his own position, their counterparts on the opposite side of the line, the two people in positions immediately following his, and their opposites. The worker in the next position down the line also reported belonging to a group of 10 people, but the membership differed. This group lacked the first two people in the preceding worker's group, but included instead the next two workers further down the line. These groups existed mainly as individual perceptions. Only in rare cases did workers agree on the definition of their groups. In the words of a member of one such group:

I'm in a team of six. One man works inside the car body right with me. We're good friends. So are the others in my group. We talk and kid all day long. Makes the job sort of fun. (Walker & Guest, 1952, p. 76)

However, only a handful of these technological groups existed at Plant X, and none of the members mentioned off-hours contact with one another.

Small groups in Hawthorne's bank wiring room

The Hawthorne studies provide an example of the association of physical proximity with the formation of groups among factory workers. The last in the series of investigations at Western Electric Company was called the Bank Wiring Observation Room. Participants installed wiring in banks of switching terminals in a special room designated for observation. A total of 14 men were involved: nine wiremen who did the actual wiring, three soldermen who soldered the connections, and two inspectors. All were experienced workers from the same shop, most about the same age. They were accustomed to setting their own pace.

After a period of unobtrusive observation in the shop, the workers moved into the observation room, which was equipped as a miniature shop with everything necessary to produce finished terminal banks. An observer sat at a desk in one corner of the room. The men worked in three teams, each consisting of three wiremen and one solderman. The observer carefully recorded their output and their activities for 6 1/2 months.

The physical layout of the shop placed the members of each team at adjacent workbenches. One team was near the truck dock, one occupied the middle of the room, and one worked in the back (Homans, 1950).

Instead of developing into three groups corresponding to the work teams, the men in the bank wiring observation room formed two groups. One was called "the group in front," consisting of most of the team by the dock, an inspector, and one member of the team that worked in the center of the room. All worked in adjacent positions. "The group in back" consisted of the team that worked in the back of the room and a wireman from the center team. As in the other group, all members occupied immediately adjacent work positions.

Each group had well-developed norms. "The group in back" tended to trade jobs (a prohibited activity), chip in money to buy candy, and engage in loud horseplay and joking. They adopted the practice of "binging," or hitting one another on the arm as a sign of disapproval. Their output was uniformly low. "The group in front" spent a good deal of time arguing, and thought their conversations were on a higher plane than those of the other group. They played a variety of games that involved small bets. They did not practice binging, but did some job trading. Their output was uniformly high.

The fact that two groups formed in the bank wiring observation room among people in adjacent workspaces agrees with the idea that proximity of workspaces encourages the formation of groups. However, other social patterns among neighboring workers might have emerged instead, including one based on three work teams, or one based on a single group of all 14 workers. This illustrates the importance of personal compatibility among the potential members of a group. (By itself, physical proximity apparently cannot even ensure that conversation will occur, much less that social ties will develop.)

Clerical groups in offices

An instance of the formation of groups in an office appeared in a small study of clerical employees (also discussed in Chapter 12). Ten female cash posters worked in a single room and recorded customers' payments for the accounting division of a large firm. Face-to-face conversation accompanied their close physical proximity (Homans, 1950). Like the men in the bank wiring observation room, the cash posters formed two more or less distinct groups. Both groups met for off-the-job activities, although their activities differed. One group comprised mostly women from the "better" suburbs. The other consisted of women from poorer districts of the inner city. As in the bank wiring observation room, the composition of the groups apparently reflected both physical proximity and personal compatibility.

Another study of clerical workers in an office also found that groups formed among people in adjacent workspaces. The study included 12 female clerks whose desks were arranged in three rows of four each with file cabinets between the rows. Conversations tended to occur between immediate neighbors in the same row (Gullahorn, 1952; see Chapter 12). Mutual friendships developed among four of the women, and four more were involved in the network of friendships; the eight may be regarded as a group. The youngest four met during off-hours and seem to have constituted a cohesive voluntary group.

In summary, a few small studies suggest that physical proximity may be associated with conversation, which was sometimes associated with mutual friendships and at times formed the basis of a group.

Physical enclosure and group cohesion

Some experts have asserted that the physical enclosure of a collection of individuals increases the chances of the development of a cohesive group. Cohesion or cohesiveness refers to the strength of the desire of the average member to remain in the group or to the strength of the ties holding the group together (see Cartwright, 1968). One expert on management wrote:

The erection of barriers between groups . . . increases the probability of in-teraction within each group . . . the increased interaction, in turn, amplifies existing relations. . . . In contrast, barriers between between groups reduce interaction between existing units. (Melcher, 1976, p. 138)

Physical enclosure might contribute to the development of cohesion in a group in three ways. First, physical barriers around a group provide a symbolic boundary, which may indicate that those inside it constitute a unit. Second, barriers around a group add to the effort required for members to converse face to face with those outside the group, which in turn may encourage conversation within it (assuming that people choose the most convenient partners in conversation). Third, the physical enclosure of a group may allow privacy for the group. Privacy may in turn permit the autonomy necessary for the group to develop its own norms, which may not coincide with the practices of the larger organization. Evidence on these ideas comes from two studies (Richards & Dobyns, 1957; Wells, 1965b), which are described in the rest of this section.

The case of the changing cage

A case study illustrates the importance of enclosure for privacy in a small group. Anthropologists studied a group of eight employees and their supervisor in the voucher-check filing unit of the Atlantic Insurance Company (Richards & Dobyns, 1957). Their job was to file canceled checks and vouchers, and to locate specific checks quickly when asked. The group had its own isolated work area, called the "voucher cage." It was surrounded on three sides by walls and separated from other employees of the audit division on the fourth side by a floor-to-ceiling expanse of steel mesh. The cage was accessible through a door in the mesh wall, and through a back door to a corridor. Both doors were kept locked; visitors rang a buzzer to gain entry. People outside the cage might have observed the group through the steel mesh, but the occupants had lined it with file cabinets and had neatly stacked empty boxes on top to hide the group from view.

The group worked well together, and had developed a friendly camaraderie. They had no trouble keeping up with the work load and even had time for games like "sniping" with rubber bands. They typically chatted with messengers who brought checks and other materials. Each afternoon one of them would go out through the back door for the group's customary snack. The voucher-check filing unit had become a cohesive group, perhaps partly as a consequence of its physical isolation.

For some time the company had been planning a consolidation of the controller's department from two floors into a single floor, and the voucher-check filing group was slated to move. The relocation took place over a single weekend; on Friday the group left their old cage and on Monday reported to a new one. The new cage, like the old one, was enclosed by walls on three sides and had steel mesh on the fourth side. The difference was that the new cage was smaller, and its only door opened into the large room containing the rest of the division. The filing cabinets were left behind for lack of space. Consequently, there was nothing to obstruct the view into the new cage from other work areas.

With their activities visible to all, the idiosyncratic practices of the group soon came to the attention of the manager, who promptly prohibited what he considered unnecessary talk. He also forbade the customary afternoon snacks, a privilege the other workers saw and wanted for themselves. (Snacks were eventually allowed for the whole department, but only at a specific time.) The cage supervisor lost autonomy as the manager began to supervise the group more closely and impose new rules – for instance, that all desks and surfaces had to be kept clean. The group fell behind schedule and began storing unfinished work in desk drawers. The manager soon had the desks replaced with new ones with less drawer-space. He transferred some employees out of the cage, which contributed to the dissolution of the group.

The case of the changing cage illustrates the tenuous character of a cohesive work-group. Apparently, the smooth operation of this group depended on its unique norms, and physical enclosure protected the norms from disruption by external forces. With the enclosure removed, the group's existence as a quasi-independent social entity ended as its members came under the full influence of the larger organization.

Groups in open offices

A less dramatic example of the importance of the physical enclosure to groups appeared in an English study of 295 clerical employees of a large insurance company (Wells, 1965b). They worked on one floor of a tall office building as members of a single department. All had the same job title: general clerk. They were relatively young, with more than two-fifths less than 20 years of age. About 200 worked in a huge, open area; the rest worked in three smaller areas housing about 30 workers each, surrounded by partitions and window walls.

The research question was whether the three enclosed sections contained more mutual friendships than the large one did. The employees completed a questionnaire in which they listed the people in the office whom they considered their friends. As expected, their responses exhibited greater internal cohesion in the enclosed areas than in the open area. Two-thirds of friendship choices within the three smaller areas were reciprocated, as compared with only 38% in the large area. (The smaller sections also contained greater proportions of social isolates.) Apparently physical enclosure was associated with mutual friendships, a critical ingredient of cohesive groups. The study lacked an assessment of group membership, although the data suggest that the smaller sections did contain some groups.

In summary, two studies provide evidence consistent with the idea that physical enclosure is associated with group cohesiveness. In the case of the changing cage, the critical factor was apparently the privacy the group obtained from enclosure, which allowed it to develop its own norms.

Seating arrangements and group discussions

When a task-oriented group assembles for a meeting its physical environment usually comprises a meeting room of some kind. Researchers have explored the hypothesis that the arrangement of the room influences the course of the meeting or the group process. Specifically, people may address their remarks in a meeting to others with whom they can easily make eye contact. Furthermore, the seating arrangement can set one person apart from the others, which may add to his or her chances of acting as leader.

Opportunities for eye-contact

A laboratory study of group discussions found a relationship between seating position and interaction patterns in groups of 10 (Steinzor, 1950). Two groups held discussions on repeated occasions around a circular table. Steinzor recorded the initiator of each remark and noted the next person to speak, in what he assumed was a response to the preceding remark. Interactions across the table occurred more often than expected by chance; interactions between people seated one or two seats apart occurred less often than expected. In other words, people tended to answer those whom they could see across the table. (This finding is sometimes called the "Steinzor effect.")

A later study found partial support for Steinzor's finding. Hearn (1957) recorded group discussions held at square tables. One-half the groups had an assigned leader who tried to influence the group, and one-half had no assigned leader. Groups with no assigned leader showed the "Steinzor effect," in which members tended to address those who sat across the table from themselves. However, in groups with strong leaders, members tended to address their neighbors (who were merely across the corner of the table). Apparently the strong leader worked against the Steinzor effect.

Perhaps the most plausible explanation of the tendency of members of group discussions to address those seated across the table is that they can easily make eye contact (see Chapter 12). Those seated on the same side of the table must turn their heads to make eye contact, and with one or more persons in between eye contact may be difficult.

A study of simulated jury deliberations found results consistent with the eye-contact hypothesis. Groups of 12 people sat around a rectangular table with one person at each end and five on each side (Strodtbeck & Hook, 1961). The researchers thought that if opportunities for eye contact influenced interaction, the most frequent participants would be those in the end seats, who could easily see all the others in the group. (Those in side seats could not readily see others on the same side of the table.) Results confirmed that the occupants of the end seats participated most in the group discussions. In another laboratory study, groups of 10 were left free to establish their own seating arrangements and, when instructed to arrive at a collective decision, tended to adopt circular seating arrangements conducive to eye contact (Batchelor & Goethals, 1972). A more recent laboratory study found similar results

(Altemeyer & Jones, 1974). Apparently the opportunity for eye contact with group members is associated with interaction.

Leadership at the head of the table

In western cultures, leaders tend to be found at the "head" of the table. In the study of jury deliberations not only were those at the ends elected leader, but those who selected end seats were also generally the members of the group who had the greatest potential for leadership – those with professional or managerial jobs (Strodtbeck & Hook, 1961). So perhaps the "head" of the table is not only a likely place for a leader to emerge, but also a likely place for someone with aspirations for leadership to sit.

Environmental psychologist Robert Sommer (1961) found leaders at the heads of tables in a study of seating preferences in discussion groups. The groups varied in size and had appointed leaders. Members chose their own seats at rectangular tables that had one seat at each end. In groups of four or more the leader generally sat in an end seat; members typically sat in side seats and hardly ever sat in the opposite end seat.

Other studies also found leadership associated with a seat in a highly visible chair. When groups of ROTC cadets and college students were observed in discussions around rectangular or V-shaped tables, those at the ends of the rectangular tables received highest ratings on leadership (Bass & Klubeck, 1953). Similarly, Hare and Bales (1963) arranged five-person groups at rectangular tables with one person at each end and three along one side. Observations of the discussions revealed that the two end seats and the center seat on the side were "high-talking seats," as predicted. These seats were also chosen most often by people with high scores on a measure of "dominance" as a personality trait, which was in turn correlated with frequency of participation in group discussions.

A laboratory study tested the idea that seating positions influence communication through the Steinzor effect, and as a consequence influence the emergence of leadership. Students in groups of five held discussions from randomly assigned seats at a rectangular table with two chairs on one of the long sides and three on the opposite side. The researchers expected and found that leaders emerged more often on the side of the table with only two seats (Howells & Becker, 1962).

In summary, available research evidence points to a clear association between leadership and seating arrangements that allow one person more opportunity than other group members for eye contact with the group. The seat at the head of the table is an example. Leaders tended to emerge in such seats, and people with aspirations to leadership tended to choose them.

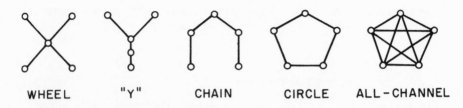

WHEEL   "Y"   CHAIN   CIRCLE   ALL-CHANNEL

Figure 14.1. Five communication networks used in laboratory research on restricted communication in groups.

Restricted communications within a group

In some circumstances, the physical environment can restrict accessibility among the members of a group through physical distance or loud noise. One question is, What effect does restriction in accessibility have on a small group?

Researchers studied restricted communications in the laboratory. Most studies created an extreme situation in which certain people in a group could only communicate directly with a limited subset of other members. The result was called a *communication network*. In the network called the "wheel," for example, one individual could communicate with all other members of the group, who in turn could communicate with nobody else. As shown in Figure 14.1, the wheel placed one member at the hub of the network. Others included the "Y," the "chain," the "circle," and the "all channel."

The most important feature of a communication network may be its degree of centralization, the extent to which communications are forced through a single individual. The wheel is most centralized, the circle and all-channel least. (Researchers have typically classified the wheel and Y as centralized.)

Social psychologist Harold Leavitt (1951) conducted perhaps the earliest study of communication networks. He invited volunteers from university classes into the laboratory in groups of five, where they sat in small carrel-like cubicles arranged in a circle. They could communicate only by passing notes through passageways between cubicles. Communication networks were constructed by blocking certain passageways. (The study included all networks shown in Fig. 14.1 except the all channel.) Each participant had a card containing several symbols, and the group's task was to discover which symbol all the members held in common. Twenty-five groups in each network each attempted to solve 16 problems. Groups in the wheel arrangement reached the fastest solutions; the circle groups sent most messages and made most errors.

Participants in the wheel arrangement reported less satisfaction than those in the circle, largely because of peripheral members' dissatisfaction. Those in central positions of the wheel and Y arrangements were relatively satisfied. Those in central positions also tended to be seen as group leaders, especially in the wheel.

After Leavitt's experiment, social psychologists studied intensively the effects of communication networks. A review of 18 subsequent laboratory experiments (Shaw, 1964) and later reviews (see Shaw, 1981) reported five consistent findings:

1. *Performance.* Centralized networks (wheel and Y) performed simple tasks faster and with fewer errors than decentralized networks did, but decentralized networks performed complex tasks faster and with fewer errors.
2. *Communication.* Members of decentralized networks sent more messages than members of centralized networks in all types of tasks.
3. *Leadership.* In centralized networks, the person in the central position consistently tended to emerge as the group leader. In decentralized networks, positions in the network were unrelated to leadership.
4. *Decision-making.* In decentralized networks members tended to distribute information to other members, and the group tried to reach consensus on a solution. In centralized networks, members tended to funnel information to the central person, who typically identified a solution and announced it to the others.
5. *Satisfaction.* The average member of a decentralized network reported greater satisfaction than the average member of a centralized network. However, the central person of a centralized network generally expressed high satisfaction.

The superior performance by centralized networks of simple tasks seems to reflect efficient communication: information typically flowed to the central person, who generated a solution. When the demands of the task were greater, the better performance of the decentralized network was probably due to more equal sharing of information and contribution by all members to the solution.

Some evidence suggests that differences in performance determined by communication networks disappear in laboratory groups who have worked together for a long time – about 60 times as long as those in the first network experiment (Burgess, 1968a,b). Other research suggests that the importance of the communication network for leadership depends on the mix of personality traits in the group; some compositions

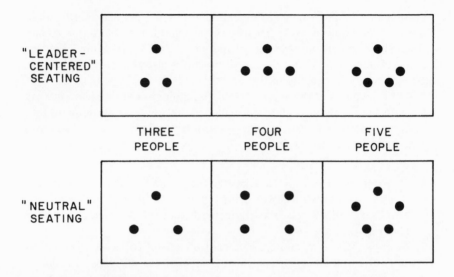

Figure 14.2. Leader-centered and non-leader-centered seating arrangements for discussions in small groups. *Source*: Adapted from Cummings, L., Huber, G.P. & Arendt, E. (1974). Effects of size and spatial arrangements on group decision-making. *Academy of Management Journal*, *17*(3), 460–475.

of individual traits may render the network relatively unimportant (Abrahamson, 1969).

One experiment produced findings consistent with the network research in face-to-face group discussions. The seating arrangement varied, and sometimes created a situation that could be described as centralized. Participants were assigned seats in group discussions consisting of three, four, or five people. In one-half the groups, one chair was placed noticeably farther from the remaining chairs than they were from each other, as shown in Figure 14.2.

Leader-centered seating arrangements placed the leader in a good position to see and address all members of the group, and in the larger groups made it difficult for the remaining members to see and address each other. The non-leader-centered groups showed greater consensus and better performance of a complex task (Cummings, Huber & Arendt, 1974). These results agree with the research on communication networks.

In summary, laboratory studies of restricted communication among the members of a group can influence its structure and process. Specifically, leaders tended to emerge in positions with relatively great access to others, and decision-making tended to become centralized in centralized networks. Whether these findings have parallels in the work place remains an unanswered question.

Summary

This chapter reviews the role of the physical environment in small groups, or units of two or more people who exert mutual influence. A few studies in factories and offices suggested an association between the development of voluntary groups with proximity among members' workspaces, including the Hawthorne study in the Bank Wiring Observation Room. Groups formed in neighboring workspaces where conversation was convenient among people who were compatible. Limited evidence also supported the idea that physical enclosure promotes group cohesiveness, particularly through its contribution to privacy. In one study enclosure apparently permitted a group to develop its own norms without external interference. Studies of the role of seating arrangements in group discussions suggested that people address those with whom they can easily make eye contact, and leaders of groups tend to occupy positions that permit maximum eye contact with members of the group. Laboratory research on communication networks associated leadership with relatively great accessibility to members of the group. Practical implications concern the use of inter-workspace proximity and physical enclosure to promote the development of cohesive groups, and the arrangement of rooms for group discussion to emphasize or deemphasize leadership.

Practical considerations

The implications of this limited research are apparently consistent with current thinking in management. Groups may form among people whose workspaces are close enough to permit convenient conversation, provided the people are compatible, and especially if the group is enclosed in its own room or area or separated from other people. Managers may want to take advantage of the physical arrangement of work areas to encourage the development of formal groups, especially autonomous groups (see Chapter 15). Similarly, informal groups might be fostered by clustering people of similar backgrounds, if voluntary association could add to employee satisfaction without interfering with their jobs. On the other hand, managers who want to discourage the development of groups might do so by avoiding enclosure of subsets of personnel. However, informal groups might develop anyway and meet in the coffee room or the parking lot.

For group discussions, the principal importance of the seating arrangement concerns the implicit designation of leadership. If one seating position gives its occupant greater visual access to the group than is possible in other positions, it is the logical location for a leader. To emphasize leadership, a manager might choose a long table with a chair at the head (and none at the other end). A circular table, on the other hand, would de-emphasize leadership.

PART IV

ORGANIZATIONS

This part of the book considers the largest unit of analysis – the organization as a whole. It is the shortest part, consisting of one chapter. The perspective taken here involves a shift from a social-psychological to a systemic view, focusing on the structure and dynamics of organizations. The scale of the physical environment is also larger. It now consists of entire buildings, especially their layout and configuration.

An organizational perspective treats the physical environment differently than a psychological or social-psychological one does. Organizations control their offices and factories, in contrast with individual workers and work-groups who may have only limited control over their environments. Organizations can build, modify, replace, or rearrange their offices and factories, like other resources under their control. So at the organizational level of analysis, the physical environment is more a malleable resource than a fixed entity.

15

OFFICES AND FACTORIES AS COMPONENTS OF ORGANIZATIONS

Scientific literature on the role of the work environment within the organization as a whole is scarce, and this chapter is correspondingly brief. An examination of the treatment of offices and factories in theories of organizations is followed by a discussion of organizational effectiveness and its potential links with the work place. Parallels between properties of organizations and the physical environment are then explored and a general hypothesis is offered: that an organization strives for congruence between certain characteristics of its offices and factories and its structure, climate, and image.

Role of offices and factories in theories of organizations

There are three types of theories on organizations, each of which treats relationships between people and their physical work environments differently. Generally, offices and factories have had a minor role. Classical theories deal with formal rules and roles in the structure of organizations; where the physical environment has had a role it concerns individual efficiency or status. Humanistic theories focus on the human psychological and social consequences of formal organizations; offices and factories represent potential sources of individual dissatisfaction. Systems theories depict organizations as dynamic entities whose components exert mutual influence. Some systems theories have an explicit place for an organization's internal physical environment, notably theories of socio-technical systems.

Classical theories

Theories of organizations generally identified as classical include Weber's concept of bureaucracy, Taylor's scientific management, and their
derivatives (see Howell, 1976; Katz & Kahn, 1978; Tausky, 1978).

Weber's formal bureaucracy. Weber's (1947) theory dealt with two characteristics of organizations that were later treated as their defining features: hierarchy of authority and roles. The theory described organizations
as formal structures of specialized interlocking roles, with specifically
defined individual duties. Each role had a position in the hierarchy of
authority as well as associated duties, both of which defined the incumbent's office or position. Weber's theory emphasized the necessity for
a unitary line of authority, uniform practices, rewards based on performance, and separation of job roles from personal lives.

Weber's theory apparently had no explicit place for the physical environment but implicitly supported the use of status symbols. The concept of "office" included a room designated for an incumbent, appropriate
for his or her rank in the hierarchy of authority.

Taylor's scientific management. Frederick W. Taylor (1911) took the
idea of specialization to its logical extreme. He argued that jobs need
to be broken down into their smallest elements, analyzed to discover
the most efficient procedures, and done according to the "one best way."
He also argued for motivation through pay. His methods of "motion
study" suggested modifications of both jobs and the tools used to do
them, all in the interest of efficiency.

Taylor's theory focused more on the design of tasks than on the
physical environment, but the emphasis on efficiency had a powerful
influence on factories, and later on offices. Taylor redesigned tools and
suggested rearrangements of work-stations for economy of motion.
Economy of time and motion became a central criterion in the design
of factories.

Scientific management depicted workers as motivated by external
forces, principly money and supervision. (This idea was later called
Theory X by McGregor, 1960.) The emphasis on supervision called for
an environment that permitted visual accessibility – or "oversight" – of
workers. The method of motion study also called for visual accessibility
of workers. Whereas Taylor apparently did not explicitly call for work
areas designed for supervision, his ideas probably did a great deal to
promote them.

According to Taylor's theory, the relationship between person and
environment can best be described by analogy to the relationship of a

cog to a machine. The problem addressed in the theory was to keep the human components of an organization operating at peak efficiency.

The theories proposed by Weber and by Taylor, called "machine theories" (Katz & Kahn, 1978), overlooked employees' needs and perceptions. They essentially dehumanized the worker, and in so doing provided an impetus for the humanistic theories.

Humanistic theories

Among the theories usually classified as outgrowths of the human relations movement, two groups of ideas have particular relevance to the work place. These include theories of job satisfaction and theories depicting organizations in terms of interpersonal relations.

Job satisfaction. Abraham Maslow (1943) suggested that each person has a hierarchy of needs, including needs for social relationships and personal growth, which the classical theories of organizations had neglected. As discussed in Chapter 4, Maslow's theory pictured the physical environment as satisfying basic needs for shelter and security. According to the theory, once these needs are satisfied, the individual gives attention to the higher-order needs.

Herzberg's theory of satisfiers and dissatisfiers depicted the physical environment as dissatisfier – a source of dissatisfaction or indifference, but not of satisfaction (see Chapter 4). According to Herzberg's theory, people gain satisfaction from such things as interesting work, autonomy, and social contact.

These theories depicted the physical environment as an element of job satisfaction, but only one of a long list of factors that potentially contribute to job satisfaction. Prominent among those factors were interpersonal relationships.

Interpersonal relationships. After the Hawthorne studies (see Chapter 3), theories of organizations began to take account of the informal and formal relationships among workers. Perhaps the leading theory on this topic was Likert's (1961) linking pin model. This model depicted the relationships of each manager and his or her subordinates as constituting a group or "family." The organization was viewed as a pyramid of overlapping families, interconnected through their common members, who were called linking pins. Unlike the classical theories, this model explicitly recognized the importance of groups or teams.

Likert's theory, like many of its predecessors, had no overt role for the physical environment. However, an earlier theory by George Homans (1950) contained an idea that was at least implicit in many of the humanistic theories: that patterns of interpersonal interaction are associated with physical proximity among workers and the technology of their jobs. Homans also postulated that the more frequent interactions are between people, the more positive their sentiments are toward each other. An implication of Homan's ideas was that cohesive groups form among people whose jobs and physical environments create opportunities for frequent interaction.

The concept of *Burolandschaft* and later ideas on open-plan offices drew upon theories that emphasized interpersonal relationships (see Chapters 2, 12, and 13). Proponents of *Burolandschaft* argued that open, undivided offices promote interaction and therefore lead to better communication, particularly among co-workers whose desks are close to each other (e.g., Lorenzen & Jaeger, 1968). Furthermore, by maximizing communication, an open-plan office was supposed to promote good interpersonal relationships. Advocates of *Burolandschaft* also drew upon systems theories of organizations to suggest that efficient communication in an open-plan office would have beneficial effects throughout the organization because of the interdependency among its elements.

Systems theories

Theories of organizations that focused on interpersonal relationships were also systems theories in that they explicitly recognized the interdependence among the components of organizations. Homans (1950) emphasized the idea that a change in one part of an organization produces corresponding changes in other parts. Other theorists argued that an organization represents an "open system" – that the relationships among internal components depend on the organization's external environment (e.g., Katz & Kahn, 1966).

The physical environment had a major role in the theory of sociotechnical systems (Trist, Higgins, Murray & Pollack, 1963; Rice, 1963; see also Cooper & Foster, 1971). The theory emphasized the importance of the fit between technology and the social structure of an organization. It suggested a general principle – that technology (task characteristics, physical layout, and equipment) needs to complement relationships among workers and their jobs. Applications of the theory usually involved work-groups. The physical environment was typically arranged to define a group's area, or to identify pieces of equipment with groups or specific members of groups.

In summary, theories of organizations have depicted the physical environment in offices and factories in rather different ways, as shown in Table 15.1. Each theory dealt with the physical environment in terms of the main focus of the theory. Weber emphasized formal roles and

Table 15.1. *Summary of roles of the physical environment in theories of organizations*

Theory of organizations	Role of the physical environment
Classical theories	
Weber: Formal organizations	Symbols of office[a]
Taylor: Scientific management	Efficiency (economy of motion)
	Supervision (visual accessibility)[a]
Humanistic theories	
Maslow: Hierarchy of needs	Satisfier of individual's basic needs
Herzberg: Satisfiers vs. dissatisfiers	Potential source of job dissatisfaction
Likert: Linking-pin model	(None explicitly stated)
Homans: Groups	Proximity and accessibility associated with patterns of interpersonal interaction[a]
Systems theory	
Trist: Sociotechnical system	Part of the technological side of an organization (key is fit with social organization)

[a] Implicit in the theory.

implicitly supported the idea of physical symbols of office. Taylor dealt with individual efficiency and job design and focused on economy of motion. Among the humanistic theories, Maslow and Herzberg depicted the environment as a potential satisfier or dissatisfier of individual needs. Homans dealt with interpersonal relationships and recognized the association between physical environments and patterns of interaction. The theory of sociotechnical systems treated the environment as part of the technological component of an organization.

In terms of the framework introduced earlier in the book (Chapter 1), theories of organizations suggest that the physical environment has a role at the individual, interpersonal, and organizational levels of analysis. If so, all three levels of analysis are important for organizational effectiveness.

Organizational effectiveness

This section explores the connections between the physical environment and organizational effectiveness – the central criterion of the adequacy of an organization. After defining what is meant by effectiveness, potential contributions by the physical environment are explored at two levels of analysis: individual and interpersonal. (The organizational level of analysis is discussed in the next section.)

Definitions

Theorists disagree about the definition of organizational effectiveness, but agree on one point: Effectiveness means more than just productivity. Current definitions are multidimensional, including a variety of criteria besides the rate of production (see Nadler, Hackman & Lawler, 1979; Smith, 1983; Steers, 1975). For example, Schein (1972) defined effectiveness in terms of communication, flexibility, creativity, and commitment within the organization.

A few theorists attempted to encompass multiple criteria through inclusive, abstract definitions of effectiveness. For instance, Chris Argyris (1964) defined effectiveness as the extent to which the organization "over time, increases outputs with constant or decreasing inputs" (p. 123), or maintains output with decreasing input. Katz & Kahn (1978) defined it as "the maximization of return to the organization by all means" (p. 255).

For present purposes, *"effectiveness"* is defined an organizations' success in maintaining (1) satisfaction and commitment among its members, (2) communication and coordination within and among its work-units, (3) adequate production, and (4) a mutually supportive relationship with its external environment. The physical environment in offices and factories has the potential to contribute to the first three of these proposed elements of effectiveness.

The individual level of analysis

An organization consists mainly of people, so its effectiveness ultimately depends on their efforts as individuals. Outcomes for the individual – job satisfaction and performance – represent key components of effectiveness. Both may be linked with the work place.

Satisfaction with the job. An individual's satisfaction with the job is important in its own right, but it is critical to organizational effectiveness because of its consistent association with relatively low rates of absence from work and low rates of turnover (see, e.g., Davis, 1977). In other words, in organizations where people experience a high level of satisfaction with their jobs, the evidence suggests that they tend to stay with their organizations and come to work regularly.

Evidence discussed earlier suggests a clear link between satisfaction with the physical environment and job satisfaction (Chapter 4). In turn, other research suggests that a variety of environmental factors are related to satisfaction with the physical environment. These include the ambient conditions – lighting, temperature, air quality, and noise, probably music, and possibly color (Chapters 5–9). Features of the workstation or workspace, such as the floorspace, equipment, chair, and capacities for personalization, privacy, and possibly comfortable conversation are also linked with satisfaction with the physical environment (Chapters 10 – 13).

The connection of the work place with an individual's job satisfaction depends on many factors and probably varies greatly from person to person. Some individuals may regard the physical environment as relatively important, because of personal preferences or job requirements. For each person, different aspects of the work place may be salient. For example, a parts inspector may regard lighting as crucial: a machine operator may see the comfort of the chair as central to his satisfaction with the physical setting.

The contribution of the physical environment to organizational effectiveness through job satisfaction depends on the extent to which each person's physical environment satisfies his or her unique needs. With the members of an organization collectively satisfied with their work environments, the aggregate can be expected to have a higher level of job satisfaction than would otherwise be the case.

Performance. Research on the psychology of the work place suggests that the physical environment influences individual performance through several psychological processes. Ambient conditions – especially heat or noise – can add to arousal, create distraction and overload, or even produce environmental stress. Performance may be improved or degraded, depending on the task.

Most of the demonstrated links between the physical environment and performance represent short-term effects. They may not persist for very long in offices or factories because of adaptation. However, adaptation itself may affect performance indirectly, through changes in work habits or expenditure of effort. If so, the question is how adaptation influences performance by individuals and how these influences contribute to the organizational effectiveness.

In the longer term, the work place can influence performance through its role in job activities. The design of equipment can promote efficiency through controls and displays. The design of work-stations can promote economy of motion through the placement of tools and materials, and through the location of work-stations in relation to frequently used work-areas. Lighting can be critical for the performance of tasks that require the visual discrimination of details. Some tasks call for relative quiet, as noise can obscure useful auditory cues. In brief, the long-term influences of the work place on individual performance depend on the details of the job and the support that the work-station gives the person for performing assigned tasks.

The contribution of the physical environment to organizational effectiveness through performance by individuals depends on the extent to which each person's work-station supports his or her job. If each job is done in a work-station that promotes economy of effort, the collective level of job performance may be higher than otherwise.

In summary, satisfaction with the physical environment is a component of job satisfaction and the physical environment is a potential source of support for the performance of specific jobs. In turn, job satisfaction and individual performance are components of the effectiveness of the organization.

The interpersonal level of analysis

The interpersonal level of analysis deals with the symbolic qualities of workspaces, influences on face-to-face conversation, and the formation and cohesion of small groups. However, potential contributions of the work place to organizational effectiveness at this level of analysis are complicated. This point is illustrated by the case of *Burolandschaft*.

The case of Burolandschaft. As outlined earlier (Chapter 2), "office landscapes" with few walls and no private offices became common in the sixties and seventies. The premise behind open offices was that communication within an organization is easier when co-workers can see each other and are located near their counterparts. The originators of the idea presented the open office as a managerial tool for improved productivity (e.g., Planas, 1974).

Exactly why an organization should become more productive in a completely open office was never quite made explicit. However, the implicit argument was that comunication would improve and that improved communication would in turn lead to higher morale, better decisions, and greater responsiveness of the organization as a whole (see, e.g., Lorenzen & Jaeger, 1968).

The open-plan office fell short of the optimistic expectations. As outlined in Chapter 12, the evidence from evaluation studies yielded mixed results on communication in open offices. Some types of communication improved in some facilities, but confidential conversation often became more difficult. At the same time, people in open offices complained about noise (see Chapter 8) and lack of privacy (Chapter 13).

Testing of the claim that open offices lead to improved productivity was hampered by the lack of an unambiguous criterion of productivity. However, a few postoccupancy evaluations of open offices incorporated ratings by employees of their performance after changing from conventional offices. Mixed results came from two large German studies (Boje, 1971; Kraemer, Sieverts and Partners, 1977) and one U.S. study (Sloan, undated). Another U.S. study showed no change in self-rated output (Zeitlin, 1969); one more showed a decline (Hundert & Greenfield, 1969). In short, some employees in some offices rated their own performance better after changing to the open plan, while others saw no change or worse performance. (Open offices were also supposed to save money and may have done so through the ability to accommodate additional employees within the same floorspace and the flexibility to rearrange offices quickly and cheaply.)

To the extent that *Burolandschaft* and the open-plan office failed to increase productivity, the failure reflects an oversimplified view of the physical environment in offices. The idea that physical accessibility generally promotes communication did not take account of different types of communication. (As outlined in Chapter 13, physical accessibility is probably most important for the choice of the partners in informal communication and for the choice of a medium of formal communication.)

Even if accessibility did lead to generally increased communication (it apparently does not), the result is not necessarily a more productive organization. There are at least two reasons why productivity might not change. First, change in an organization rarely occurs as a consequence of change in only one of its elements (such as the physical layout), while other aspects remain unchanged (Katz & Kahn, 1978). In the case of open offices, employees' jobs and their interrelations usually remained the same – only the physical layout changed. Forces tending toward stability in the organizations probably compensated for disruptions in patterns of activity brought about by the new offices. Second, an organization can only benefit from greater communication when it is insufficient in the first place. In an organization in which communication is already adequate, spending more effort or time at it could detract from other activities that promote effectiveness. If *Burolandschaft* led to improved communication, it probably did so only in organizations with deficient communication. And the benefits could only accrue within the context of broader organizational change.

In brief, the case of *Burolandschaft* illustrates the complexity of the connection between the work place and communication. The relationship depends on the types of communication involved and the pattern of communication that exists within the organization. Furthermore, a successful effort to introduce change in an organization probably requires more than just alteration of the physical environment.

Interpersonal relations and organizational effectiveness. The work place may contribute to organizational effectiveness through interpersonal relations in at least three ways: through individual satisfaction or performance, through links with communication, and through support of the organization's structure. However, the evidence for such contributions is indirect at best.

Research evidence does suggest that satisfaction with the work environment depends on characteristics of the work place relevant to interpersonal relations. For instance, environmental satisfaction has been found higher in workspaces that appropriately display status or express the occupant's self-identities through personalization (see Chapter 11). Similarly, satisfaction with the environment has been linked with privacy (Chapter 13). It is possible (but not empirically demonstrated) that in workspaces that allow comfortable conversation, occupants perform more effectively if their jobs require frequent conversations. Similarly, in workspaces conducive to informal conversation, workers may gain satisfaction from friendly relations with co-workers. Through such influences on individual satisfaction and performance, the work place could potentially contribute to organizational effectiveness.

If the work place contributes to organizational effectiveness through its links with communication, it may do so either as a source of symbolic messages or as an influence on choices in communication. As a symbolic medium, the work place can convey information about status. It is possible that appropriate status symbols add to the effectiveness of the organization. For instance, clear status markers may save time by preventing confusion about peoples' positions. However, the role of the work place as a symbolic medium is limited to conveying information about existing properties of the organization.

Another important symbolic function of the work place concerns the identity of work-groups, teams, and subunits of the organization. For instance, work-groups may be symbolically designated through arrangements of furniture, enclosure by partitions or walls, or locations in separate buildings. However, the symbolic designation of work-groups can only contribute to the effectiveness of an organization in which work-groups are integral components. (In small organizations or subdivisions managed as if they had no subgroups, symbolic boundaries could actually detract from the coordination of efforts.)

If the physical environment enters into individual choices in communication, it may contribute to the effectiveness of the organization, under some circumstances. For instance, in a research firm where informal communication is important for creativity, an environment conducive to conversation may encourage scientists to talk. In a publishing or advertising organization, where formal, collaborative efforts are commonplace, the existence of comfortable conference rooms may lead to more frequent or longer meetings, offering more opportunities for joint efforts, which in turn could contribute to production. However, the work place seems likely to contribute to organizational effectiveness only if it encourages choices in communication consistent with the organization's operations.

In brief, a link of the work place with organizational effectiveness through interpersonal relations depends on characteristics of the organization. Work places may symbolize status or group identity and may figure in choices in communication. Whether this contributes to the general effectiveness of the organization depends on which qualities are symbolized, which choices are encouraged, and how consistent the symbolic messages or choices in communication are with processes of the organization. In other words, the role of the work place in interpersonal relations is a problem for the organizational level of analysis.

Properties of organizations and work places

A central premise of the organizational level of analysis is that features of the work environment reflect or augment properties of the organization. This section outlines the basis for such a premise and discusses some possible connections between features of the work place and organizational structure, climate, and image.

Does the work place mirror the organization?

At least four more or less distinct lines of thought suggest that buildings mirror the organizations that occupy them. First, an historical analysis of thinking by architects and designers indicates at least an implicit acceptance of a connection between properties of organizations and features of buildings (see the historical description by Duffy, 1974a). Second, environmental psychologist William Michelson (1970) advanced the hypothesis of congruence between buildings and people. He suggested that people attempt to create environments congruent with their activities and that buildings incorporate characteristics consistent with the activities of occupants. Third, systems theory implies, among other things, that the components of a system tend toward mutual accommodation, in the service of equilibrium within the system (see Berrien,

1983). Fourth, the theory of sociotechnical systems suggests that organizations operate effectively only when their technological components, including buildings, operate in concert with their social and psychological elements (see Trist et al., 1963).

All these perspectives imply that buildings reflect the properties of organizations. The two systems theories further imply a dynamic striving toward consistency between organizations and buildings. In other words, when buildings fail to mirror organizations, the discrepancy is thought to impel corrective action within the organization. If so, it should be possible to identify specific features of organizations with parallels in features of buildings.

Organizational structure and features of work places

This section discusses the possibility that buildings reflect aspects of an organization's structure. Structure refers to relatively stable characteristics of organizations, particularly its work roles, work-units, and their interrelationships (see, e.g., James & Jones, 1976; Payne & Pugh, 1983). A discussion of the dimensions of organizational structure is followed by an outline of an hypothesis proposed by Francis Duffy (1974b). A list of parallel features of organizational structure and buildings is proposed and a few examples described.

Dimensions of organizational structure. Researchers have attempted to identify dimensions of organizational structure. A dimension is a structural property that can be defined and measured on a single continuum in an organization. Empirical research and theoretical analysis have converged on a fairly consistent list of dimensions. A review of the literature up to 1976, including some empirical studies, identified seven dimensions (James & Jones, 1976):

1. *Size* of the organization (total number of people and net assets)
2. *Centralization* of decision-making, authority, and control in highest-ranking positions
3. *Configuration* of roles and work-units, including the number and size of subdivisions or subgroups, the number of levels in the hierarchy, the span of control (number of supervisees per supervisor), and tall versus flat shape of the organization (tall means many levels of authority with relatively narrow spans of control)
4. *Formalization* of roles, including the extent to which roles are specified, the emphasis on status, and the emphasis on formal channels and written communication
5. *Specialization*, or the number of different jobs or specialties

6. *Standardization* of procedure and specification of tasks

7. *Interdependence* among components of the organization or among tasks

These seven dimensions agree closely with a list identified in another review, by Payne and Pugh (1983). However, these investigators included some of the dimensions as context rather than as structure. Context includes size, interdependence, technology, and other characteristics.

Theorists have called for further research on the dimensions of organizational structure. However, the list presented here provides a starting point for considering the relationship between properties or organizational structure and properties of work places.

Duffy's hypothesis. Architect Francis Duffy (1974a–c) presented what seems to be the only published theory on the connections between organizational structure and the work place. His central hypothesis held that two complex qualities of organizations – bureaucracy and interaction – are associated with two qualities of office environments – differentiation and subdivision.

Duffy's term *bureaucracy* referred to the "tightness with which members of an organization are bound together" (1974c, p. 221). It included the degree of centralization of decision-making, the predominance of professional employees, the importance of the hierarchy of authority, the specification of rules for various jobs, the importance of following the rules, and other features. *Interaction* referred to the frequency and importance of communication among co-workers and between workers and their visitors. (Duffy's bureaucracy encompasses several of the dimensions of organizational structure outlined earlier: centralization, specialization, formalization, standardization, and elements of configuration. Interaction resembles interdependence.)

Duffy's dimensions of the physical environment comprised differentiation and subdivision. *Differentiation* referred to the variety among individual workspaces in floorspace and furniture. Undifferentiated environments were said to contain uniform or similar workspaces, whereas differentiated layouts had several types of workspaces. *Subdivision* referred to the presence of screens or partitions between workspaces. Subdivided layouts were said to contain conventional private offices or enclosed workspaces; unsubdivided layouts were open. Figure 15.1 shows four office layouts that illustrate high and low differentiation and high and low subdivision.

Duffy theorized that organizations with a high degree of bureaucracy have highly differentiated office environments. By contrast, nonbureaucratic organizations were supposed to have relatively undifferen-

LOW SUBDIVISION,
HIGH DIFFERENTIATION

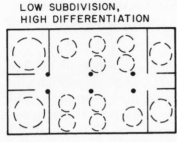

EXAMPLE: "CLERICAL" OFFICE

HIGH SUBDIVISION,
HIGH DIFFERENTIATION

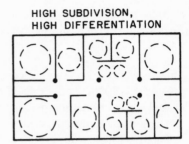

EXAMPLE: "CORPORATE"
HEADQUARTERS

LOW SUBDIVISION,
LOW DIFFERENTIATION

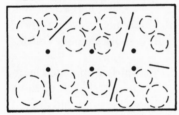

EXAMPLE: "DESIGN" OFFICE

HIGH SUBDIVISION,
LOW DIFFERENTIATION

EXAMPLE: "RESEARCH" OFFICE

Figure 15.1. Four office layouts reflecting high or low subdivision and high or low differentiation of the physical environment. *Source*: Duffy, F.C. (1974a). Office design and organizations: 1. Theoretical basis. *Environment and Planning B, 1,* 105–118.

tiated and homogeneous offices. Organizations with high needs for interaction were supposed to have open, unsubdivided offices, whereas organizations with little interaction were thought to occupy highly subdivided offices. (Duffy apparently accepted the idea that communication is associated with visual accessibility.)

An empirical test of the hypothesis generally failed to confirm it. Duffy (1974b) surveyed 361 office employees from a total of 16 small organizations, and recorded physical properties of their workspaces. He developed indexes of bureaucracy, interaction, differentiation, and subdivision on the basis of the surveys and physical measurements. As expected, organizations with relatively high average frequency and importance of internal communication had relatively unsubdivided offices. However, several other indexes of communication were unrelated to subdivision (see Chapter 12) and, contrary to expectations, highly centralized organizations had relatively unsubdivided, undifferentiated layouts.

The unexpected association of centralization with unsubdivided, undifferentiated layouts apparently resulted from the tendency of people with professional training or high rank to have enclosed, differentiated workspaces. Organizations with a large proportion of professionals or employees of "high standing" were relatively decentralized and allowed their members to share in the decision-making process. (This is consistent with other research, such as that conducted by Hage & Aiken, 1967.) Most of the correlations among properties of organizations and office environments could be traced to the proportion of people with professional training.

In retrospect, Duffy's hypothesis apparently used overinclusive dimensions of organizational structure. The elements of bureaucracy included several important structural dimensions, each of which could be related to different features of the environment. A component of differentiation – specialization (the proportion of professionals) – turned out to be a key feature of organizations. Duffy's physical variables also may have been too inclusive. For instance, "subdivision" referred to the enclosure of individual workspaces as well as the enclosure of subgroups of the organization. In brief, the relationships between organizational structure and features of the physical environment are probably more complex than Duffy had hypothesized.

An alternative hypothesis: parallels between organizational structure and features of work places. An alternative to Duffy's hypothesis may be built on the concept of congruence. A general hypothesis is that each structural dimension of an organization is reflected in one or more physical properties of the work place, in a way that makes the physical structure congruent with the organization (see Michelson, 1977).

Table 15.2 lists the dimensions of organizational structure outlined earlier and proposes parallel dimensions of the physical environment. The table represents an elaborate hypothesis involving eight dimensions of organizations and 11 features of the physical environment proposed as congruent with the dimensions.

The size of an organization may be reflected in its space – the number and size of its buildings. As the number of people in the organization increases, so does its requirement for floorspace appropriate for its people and resources.

The extent to which an organization incorporates technology partially determines its degree of automation. A highly automated organization,

Table 15.2. *Dimensions of organizational structure and properties of physical environments hypothesized as parallel*

Dimensions of organizational structure	Properties of the physical environment
Size: the total number of people and net assets	*Space*: the amount of floorspace in buildings
Technology: the extent to which processes in the organization incorporate technology	*Automation*: the proportion of space devoted to machinery and equipment
Configuration: including numbers and sizes of work-units and the number of levels in the hierarchy	*Delineation of work-units*: through location, enclosure, and physical boundaries
	Differentiation by rank: of groups or individuals, using status markers
Interdependence: among work units and tasks, including work-flow	*Proximity of work-units*: adjacent in the work flow
Specialization: the number of different jobs and tasks included in the organization	*Differentiation by job or task*: of work areas for work-units or individuals
	Enclosure of task areas or work-spaces: for specific tasks or jobs
Centralization: of decision-making, authority, and control to the highest-ranking members of the organization	*Uniformity of workspaces*: within ranks and jobs
	Visual accessibility of work-spaces: within subdivisions, for supervision
Formalization of roles: including role-specification, emphasis on status, and emphasis on formal channels	*Differentiation by rank*: of individual workspaces
	Uniformity of workspaces within ranks
Standardization: of procedures and specification of tasks	*Rigidity of layout*: within buildings and work-units

such as a robot automobile factory, necessarily devotes a relatively large share of its space to machines and equipment. By contrast, a relatively labor-intensive operation such as a factory that does manual assembly of automobiles has to accommodate more people and fewer machines.

The structural configuration of an organization may be reflected in its physical configuration. Specifically, its subdivisions may be delineated by separate locations or buildings or floors within a building. (If not, the subdivisions may have to be delineated in other ways, such as signs or insignia, to avoid confusion among the workers or their visitors.) The status hierarchy of an organization may be reflected by status markers to differentiate groups and individuals. For instance, some factories provide more lavish accommodations for office staff, as a group, than for lower-ranking production workers. Within groups, higher-ranking positions may be differentiated through the status markers incorporated in workspaces. (Evidence for differentiation among individuals by rank is summarized in Chapter 11.)

The degree of interdependence among the work-units or tasks within an organization depends on the nature of its products and on the details of its processes. In offices, the products usually represent information of some kind, and underlying patterns of interdependence may be rather complex. Consequently an office may have an elaborate work-flow, involving both electronic exchange and the physical transfer of paper. In factories with one or more production lines, work-flow involves materials and products that move through the plant.

For a physical work environment to tbe congruent with the organization, it needs to accommodate the work-flow with maximum economy of motion. So work-units or individuals adjacent in the work-flow (or interdependent in their tasks) need to be accessible to one another. Accessibility usually requires physical proximity, and in some cases it requires pathways through walls or other barriers. However, if work-flow is electronic, and if people can gain access to one another through electronic media, physical accessibility may not be critical to work-flow. In general, the greater the interdependence, the more likely the use of a physical layout based on accessibility among work-units.

For organizations with a high degree of specialization, a congruent work place contains corresponding diversity of work-areas and work-spaces. Assuming that each job or task has unique requirements for equipment and working conditions, it is reasonable to expect differentiation of workspaces by jobs. Furthermore, specialization may call for physical separation or compartmentalization of tasks (see Bechtel, 1976). Operations that create noise, dust, or fumes may need to be isolated. People in highly demanding jobs may need enclosed workspaces to insulate against distraction. Workers who converse often may need to be isolated to ensure confidentiality or contain noise. In general, the greater the specialization, the more likely an organization is to have work-areas physically enclosed and differentiated by job.

In highly centralized organizations, work environments may contain highly uniform workspaces that allow visual supervision. Uniform work-spaces reflect minimal latitude for decisions about the work place in lower ranks. (In contrast, diverse and personalized workspaces imply greater latitude in decisions about the work place, which may or may not reflect a policy of decentralization in other matters.) Relatively open work-areas that make for visual supervision are consistent with a philosophy of management that emphasizes supervision.

In organizations with a high degree of formalization, a congruent environment emphasizes formal rules, roles, ranks, and relationships. An office or factory may extend its formal rules to include the regulation of workspaces, which may result in outward uniformity and minimal latitude for personalization (Duffy & Worthington, 1977). Roles may be symbolized in workspaces differentiated by jobs; people in different specialities may occupy workspaces with visible differences related to their work. The work place may also symbolize individual status through workspaces differentiated by rank (i.e., with status markers). Workgroups and subunits may be differentiated according to their relative influence in the organization (e.g., the production department may have more space and more windows than the public relations department).

In an organization with highly standardized procedures, a congruent environment is likely to have a rigidly fixed arrangement. For instance, an office with closely specified rules may also have a fixed layout delineated by structural walls. By contrast, in an organization in which the rules are not closely defined (or frequently subject to change and not easily standardized), the layout may also be flexible. The office may use moveable partitions or modular workspaces. (This proposition resembles Weick's 1979 argument that the equivocality or uncertainty inherent in an organization's structure reflects the uncertainty inherent in its surroundings.)

In summary, eight dimensions of organizational structure are hypothesized as having parallels in features of the physical environment, which tend toward congruence with the organizational structure. This idea represents an hypothesis yet to be tested in empirical research.

Examples of parallels between organizational structure and work places. Office planners and designers have commented on the importance of the consistency between the structural properties of organizations and their buildings. For instance, Moleski and Lang (1982) noted the importance of designing offices to reflect the power hierarchy and other elements of the organization. In reviewing a new building, Duffy (1978) pointed out that "hierarchical differences are reinforced by physical differences between offices occupied by officials of various degrees of grandeur" (p. 598). Similarly, Duffy (1977) noted that two other office buildings represented "attempts to solve the difficult problem of identifying places for small groups within the open plan" (p. 941). Jockusch (1982) also emphasized the importance of office spaces designed to accommodate work-groups.

Factories have also been designed to accommodate and support organizational structures. The most dramatic examples concern factories designed for work-groups, such as the well-known Volvo factory in Kalmar, Sweden.

The Volvo Corporation designed its automobile factory for work by autonomous groups instead of individuals. The result was a redesigned organization in which jobs and supervisory relationships were quite different from those in a traditional automobile factory. Instead of working at one repetitive procedure under close supervision of a foreman, Volvo workers worked at varied tasks in groups with minimal supervision. The groups of 15 to 20 workers had the responsibility of assembling and installing a major component of the automobile such as the steering assembly. Within the groups workers could divide the labor as they chose (e.g., Dowling, 1973).

The Volvo factory provided environmental support for the autonomous work groups by giving each group its own designated work-area (see Fig. 15.2). The new building consisted of joined hexagonal wings. The external walls had large windows; most of the groups had areas next to the window walls. The groups' areas had entrances, separate locker rooms, carpeted coffee rooms, showers, and saunas. The groups were responsible for their own cleaning and maintenance. Production areas had baffled ceilings designed to absorb sound and had specially designed heating, ventilation, and air-conditioning systems.

Operations were highly automated. The groups received materials at their own areas, and mobile carriers brought partially assembled automobiles for installation of the group's component. Each group's area had buffer zones to park incoming and outgoing carriers. The groups were free to develop their own procedures.

A 1976 evaluation of the new Volvo plant suggested that the new design had been successful. On balance, the new plant had been about as productive as a traditional assembly line. However, it reportedly had less absenteeism and turnover and required fewer supervisory personnel (see Katz & Kahn, 1978).

One view of the apparent success of the Volvo factory comes from ecological psychology (see Barker, 1960, 1968; Wicker, 1979). The theory treats the physical environment as part of a behavior setting, or a set of interrelated roles, with people to carry them out, a defined physical location, and associated equipment, props, and materials. Examples include offices and factories, where the interrelated roles are jobs. A central hypothesis of ecological psychology concerns over- and understaffing: occupants of a behavior setting containing fewer people than optimal for carrying out the roles feel highly motivated and involved, and accept extra responsibility to help preserve the setting. By contrast,

Figure 15.2. Group working area in the Kalmar Volvo Plant. A Volvo sits on its motorized carrier in the foreground, while members of the group relax by the windows of their breakfast room in the background. *Source:* Photograph provided by Volvo of America Corporation, Rockleigh, NJ.

overstaffing leads to lower motivation, reduced involvement, and even alienation.

An ecological analysis of the Volvo factory suggests that the new building and reorganized jobs redefined the behavior setting. What had been a large unitary factory became a cluster of small, self-contained, interconnected behavior settings. Each worker's role went from one of hundreds on the assembly line, to one of a small group of 15 or 20 workers. In the groups each worker's contribution was probably more apparent than in the old assembly line. (Perhaps the workers viewed their contributions as relatively insignificant in the traditional arrangement, which alienated them. This could help explain the high rates of absence.) In effect, the creation of autonomous work groups with separate areas transformed each worker into a bigger fish in a small pond.

The Volvo factory is one of a growing number of factories to reorganize for assembly by autonomous groups. Similar experiments occurred at Saab-Scania, in Sweden, and in other factories in Norway and earlier in India (Katz & Kahn, 1978). A growing number of such experiments has been described in factories in the United States (see Zager & Rosow, 1982).

Organizational climate and image

This section considers the connection between the physical environment and two other features of organizations: climate and image. After a discussion of the definitions and components of climate and image, some possible parallels in the work place are outlined.

Definitions. Whereas the term *structure* refers to the formal characteristics of an organization, *climate* is a broader and less precise term. It usually refers to the unique values, style, culture, or collective personality of an organization. According to Porter, Lawler, and Hackman (1975), climate means "the typical or characteristic day-to-day properties of a particular work environment – its nature as perceived and felt by those who work in it or are familiar with it" (p. 456).

However, theorists disagree about the definition of climate. To some it is a collective perception among the members of the organization about the quality of life there (e.g., Tagiuri & Litwin, 1968). To others it is a property of an organization that can be defined and measured independently of individual perceptions (e.g., Payne & Pugh, 1983). Other researchers have argued that climate is not even a property of the organization, but a property of individual perceptions (e.g., Schneider, 1975). However, critics pointed out that if climate is psychological, it is difficult to distinguish from other perceptions related to work, such as job satisfaction and job characteristics (e.g., Guion, 1973).

For present purposes, the term *climate* refers to perceptions of the quality or style of an organization shared among the members of the organization. (This broad definition includes members' shared perceptions of the structure of an organization, and collective perceptions of jobs and their characteristics.)

If possible, the concept of image as applied to organizations is even more vague than "climate." It seems to refer to shared perceptions of an organization held among people outside it. By this definition, image is the public counterpart of the climate of an organization.

Elements of organizational climate. Researchers have defined dimensions of organizational climate similar to those defined for structure. The literature on climate shows less agreement. The following list culled from a review of earlier research represents a reasonably good synthesis (Campbell, Dunnette, Lawler & Weick, 1975, p. 306):

1. *Individual autonomy*, or freedom and responsibility in decision-making
2. *Degree of structure imposed* on the position, including the closeness of supervision and the specification of the details of jobs
3. *Reward orientation*, including general satisfaction and orientation toward profit, promotion, and achievement
4. *Consideration, warmth, and support*, particularly from supervisory practices
5. *Cooperative interpersonal relations among peers*, including presence of conflict, tolerance for conflict, and cooperation among peers (Campbell et al. said they were tempted to add this fifth dimension to their list, but did not add it.)

Organizational climate, image, and the work place. We uncovered no empirical studies of the connection between climate or image and properties of the work place. However, organizational consultants Steele and Jenks (1977) provided a perspective on the use of the physical environment to stimulate change in organizational climate. They identified their own dimensions of climate: (1) "stimulating energy," (2) "improving the distribution of energy," (3) "increasing pleasure," and (4) "improving growth possibilities" (p. 132).

To stimulate energy in an organization, Steele and Jenks suggested the use of visual stimulation (e.g., colors or graphics), central gathering places, and more meeting places, as well as changing the size of spaces to fit "task needs." To improve the distribution of energy, these investigators advocated reducing the "boundary barriers" between groups, reducing actual and functional distances, reducing the "status function" (i.e., status symbols), and building in flexibility. To increase pleasure, they recommended support for personalization, livening up "dead zones" such as corridors and supply rooms, and avoiding sterility. Finally, to improve the possibilities of "growth" (psychological development of individuals), they recommended creating "demand qualities" (by leaving parts of the setting unfinished), sharing decisions about the physical environment, and providing technical support for "tinkering" by individuals who want to alter their settings.

Steele and Jenks's ideas apparently have not been tested in research, although they have been tried in some organizations. Some of their suggestions could result in a favorable climate. For instance, the encouragement of personalization is consistent with a high degree of individual autonomy, which in turn is associated with job satisfaction. The livening up of hallways may convey a general orientation toward employee satisfaction. On the other hand, some of Steele and Jenks's suggestions may lead to unexpected results. For instance, the reduction of barriers between groups may not produce a favorable climate – instead it could undermine the identity of existing groups. Similarly, the addition of more meeting places may not improve the climate if such places are already available, or if they are not used for meetings.

A general hypothesis on the connection of the work place with climate and image is that organizations express their central values in their offices and factories. If so, climate is reflected in the work place (but the work place does not necessarily dictate the climate). For instance, an organization that places a high value on the satisfaction of its members may provide a comfortable work place suited to each individual's needs. By contrast, an organization with little orientation toward employee satisfaction may provide less comfortable accommodations. (However, a lavish office with each workspace tailored to its occupant may not guarantee a positive climate, although it would probably be associated with a high level of satisfaction with the environment.)

For now, the connection between the work place and organizational climate and image seems to be a matter of speculation.

Summary

This chapter discusses the place of offices and factories within the organization as a whole, a topic on which the literature is limited. The treatment of the work place according to theories of organization is considered first. Then possible contributions of the work environment to organizational effectiveness are addressed. Parallels between properties of the physical environment and of the organization are discussed as well.

The role of offices and factories in theories of organizations has varied, but generally the work place has a relatively minor role. Theories of organizations fall into three general categories: (1) classical theories that focus on formal roles; (2) humanistic theories that focus on job satisfaction or interpersonal relations; and (3) systems theories that focus on the interrelations among components of an organization. Among the classical perspectives, Weber's theory of bureacracy focues on formal roles, and implicitly treats the work place as a symbol of office. Taylor's scientific management treats it as a source of influence on individual efficiency, through its support of economy of motion. Humanistic theories related to job satisfaction, by Maslow and by Herzberg, treat the work place as a potential satisfier or dissatisfier of individual needs. These theories suggest that people overlook a satisfactory environment. Humanistic theories based on interpersonal relations, proposed by Homans and by Likert, point to a link between physical accessibility and patterns of interaction among co-workers. Among systems theories, the theory of *sociotechnicial systems* treats the work environment as part of the technical component of an organization, which ideally is meshed with the social component. Taken together, the theories of organizations suggest a role for the physical environment at the level of the individual worker, interpersonal relations, and the organization as a whole.

The contribution of the work place to organizational effectiveness may involve the individual, interpersonal, and organizational levels of analysis. Effectiveness is a general criterion of success of an organization that subsumes individual satisfaction, coordination and communication, production, and a mutually supportive relationship with the organization's external surroundings. For the individual, research and theory suggest that many facets of the work environment can influence satisfaction, some can influence performance, and both are elements of organizational effectiveness. Contributions of a work place to effectiveness through interpersonal relationships are less clear and probably more complex. They depend on symbolic qualities of the environment, its role in the accessibility of workers to one another and their choices in communication, and the consistency between these and properties of the organization.

For the organization, offices and factories may contribute to its effectiveness by supporting or reinforcing certain of its characteristics, including aspects of its structure, climate, and image. Structure refers to relatively stable features, especially roles, work-units, and their interrelationships. (Dimensions of organizational structure include size, centralization, configuration, formalization, standardization, specialization, and interdependence.) Climate refers to shared perceptions of the quality of life within the organization among its members. Image refers to shared perceptions of an organization among nonmembers.

A general hypothesis holds that organizations strive for congruence between features of their offices and factories and corresponding dimensions of their structure, climate, and image.

Practical considerations

Despite the lack of direct, empirical evidence, it is difficult to deny the potential importance of the physical working environment for an organization's effectiveness. The work place apparently can influence individual satisfaction and performance; it also seems to have a role in communication and in the formation of groups. These in turn can contribute to organizational effectiveness.

When considering the organization as a whole, planners of offices and factories need to pay particular attention to the organization's structure, climate, and image. For all three, the physical environment apparently needs to be congruent with corresponding features of the organization for greatest effectiveness.

The structure of an organization encompasses formally defined roles, work-units, and their interrelationships, which under ideal circumstances are mirrored in offices and factories. Individual roles are expressed through the design of work-stations and workspaces. Ideally, variations among work-stations are consistent with the range of jobs and specialties in the organization (its degree of specialization). However, work-stations also vary as a function of rank or status, depending on how formalized and centralized the organization is, how tall the hierarchy is, and how strongly status is emphasized. One way or another, the organization's treatment of status and authority is likely to be expressed in the differences, or lack of them, among its work-stations.

The use of the environment to define work-units depends on the configuration of the organization and on the interdependence among its parts. Work-units integral to the organization may be appropriately delineated through physical enclosure or through separation among units by distance. However, physical distance or boundaries among work-units must also ensure an appropriate degree of accessibility, particularly between work-units adjacent in the local workflow. The planner's problem is to provide enough separation among work-units to allow each to develop its own identity but still provide enough accessibility to permit sufficient interunit contact.

If an organization emphasizes small, cohesive work-groups, each should have enough physical separation from other work-groups to permit the development of its own norms without external interference. At the same time, the members within each work-unit need to be accessible enough to one another to maintain informal, face-to-face contact while working, but separate enough for adequate privacy. This has sometimes been achieved in offices by giving work-units their own wings or suites of workspaces opening onto central clerical and conference areas.

An important issue for planners concerns the stability or permanence of roles and work-units in an organization (as opposed to fluidity). In an organization with a stable, well-defined structure that seems likely to endure, a planner can introduce fixed boundaries among work-units and work-stations. However, if an organization has only a loosely de-fined structure, or if the current structure is only temporary, internal boundaries may need to be easily modified. Modular work-stations, movable partitions, and portable equipment can provide flexibility.

The use of the physical environment to express organizational climate is more subtle and less clear cut than the expression of structure. In effect, the work place is a medium for the expression of the "personality" of the organization. The architect or office planner has to choose the ones most representative of key values of the organization. For instance, organizations that emphasize egalitarianism might have homogeneous work-stations. Organizations that emphasize egalitarianism, autonomy, and individuality might have work-stations that appear to be hetero-geneous (because of individual personalization or participation in their design) but have few of the differences usually associated with status. An organization that places a strong value on individual comfort may call for a plush office or factory; an organization the emphasizes spartan efficiency may try to avoid any appearance of plushness.

For an organization's image – or public face – the first issue is whether the organization wants one at all. Some organizations attempt to have no image; accordingly, their buildings are hidden from public view and inaccessible to outsiders. Others have highly visible buildings and an open-door policy.

If an organization does want an image, it is probably most clearly connected with aspects of the office or factory that are directly visible or accessible to the public. The exteriors of buildings provide an obvious medium for the expression of corporate identity.

In organizations that allow public entry into their facilities, a variety of features may express an organization's image: the size, shape, and design of the entrance; the size, layout, and decoration of entry hall or foyer; the lighting; the artwork (if any); the furnishings, and so on. Depending on how much of the office or factory is accessible, the public image may begin to resemble the organization's internal climate.

Part V

THE FUTURE

The last part of the book deals with the future of the work place. Chapter 16 discusses the evolutionary trends that have shaped offices and factories in the past, and speculates on their continuation into the future. Chapter 17, the concluding chapter, summarizes the research and theory reviewed in earlier chapters, and offers a list of priorities for future research on the psychology of the physical environment in offices and factories.

16
THE FUTURE OF OFFICES AND FACTORIES

Offices and factories have changed during the past century and promise to continue to change. We can only speculate about the shape of things to come, but many experts have offered forecasts. This section summarizes, and adds to, current speculation. Trends are identified that seem likely to play a major role in future evolution of offices and factories, and critical issues for the relationship of workers and their future environments are specified. After the process of evolutionary change is outlined, offices and factories are discussed separately. The chapter concludes by identifying critical issues for the psychology of the work place.

Process of change in the work place

Perhaps the best basis for forecasting the future course of evolution in the office and factory comes from an examination of conditions surrounding their earlier evolution. Past changes have common elements that suggest hypotheses for the future.

Past changes

The history of offices and factories (outlined in Chapter 2) indicates that change usually reflected one of two motives: (1) to improve efficiency or productivity through greater comfort, convenience, or safety of workers; or (2) to satisfy demands pressed by unions or government. For example, soon after 1900 many U.S. factories installed electrical ventilation fans, partly in response to the promptings of unions, and partly in the belief that workers in well-ventilated factories work more productively.

Even the most rapid evolutionary changes in the work place took more than a decade to become widespread. Obsolete environments persisted long after newer ones appeared. For example, electrically lit factories were commonplace in 1900, only a decade after first becoming feasible. But even in the 1980s it is still possible to find factories in which the only light comes from old-fashioned skylights.

Evolution of the work place occurred slowly for at least two reasons. The costs and time required for renovation of existing buildings probably posed barriers to quick changes, even where the owners were convinced that the investment would pay a return. New buildings required years to plan and build, and owners may have been reluctant to incorporate untried technologies. Each new building may have incorporated lessons learned from its predecessors, but it took time.

When change did come to the work place, it often involved the introduction of relatively new technology. For example, many companies of the 1930s housed their expanding clerical staffs in the large, open offices that became feasible with the advent of electrical air-conditioners. Earlier offices usually occupied smaller rooms, where windows provided the necessary ventilation and light. (Other crucial developments, especially steel-frame construction and electric lighting, came earlier.) Organizations were growing larger and more centralized at the time, so the open spaces met a need. In brief, the office changed when the necessary technology was available, and when the changing structure of organizations created a need for it.

Even when new technology was available, evolutionary change sometimes waited decades until favorable conditions prevailed. The most conspicuous example concerned the electric light, which was commercially available around 1880 but only became common in offices after 1930. Until then, most offices drew their light from windows, although many offices were inadequately lit even by existing standards. Several events favored the adoption of electric lighting in offices of the 1930s. Electrical utility companies were providing and advertising inexpensive power. New electrical air conditioners allowed interior rooms to be kept comfortable in summer. And perhaps most important, lighting came to be regarded as an aid to efficiency. This occurred after widely publicized accounts of improved production in factories with electric lights.

The combination of technological advance and organizational change apparently precipitated some evolutionary changes in offices and factories. However, the degree of organizational change varied, from practically none to major reorganization. In cases involving minimal change, organizations substituted a new technology for an existing one, to increase comfort, convenience, or efficiency. (Comfort and efficiency were regarded as closely related to each other for several decades.) For example, the introduction of electric lighting into the office called for little change in the organizations that adopted it. The introduction of the manual typewriter into the office, and later the electric typewriter, merely let people work faster and more efficiently at the same job as before. The details of the jobs changed, but the tasks to be accomplished were practically the same. However, the new technology may have changed work roles through a shift in the ratio of workers to supervisor. Offices and factories contain other examples, predominantly involving new equipment of relatively low unit cost.

Some technological advances brought organizational change through shifts in the relative proportions of certain types of workers. This in turn led to changes in the amounts and types of space they needed. For example, the mainframe computers of the 1960s replaced many clerical workers in offices, but created a demand for a small number of technical workers. One office planner wrote, "an insurance company headquarters is now primarily a computer center where it was formerly a hive of clerical workers" (Pile, 1978, p. 16). The office environment saw the gradual replacement of some huge clerical "pool" offices of the 1930s. These were supplemented by enclosed areas capable of accommodating computers, their noisy supporting equipment, and their relatively few skilled operators. At about the same time, the "programmable controller" (a type of computerized monitor for factory machines) replaced some workers, leaving the factories to accommodate fewer people, including some with greater technical skills.

When technological innovaton led to the replacement of people with machines, change occurred slowly, over several decades. The slow pace of change probably reflects the time required for rebuilding offices and factories. It also may reflect the practice of reducing personnel gradually through attrition. Faster changes, even where they could have been accomplished, might have been resisted by workers and their unions.

Some changes in the work place supported major restructuring of jobs or roles. These changes involved alterations in the physical separation among workers. The most dramatic examples occurred in factories built to accommodate work by groups or teams. New floor plans contained areas designated for work-groups, where the members of each group could conveniently work together but were separated from other groups. The technology necessary for work groups was generally quite simple and well established, as in the famous Volvo plant. (Chapter 14 describes this and other examples.)

The introduction of *Burolandschaft* into offices was supposed to involve organizational change, but it apparently did not (see Chapters 2 and 12). Companies introduced the new office technology (modular, movable workspaces) to replace existing technology (built-in walls) and reportedly realized lower costs and greater flexibility. However, the organizations themselves seem to have undergone little if any change. What was billed as reorganization turned out to be replacement of existing technology by more advanced technology, in the service of organizational goals.

Burolandschaft illustrates a common feature of past evolutionary changes in the work place: a general tendency of promoters of change to overestimate the pace of change. What now appears as evolution was often heralded as revolution, when optimistic forecasters predicted rapid and dramatic changes to accompany developments in the physical environment. Such optimism occurred not only with *Burolandschaft*, but with the electric light, the telephone, and other innovations. In retrospect, changes in the work place were typically slower than predicted.

Another feature of evolutionary change illustrated by *Burolandschaft* is the tendency of promoters to depict the physical environment as an agent of organizational change. The premise underlying this view is that the environment creates change by prompting people to adjust their behavior and, through collective changes, to influence the whole organization. In the case of *Burolandschaft*, open offices were supposed to stimulate conversation between neighbors and thereby increase communication throughout the organization. *Burolandschaft* apparently failed to produce the anticipated increases in communication, consistent with the failure of many earlier attempts to create organizational change through individuals (see Katz & Kahn, 1978). Far from being an agent of change, the physical environment has usually been its servant.

In summary, past changes in the office and factory grew out of a desire to improve efficiency or to satisfy forces from outside the organization. Many changes came from the substitution of new technology for existing technology, with little accompanying change in organizations that used them. In some cases, organizational change created a need for alteration of the physical environment, with accompanying changes in the numbers of workers or their work roles. However, proponents of change often overestimated the impact of new technology.

Hypotheses for future change

Technological development provides the driving force behind change in the work place, but offices and factories only seem to change under certain circumstances:

1. When new technology is seen as allowing more efficient performance of existing tasks without substantial changes in numbers of workers or their jobs, organizations replace the existing technology and revise offices or factories to accommodate it.
2. When new technology offers improved efficiency, but also requires substantial changes in the number of workers or in their work roles, the pace of change slows as the requirement for organizational change increases.
3. With planned reorganization of work roles, change comes quickly in the office or factory to complement and support the reorganization, incorporating the most advanced available technology.

In short, the evolution of offices and factories is expected to occur through adoption of technological advances that serve organizational goals, within limits set by the pace of organizational change.

Changes in the office

Forecasts of change in the office usually point to a cluster of advances in technology collectively called the "paperless office," the "electronic office," or the "automated office." This section outlines these innovations and their likely offspring, and discusses some less publicized innovations, along with implications of new technology for change in the office.

Advances in office technology

The paperless or electronic office represents a vision of the immediate future based on existing, commercially available equipment (see J. Stewart, 1980). One forecast includes an account of the experiences of an actual user of a prototype office:

I go into my office, sit down at a TV screen with a typing keyboard, and call up an index of what's in my electronic "inbox." I can select any or all of the documents for display on the screen . . . I display my calendar for the rest of the week. Finally, I call up the phone log for my telephone messages. So far I haven't touched a single piece of paper. My secretary uses the system's word-processing capability for doing memos. Documents are created, edited on the screen, and kept on disks. They are transmitted electronically and instantaneously. (Ruff & Associates, 1978, p. 23).

This fairly typical example illustrates most of the elements of a paperless office, which usually reside in a VDT with a keyboard, and a nearby telephone or picture-phone. The equipment allows the electronic storage, retrieval, and display of existing documents, the electronic composition and editing of text, the instantaneous transfer of printed text, and the convenient use of advanced telecommunications.

Storage and retrieval of information. Computers conveniently store increasingly massive amounts of information, and people can use sophisticated supporting technology to gain access to and manipulate it. Powerful microcomputers that fit conveniently on a conventional desk top can accomplish tasks once relegated to mainframe computers. Computer files are portable (they can be recorded on small, removable disks or on magnetic tape). With the aid of widely available software (programs for computers), numerical files can be quickly analyzed, and the results displayed as multicolored graphs, charts, or schematic diagrams.

Computers permit quick access to large, remote data bases, which can be consulted on specific issues. For example, a congressional liaison worker kept a computer file of all incoming and outgoing correspondence. When a letter came from a constituent concerning competition in the sale of eggs, the computer file was asked about other letters on the same topic, other letters by the same person, and replies by the congressional office (Vail, 1978). The same liaison worker could have telephoned any of several national data bases using a *modem* (a device that links computers through phone lines) and had a high-speed printer print the references to selected publications of the economics of egg production.

Publicity has focused on the computer to the exclusion of another important and spreading technology: *microfiche* and *microfilm*. These are miniature photographs of documents stored on transparent film that can be projected at readable size onto a lighted screen. Microfiche are flat sheets; microfilms are strips of film rolled onto spools. Commercially available microfiche and microfilm readers are compact enough to fit on conventional desk tops, and even in desk drawers. An advantage of microfilm and microfiche is that their use requires practically no special skill or training.

Advancing technology for the storage and retrieval of information will probably allow more and more data to be stored in smaller and smaller packages. At the same time, the demands in future offices for information will probably continue to increase. The result may be vastly more efficient handling of information, with much more information to handle.

Composition and editing of text. A word processor combines VDT with a high-speed printer and a specially programmed computer. The combination permits its user to type text, see it displayed, and edit it, all electronically. The user can instruct the word processor to print a document onto paper, or send it to a central storage site, send it to specific recipients who have VDTs of their own, or convert it to electronic mail. Variations of this technology also exist for composing, editing, and transferring drawings and diagrams.

Forecasters have claimed that the technology for a voice-activated word processor is imminent (e.g., Toffler, 1980; Uttal, 1982). If so, the potential exists for a machine that takes dictation, displays the text, incorporates editorial changes upon spoken command, and electronically sends the resulting document through a central network to remote locations, where recipients read it on their VDTs, respond, and store the whole exchange in their own computer files.

The emerging technology seems likely to transform secretarial and clerical work. Once machines can convert dictation into finished text, typists might become unecessary:

When you had a clay tablet, you needed a scribe who knew how to bake clay and chisel marks on it . . . today we have scribes called typists. But as soon as the new technology makes it easier to capture the message, to correct it, store it, retrieve it, send it and copy it, we will do all those things for ourselves – just like writing and talking. (Toffler, 1980, p. 191, quoting Vince Giuliano)

However, it is debatable as to whether the machines will replace secretaries or will simply change their duties.

Electronic transfer of text. A collection of innovations loosely called electronic mail allows convenient, instantaneous transmission and reception of printed text, and in some cases even the transmission of diagrams or drawings. Word processors or computers are linked through telephone lines, cable networks, or microwave transmitters; photocopiers are similarly linked; telephone systems can be augmented with printers and displays. As a result, office workers can rely on several systems to exchange written messages quickly with or without paper. (Even the exchange of paper has speeded up with the advent of overnight couriers.)

Advanced telecommunications. The standard telephone gained some new capabilities in the 1970s. Calls could be forwarded (automatically and temporarily routed from one destination to another). New systems permitted conference calls (more than two people talking simultaneously). Telephones became increasingly portable: some versions were designed for use in moving automobiles; others were "wireless." Advancing technology will probably yield inexpensive, compact, portable communicators that allow people to converse conveniently from practically anyplace, no matter how remote.

A variation of the telephone, called the picture-phone, supplies both oral and visual channels; it can be used simultaneously by groups of people in video-conferences. Centers for video-conferences became fairly common during the early 1980s. Meetings conducted through such centers replaced some old-fashioned business meetings involving personal travel. In theory, at least, picture-phones eventually could replace conventional telephones, and video-conferences could replace business meetings, as the technology for video-conferences grows less expensive and more compact.

Another, less publicized development could affect the future of telecommunications: the speech compressor. This machine

speeds up the rate of recorded speech without increasing its pitch, thus avoiding the "Donald Duck" sound we commonly hear when a tape recording is running fast. With a speech compressor, the listener hears the person on the tape talking faster but sounding much the same otherwise. Models in use today can produce speech rates of 300 to 400 words per minute, which is as fast as many people can read. (Vail, 1978, p. 32)

Speech can also be synthesized by machines (Kornbluth, 1982). Voice messages can be converted into computerized signals and transmitted as voice mail to remote destinations (Uttal, 1982).

In brief, existing or imminent technology provides convenient remote communication involving visual, oral, and written channels and permits instant conversion of voice messages to written ones, and vice versa.

Advanced environmental monitoring and control. The ambient environment in a typical office is controlled from a central HVAC (heating, ventilation, and air conditioning) system. The temperature is monitored by sensors in various parts of the building; the central processor starts or stops coolers or heaters, and (in some applications) opens and closes mechanical air vents to maintain the desired temperature in each part of the building. Advances in the technology of temperature sensors, airflow sensors, central processors, thermostats, and supporting equipment promise to make HVAC systems more responsive to local variations in conditions, and therefore more responsive to local users. If current trends continue, the potential will soon exist for offices to incorporate systems that allow each individual in his or her workspace to exert substantial control over the ambient conditions there. One expert envisions offices in which each worker can directly control the temperature, the amount and direction of air flow, the intensity and quality of lighting, and the ambient sound in his or her workspace (Lerner, undated).

In summary, advances in technology relevant to the office create the potential for substantial change in office work, and in the office environment. Whether this potential will be realized, how soon, and with what implications, represent key issues for the office of the future.

Evolution of the office

Few experts question the claim that the typical office of the future will incorporate electronic technology. Indeed, forecasters have treated the paperless office as a foregone conclusion since the mid-1970s, and some have openly wondered what is detaining its arrival (e.g., Uttal, 1982).

Current debate on the future of the office focuses on three questions: (1) To what extent will office work migrate into employee's homes? (2) To what degree will telecommunications replace personal meetings? (3) Will employees participate more in the design of offices? Depending on the answers to these questions, future office environments may differ considerably from those that exist today. However, experts disagree about the potential for change.

Office work at home. Until Alvin Toffler's book *The Third Wave* appeared in 1980, few experts ventured to predict that substantial amounts of office work would occur in employees' homes. However, Toffler's concept of the "electronic cottage" prompted serious debate. Given the choice of using a computer at home to perform tasks usually done in office buildings, he claimed, many would choose to stay at home.

On the opposite side of the debate, futurist John Naisbett (1982), argued that, if anything, automation makes people even *more* eager for the social contact they obtain in the office. The electronic cottage, he claimed, would isolate office workers, and they would strenuously resist.

Evidence consistent with Naisbett's views came from a survey of the opinions of 60 New York stockbrokers whose work involved virtually constant use of computer terminals and telephones in dealing with clients. The survey revealed "a very general sentiment against working only at home." One participant explained his resistance to home work: "this type of industry requires moment-by-moment interaction with co-workers for advice and motivation" (Becker, 1981, p. 193, citing an unpublished study).

So far, events have favored Naisbett's view more than Toffler's. Despite the availability of the technology to support home office work in the seventies, apparently only a tiny fraction of office work took place in homes during the subsequent decade.

On the other hand, past changes in the office environment happened slowly, so perhaps the rarity of home office work only indicates that the change had not yet had time to take hold. Ample precedent does exist for office work at home. Indeed, the practice of working in office buildings only originated during the Industrial Revolution (see Chapter 2). And even now, many self-employed and professional people work at home, continuing the preindustrial tradition. People who routinely work at home include writers, editors, painters, photographers, brokers, sculptors, architects, counselors, designers, consultants, and others (see Campbell, 1982). However, for approximately the past 100 years, employees of large organizations have performed office work almost exclusively in office buildings.

During the 1970s it was so unusual for employees to work at home that an exception made front-page news in *The Wall Street Journal* (Evans, 1976). The story described a group of Weyerhaeuser executives who assembled at a vice-president's suburban home for nearly a week to draft a booklet on employee conduct. The story told of executives working for other companies who wrote speeches, did special projects, or performed creative work. Some routinely spent part of their workweek at home. They had a more or less explicit understanding with their companies that they could schedule working hours as they pleased, but they were responsible for producing specific results. The vice-president at Weyerhaeuser described the agreement this way:

Working at home is consistent with our shift toward flexible hours ... the important thing is getting your job done. It's incidental to us where you do it. (Evans, 1976, p. 1)

What the executives did in their homes resembled the work that self-employed professionals do, but the executives were doing it as employees of large companies.

For an organization to allow its executives to do even creative work at home during a regular work-day represents a departure from prevailing practice. Executives generally have considerable autonomy in their jobs, and may spend a large fraction of their time away from their offices traveling or at meetings. However, their jobs are traditionally tied to their offices, where day-to-day contacts take a major share of their efforts (see Poppel, 1982). So ingrained is the bond between the job and the physical setting that some companies even provide special facilities in the building for those who need to work away from their offices to avoid distraction. An example is McDonald's "think tank" (see Chapter 12). For office work at home to become more than an occasional aberration among executives, the implicit ties between job and office must weaken.

Large organizations of the seventies and early eighties occasionally permitted small numbers of clerical or professional employees to work at home, to accommodate their work habits or their inability to come to the office. Some publicized examples concern computer programmers. For instance, Digital Equipment Corporation had several hundred employees working at home. Data General Corporation had about 25 terminals used "by 50 or 60 people when they preferred to work at home" (Vicker, 1981, p. 56). However, we found no evidence to indicate whether these examples represented isolated instances or widespread practice in the computer industry.

During the late seventies, some companies experimented with clerical work in the "electronic cottage," involving a few employees who could not work in the office. For example Jane Adams, a secretary at the Afgar Company for more than 2 years, had her first child and was reluctant to continue working at the office.

The company simply arranged to have a remote dictation unit and a computer terminal installed in Jane's home . . . it also had a separate phone line installed. Today Jane attends to her household chores, mothers her new daughter, and periodically checks the incoming dictation unit to see if any typing needs to be done. When there is some, she sits at her terminal, transcribes the dictation, and then registers its location in a computer file so her boss can find it. (Vail, 1978, p. 32).

She worked flexible hours, including some times during evenings and weekends, but she could take time off during the regular work-week if she chose to.

For the Afgar Company to send clerical work to Jane Adams's house represented a much greater departure from prevailing practice than Weyerhaeuser's letting a group of executives meet for a few days at a vice-president's home. By allowing Jane Adams to work outside its premises while treating her as an employee (and not a contractor), the company broke with several long-standing traditions. It allowed a relatively low-ranking employee to schedule her own work. It gave up the visual supervision so common in clerical work and instead trusted her to work unsupervised. By allowing her to work outside its premises, the company relinquished control over her working conditions and left open the possibility that her work would be hampered by distractions around the house. The company's equipment also resided outside its premises, adding other risks. However, while the organzation lost some control, it did retain the services of Jane Adams.

Other companies besides Afgar reportedly tried sending clerical work to employees' homes on a limited basis. Continental Illinois Bank arranged for four employees to work at home. The employees said they liked the arrangement, and the bank's management liked it too (Vicker, 1981).

However, problems soon began to surface. Continental Illinois Bank developed difficulties in coordinating the efforts of the workers at home: "It took three people at the office to transfer the work of four people at home," (Johnson, 1983, p. 37). A medical transcription company reported that when its patients became concerned over the confidentiality of their files, its brief venture into home office work ended. Other employers expressed concern about resistance by labor unions and about restrictions posed by laws and regulations. Even so, advocates still contend that office work at home is the "wave of the future."

In brief, the possibility of office work in employee's homes is just that – a possibility. Few organizations have reported trying it. Occasional publicized experiments have involved only a fraction of the employees of any one company and originated primarily to accommodate the convenience of employees.

A critical and unanswered question is, how many employees would work at least part time at home if given the opportunity? Office work at home is unlikely to become common unless a substantial fraction of employees prefer it, and so far there is little evidence that they do.

Assuming that some employees want it, widespread office work at home would require organizational change. The roles of employee and supervisor would need to be redefined, giving the employees more autonomy, flexibility, and responsibility. Perhaps more importantly, while at home the employees would give up personal accessibility to co-workers, opportunities for face-to-face conversation, and the associated informal contact. Electronic communication might substitute for some of the lost contact, but the replacement might be unsatisfactory (Naisbett, 1982). Organizations that depend on informal, face-to-face interaction for internal communication would need to adjust to the decreased opportunities for personal meetings.

Some organizations have partly set the stage for office work at home by introducing flexible scheduling of work (Abbott, 1978; Toffler, 1980). Under *flextime*, everyone on the staff of an organization is expected to be in the building during certain core times. This allows workers to schedule personal meetings during their coinciding hours in the office. To the extent that flextime is feasible, employees could work part-time at home.

However, for office work at home to become common, it has to serve organizational goals. One possible goal concerns the accommodation of employees' convenience, a goal that seems to underlie the movement toward flextime. Another possible goal is economy, which could come from savings realized by providing less office space for larger staffs. (However, these savings could be partly offset by hidden costs of cottage work, such as expensive insurance against accidents to personnel or equipment.) To the extent that organizations value the convenience of their employees, or expect to save money, they have reason to support cottage work.

If work at home does become as common as Toffler (1980) predicts, the requirement for organizational change will probably make the transition a slow one. The only conditions likely to promote revolutionary change include conscious attempts to design – and build from scratch – new organizations based primarily on cottage work.

A shift toward office work at home could have a powerful impact on the use of space in offices. While employees work at home they leave workspaces at the office vacant. Organizations could take advantage by eliminating personal workspaces, and instead letting people share a pool of work-stations. (This arrangement resembles the nonterritorial office discussed in Chapter 11.) For example, 100 office employees who worked mainly at home might share only 50 work-stations in an office building, along with appropriate conference rooms. When employees did come to the office, they might go to vacant spaces or to meetings. Under this scenario, the office building of the future would be a conference center and a checkpoint for a mobile work force.

A critical implication of a mobile office staff that shares work-stations is a potential loosening of the psychological ties between people and the office. If employees spend part of their work time at home, they have more than just one place of work (unless they work exclusively at home). No longer would the job be identified completely with the office building. This could lead to a weakening of three processes described earlier as important in the work environment: (1) the use of workspaces to symbolize status (Chapter 11); (2) the tendency of workers to express their personalities through their workspaces (Chapter 11); and (3) the capacity of the organization to convey its values to employees through their workspaces (Chapter 15). The weakening of these symbolic bonds could conceivably lead people to feel less committed to the organization. At the same time, commitment by the organization to its employees could also weaken.

A second implication of office work at home concerns the organization's loss of control over the conditions of work. Whereas an organization can control the environment in the office, it cannot determine that the employee's home provides an adequate work setting. It has no control, for instance, over the presence of preschool children, or pets, or visiting neighbors. It cannot ensure a comfortable temperature or adequate ventilation. (On the other hand, residents would probably make their homes as comfortable as they could for themselves.)

Where organizations cannot control the conditions of work, they can increase their attention to the results. For instance, instead of paying clerical employees by the hour or the week, a company might pay for completed units of work, such as invoices, pages, or the like. (This possibility has inspired serious reference to the "electronic sweatshop," recalling times when companies mercilessly exploited cottage workers.) Cottage employees might become contractors, with the organization taking responsibility for very little besides supplying the work and paying for the product.

In summary, office work at home is rare, except by the self-employed, but may be feasible in organizations that redefine work roles and use electronic communication. If substantial numbers of employees prefer working part time at home, and if organizations try to satisfy their employees (or try to save money on office space), they might move slowly toward a version of the "electronic cottage." Implications could include the disappearance of some personal workspaces and the weakening of symbolic ties between people and their office buildings, which now include the use of workspaces to signal status, express the worker's self-identity, and reflect the organization's values. Organizations would lose control over employees' working conditions, and might focus more on the results of the work. The "electronic cottage" could eventually change the role of employee to that of contractor and the role of the office building to that of conference center and checkpoint. However, office work at home is unlikely to become common unless a substantial fraction of workers prefer it, and there is no evidence that they do.

Electronic communication. The advent of electronic mail, advanced telephones, picture-phones, interactive computer links, and related innovations raises the possibility that office workers in the future will communicate less through face-to-face conversations and more through electronic media. The new technology permits office employees to work at home, or practically anyplace else, while still maintaining moment-to-moment contact with co-workers.

A substantial shift toward telecommunications among office workers would probably lead to changes in the office environment. If electronic communications begins to replace face-to-face meetings, offices of the future might accommodate the new media by providing specialized facilities such as video-conference centers. The most extreme scenario pictures people as communicating primarily through electronic media and rarely seeing one another in person. This improbable occurrence would largely eliminate the need for central office buildings.

The key question is, can new forms of telecommunication replace a substantial fraction of face-to-face meetings among office workers? The answer depends upon the willingness of workers to exchange the rich and varied exchange available in a personal conversation for the expediency of a video-conference, electronic message, or interactive computer session.

One possibility is that electronic communication will replace meetings that people regard as least important. People may still prefer face-to-face conversation for exchanges involving strangers, prolonged meetings, negotiation, persuasion, or informal conversation (see Chapter 12).

Organizations experimented in the early eighties with video-conferences to save travel. For instance, a group of 10 executives of Westinghouse, including six from New York and four from Pittsburgh, held a meeting from their own cities through AT&T's Picturephone centers. The six New Yorkers avoided the trip, which would have taken 4 hours each way, instead walking 10 minutes to a building near their offices.

[T]hey sat side by side in a 16 by 20 foot conference room in front of a
bank of four television cameras and two large monitors. Each participant
was strung with a microphone around his neck. (Hilton, 1981, p. 23)

The Pittsburgh executives occupied a similar room in their city. The conference proceeded as planned, closely following the agenda, with little banter and digression. Participants did have some minor troubles, such as knowing when to talk ("everyone spoke at once") and how to proceed. One participant commented, "we were a little stilted and formal with each other. Frankly, I missed the camaraderie, too. But I spent another six hours at my desk in New York" (p. 23).

So far organizations have approached video-conferences slowly and cautiously. By 1983, only "about 12 large corporations [had] installed their own video conference equipment. And American Bell rent[ed] video-conference rooms to the public in only 11 cities" (Gottschalk, 1983, p. 35). The hesitant response to video-conferences at least partly reflects the discomfort and unfamiliarity among users: "we've found that people feel awkward on video-conferences, and it inhibits creativity . . . ," said a manager whose company tried and rejected the idea. Another expert noted:

[P]eople who have watched television for twenty years have built up all
kinds of cultural expectations . . . they expect to see . . . polished performers
reading a script without a hair out of place. In contrast, executives or

managers . . . tend to have their ties askew, don't always look at the camera, . . . and seem unsure what to say. (p. 35)

Some people at video-conferences were embarrassed by being on camera when they believed they weren't. Others were discomfited by the unexpected appearance of their superiors in the audience. Technical problems also occurred, such as the bright footlighting that made one group of executives look like a "satanic worship society" (Gottschalk, 1983).

The examples suggest that video-conferences can replace meetings only when individual users develop enough skill to feel comfortable using the new medium. The same was probably true of telephones when they first began to appear in office buildings in the late 1800s.

One area in which video-conferences are already replacing meetings is in education, through televised seminars, lectures, and workshops. Seminars demand less of participants than meetings do; those who attend seminars can just sit and listen as if watching TV, perhaps interjecting questions by telephone or VDT. Producers of "TV seminars" report that large audiences have simultaneously attended televised lectures in cities across the country. Such seminars allow busy lecturers to reach large audiences without traveling. Participants can see valuable presentations without leaving their own cities. Unfortunately, some promising TV seminars failed to attract enough subscribers to meet expenses, prompting one expert to observe that the successful seminar needs to provide information either to help viewers make money or to help them stay out of jail (Bulkeley, 1981).

The anecdotes suggest that a video-conference represents an acceptable substitute for a meeting only when travel makes the meeting difficult or impossible. Like a telephone call, a video conference represents the choice of expediency. It is selected when the meeting is not important enough to warrant the time and expense of travel but still has a high enough priority to warrant an exchange involving voice and visual communication. One expert suggested that office workers use video-conferences for lower-level, lower-risk meetings (Gottschalk, 1983).

A video-conference clearly provides a pale substitute for a meeting. Participants can see and hear one another but still cannot perceive the peripheral cues that let them feel truly acquainted. And no video-conference call permits conversants to go to a restaurant, a bar, a museum, or another local attraction after finishing the formal agenda. Such joint activities may provide a backdrop for the kind of contact that builds personal relationships. By eliminating travel, video-conferences also eliminate stimulation and new experience. Electronic meetings may be efficient, but are certainly not personal or stimulating.

The fact that a video-conference represents an expedient substitute for a meeting makes the conference itself into a message. The initiator of an electronic conference says, in effect, that the purposes of the meeting, or the people involved, do not warrant a personal trip. When someone wants to convey the message that "this is a top-priority meeting," he or she probably travels. In short, face-to-face meetings are in no danger of extinction. Video-conferences, like telephone calls, may take a share of routine communication, but only a share.

Electronic communications will probably lead to changes in the office environment. One likely change is the appearance of video-conference centers in office buildings of even modest size. Advancing technology will also create the possibility of an inexpensive picture-phone on every desk, but office workers may keep this innovation at a distance. An old-fashioned telephone lets people talk without attending to appearances. A picture-phone on the desk would literally put its user on camera, and make appearances important. This could give people more communication than they want. On the other hand, a video-conference center in the office building would provide convenient access to picture-phones when needed, but enough control over their use to avoid unwanted TV appearances.

If large numbers of office workers begin to work part time at home, the office building might evolve into a communications center, where the occupants spend most of their time holding meetings, video-conferences, computer conferences, and the like. The vision of the office as a "social watering hole" (see Chapter 13) could become its primary mission. If so, office buildings will probably begin to resemble small convention centers more than concentrations of work-stations.

In summary, electronic communication provides a potential substitute for face-to-face meetings, but it is likely to replace only those meetings with lowest priority. Telecommunication permits visual and auditory exchange but provides only a pale substitute for a personal meeting. Anecdotes concerning video-conferences suggest that people have difficulty in becoming accustomed to these media; organizations have moved very slowly to adopt them. Facilities for video-conferences will probably become common in office buildings of the future, but picture-phones may not appear anytime soon on individual desks.

Participation by employees in the design of offices. Some experts envision a greatly expanded role of employees in the design of offices of the future. Paul Dickson's (1975) book, *The Future of the Workplace*, pointed to the unique experiment at the Federal Aviation Administration building in Seattle in which workers exercised substantial responsibility in the design of their new offices (see Chapter 11). Designer Walter Kleeman (1982) noted that participative design offers potential solutions to problems experienced by office workers who are confronted with a changing technology. Environmental psychologist Franklin Becker (1981) criticized traditional practices of organizations, which have given workers at most a minor part in decisions concerning their environments.

Ideally, participative design offers the potential for tailoring the work place to its users. To the extent that office workers have a voice in decisions about the size, furnishing, color, arrangement, lighting, or layout of their workspaces, the environment may meet their needs better than it would without their participation. Even if the resulting environment is practically the same as one planned entirely by a team of architects and designers, the act of participation by itself could make the environment more satisfying to the workers who use it. (Research described in Chapter 11 suggests that participation is associated with satisfaction with the work environment.) However, office workers may have only limited knowledge and understanding of the impact of the environment, so their participation would need guidance by experts.

Barriers to the use of the participative design come from the practical difficulties involved in its introduction. One serious obstacle is the lack of an organizational vehicle for incorporating employees in the planning of their environments. Indeed, organizations seem to have long-standing procedures that exclude employees' participation (Becker, 1981). Participative design clearly calls for substantial organizational change.

Organizational change to accommodate participative design might be slow and difficult, for two reasons. First, the professional architects, planners, and designers who now have responsibility for designing offices may resist a change that would restrict their autonomy and complicate their jobs. (Involvement of office workers in decisions about their workspaces could add substantially to the time and personnel required to plan an office building or a renovation.) If office planners did resist the change, their resistance might be sufficient to stop it entirely. Office planners represent a powerful coalition within an organization, and they may have a strong interest in maintaining the status quo. Such coalitions generally impede organizational change (Katz & Kahn, 1978). Furthermore, the cooperation of office planners would be essential in implementing participative design, and they might not cooperate.

A second practical problem is that organizations need persuasive reasons to revise existing procedures in favor of participative design. The potential benefits of such changes might include improved satisfaction among employees or improved efficiency brought about by better designed offices. However, participation would carry costs, particularly the time spent by employees in participating and in organizing themselves to do it. The management of an organization would have to be convinced that the potential benefits justified the costs.

On the other hand, some developments favor participative design of offices. One is a wider trend toward participative management. Experts point out that management is increasingly involving workers in decisions affecting their work (e.g., Peters & Waterman, 1982; Zager & Rosow, 1982). Another favorable development concerns the increasing use of modular workspaces. Since the advent of systems furniture (see Chapter 2), partitions and furniture that define workspaces are portable and often interchangeable, so they can easily be rearranged. In consequence, the layout of an office can be changed relatively quickly and inexpensively. Such flexibility gives the occupants the opportunity to tailor certain aspects of the environment to their needs. (Whether the organization permits them to take advantage of this capacity is a separate question.)

In summary, participation by workers in decisions about their offices ideally offers a means of tailoring the environment to its occupants, but practically entails some problems. Barriers to participative design include the need for organizational change, possible resistance to change by office planners, and the need by organizations for a persuasive reason to adopt it. On the other hand, the trends toward participative management and the widespread use of flexible, modular workspaces could presage more participative design.

Changes in the factory

Potential changes in the factory can be summed up in one word: automation. This section outlines some of the innovations in automation that have occurred or are imminent in factories, and their implications for work environments of the future.

Advances in automation

Automation of the factory comprises the use of machines to do operations formerly done by hand. Practically every facet of manufacturing is involved. With the advent of computerized controllers and robots, it is technically possible to manufacture many products untouched by human hands (see Forester, 1980). Automation involves advances in the technology of manufacturing and in the physical environment of the factory.

Technology of manufacturing. Advances in microelectronics, computers, and associated equipment permit automation of at least six facets of manufacturing (Bessant, Braun & Moseley, 1980; Toffler, 1980):

1. *Transfer of materials, parts, and products.* Computerized carriers can move materials through factories from warehouse to production and from production to shipping, and all steps in between. In the manufacture of paper, for example, automated carriers move finished rolls of paper from production line to warehouse and onward to waiting trucks or trains.
2. *Regulation of physical conditions in production.* Through sensors and computer-controlled systems, it is possible to closely monitor and regulate temperature, humidity, pressure, and other factors in a production line and its surrounding environment.
3. *Automated operations.* Machines with computerized controllers and robots can perform a wide range of operations, including cutting, drilling, machining, and welding; mixing and pouring; painting and spraying; assembly of some components; and other operations (see Zermeno, Moseley & Braun 1980). In some industries, all operations along an entire production line can be automated (e.g., pharmaceuticals, food, beverages, plastics).
4. *Small-batch production.* Computer-controlled production machines can be programmed to produce small batches of items of a given size or type, then reprogrammed to make another type of item. For example, a computerized laser can cut cloth to a pattern fast enough to be economical while cutting one piece at a time. As a result, the manufacturer can produce a piece of clothing of a selected size and pattern on demand (Toffler, 1980).
5. *Sampling and quality control.* In operations that require frequent sampling and analysis (e.g., foods, beverages, metals, chemicals), it can be done by computerized robots. Some kinds of inspection can be automated through the use of mechanized scanners, photoreceptors, sensors, and cameras. The result is the potential for a new standard of quality control.
6. *Integration and coordination of manufacturing processes.* Computers can be used to control and coordinate whole factories, including inventories of supplies, records of routine maintenance, allocation of work, inventories of finished product, warehousing, sales records, shipping, and billing.

In brief, it is technically possible to automate most aspects of manufacturing. Even the design of manufacturing processes can be automated (Gold, 1982).

Physical evironment. The physical environment for factory workers has the potential to be as comfortable as that in an office. Many of the most dirty and hazardous jobs have been automated, and others soon will be. Many of the remaining jobs in factories involve the programming, monitoring, and control of machines in quiet, self-contained production lines. Advances in heating, ventilation, and air-conditioning systems, along with advances in lighting and acoustics, have already made it possible for factories to be quite comfortable.

Monitoring and inspection of processes in hostile environments can be done remotely. (In the manufacture of metals, remote monitoring is already occurring.) As a result, it is technically feasible to provide a comfortable environment for factory workers in most industries.

Evolution of the factory environment

Evolutionary change in the physical environment of the factory represents a component of broader change in the technology of manufacturing. Technological change also involves evolution in jobs and organizations (see Tushman & Moore, 1982), which themselves may call for new physical accommodations in the factory.

Forecasts concerning environments in factories are more difficult than in the office, for two reasons. First, factories are more varied, because of their greater variety in technology. Second, the configurations of factories depend on their products, and the types of products manufactured depend on a variety of other factors, including the availability of labor, materials, and markets.

Within the context of varied and unpredictable changes in manufacturing, at least four questions arise concerning the relationship between people and their physical environments: (1) Will the factory incorporate a rising standard of physical comfort for workers? (2) Will factories begin to use modular work-stations similar to those found in offices? (3) To what extent will factories be designed to accommodate workgroups or teams? (4) To what extent will factory work be done in workers' homes?

A rising standard of comfort? It is now technically possible to design comfortable factory environments in many industries, and the future may bring new reasons for doing so. One may be the need to attract highly skilled employees through a pleasant work place. Experts expect automation to bring a decrease in the total number of jobs in any one factory. However, the fewer jobs may require greater skill, and skilled employees may be costly to recruit and replace. If so, organizations may devote more resources to attracting and retaining employees, including comfortable factory environments.

A higher standard of comfort in factories may also grow out of the need for special conditions in certain industrial processes. For example, the assembly of some types of computer chips requires a dust-free atmosphere. Some operations in food- or beverage-processing require constant temperatures and humidities. Where factories have the means to monitor and control the ambient environment, these may be used to regulate the environment of people as well as processes. This may become even more feasible as the number of workers declines.

A third reason for a rising standard of comfort in factories concerns the automation of jobs that place people in uncomfortable or hazardous conditions. As such jobs are automated, reasons for subjecting people to harsh conditions may begin to disappear. And workers may demand more comfortable environments when there is no obvious reason not to have them.

The standard of comfort may also rise because of improvements in the technology of HVAC. As factories are built, they are likely to use the latest equipment. So as older factories are replaced by newer ones, the standard of comfort may advance with the capacities of HVAC equipment.

In brief, the standard of comfort in factories may rise for at least four reasons: (1) advances in the technologies of environmental control, (2) automation of jobs done in hostile conditions, (3) the need to maintain special conditions in certain industrial processes, and (4) the need to attract and retain skilled workers.

Modular work-stations? During the past 15 years, offices have increasingly incorporated modular work-stations assembled from interchangeable, interlocking, and portable components. It seems probable that this trend will spread to factories, particularly in the so-called high-tech industries involving electronics. Modular work-stations are already available for factories, as in the example depicted in Figure 16.1.

Accommodation of work-groups? If the current trend toward the design of jobs for groups continues (e.g., Zager & Rosow, 1982), it seems likely that factories will be designed accordingly. If so, more factories may resemble the Volvo plant (described in Chapter 15) with separate areas designated for groups.

However, current trends toward the use of work-groups may not continue. One reason for assembly by groups is to build variety, autonomy, and cooperation into otherwise monotonous jobs (see Hackman & Oldham, 1981). However, the monotonous jobs now being assigned

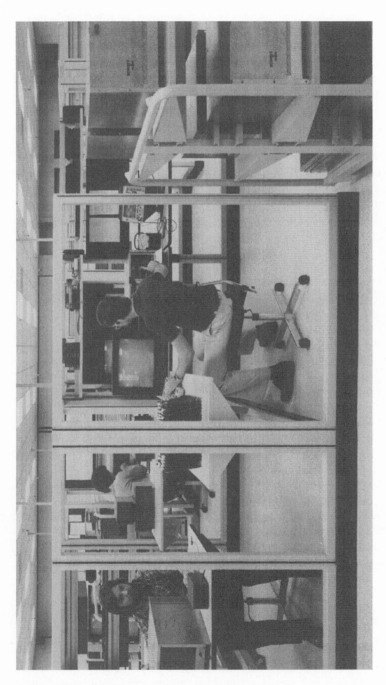

Figure 16.1. An example of modular work-stations for factories: Action Factory™ by Herman Miller, Inc. *Source:* Photograph provided courtesy of Herman Miller, Inc., Zeeland, MI.

to groups could begin to disappear. As assembly is automated, more factory work may be done by fewer people (Main, 1982). Some of the remaining work may be more technically demanding; some may involve little more than overseeing and maintaining machines as they operate. It remains to be seen whether the next generation of factory jobs can or will be designed for work-groups.

Cottage industry? Factory work could conceivably begin to move into workers' homes. The availability of inexpensive computers and industrial machines may permit people to produce and market certain products on a small scale. Traditional cottage industry has often involved clothing, foods, and handicrafts (e.g., Kilpatrick, 1981). Advances in communication could even create more possibilities for marketing out of the home than ever existed before. However, experts have erroneously predicted a trend toward greater cottage industry before (e.g., Hubert, 1897, p. 310).

Electronic communications in combination with robots could create a new type of cottage industry based on the remote monitoring or operation of factory machines. If industrial processes can be operated remotely, there is no technical reason why workers could not operate them from home. It is conceivable that the majority of jobs involving the monitoring of machines could be done through video display terminals or home computers. Perhaps even such jobs as machining could be done from home.

Although the potential for remote factory work probably exists now, it may be slow to develop. Some of the same concerns raised by home office work also apply to home factory work. Employees may sacrifice the social contact they obtain at factories (in some jobs it may be minimal anyway). Organizations may have to change, incorporating new designs for jobs and new relationships with workers. (For example, workers might become contractors.) And organizations would need reasons to change; for example, cottage work would have to either save money or promote satisfaction among employees. To the extent that factory work at home requires organizational change, it may develop slowly if at all.

In summary, future factories may bring a rising standard of comfort, increasing use of modular work-stations, greater accommodation of work-groups, and the possibility of more cottage industry or remote factory work. However, only the rising standard of comfort represents a likely change; the others are doubtful.

Issues for environmental psychology

The future evolution of offices and factories raises at least three issues for a psychology of the work place. First, change itself represents a topic for study. Little is known about the conditions that precipitate change, or the processes through which it occurs. A second issue concerns adaptation by individuals, who not only may see changes in the physical environment but their jobs and the supporting technology as well. The question is, how do individuals accommodate to changes in job, technology, and environment, as all three evolve? Third, organizations are changing, and the dynamics of organizational change are still not well understood. In particular, a question for the psychology of the work place concerns the role of the work environment in the evolution of organizations. Evolution of offices and factories seems to grow out of organizational change, but perhaps some change also grows out of the environment. These and other issues remain for the future.

Summary

This chapter speculates on the future of offices and factories, on the basis of history and current literature. After a general discussion of the process of change in the work place, some advances in technology in the office and factory are described along with their possible implications.

Past changes in the work environment have generally grown out of applications of new technology designed to improve efficiency or to satisfy pressures from outside the organization. Some changes in the work place have involved the substitution of a new technology for an older one, with little concomitant change in organization. Others have involved substantial changes in organizations, such as modifications of jobs or numbers of employees. Changes in offices and factories have usually proceeded at the pace of organizational change, sometimes quite slowly.

Advancing technology has created the possibility of electronic or "paperless" offices, in which people do most of their work through computers combined with electronic communication. One question for the office of the future concerns the possibility that workers will do part or all of their work from their homes. The electronic cottage may be convenient, but would call for the sacrifice of some face-to-face contact with co-workers. Even so, it seems likely that future office workers will spend a larger fraction of their workdays at home.

A related question for the office of the future concerns the possibility that electronic media for communication, such as video-conferences, will replace face-to-face meetings. Electronic communication may be expedient, but it sacrifices much of the richness of personal meetings. So electronic communication seems unlikely to replace more than a fraction of personal meetings, probably the least important ones.

The future of offices also concerns the question of the possibility of greater participation by workers in the design of their workspaces. According to experts, participative design promises to improve the work place. However, the necessity for change in current practices by organizations probably will make the shift to participative design a slow one.

Technological advances allow the potential for automation of many aspects of manufacturing and stringent control over working conditions. Within the context of increasing technical possibilities, one question for the future of factories is whether the standard of comfort will rise. For several reasons, it seems likely to do so.

A second question for the factory of the future concerns the use of modular work-stations analogous to those used in offices. The prevalence of modular work-stations seems likely to increase.

A third question concerns the accommodation of work-groups in factories. If the trend continues toward the increasing use of work-groups, the physical environment may be modified to accommodate them. However, it is difficult to tell how long the trend toward work-groups will continue.

A fourth question for factories of the future concerns "cottage industry," or factory work at home. Even if technically feasible, it may be slow in coming, for several reasons. The main obstacle is the necessity of organizational change.

For a psychology of the work place, the future raises several issues, including processes of change and patterns of adaptation among individuals and organizations.

17
CONCLUSIONS

This chapter summarizes the conclusions suggested by the research and theory described in the rest of the book. It also identifies unanswered questions and sets priorities for future studies. First, the current research literature and its limitations are considered and a context established for substantive conclusions about the work place. The three units of analysis – the individual, interpersonal relationships, and the organization – are then discussed in turn. The chapter ends with a wish list of priorities for future research.

Existing research and theory

The research and theory on the psychology of the work place reviewed in earlier chapters are extensive in some areas but in general are limited. Available theories can account for some of the empirical findings, but they leave gaps. Even so, the literature provides a basis for tentative conclusions.

1. *Empirical research is limited.* This book cites 290 empirical studies related to the psychology of the work place. However, the research literature reviewed here is far from satisfactory. For some topics there were only a handful of studies; for others there were many laboratory experiments but few field studies. Factories have been particularly infrequent sites of research. For very few questions did a sizeable body of evidence exist, containing a balanced combination of laboratory and field research.

Empirical research seems to have been limited mainly by the kinds of questions asked in the past, as well as the methods used to study them.The oldest questions concerned the influences of the ambient environment on individual performance, and the predominant strategy of early research was the laboratory experiment (e.g., J.J.B. Morgan, 1916). Following precedent, more than half the empirical studies cited in earlier chapters comprised laboratory experiments on the effects of ambient conditions on individual performance (see Table 3.3).

After the Hawthorne studies, research reports on job satisfaction began to appear, and surveys became common. At the same time research began to focus on the role of the physical environment in interpersonal relations. There were field studies on this topic, but very few. Only lately have psychologists begun to ask questions about the role of the physical environment in the organization. Accordingly, studies at the level of the organization have been rarest of all.

2. *Current theories deal with many issues, but leave important gaps.* The oldest and best developed theories concern the influence of the work place on performance and grow out of laboratory experiments. The concepts of arousal and overload deal with the short-term influences of the environment that can be studied in the laboratory. Unfortunately, these concepts do not deal as well with long-term influences on performance (which, coincidentally, have not been studied as much).

Theories on the role of the environment in individual satisfaction are chiefly derived from industrial psychology. They treat satisfaction with the physical environment as a component of job satisfaction. Unfortunately, theories on job satisfaction do not deal adequately with the tendency of people to become unconscious of their physical surroundings as time passes.

Theories about the role of the physical environment in interpersonal relationships and organizations represent little more than isolated hypotheses or tentative applications of general theories. For instance, Altman's theory of privacy regulation (see Chapter 13) provides a general perspective on the use of physical settings to establish social boundaries and regulate interpersonal exchange. But how the theory applies in offices and factories remains to be specified. Similarly, systems theory (Chapter 15) provides a general perspective on the role of the physical environment in organizations. The theory implies that organizations strive for congruence between their social structures and properties of their offices and factories. However, this is only an hypothesis and if accurate, the details remain to be worked out.

3. *Current literature warrants tentative conclusions.* Taken together, the empirical research and related theory provide a basis for plausible hypotheses on most of the issues addressed in this book. Some hypotheses have fairly adequate research support. Many others represent little more than educated guesses. For one reason or another, many conclusions must be tentative.

The individual and the work place

Conclusions on the relationship between the individual worker and the physical environment concern the environment as a whole and its specific properties. These include lighting and windows, temperature and air, noise, music, color, and work-stations and supporting facilities.

The work place as a whole

4. *Short-term influences on performance can involve psychological arousal, stress, overload, or fatigue.* All these processes have been connected with short-term improvements in performance, short-term decrements, or both. The effects apparently depend on characteristics of the task and of the individual. However, they can change over time, or even disappear, through *adaptation*.

5. *Long-term influences on performance depend on adaptation but are not well understood.* Perceptual adaptation involves the well-established tendency of people to perceive extreme or intense environmental conditions as less extreme or intense with the passage of time. Behavioral adaptation involves changes in habits to accommodate the environment. Both forms of adaptation probably attenuate the influences of the environment on performance. However, they remain virtually unexplored in the work place.

UNANSWERED QUESTION: How do people adapt to physical environments in offices and factories, with what consequences for satisfaction and performance?

6. *Satisfaction with the physical environment is a component of job satisfaction.* Research on job satisfaction leaves little doubt that the physical environment in offices and factories contributes to a person's general satisfaction with the job. At the very least, inadequate or uncomfortable work places are associated with dissatisfaction with the environment. However, consequences of the physical environment for job satisfaction have varied widely from one person to another. One possible reason is variation in the extent to which the physical environment fulfills peoples' needs. It may gain importance to the individual's satisfaction as it leaves basic needs unfulfilled. Research evidence is generally consistent with the idea that the environment operates more as a "dissatisfier" in that it creates dissatisfaction when inadequate.

UNANSWERED QUESTION: What factors differentiate people who attach great importance to their physical environments from those who attach relatively little importance to it?

7. *Workers in offices and factories may overlook or ignore their physical environments.* Two major theories on job satisfaction suggest that workers pay little attention to the work place as long as it is adequate. Satisfaction is thought to come from other aspects of the job, such as the work itself. However, workers may be unaware of the extent to which the physical environment contributes to their satisfaction, because of adaptation, habits of attribution, or a tendency to ignore low-priority inputs.

UNANSWERED QUESTION: To what extent does the physical environment contribute to job satisfaction through processes beyond conscious awareness?

Lighting and windows

8. *The intensity of lighting affects performance by influencing the visibility of details.* For tasks involving visual discrimination of small details, research suggests an association between the intensity of lighting and performance. (Performance has been relatively poor in dim light.) Laboratory research has shown that intensified light improves the visibility of details. The effect of lighting is most pronounced for difficult discriminations, but minimal for easy ones. Furthermore, the intensity of lighting seeems to follow a principle of diminishing returns: added light brings smaller and smaller gains in visibility. As people age, the optimal intensity of lighting increases. On average, an older worker requires brighter light than a younger worker for the same task.

UNANSWERED QUESTION: Does the intensity of lighting affect performance for reasons other than its influence on the visibility of details?

9. *Glare can create dissatisfaction and distraction.* Bright reflections from reading materials or equipment, or bright lights in a worker's field of vision, can create uncomfortable or debilitating glare. Evidence is scant but consistent in associating glare with dissatisfaction with the environment. One laboratory study found that bright light within the field of vision led to involuntary diversion of the individual's gaze; such phototropism may render glare a potent source of distraction.

UNANSWERED QUESTION: What are the major sources of glare in offices and factories, and what proportions of employees are bothered by them?

10. *Intensity of lighting is associated with satisfaction with the environment, up to a point.* Research in offices suggests that brighter light brings greater satisfaction, but there is an optimum range beyond which the light becomes too bright. Very bright light can apparently bring complaints and eye problems. (Official standards call for brighter lighting in the United States than in other industrial nations; there is reason to suspect that the U.S. standards may be excessive.)

11. *People respond favorably to windows.* Limited evidence suggests that office employees appreciate working near windows for the view outside, as well as for the natural lighting.

UNANSWERED QUESTION: To what extent does a nearby window contribute to a worker's satisfaction with the physical environment?

Temperature and air

12. *Temperature represents a common source of dissatisfaction in the work place.* Surveys among office and factory workers found that from one-tenth to one-half complained about the temperature. Workers sometimes found their environments too cold, sometimes too hot, and sometimes too variable. These complaints may reflect inadequacies in heating or cooling of offices and factories. They probably also reflect the wide variation in individual preferences regarding indoor climate. The relationship of dissatisfaction with the temperature and dissatisfaction with the job remains largely unexplored.

UNANSWERED QUESTION: Do people prefer variable climatic conditions over constant conditions and, if so, what ranges of variation?

13. *Uncomfortable but tolerable heat is associated with relatively poor performance of several types of tasks.* This hypothesis has fairly strong support. Four of six studies in factories, and one in an office, found warm temperatures to be associated with relatively low output. An extensive literature of laboratory experiments has found tolerable heat associated with relatively poor performance in four types of tasks: (1) sustained mental tasks that called for fine motor coordination or rapid scanning and lasted at least 60 minutes; (2) motor tasks that called for continuous eye–hand coordination and lasted at least 30 minutes; (3) highly demanding vigilance tasks that continued for 2 hours; and (4) dual tasks. The decrements in performance in the laboratory occured at temperatures uncomfortable enough to bring complaints in most work places.

14. *Air pollution may create dissatisfaction.* A few surveys suggest that air pollution annoys workers in offices and factories. A large fraction of non-smokers may be particularly irritated by cigarette smoke from their co-workers who smoke.

Noise

15. *Noise represents a potent source of dissatisfaction among office workers.* Surveys found from 20% to 50% of office workers annoyed by unwanted sounds, particularly in open offices. Sources of noise especially associated with dissatisfaction included conversations among co-workers and the ringing of telephones. One study found noise from conversations among co-workers to be associated with dissatisfaction with the job.

UNANSWERED QUESTION: How prevalent are complaints about noise among factory workers, from what sources, and with what consequences for their satisfaction?

16. *Predictable noise is associated with influences on performance of several types of tasks in the laboratory.* Studies of regular or constant noise found it to be associated with decrements in performance in four circumstances: (1) at onset or offset of noise during clerical tasks; (2) during some highly demanding motor tasks; (3) during highly demanding vigilance tasks, when the noise was very intense (100 decibels); and (4) during dual tasks with very intense noise (100 decibels). (On the other hand, constant sound enhanced performance in certain special circumstances.) The effects of predictable noise appeared to reflect an increase in arousal caused by loud noise, the masking of valuable auditory feedback by noise, or distortions in judgment brought on by arousal in loud noise.

UNANSWERED QUESTION: To what extent is predictable noise associated with decrements or increments in performance in offices or factories?

17. *Unpredictable noise is associated with relatively poor performance of most tasks in the laboratory.* Laboratory studies of intermittent or irregular noises found them to be associated with decrements in performance under five circumstances: (1) during clerical tasks immediately after onset or change in noise; (2) during mental tasks involving mental calculation or short-term recall; (3) during highly or moderately demanding motor tasks; (4) during all but the simplest forms of vigilance; and (5) during dual tasks. Decrements in performance generally involved errors and apparently reflected distraction of attention. Some research found errors particularly likely to occur during the few seconds following loud bursts of noise. Most of the findings concerned relatively brief work-sessions, so they could not take account of adaptation.

UNANSWERED QUESTION: To what extent is unpredictable noise associated with errors in the long-term performance of tasks in offices or factories?

Music

18. *A large proportion of factory workers may prefer to work to music.* Three early studies in factories found that more than 85% of the workers said they enjoyed listening to recorded music while doing repetitive jobs. (The most recent study cited on this point was published in 1966.)

19. *Music may bring slight increases in output in factory work.* Research on the effects of music on factory workers showed small, but consistent, gains in output. (Only a few of the gains were statistically significant, so this is merely a plausible hypothesis.)

UNANSWERED QUESTION: How prevalent is the use of recorded background music in modern offices and factories and what, if any, effects does it have on workers?

Color

20. *Color has no demonstrated effect on satisfaction or performance.* Experts have made extravagant claims about the influences of color, but research supplies essentially no corroboration for these claims. If color contributes to satisfaction, it probably does so through favorable attitudes, which may develop when the colors in a work place agree with occupants' preferences. However, these attitudes may diminish in intensity as time passes and perceptual adaptation occurs.

21. *Color may influence perceptions of the size or temperature of a room.* This is a tentative conclusion. Limited evidence suggests that light colors make a room appear relatively large. Experts claim that some colors make walls appear closer than they are ("advancing" colors), while others create the illusion of distance ("receding" colors). One out of our four laboratory studies suggests that in "warm" colors people actually experience slightly warmer temperatures.

UNANSWERED QUESTION: Can color schemes influence workers' moods or attitudes, and if so, do they affect job satisfaction?

Work-stations

22. *Satisfaction and performance in a work-station depend on a variety of features and on the characteristics and activities of the occupant.* A work-station contains a variety of components, each with many important details. The individual's comfort, satisfaction, and performance depend on these and on his or her bodily dimensions, tasks, and specific work habits. As a result, the relationship between person and work-station is highly complex.

23. *Key components of work-stations include displays and controls of equipment and supportive items such as chairs and work-surfaces.* The model of the man–machine system emphasizes the importance of displays and controls. Surveys of office employees indicate the importance of chairs and work-surfaces, as well as the layout of the work-station for ease of access to equipment, tools, materials, and supplies. Research has seldom dealt with the question of long-term adaptation in work-stations.

UNANSWERED QUESTION: Over the long term, how are features of work-stations associated with adaptive changes in habits of work, and how are these changes related to individual satisfaction or performance?

24. *The amount of floorspace included in the work-station is associated with satisfaction with the environment.* This tentative conclusion is based on two field studies. Floorspace may also be related to other outcomes, such as performance, through its relevance to crowding or interference of workers with one another's activities. Floorspace is also a traditional symbol of status, and its connection with satisfaction with the environment may reflect its symbolic properties.

25. *A large fraction of U.S. office workers find their chairs comfortable.* This conclusion is based on three surveys done in the United States. One survey found that only about one-third of the participants rated their chairs comfortable, while another found more than 80% of those surveyed to be comfortable in their chairs.

26. *Equipment in offices and factories can create discomfort, stress, and possibly job dissatisfaction.* This conclusion is illustrated by extensive research on video display terminals (VDTs) in the office. Adverse effects on job satisfaction may stem from changes in job characteristics brought about by the design or capabilities of new equipment.

UNANSWERED QUESTION: What long-term effects does an uncomfortable or stress-producing piece of equipment have on the user?

Supporting facilities

27. *Practically no evidence exists on the psychological impact of supporting facilities such as restrooms, lounges, and eating areas.*

UNANSWERED QUESTION: What qualities of supportive facilities are related to workers' satisfaction with their physical environments?

Interpersonal relations

Conclusions at the level of interpersonal relationships concern the role of the physical environment in social-psychological processes. These include symbolic messages, communication, privacy, and the formation and cohesion of groups.

Symbolic workspaces

28. *Given the opportunity, a large proportion of office workers personalize their workspaces with work-related or personal objects.* This conclusion is based on one study, so it is tentative.

UNANSWERED QUESTION: In factories in which people have individually assigned work-stations, how prevalent is personalization?

29. *Personalization of workspaces is associated with satisfaction with the physical environment.* This tentative conclusion is based on indirect evidence from a handful of studies in nonwork settings and on one study of office workers.

UNANSWERED QUESTION: To what extent is personalization of workspaces associated with job satisfaction?

30. *Workers treat their workspaces as territories (zones of control) and use them to regulate social contact.* This plausible hypothesis derives from Altman's (1975) theory of the regulation of social contact, but it apparently has no empirical support in offices or factories. One study suggested that some office workers are more territorial than others.

31. *Participation by workers in the design of workspaces, while rare, is associated with satisfaction with the environment.* Surveys of office workers found that only a small fraction of them participated in the design of their workspaces. One study found that among those who did participate, satisfaction with the environment and job was higher. (Another study found that minimal participation was associated with lower satisfaction than no participation; only those with substantial participation had greater satisfaction with the environment.) Higher satisfaction could be an outcome of self-expression through the environment or a concomitant of job autonomy.

32. *Many features of workspaces symbolize status in the organization's hierarchy of power.* Research and anecdotes suggest that traditional signs of rank include location, accessibility, floorspace, furnishings, personalization, and other features. These items are widely used and recognized as status markers, but no single item seems to approach universal use. Limited evidence suggests that scarce resources are the most desirable status markers.

33. *Congruence between formal rank and physical features of workspaces is associated with satisfaction with the environment.* This hypothesis derives from Adam's (1953) theory of status congruency and is supported by research on one relatively large sample of office workers.

Communication

The role of the physical environment in interpersonal communication hinges primarily on its influences on the convenience or comfort of face-to-face conversations. Most of the relevant research consists of field studies on the relationship between proximity and communication and on laboratory studies on conditions surrounding conversations.

34. *The use of face-to-face conversation as a medium of formal communication increases with the proximity of conversants' workspaces.* This is a plausible hypothesis. Analysis suggested that for formal communication where the initiator has discretion about the medium, the choice of face-to-face conversation over other media depends on convenience. (For formal exchanges that seem to demand a face-to-face conference, convenience may be a relatively minor concern.) Two field studies of offices found that the amount of time spent in formal face-to-face communication was unrelated to the average inter-workspace proximity. Two other studies of offices indirectly suggested that conversations between specific pairs of people were associated with the proximity of their workspaces.

UNANSWERED QUESTION: Under what conditions do people choose to conduct formal communication by means of face-to-face conversation?

35. *The likelihood of informal conversation between co-workers increases with the proximity of their workspaces.* This conclusion represents a hypothesis that has limited but consistent support. For informal conversation, the initiator has discretion about his or her partner or may make the choice partly upon the basis of convenience. A few field studies and case studies provided evidence consistent with this idea.

36. *Office and factory workers tend to choose friends from among co-workers who occupy nearby workspaces.* A few field studies found friendships among people in adjacent workspaces, where conditions allowed them to talk with each other during work. However, friendships only formed among a fraction of the neighboring workers who conversed, and often involved people with similar backgrounds.

37. *Visual accessibility among workspaces in open offices is not consistently associated with communication.* Studies that assessed ratings of communication in open offices found mixed results. Open offices were sometimes associated with relatively frequent informal contact or interdepartmental contact. However, open offices were often associated with difficulties in holding confidential conversations.

38. *Gathering places for conversation outside of workspaces develop in convenient, central areas used for everyday activities.* This is a plausible hypothesis based mostly on anecdotes and experts' opinions.

UNANSWERED QUESTION: What environmental conditions are conducive to the development of gathering places in offices or factories?

39. *Arrangements for comfortable conversation provide opportunities for eye contact at distances of up to about 10 feet.* Research evidence suggests that people can easily adapt to a variety of seating arrangements. However, beyond a certain distance it may be difficult to converse.

40. *Conversations held across desks or tables involve greater psychological distance than do those without desks or tables.* A handful of studies of offices consistently suggests that desks or tables are seen as psychological barriers. In some circumstances, however, psychological distance may be preferred.

41. *Conversations held in comfortable or pleasant environments are relatively long and positive.* This is a tentative hypothesis based on mixed evidence. An early laboratory study found pleasant surroundings to be associated with relatively positive responses to pictures of other people. Other studies found noise or heat to be associated with insensitivity or negative attitudes. Nevertheless, other evidence suggested that shared stress can lead to liking or attraction between people working in the same environment.

UNANSWERED QUESTION: Do pleasant settings lead to favorable attitudes among co-workers?

42. *As background noise becomes louder, conversation becomes more difficult.* This is well established. Acousticians have specified the relationship between intensity of background noise and the maximum distance at which a conversation can take place in a normal voice under various conditions of noise.

Privacy

Privacy refers to the management of information or the regulation of interaction. In work environments, privacy usually connotes an intentional retreat from unwanted observation, audition, distraction, or interruption. Among the resources for privacy in a work environment is physical enclosure of workspaces. Of the few studies on privacy, most concerned physical enclosure.

43. *Both actual and desired physical enclosure vary among individuals and among jobs.* Studies of office workers' preferences on the number of people per room found that only a fraction preferred private offices. For many, the optimal number of people per room was between two and seven per room. (However, in one study most office workers occupied rooms with more people than they preferred.) Field studies of offices consistently found people in high-ranking jobs (such as managers, supervisors, and professionals) in relatively enclosed workspaces, consistent with the idea that enclosure symbolizes status.

44. *Physical enclosure of workspaces is associated with privacy, but the relationship depends on the job.* The association between enclosure and privacy is fairly well established, but the evidence that it varies by job is limited. One study found particularly strong connections between physical enclosure and conversational privacy among managers and between enclosure and isolation from intrusions among professional and technical employees.

45. *Privacy is associated with satisfaction with the physical environment.* Several field studies found privacy to be correlated with environmental satisfaction. In one study, different facets of privacy were particularly related to environmental satisfaction in different jobs.

UNANSWERED QUESTION: Are job-related forms of privacy associated with job performance?

Small groups

46. *Small informal groups tend to form among workers whose workspaces are close together.* A few studies suggest an association between proximity of workspaces and the formation of small groups. This occurred in conditions that permitted conversation among people while they were at their workspaces. Informal groups apparently developed only among people who were personally compatible (a small fraction of those whose workspaces were easily accessible).

47. *Physical enclosure of a small group is associated with cohesion.* This conclusion is plausible but not well established. One case study showed that a cohesive group dissolved when it lost the physical enclosure that supplied privacy and allowed maintenance of its norms. Another field study found mutual friendships more common in small, enclosed office areas than in a large, open area.

UNANSWERED QUESTION: Does the physical enclosure of work-groups in offices or factories enhance their cohesiveness?

48. *In group discussions, people tend to address those with whom they can easily make eye contact.* Several laboratory studies found seating arrangements that allow eye contact to be associated with a relatively high likelihood of conversation. (If so, a circular seating arrangement may be most conducive to interchange in a group.)

49. *In group discussions, leadership is associated with relatively prominent or visually accessible positions.* Laboratory research on group discussions at rectangular tables found that potential leaders tended to choose a chair at the "head" of the table and that occupants of these chairs tended to emerge as leaders. Similarly, laboratory studies of restricted communication in groups found leaders most often in central positions in artificial communication networks.

Organizations

Conclusions on the role of the work place in the organization as a whole concern two issues: the contribution of the physical environment to organizational effectiveness, and the connection between properties of organizations and characteristics of offices and factories.

50. *The physical work environment contributes to organizational effectiveness through influences on individuals, interpersonal relationships, and the organization.* Effectiveness is defined in terms of multiple criteria, including individual performance and satisfaction, interpersonal communication, cohesion of work-groups, and the integration of the organization. There is evidence that the physical environment has a role at the levels of the individuals and interpersonal relationships. However, evidence at the level of the organization is scarce.

UNANSWERED QUESTION: Do properties of offices and factories at the scale of the organization contribute to organizational effectiveness?

51. *Physical characteristics of offices and factories mirror the organization's structure.* The plausible hypothesis has little supporting evidence. A correspondence may exist between specific dimensions or properties of work places and dimensions of organizational structure.

UNANSWERED QUESTION: Do physical characteristics of work places mirror aspects of organizational structure? (If so, which ones, and how closely?)

52. *Organizations strive for congruence between properties of their work places and aspects of their structures.* This is also an hypothesis, and it represents another unanswered question.

53. *Physical characteristics of offices and factories may mirror an organization's climate and image.* This is a speculative hypothesis more than a conclusion. Organizational climate has been defined in many ways. (Experts disagree about not only its definition, but also its usefulness.) Climate often refers to shared perceptions of qualities of an organization among its members – regarding such things as efficiency, cohesiveness, responsiveness, progressiveness, openness vs. secrecy, and so on. Similarly, image refers to shared perceptions of qualities of an organization by non-members, including customers and the general public. It seems likely that features of the work place contribute to, or even help create, such perceptions.

UNANSWERED QUESTION: Are features of the work places associated with shared perceptions of the organization among members or non-members? (If so, which features?)

Work places of the future

Conclusions about the future of work places represent nothing more than educated speculations. They are based on the history of offices and factories and on current literature.

54. *The future evolution of offices may depend on the extent of the use of new technology for communication.* Advances in the technology of information processing, including new types of computers and electronics, have created new possibilities for office work. The technology raises two questions: (1) to what extent will office work of the future occur in workers' homes, and (2) to what extent will electronic forms of communication replace face-to-face meetings? If home office work or electronic meetings become popular, the character of the office environment may change – it may resemble a conference center more than a concentration of work-stations.

55. *The future evolution of factories hinges on the incorporation of automation.* Factories of the future appear likely to take advantage of major advances in automation and integration of operations. The increasing use of computer-aided manufacturing and robotics appears inevitable, although the pace of change is difficult to predict. As factories incorporate more automation, one likely consequence is change in the numbers and characteristics of jobs. Accompanying evolution of the physical working environment depends on at least three key questions: (1) To what extent will factories incorporate a rising standard of comfort? (2) To what degree will work in future factories be organized around groups or teams? (3) To what extent will factory work occur in workers' homes, either as cottage work or as remote control of factories? Depending on the answers to these questions, factories of the future could be rather different from what they are now.

Priorities for future research

Given a research literature that leaves so many unanswered questions, an obvious conclusion is that much research needs to be done. However, some questions appear more urgent than others. For each of the three units of analysis, this section identifies a few key issues, after setting priorities on the units of analysis themselves.

Units of analysis

So far, research has focused most on the individual and least on the organization as a whole. In future, these priorities need to be reversed: organization first, individual last.

The most pressing area for empirical study of the physical work environment concerns connections between work places and organization as a whole. In particular, researchers need to identify parallels between physical properties of offices and factories and aspects of organizational structure.

Questions concerning interpersonal relationships also need to be pursued, although some research has already been done. Key questions concern communication and the formation of groups.

Research on the relationship between the individual and the work place has gone sufficiently far in some areas and not far enough in others. However, research focusing on the individual has a longer history and has resulted in a larger literature than for other units of analysis. For this reason alone, future studies need to emphasize interpersonal relationships and organizations.

The individual and the work place

Future research on the relationship between the individual and the work place needs to depart from past precedent in two ways: settings for research and questions for study.

Settings for research. Earlier research emphasized the laboratory over the work place. The factory was particularly neglected. As a result, the literature contains ample evidence on questions that can be answered in the laboratory. On the other hand, many questions concerning offices and factories remain to be studied.

Future research needs to emphasize actual work environments, especially factories. When the laboratory is used, it should be as an occasional adjunct to naturalistic research. A lack of methods need not impede research in natural settings; adequate methods exist (see, e.g., Zeisel, 1980).

Questions for study. Perhaps the most urgent issues at the level of the individual concern adaptation. Over the long term, how do people adapt to work environments? To what extent does adaptation involve changes in job activities? Does adaptation carry costs?

Interpersonal relationships

Research on the connection between work places and interpersonal relationships essentially needs to continue along the same lines as in the past. Many of the key questions have been addressed, but only in a handful of studies.

One of the most urgent questions concerns the role of the physical environment in communication. Future studies need to distinguish between formal and informal exchange and to investigate links between choices in communication and proximity of workspaces for pairs of people.

Another pressing issue concerns the formation and cohesion of groups. A few small studies suggest plausible hypotheses, but these need to be tested in work places.

A third issue, largely uninvestigated, is the role of environmental factors in gathering places.

The organization

If the psychology of work places has an uncharted frontier, it is the connection between physical environments and organizations. Research on this issue is so scarce that even the exploratory work remains to be done. Yet organizational effectiveness is a central issue in industrial-organizational psychology. An interesting question is whether organizational structure is mirrored in the work place. This issue remains largely unexplored.

In brief, research on the psychology of the work places leaves a substantial agenda of unanswered questions. At the top of the list is research on the organization as a whole.

Summary

This final chapter presents a series of 55 conclusions on the psychology of the work place along with some unanswered questions. The conclusions deal with the current literature on offices and factories; the influence of the work place at the levels of the individual, interpersonal relationships, and the organization; and the future of the work place. Priorities for future research are suggested.

Current literature on the psychology of the work place, at least as reviewed here, is quite limited. For only a few questions does the empirical evidence provide enough support to warrant a strong conclusion. For most issues, conclusions are limited.

For the individual worker, key outcomes include satisfaction with the physical environment as well as job satisfaction and job performance. Aspects of the work place potentially related to these outcomes include lighting and windows; temperature and air; noise; music; color; workstations; and supporting facilities. Of 27 specific conclusions on these issues, perhaps three or four are well established.

At the level of interpersonal relationships, key issues concern symbolic qualities of workspaces; face-to-face communication; privacy; and the formation or cohesion of groups. All these processes potentially involve a variety of aspects of the physical environment, particularly the characteristics of individual workspaces that differentiate people or limit their accessibility. A total of 22 specific conclusions are advanced. Of these, perhaps three are well established.

Research and theory are least well developed the level of the organization. The central issues concern the contribution of the physical environment of organizational effectiveness and the possibility that characteristics of the work place mirror characteristics of the organization's structure or climate. Four conclusions are advanced, all of which are tentative.

Speculations on the future of the work place are based on extensions of history and current literature. The key questions concern the pace of automation in offices and factories as well as the concomitant pace of organizational change.

There is no shortage of topics for future research, but the issues of highest priority involve the organization as a whole. Future research needs to emphasize actual work setting over the laboratory and to focus particularly on the factory.

REFERENCES

Aaronson, B. S. (1970). Some affective stereotypes of color. *International Journal of Symbology*, 2(1), 15–27.

Abbott, W. (1978). Work in the year 2001. In E. Cornish (Ed.), *1999: The World of Tomorrow*. Washington, DC: World Future Society.

Abrahamson, M. (1969). Position, personality, and leadership. *Psychological Record, 19*, 113–122.

Acking, C. A. & Kuller, R. (1972). The perception of an interior as a function of its color. *Ergonomics, 15*(16), 645–654.

Adams, E. T. (1896). Artistic engine-room interiors. *The Engineering Magazine, 10*(6), 1046–1058.

Adams, J. S. (1965). Inequity in social exchange. In L. Berkowitz (Ed.), *Advances in Experimental Social Psychology*, Vol. 2 (pp. 267–299). New York: Academic Press.

Adams, S. (1953). Status congruency as a variable in small group performance. *Social Forces, 32*(1), 16–22.

Aiello, J. R. & Thompson, D. E. (1980). When compensation fails: Mediating effects of sex and locus of control at extended interaction distances. *Basic and Applied Social Psychology, 1*(1), 65–82.

Aiello, J. R., Epstein, Y. M. & Karlin, R. (1975). Effects of crowding on electrodermal activity. *Sociological Symposium, 14*, 43–57.

Aldrich, H. E. (1979). *Organizations and environments*. Englewood Cliffs, NJ: Prentice-Hall.

Aldrich, H. E. & Pfeffer, J. (1976). Environments of organizations. *Annual Review of Sociology, 2*, 79–105.

Alford, L. P. (Ed.). (1924). *Management's Handbook*. New York: Ronald Press.

Allen, E. C. & Guilford J. P. (1936). Factors determining the affective values of color combinations. *American Journal of Psychology, 48*(4), 643–648.

Allen, L. (1901). Heating and ventilating the machine shop. *The Engineering Magazine, 21*(1), 75–80.

Allen, M. A. & Fischer, G. J. (1978). Ambient temperature effects on paired associate learning. *Ergonomics, 21*(2), 95–101.

Allen, R. W., Ellis, M. D. & Hart, A. W. (1976). *Industrial Hygiene*. Englewood Cliffs, NJ: Prentice-Hall.

Allen, T. J. & Gerstberger, P. G. (1973). A field experiment to improve communications in a product engineering department: The nonterritorial office. *Human Factors, 15*(5), 487–498.

Allport, F. H. (1920). The influence of the group upon association and thought. *Journal of Experimental Psychology, 3*(3), 159–182.

Altemeyer, R. A. & Jones, K. (1974). Sexual identity, physical attractiveness, and seating position as determinants of influence in discussion groups. *Canadian Journal of Behavioral Science, 6*(4), 357–375.

Altman, I. (1973). Some perspectives on the study of man–environment phenomena. *Representative Research in Social Psychology, 4*, 109–126.

Altman, I. (1974). Privacy: A conceptual analysis. In D. H. Carson (Ed.), *EDRA 5: Man–Environment Interactions: Evaluations and Applications, The State of the Art in Environmental Design Research – 1974* (pp. 3–28). Milwaukee: Environmental Design Research Association.

Altman, I. (1975). *The Environment and Social Behavior*. Monterey, CA: Brooks/ Cole.

Altman, I. (1976). Privacy: A conceptual analysis. *Environment and Behavior, 8*, 7–29.

Altman, I. (1977). Privacy regulation: Culturally universal or culturally specific? *Journal of Social Issues, 33*(3), 66–84.

Altman, I. & Chemers, M. (1980). *Culture and Environment*. Monterey, CA: Brooks/Cole.

Altman, I. & Vinsel, A. M. (1978). Personal space: An analysis of E. T. Hall's proxemics framework. In I. Altman & J. Wohlwill (Eds.), *Human Behavior and Environment: Advances in Theory and Research*, Vol. 2 (pp. 181–254). New York: Plenum.

Appley, M. H. & Trumbull, R. (1967). On the concept of psychological stress. In M. Appley & R. Trumbull (Eds.), *Psychological Stress* (pp. 584–595). New York: Appleton-Century-Crofts.

Archea, J. (1977). The place of architectural factors in behavioral theories of privacy. *Journal of Social Issues, 33*(3), 116–137.

Ardrey, R. (1966). *The Territorial Imperative*. New York: Dell.

Argyle, M. & Dean, J. (1965). Eye contact, distance and affiliation. *Sociometry, 28*, 289–304.

Argyris, C. (1964). *Integrating the Individual and the Organization*. New York: Wiley.

Armstrong, R. B. (1972). *The Office Industry: Patterns of Growth and Location*. Cambridge, MA: M.I.T. Press.

Arnaud, L. (1952). The tall building in New York in the twentieth century. *Journal of the Society of Architectural Historians, 11*(2), 15–18.

Arnold, H. L. (1896a). Modern machine-shop economics. II. *The Engineering Magazine, 11*(2), 263–269.

Arnold, H. L. (1896b). Modern machine-shop economics. III. *The Engineering Magazine, 11(3)*, 469–477.

Aronson, E. & Carlsmith, J. M. (1968). Experimentation in social psychology. In G. Lindzey & E. Aronson (Eds.), *The Handbook of Social Psychology*. 2nd ed., Vol. II (pp. 1–79). Reading, MA: Addison-Wesley.

"As They Used to Look." (1917). *System, The Magazine of Business, 32*, 728–729.

Averill, J. R. (1973). Personal control over aversive stimuli and its relation to stress. *Psychological Bulletin, 80*(4), 286–303.

Ayoub, M. M. (1973). Work place design and posture. *Human Factors, 15*(3), 265–268.

Ayres, L. P. (1911). The influence of music on speed in the six day bicycle race. *American Physical Education Review, 16*, 321–324.

Azer, N. Z., McNall, P. E. & Leung, H. C. (1972). Effects of heat stress on performance. *Ergonomics, 15*(6), 681–691.

Babbie, E. R. (1975). *The Practice of Social Research*. Belmont, CA: Wadsworth.

"Background Music: But It's Good For You." (1963, August 30). *Time*, p. 34ff.

Balzer, R. (1976). *Clockwork: Life in and Outside an American Factory*. Garden City, NJ: Doubleday.

Baritz, L. (1960). *The Servants of Power: A History of the Use of Social Science in American Industry*. Middletown, CT: Wesleyan University Press.

Barker, R. G. (1960). Ecology and motivation. In M. Jones, R. Barker, D. Taylor, W. Toman, R. White, F. Heider & D. Rapaport (Eds.), *Nebraska Symposium on Motivation*, Vol. 8 (pp. 1–50). Lincoln: University of Nebraska Press.

Barker, R. G. (1968). *Ecological Psychology*. Palo Alto, CA: Stanford University Press.

Barnaby, J. (1924). Office management. In L. P. Alford (Ed.), *Management's Handbook* (pp. 370–424). New York: Ronald Press.

Barnard, C. I. (1946). Functional pathology of status systems in formal organizations. In W. F. Whyte (Ed.), *Industry and Society* (pp. 46–83). Chicago: McGraw-Hill.

Barnett, J. (1974). The future of the office building. *Architectural Record, 155*, 127–130.

Barnum, G. (1971). The story of a Fall River mill girl. In L. Stein & P. Taft

(Eds.), *Workers Speak: Self Portraits* (pp. 28–30). New York: Arno – The New York Times.

Bass, B. M. & Klubeck, S. (1952). Effects of seating arrangement on leaderless group discussions. *Journal of Abnormal and Social Psychology, 47,* 724–727.

Batchelor, J. P. & Goethals, G. R. (1971). Spatial arrangements in freely formed groups. *Sociometry, 35*(2), 270–279.

Bates, A. (1964). Privacy – A useful concept. *Social Forces, 42,* 429–434.

Baum, A. & Davis, G. E. (1976). Spatial and social aspects of crowding perception. *Environment & Behavior, 8,* 527–545.

Baum, A. & Epstein, Y. (Eds.). (1978). *Human Response to Crowding.* Hillsdale, NJ: Lawrence Erlbaum.

Baum, A., Singer, J. & Baum, C. (1981). Stress and the environment. *Journal of Social Issues, 37*(1), 4–35.

Beardsley, E. L. (1971). Privacy: Autonomy and selective disclosure. In J. R. Pennock & J. W. Chapman (Eds.), *Privacy* (pp. 56–70). New York: Atherton Press.

Beatty, J. (1965, August 28). Trade winds. *Saturday Review,* p. 12.

Bechtel, R. B. (1976). *Enclosing Behavior.* Stroudsburg, PA: Dowden, Hutchinson & Ross.

Becker, F. D. (1981). *Workspace: Creating Environments in Organizations.* New York: Praeger.

Bedford, T. (1961). Researches on thermal comfort. *Ergonomics, 4,* 289–310.

Bedford, T. (1964). *Basic Principles of Ventilation and Heating.* London: H. K. Lewis & Co.

Bell, C. R., Provins, K. A. & Hiorns, R. W. (1964). Visual and auditory vigilance during exposure to hot and humid conditions. *Ergonomics, 7*(3), 279–288.

Bell, P. A. (1978). Effects of noise and heat stress on primary and subsidiary task performance. *Human Factors, 20*(6), 749–752.

Bell, P. A. (1981). Physiological, comfort, performance, and social effects of heat stress. *Journal of Social Issues, 37*(1), 71–94.

Bell, P. A., Fisher, J. D. & Loomis, R. J. (1978). *Environmental Psychology.* Philadelphia: W. B. Saunders.

Bell, P. A., Loomis, R. & Cervone, J. (1982). Effects of heat, social facilitation, sex differences, and task difficulty on task performance. *Human Factors, 24,* 19–24.

Bennett, C. (1977). *Spaces for People: Human Factors in Design.* Englewood Cliffs, NJ: Prentice-Hall.

Bennett, C. & Rey, P. (1972). What's so hot about red? *Human Factors, 14*(2), 149–154.

Benson, B. E. (1945). *Music and Sound Systems in Industry.* New York: McGraw-Hill.

Berg, L. D. (1892). Iron construction in New York City. *Architectural Record, 1*(4), 448–469.

Bergum, B. & Lehr, D. (1963). Effects of authoritarianism on vigilance performance. *Journal of Applied Psychology, 47*, 75–77.

Berkowitz, L. & Walster, E. (Eds.). (1976). *Equity Theory: Toward a General Theory of Social Interaction. Advances in Experimental Social Psychology*, Vol. 9. New York: Academic Press.

Berkun, M. M. (1964). Performance decrement under psychological stress. *Human Factors, 6*(1), 21–30.

Berrien, F. K. (1946). The effects of noise. *Psychological Bulletin, 43*, 141–161.

Berrien, F. K. (1983). A general systems approach to organizations. In M. D. Dunnette (Ed.), *Handbook of Industrial and Organizational Psychology* (pp. 41–62). New York: Wiley.

Berry, P. C. (1961). Effect of colored illumination upon perceived temperature. *Journal of Applied Psychology, 45*(4), 248–250.

Bertalanffy, L. Von. (1950). An outline of general systems theory. *British Journal of Philosophical Science, 1*, 134–165.

Bessant, J., Braun, E. & Moseley, R. (1980). Microelectronics in manufacturing industry: The rate of diffusion. In T. Forester (Ed.), *The Microelectronics Revolution* (pp. 198–218). Oxford: Basil Blackwell.

Beutell, A. W. (1934). An empirical basis for a lighting code. *Illuminating Engineering, 27*, 5–16.

Birren, F. (1963). *Color, a Survey in Words and Pictures*. New Hyde Park, NY: University Books.

Birren, F. (1968). *Color for Interiors*. New York: Whitney Library of Design.

Black, F. W. & Milroy, E. A. (1967). Experience of air-conditioning in offices. *Arena, 82*, 157–163.

Blackwell, H. R. (1959). Development and use of a quantitative method for specification of interior illumination levels on the basis of performance data. *Illuminating Engineering, 54*, 317–353.

Blackwell, H. R. & Smith, S. W. (1970). Additional visual performance data for use in illumination specification systems. *Illuminating Engineering, 65*, 389–410.

Blackwell, P. J. & Belt, J. A. (1971). Effect of differential levels of ambient noise on vigilance performance. *Perceptual and Motor Skills, 32*, 734.

Blair, R. N., & Winston, C. W. (1971). *Elements of Industrial Systems Engineering*. Englewood Cliffs, NJ: Prentice-Hall.

Blake, P. (1977). *Form Follows Fiasco: Why Modern Architecture Hasn't Worked*. Boston, MA: Little, Brown.

Blum, M. L. & Naylor, J. C. (1968). *Industrial Psychology: Its Theoretical and Social Foundations*. New York: Harper & Row.

Boggs, D. H. & Simon, J. R. (1968). Differential effects of noise on tasks of varying complexity. *Journal of Applied Psychology, 52*(2), 148–153.

Boje, A. (1971). *Open Plan Offices*. London: Business Books. (German edition published 1968.)

BOSTI (1980a). The Impact of Office Environment on Productivity and Quality of Working Life: First Interim Report. Buffalo, NY: Buffalo Organization for Social and Technological Innovation.

BOSTI (1980b). The Impact of Office Environment on Productivity and Quality of Working Life: Second Interim Report. Buffalo, NY: Buffalo Organization for Social and Technological Innovation.

BOSTI (1981). The Impact of Office Environment on Productivity and Quality of Working Life: Comprehensive Findings. Buffalo, NY: Buffalo Organization for Social and Technological Innovation.

Bowden, E. W. (1946). Current danger in penny-wise savings. *Architectural Record, 100*(6), 101.

Bowles, R. S. (1962). Color in your plant – Helpful or harmful? *Factory, 119*, 92–95.

Boyce, P. R. (1973). Age, illuminance, visual performance, and preference. *Lighting Research and Technology, 5*, 125–144.

Boyce, P. R. (1974). Users' assessments of a landscaped office. *Journal of Architectural Research, 3*(3), 44–62.

Boyce, P. R. (1975). The luminous environment. In D. Canter & P. Stringer (Eds.), *Environmental Interaction: Psychological Approaches to Our Physical Surroundings* (pp. 81–124). New York: International Universities Press.

Boyce, P. R. (1981). *Human Factors in Lighting*. London: Applied Science Publishers.

Branton, P. (1969). Behaviour, body mechanics and discomfort. *Ergonomics, 12*(2), 316–327.

Broadbent, D. E. (1953). Noise, paced performance, and vigilance tasks. *British Journal of Psychology, 44*(4), 295–303.

Broadbent, D. E. (1954). Some effects of noise on visual performance. *Quarterly Journal of Experimental Psychology, 6*(1), 1–5.

Broadbent, D. E. (1957a). Effects of noise on behavior. In C. M. Harris (Ed.), *Handbook of Noise Control* (pp. 10–1 to 10–34). New York: McGraw-Hill.

Broadbent, D. E. (1957b). Effects of noises of high and low frequency on behaviour. *Ergonomics, 1*, 21–29.

Broadbent, D. E. (1958). Effect of noise on an "intellectual" task. *Journal of the Acoustical Society of America, 30*, 824–827.

Broadbent, D. E. (1971). *Decision and Stress*. London: Academic Press.

Broadbent, D. E. (1976). Noise and details of experiments: A reply to Poulton. *Applied Ergonomics, 7*(4), 231–235.

Broadbent, D. E. (1979). Human performance and noise. In C. M. Harris (Ed.), *Handbook of Noise Control*, 2nd ed. (pp. 17–1 to 17–20). New York: McGraw-Hill.

Broadbent, D. E. & Gregory, M. (1963). Vigilance considered as a statistical decision. *British Journal of Psychology, 54*, 309–323.

Broadbent, D. E. & Gregory, M. (1965). Effects of noise and of signal rate upon vigilance analyzed by means of decision theory. *Human Factors, 7,* 155–162.

Broadbent, D. E. & Little, E. A. (1960). Effects of noise reduction in a work situation. *Occupational Psychology, 34*(1), 133–140.

Broady, M. (1966). Social theory in architectural design. *Arena, 81,* 149–154.

Brookes, M. J. (1972a). Changes in employee attitudes and work practices in an office langscape. In W. J. Mitchell (Ed.), *Environmental Design: Research and Practice. Proceedings of the ERDA3/AR 8 Conference, UCLA. January 1972.* (pp. 14–1–1 to 14–1–9). Los Angeles, CA: University of California Press.

Brookes, M. J. (1972b). Office landscape: Does it work? *Applied Ergonomics, 3*(4), 224–236.

Brookes, M. J. & Kaplan A. (1972). The office environment: Space planning and affective behavior. *Human Factors, 14*(5), 373–391.

Brown, J. A. C. (1954). *The Social Psychology of Industry.* Baltimore, MD: Penguin Books.

Bulkeley, W. M. (1981, October 15). The latest in seminars: A TV hookup. *The Wall Street Journal,* p. 31.

Burandt, U. & Grandjean, E. (1963). Sitting habits of office employees. *Ergonomics, 6*(2), 217–228.

Burger, J. M. (1983). Verbal message inhibition through nonverbal communication within an open space office. Unpublished paper presented at the 91st Annual Conference of the American Psychological Association, Anaheim, CA.

Burgess, R. L. (1968a). Communication networks: An experimental reevaluation. *Journal of Experimental Social Psychology, 4,* 324–337.

Burgess, R. L. (1968b). An experimental and mathematical analysis of group behavior within restricted networks. *Journal of Experimental Social Psychology, 4,* 338–349.

Burris-Meyer, H. (1943). Music in industry. *Mechanical Engineering, 65*(1), 31–34.

Bursill, A. E. (1958). The restriction of peripheral vision during exposure to hot and humid conditions. *Quarterly Journal of Experimental Psychology, 10,* 113–129.

Burtt, H. E. (1948). *Applied Psychology.* New York: Prentice-Hall.

Business Etiquette Handbook (1965). West Nyack, NY: Parker Publishing.

Buzzard, R. B. (1973). A practical look at industrial stress. *Occupational Psychology, 47,* 51–61.

Cahn, W. (1972). *A Pictorial History of American Labor.* New York: Crown.

Cakir, A., Hart, D. J. & Stewart, T. F. M. (1980). *Visual Display Terminals: A Manual Covering Ergonomics Workplace Design Health and Safety Task Organization.* Chichester: Wiley.

Campbell, B. (1982, June). Homework. *Working Woman*, pp. 72–75.

Campbell, D. E. (1978). The effects of different office arrangements on visitors. Unpublished paper presented at the 86th Annual Convention of the American Psychological Association, Toronto.

Campbell, D. E. (1979). Interior office design and visitor response. *Journal of Applied Psychology, 64*(6), 648–653.

Campbell, D. E. (1980). Professors and their offices: A survey of person–behavior–environment relationships. In R. Stough & A. Wandersman (Eds.), *Optimizing Environments: Research, Practice and Policy* (pp. 227–237). Washington, DC: Environmental Design Research Association.

Campbell, D. T. & Stanley, J. C. (1963). *Experimental and Quasi-experimental Designs for Research*. Chicago: Rand-McNally.

Campbell, J. P., Dunnette, M. D., Lawler, E. E. & Weick, K. E. (1975). Environmental variation and managerial effectiveness. In R. M. Steers and L. W. Porter (Eds.), *Motivation and Work Behavior* (pp. 301–314). New York: McGraw-Hill.

Canter, D. (1968). Office Size: An example of psychological research in architecture. *Architects Journal, 147*(7), 881–888.

Canter, D. (Ed.). (1970). *Architectural Psychology*. London: Royal Institute of British Architects.

Canter, D. & Stringer, P. (1975). *Environmental Interaction: Psychological Approaches to Our Physical Surroundings*. New York: International Universities Press.

Carpenter, C. R. (1958). Territoriality: A review of concepts and problems. In A. Roe & G. Simpson (Eds.), *Behavior and Evolution* (pp. 224–250). New Haven, CT: Yale University Press.

Cartwright, D. (1968). The nature of group cohesiveness. In D. Cartwright & A. Zander (Eds.), *Group Dynamics: Research and Theory*, 3rd. ed. (pp. 91–109). New York: Harper & Row.

Cartwright, D. & Zander, A. (Eds.). (1968). *Group Dynamics: Research and Theory*, 3rd ed. New York: Harper & Row.

Cavanaugh, W. J., Farrell, W. R., Hirtle, P. W. & Watters, B. G. (1962). Speech privacy in buildings. *Journal of the Acoustical Society of America, 34*(4), 475–492.

Chapanis, A. (1976). Engineering psychology. In M. D. Dunnette (Ed.), *Handbook of Industrial and Organizational Psychology* (pp. 697–744). Chicago: Rand-McNally.

Chapman, D. (1967). Design, status and morale. *Arena, 82*, 156.

Chapman, S. D. (1974). The textile factory before Arkwright: A typology of factory development. *Business History Review, 48*(4), 451–478.

Chase, M. (1982, December 3). Computer-chip makers take an interest in factory process. *The Wall Street Journal*, p. 33.

Chase, S. (1929). *Men and Machines*. New York: Macmillan.

Chatterjee, A. & Krishnamurty, V. (1972). Differential effect of noise as an environmental stress. *Behaviorometric, 2*(1), 1–8.

Chiles, W. D. (1958). Effects of elevated temperatures on performance of a complex mental task. *Ergonomics, 2*(1), 89–96.

Choungòurian, A. (1968). Colour preference and cultural variation. *Perceptual and Motor Skills, 26*, 1203–1206.

Clark, K. S. (1929). *Music in Industry*. New York: National Bureau for the Advancement of Music.

Clark, W. C. & Kingston, J. L. (1930). *The Skyscraper: A Study in the Economic Height of Modern Office Buildings*. New York: American Institute of Steel Construction.

Clearwater, Y. A. (1979). Social–Environmental Relationships in Open and Closed Offices. Doctoral dissertation, University of California, Davis, 1979.

Cohen, A. (1968). Noise effects on health, productivity, and well-being. *Transactions of the New York Academy of Science, 30*(7), 910–918.

Cohen, S. (1978). Environmental load and the allocation of attention. In A. Baum, J. E. Singer & S. Valins (Eds.), *Advances in Environmental Psychology* (pp. 1–29). Hillsdale, NJ: Lawrence Erlbaum.

Cohen, S. (1980a). The aftereffects of stress on human performance and social behavior: A review of research and theory. *Psychological Bulletin, 88*(1), 82–108.

Cohen, S. (1980b). Cognitive processes as determinants of environmental stress. In I. Sarason & C. Spielberger (Eds.), *Stress and Anxiety*, Vol. 7 (pp. 171–183). Washington, DC: Hemisphere Press.

Cohen, S., Glass, D. C. & Phillips, S. (1979). Environment and health. In H. E. Freeman, S. Levine, & L. G. Reeder (Eds.), *Handbook of Medical Sociology* (pp. 134–149). Englewood Cliffs, NJ: Prentice-Hall.

Cohen, S. & Lezak, A. (1977). Noise and inattentiveness to social cues. *Environment and Behavior, 9*, 559–572.

Cohen, S. & Spacapan, S. (1978). The aftereffects of stress: An attentional interpretation. *Environmental Psychology and Nonverbal Behavior, 3*(1), 43–57.

Coleman, A. D. (1968). Territoriality in man: A comparison of behavior in home and hospital. *American Journal of Orthopsychiatry, 38*(3), 464–468.

Collins, B. L. (1975). Windows and people: A literature survey. Washington DC: U. S. Department of Commerce, National Bureau of Standards, Building Science Series, #700.

Colquhoun, W. P. & Goldman, R. F. (1972). Vigilance under induced hyperthermia. *Ergonomics, 15*(6), 621–632.

Condit, C. W. (1960). *American Building Art: The Nineteenth Century*. New York: Oxford University Press.

Conrath, C. W. (1973). Communication patterns, organizational structure, and man: Some relationships. *Human Factors, 15*(5), 459–470.

Conroy, J. & Sundstrom, E. (1977). Territorial dominance in a dyadic conversation as a function of similarity of opinion. *Journal of Personality and Social Psychology, 35*(8), 570–576.

Conroy, W. (1933). And for the plant layout: Motion economy. *Factory Management and Maintenance, 91*(4), 153–154.

Conte, J. A. (1966). A study of the effects of paced audio rhythm on repetitive motion. *Journal of Industrial Engineering, 17*(31), 163–169.

Cook, T. & Campbell, D. T. (1983). The design and conduct of quasi-experiments and true experiments in field settings. In M. D. Dunnette (Ed.), *Handbook of Industrial and Organizational Psychology* (pp. 223–326). New York: Wiley.

Coombs, O. (1977, October 31). True tales of the New York workplace. *New York*, p. 69ff.

Cooper, R. & Foster, M. (1971). Sociotechnical systems. *American Psychologist, 26*, 467–474.

Cooper, C. L. & Payne, R. (Eds.). (1978). *Stress at Work*. Chichester: Wiley.

Copley, F. B. (1920). Private office – Entrance next door. *American Magazine, 90*, p. 60ff.

Corlin, L. (1977). Retla open plan executives back to private offices. *Contract, 18*, 84–87.

Corso, J. F. (1952). The effects of noise on human behavior. U. S. Air Force Report No. WADR-TR-53-81, Wright-Patterson Air Force Base, OH.

Cottrell, N.B. (1972). Social facilitation. In C. G. McClintock (Ed.), *Experimental Social Psychology*. New York: Holt, Rinehart & Winston.

Cottrell, N. B., Rittle, R. H. & Wack, D. L. (1967). The presence of an audience and list-type (competitional or non-competitional) as joint determinants of performance in paired-associate learning. *Journal of Personality, 35*, 425–434.

Cottrell, N. B., Wack, D. L., Sekrack, G. J. & Rittle, R. H. (1968). Social facilitation of dominant responses by the presence of an audience and the mere presence of others. *Journal of Personality and Social Psychology, 9*, 245–250.

Cowan, P., Fine, D., Ireland, J., Jordan, C., Mercer, D. & Sears, A. (1960). *The Office: A Facet of Urban Growth*. New York: American Elsevier.

Cummings, L. L., Huber, G. P. & Arendt, E. (1974). Effects of size and spatial arrangements on group decision making. *Academy of Management Journal, 17*(3), 460–475.

Dainoff, M. J., Happ, A. & Crane, P. (1981). Visual fatigue and occupational stress in VDT operators. *Human Factors, 23*(4), 421–438.

Dannenbaum, A. (1945). The effect of music on visual acuity. *Sarah Lawrence Studies, 4*, 18–26.

Davenport, W. G. (1974). Arousal theory and vigilance: Schedules for background stimulation. *Journal of General Psychology, 91*(4), 51–59.

Davies, D. R. (1968). Physiological and psychological effects of exposure to high intensity noise. *Applied Acoustics, 1*(3), 215–233.

Davies, D. R. & Hockey, G. R. J. (1966). The effects of noise and doubling the signal frequency on individual differences in visual vigilance performance. *British Journal of Psychology, 57,* 381–389.

Davies, D. R., Hockey, G. R. J. & Taylor, A. (1969). Varied auditory stimulation, temperament differences and vigilance performance. *British Journal of Psychology, 60*(4), 453–457.

Davies, D. R. & Jones, D. M. (1975). The effects of noise and incentives upon attention in short-term memory. *British Journal of Psychology, 66*(1), 61–68.

Davies, D. R., Lang, L. & Shackleton, V. J. (1973). The effects of music and task difficulty on performance at a visual vigilance task. *British Journal of Psychology, 64*(3), 383–389.

Davis, G. & Altman, I. (1976). Territories at the work-place: Theory into design guidelines. *Man–Environment Systems, 6,* 46–53.

Davis, K. (1953). Management communication and the grapevine. *Harvard Business Review, 31,* 43–49.

Davis, K. (1977). *Human Behavior at Work,* 5th ed. New York: McGraw-Hill.

Davison, H. J. (1918). The effect of color on mental and physical wellbeing – A study in psychological reaction. *The Modern Hospital, 10,* 277–279.

Deasy, C. M. (1974). *Design for Human Affairs.* New York: Wiley.

Deaux, K. & Wrightsman, L. S. (1984). *Social Psychology in the Eighties,* 4th ed. Monterey, CA: Brooks/ Cole.

Dempsey, F. (1914). Nela Park: A novelty in the architectural grouping of industrial buildings. *Architectural Record, 35*(6), 469–504.

Dickson, P. (1975). *The Future of the Workplace: The Coming Revolution in Jobs.* New York: Weybright & Talley.

Diemer, H. (1921). *Factory Organization and Administration,* 3rd ed. New York: McGraw-Hill.

Doering, J. R. (1977). Combined Effects of Noise, Illumination and Task Complexity on Task Performance. Masters Thesis, University of Wisconsin, Oshkosh.

Douglass, L. (1947). New departures in office building design. *Architectural Record, 102*(4), 119–122.

Dowling, W. F. (1973). Job redesign on the assembly line: Farewell to blue collar blues? *Organizational Dynamics,* 51–67.

Draeger, S. (1977, June). Using colors in the office. *The Office,* 61–64.

Dravnieks, A. & O'Neill, H. J. (1979). Annoyance potential of air pollution odors. *American Industrial Hygiene Journal, 40,* 85–95.

Dreyfuss, H. (1966). *The Measure of Man: Human Factors in Design.* New York: Whitney Library of Design.

Dubin, R. (1958). *The World of Work: Industrial Society and Human Relations.* Englewood Cliffs, NJ: Prentice-Hall.

Dubos, R. (1980). *Man Adapting*, 2nd ed. New Haven, CT: Yale University Press.

Duffy, E. (1962). *Activation and Behavior*. New York: Wiley.

Duffy, F. C. (1968). User and the office building. *Building Research 5*, 31–37.

Duffy, F. C. (1969). Role and status in the office. *Architectural Association Quarterly, 1*, 4–13.

Duffy, F. C. (1974a). Office design and organizations: 1. Theoretical basis. *Environment and Planning B, 1*, 105–118.

Duffy, F. C. (1974b). Office design and organizations: 2. The testing of a hypothetical model. *Environment and Planning B, 1*, 217–235.

Duffy, F. C. (1974c). Office Interiors and Organizations: A Comparative Study of the Relation Between Organizational Structure and the Use of Interior Space in Sixteen Office Organizations. Doctoral Dissertation, Architecture, Princeton Univeristy.

Duffy, F. C. (1977, May 18). Appraisal [of Hillingdon Civic Center]. *Architects Journal*, pp. 939–943.

Duffy, F. C. (1978, March 29). Three offices: Reading. *Architects Journal*, pp. 593–604.

Duffy, F. C. (1980). Office buildings and organizational change. In A. D. King (Ed.), *Buildings and Society: Essays on the Social Development of the Built Environment* (pp. 254–280). London: Routledge & Kegan Paul.

Duffy, F. C., Cave, C. & Worthington, J. (Eds.). (1976). *Planning Office Space*. London: Architectural Press.

Duffy, F. C. & Worthington, J. (1977). Organizational design. *Journal of Architectural Research, 6*(1), 4–9.

Duncan, J. S. (1915). *Principles of Industrial Management*. New York: Appleton.

Dunnette, M. D. (Ed.). (1983). *Handbook of Industrial and Organizational Psychology*. New York: Wiley.

Edney, J. J. (1974). Human territoriality. *Psychological Bulletin, 81*, 959–975.

Egan, M. D. (1972). *Concepts in Architectural Acoustics*. New York: McGraw-Hill.

Ellis, P. & Duffy, F.C. (1980, May). Lost office landscapes. *Management Today*, p. 47ff.

Elton, P. M. (1920). A Study of Output in Silk Weaving During Winter Months. Industrial Fatigue Research Board, Report No. 9. London: H. Majesty's Stationery Office.

Eschenbrenner, A. J. (1971). Effects of intermittent noise on the performance of a complex psychomotor task. *Human Factors, 13*(1), 59–63.

Esser, A. H. (1970). Interactional hierarchy – Power structure in a psychiatric ward. In S. Hutt & C. Hutt (Eds.), *Behaviour Studies in Psychiatry* (pp. 25–59). Oxford: Pergamon.

Estabrook, M. & Sommer, R. (1972). Social rank and acquaintanceship in two academic buildings. In W. Graham & K. H. Roberts (Eds.), *Comparative*

Studies in Organizational Behavior (pp. 122–128). New York: Holt, Rinehart & Winston.

Evans, C. A. (1976, December 14). A way to improve office's efficiency: Just stay at home. *The Wall Street Journal*, p. 1.

Evans, G. W. (1978). Human spatial behavior: The arousal model. In A. Baum & Y. Epstein (Eds.), *Human Response to Crowding* (pp. 283–302). Hillsdale, NJ: Lawrence Erlbaum.

Evans, G. W. & Jacobs, S. V. (1981). Air pollution and human behavior. *Journal of Social Issues, 37*(1), 95–125.

Evans, G. W. (1979). Behavioral and physiological consequences of crowding in humans. *Journal of Applied Social Psychology, 9*, 27–46.

Evans, S. (1968, February). Lighting and productivity: How one boosts the other. *Administrative Management*, pp. 28–30.

Eysenck, H. J. (1941). A critical and experimental study of colour preferences. *American Journal of Psychology, 54*, 385–394.

Fanger, P. O. (1972). Improvement of human comfort and resulting effects on working capacity. *Biometeorology, 5*(2), 31–41.

Fanger, P. O., Breum, N. O. & Jerking, E. (1977). Can color and noise influence man's thermal comfort? *Ergonomics, 20*(1), 11–18.

Farbstein, J. D. (1975). Organization, Space and Activity: The Relationship of Task and Status to the Allocation and Use of Space in Certain Organizations. Doctoral Dissertation, Environmental Studies, University of London.

Faulkner, T. W. & Murphy, T. J. (1973). Lighting for difficult visual tasks. *Human Factors, 15*(2), 149–162.

Faunce, W. A. (1958). Automation in the automobile industry: Some consequences for in-plant social structure. *American Sociological Review, 23*, 401–407.

Ferguson, G. S. (1983). Employee satisfaction with the office environment: Evaluation of a causal model. In D. Amedeo, J. Griffin & J. Potter (Eds.), *EDRA 1983: Proceedings of the Fourteenth International Conference of the Environmental Design Research Association* (pp. 120–128). Washington, DC: Environmental Design Research Association.

Festinger, L., Schachter, S. & Back, K. (1950). *Social Pressures in Informal Groups: A Study of Human Factors in Housing*. New York: Harper.

Fetridge, C. & Minor, R. (Eds.). (1975). *Office Administration Handbook*, 5th ed. Chicago: Dartnell Press.

Fine, B. J., Cohen, A. & Crist, B. (1960). Effects of exposure to high humidity at high and moderate ambient temperature on anagram solution and auditory discrimination. *Psychological Reports, 7*, 171–181.

Fine, B. J. & Kobrick, J. L. (1978). Effects of altitude and heat on complex cognitive tasks. *Human Factors, 20*(1), 115–122.

Finkelman, J. M. & Glass, D. C. (1970). Reappraisal of the relationship between noise and human performance by means of a subsidiary task measure. *Journal of Applied Psychology, 54*(3), 211–213.

Fitch, J. M. (1948). *American Building.* Cambridge, MA: Houghton Mifflin.

Fitzgibbons, R. M. (1977, October 31). Visible means of support. *New York, 19*, 65–67.

Flynn, J. E., Spèncer, T. J., Martyniuk, O. & Hendrick, C. (1973). Interim study of procedures for investigating the effect of light on impression and behavior. *Journal of the Illuminating Engineering Society, 3*(2), 87–94.

Ford, A. (1929). Attention-automatization: An investigation of the transitional nature of mind. *American Journal of Psychology, 41*(1), 1–32.

Forester, T. (Ed.). (1980). *The Microelectronics Revolution.* Oxford: Basil Blackwell.

Forster, P. (1978). Attentional selectivity: A rejoinder to Hockey. *British Journal of Psychology, 69*, 505–506.

Forster, P. & Grierson, A. T. (1978). Noise and attentional selectivity: A reproducible phenomenon? *British Journal of Psychology, 69*, 489–498.

Fox, J. G. (1971a). Background music and industrial efficiency – A review. *Applied Ergonomics, 2*(2), 70–73.

Fox, J. G. (1971b). The influence of background music on productivity. *Factory Management, 40*, 25–28.

Fox, J. G. & Embrey, E. D. (1972). Music – An aid to productivity. *Applied Ergonomics, 3*(4), 202–205.

Fraser, R. *Work: Volume 2: Twenty Personal Accounts.* Baltimore, MD: Penguin Books.

Freeburne, C. M. & Fleischer, M. S. (1952). The effect of music distraction upon reading rate and comprehension. *Journal of Educational Psychology, 43*, 101–109.

Freedman, J. L., Klevansky, S. & Ehrlich, P. (1971). The effect of crowding on human task performance. *Journal of Applied Social Psychology, 1*, 7–26.

Friedmann, G. (1955). *Industrial Society: The Emergence of the Human Problems of Automation.* Glencoe, IL: The Free Press.

Fucigna, J. T. (1967). The ergonomics of offices. *Ergonomics, 10*(5), 589–604.

Galitz, W. D. (1980). *Human Factors in Office Automation.* Atlanta, GA: Life Office Management Association.

Galloway, L. (1919). *Office Management: Its Principles and Practice.* New York: Ronald Press.

Garnsey, J. E. (1948). Functional color in industrial buildings. *Architectural Record, 104*(2), 118–123.

Gatewood, E. L. (1921). An experiment in the use of music in an architectural drafting room. *Journal of Applied Psychology, 5*, 350–358.

Geen, R. G. & Gange, J. J. (1977). Drive theory of social facilitation: Twelve years of theory and research. *Psychological Bulletin, 84*(6), 1267–1288.

George, C. S. (1968). *The History of Management Thought*. Englewood Cliffs, NJ: Prentice-Hall.

Geran, M. (1976). Does it work? *Interior Design, 47*(2), 114–117.

Gerlach, K. A. (1974). Environmental design to counter occupational boredom. *Journal of Architectural Research, 3*(3), 15–19.

Gerstberger, P. & Allen, T. J. (1968). Criteria used by research and development engineers in the selection of an information source. *Journal of Applied Psychology, 52*(4), 272–279.

Gilbreth, L. M. (1931). Motion study. In W. J. Donald (Ed.), *Handbook of Business Administration* (pp. 628–643). New York: McGraw-Hill.

Giuliano, V. E. (1982). The mechanization of office work. *Scientific American, 247*(3), 149–164.

Givoni, B. (1976). *Man, Climate and Architecture*. London: Applied Science Publishers.

Givoni, B. & Rim, Y. (1962). Effects of the thermal environment and psychological factors upon subjects' responses and performance of mental work. *Ergonomics, 5*(1), 99–114.

Gladstones, W. H. (1969). Some effects of commercial background music on data preparation operators. *Occupational Psychology, 45*, 213–222.

Glass, D. C. & Singer, J. E. (1972). *Urban stress: Experiments on Noise and Social Stressors*. New York: Academic Press.

Glass, D. C., Singer, J. E. & Friedman, L. N. (1969). Psychic costs of adaptation to an environmental stressor. *Journal of Personality and Social Psychology 12*(3), 200–210.

Goddard, J. B. (1973). *Office Linkages and Location: A Study of Communications and Spatial Patterns in Central London*. Oxford: Pergamon.

Goffman, E. (1959). *The Presentation of Self in Everyday Life*. Garden City, NJ: Doubleday-Anchor.

Gold, B. (1982). CAM [Computer Aided Manufacturing] sets new rules for production. *Harvard Business Review, 60*(6), 88–94.

Goodrich, R. (1982). Seven office evaluations: A review. *Environment and Behavior, 14*, 353–378.

Gorman, T. (1982, February). Safety VDTs. *Working Woman*, p. 30ff.

Gottschalk, E. C. (1983, June 26). Firms are cool to meetings by television. *The Wall Street Journal*, p. 35ff.

Greene, T. & Bell, P. A. (1980). Additional considerations concerning the effects of "warm" and "cool" wall colours on energy conservation. *Ergonomics, 23*, 949–954.

Grether, W. F. (1971, June). Noise and human performance. Report No. AMRL-TR-70-29. Wright-Patterson Air Force Base, OH.: Aerospace Medical Research Laboratory, Aerospace Medical Division (NTIS No. AD-729-213).

Grieve, J. I. (1960). Thermal stress in a single storey factory. *Ergonomics, 3*(4), 297–306.

Griffiths, I. D. (1975). Thermal comfort: A behavioral approach. In D. Canter & P. Stringer (Eds.), *Environmental Interaction: Psychological Approaches to Our Physical Surroundings* (pp. 21–52). New York: International Universities Press.

Griffiths, I. D. & Boyce, P. R. (1971). Performance and thermal comfort. *Ergonomics, 14*(3), 457–468.

Griffitt, W. (1970). Environmental effects on interpersonal affective behavior: Ambient effective temperature and attraction. *Journal of Personality and Social Psychology, 15*, 240–244.

Griffitt, W. & Veitch, R. (1971). Hot and crowded: Influences of population density and temperature on interpersonal affective behavior. *Journal of Personality and Social Psychology, 17*, 92–98.

Grimaldi, J. V. (1958). Sensori-motor performance under varying noise conditions. *Ergonomics, 2*(1), 34–43.

Grivel, F. & Barth, M. (1980). Thermal comfort in office spaces: Predictions and observations. In E. Fernandes, J. Woods & A. Faist (Eds.), *Building Energy Management* (pp. 681–693). Oxford: Pergamon.

Grobman, K. (1970). Informal office layout for employee interaction. *The Office, 71*(6), 12–14.

Guilford, J. P. (1934). The affective value of color as a function of hue, tint, and chroma. *Journal of Experimental Psychology, 17*, 342–370.

Guilford, J. P. & Smith, P. C. (1959). A system of color preferences. *American Journal of Psychology, 72*(4), 487–502.

Guion, R. M. (1973). A note on organizational climate. *Organizational Behavior and Human Performance, 9*, 120–125.

Gullahorn, J. T. (1952). Distance and friendship as factors in the gross interaction matrix. *Sociometry, 15*, 123–134.

Gundlach, C. & Macoubrey, C. (1931). The effect of color on apparent size. *American Journal of Psychology, 43*, 109–111.

Guth, S. K. & Eastman, A. A. (1955). Lighting for the forgotten man. *American Journal of Optometry, 32*, 413–421.

Gutman, R. (1966). Site planning and social behavior. *Journal of Social Issues, 2*, 103–105.

Haber, R. N. (1958). Discrepancy from adaptation level as a source of affect. *Journal of Experimental Psychology, 56*(4), 370–375.

Hack, J. M., Robinson, H. W. & Lathrop, R. G. (1965). Auditory distraction and compensatory tracking. *Perceptual and Motor Skills, 20*, 228–230.

Hackman, J. R. & Oldham, G. R. (1981). *Work Redesign*. Reading, MA: Addison-Wesley.

Hage, J. & Aiken, M. (1967). Relationship of centralization to other structural properties. *Administrative Science Quarterly, 12*, 72–92.

Hall, E. T. (1959). *The Silent Language*. Greenwich, CT: Fawcett.

Hall, E. T. (1966). *The Hidden Dimension*. Garden City, NY: Doubleday.

Hall, P. G. (1975). *Urban and Regional Planning: Problems in Modern Geography*. N. Pomfret, VT: David & Charles.

Halse, A. O. (1968). *The Use of Color in Interiors*. New York: McGraw-Hill.

Hamilton, P. & Copeman, A. (1970). The effect of alcohol and noise on components of a tracking and monitoring task. *British Journal of Psychology, 61*, 149–156.

Hansen, R. A. (1974). Unintelligibility, not audibility, determines acoustical privacy in an open plan. *Contract, 15*(2), 42–47.

Hansen, W. B. & Altman, I. (1976). Decorating personal places: A descriptive analysis. *Environment and Behavior, 8*(4), 491–504.

Hanson, A. (1978). Effects of a move to an open landscape office. *Dissertation Abstracts International, 39*(6), 3046B.

Hard, W. (1907). Where poison haunts man's daily work. *Munsey's Magazine, 37*, 717–721.

Hard, W. (1908). Pensioners of peace. *Everybody's Magazine, 19*(4), 522–533.

Hardy, H. C. (1957). A guide to office acoustics. *Architectural Record, 121*(2), 235–240.

Hare, A. P. & Bales, R. F. (1963). Seating position and small group interaction. *Sociometry, 26*, 480–486.

Harmon, F. L. (1933). The effects of noise upon certain psychological and physiological processes. *Archives of Psychology, 23*(147), 1–81.

Harris, C. S. (1972). Effects of intermittent and continuous noise on serial search performance. *Perceptual and Motor Skills, 35*, 627–634.

Harris, T. G. (1977, October 31). Psychology of the New York work space. *New York*, pp. 51–54.

Hartley, L. R. (1973). Effect of prior noise or prior performance on serial reaction. *Journal of Experimental Psychology, 101*(2), 255–261.

Hartley, L. R. (1974). Performance during continuous and intermittent noise and wearing ear protection. *Journal of Experimental Psychology, 102*(3), 512–516.

Hartley, L. R. & Adams, R. G. (1974). Effect of noise on the Stroop test. *Journal of Experimental Psychology, 102*(1), 62–66.

Harvey, J. H. (Ed.). (1981). *Cognition, Social Behavior, and the Environment*. Hillsdale, NJ: Erlbaum.

Hawley, M. E. and Kryter, K. D. (1957). Effects of noise on speech. In C. M. Harris (Ed.), *Handbook of Noise Control* (pp. 1–1 to 1–26). New York: McGraw-Hill.

Hayward, S. C. & Franklin, S. S. (1974). Perceived openness – enclosure of architectural space. *Environment and Behavior, 6*(1), 37–52.

Hearn, G. (1957). Leadership and the spatial factor in small groups. *Journal of Abnormal and Social Psychology, 54*, 269–272.

Hebb, D. O. (1949). *The Organization of Behavior: A Neuropsychological Theory*. New York: Wiley.

Hedge, A. (1982). The open-plan office: A systematic investigation of employee reactions to their work environment. *Environment and Behavior, 14*(5), 519–542.

Heller, J., Groff, B. & Solomon, S. (1977). Toward an understanding of crowding: The role of physical interaction. *Journal of Personality and Social Psychology, 35*, 183–190.

Helson, H. (1964). *Adaptation-Level Theory: An Experimental and Systematic Approach to Behavior.* New York: Harper & Row.

Helson, H. & Lansford, T. (1970). The role of spectral energy source and background color in the pleasantness of object colors. *Applied Optics, 9*(7), 1513–1562.

Henderson, R. L., McNelis, J. F. & Williams, H. G. (1975). A survey of important visual tasks in offices. *Lighting Design and Application, 5*, 18–25.

Herbert, R. K. (1978). Use of the articulation index to evaluate acoustical privacy in the open office. *Noise Control Engineering, 11*(2), 64–67.

Herzberg, F. (1966). *Work and the Nature of Man.* Cleveland: World Publishing.

Herzberg, F., Mausner, B., Peterson, R. O. & Capwell, D. F. (1957). *Job Attitudes: Review of Research and Opinion.* Pittsburgh: Psychological Service of Pittsburgh.

Herzberg, F., Mausner, B. & Snyderman, B. (1959). *The Motivation to Work.* New York: Wiley.

Hevner, K. (1935). Experimental studies of the affective value of colors and lines. *Journal of Applied Psychology, 19*, 385–389.

Hicks, P. E. (1977). *Introduction to Industrial Engineering and Management Science.* New York: McGraw-Hill.

"The Higher the Rank, the More Enclosure at PRUPAC's Open Plan Headquarters." (1977). *Contract, 18*(11), 56–60.

Hill, G. (1893). Some practical limiting conditions in the design of the modern office building. *Architectural Record, 2*(4), 445–468.

Hill, L., Flack, M., McIntosh, J., Rowlands, R. A. & Walker, H. (1913). The influence of the atmosphere on your health and comfort in crowded places. *Smithsonian Miscellaneous Collections, 60*(23), publication no. 2170.

Hilton, J. (1981, July 13). Face to camera at an actual teleconference. *The Wall Street Journal*, p. 23.

Hirt, E. & Kimble, C. E. (1981). The home-field advantage in sports: Differences and correlates. Unpublished paper presented at the annual conference of the Midwestern Psychological Association, Detroit.

Hockey, G. R. (1970a). Effects of loud noise on attentional selectivity. *Quarterly Journal of Experimental Psychology, 22*, 28–36.

Hockey, G. R. (1970b). Signal probability and spatial locations as possible bases for increased selectivity in noise. *Quarterly Journal of Experimental Psychology, 22*, 37–42.

Hockey, G. R. (1972). Effects of noise on human efficiency and some individual differences. *Journal of Sound and Vibration, 20*(3), 299–304.

Hockey, G. R. (1978). Attentional selectivity and the problems of replication: A reply to Forster & Grierson. *British Journal of Psychology, 69,* 499–503.

Hollingworth, H. L. & Poffenberger, A. T. (1926). *Applied Psychology.* New York: Appleton.

Holtzman, M. J. (1978). There's more to perks than coffee. *Hardware Age, 215,* 75–82.

Homans, G. C. (1950). *The Human Group.* New York: Harcourt, Brace & World.

Homans, G. C. (1954). The cash posters: A study of a group of working girls. *American Sociological Review, 19,* 724–733.

Hopf, H. A. (1931). Physical factors. In W. J. Donald (Ed.), *Handbook of Business Administration* (pp. 749–771). New York: McGraw-Hill.

Hopkinson, R. G. & Longmore, J. (1959). Attention and distraction in the lighting of work-places. *Ergonomics, 2,* 321–334.

Hoppock, R. (1935). *Job Satisfaction.* New York: Harper & Brothers.

Houghten, F. C. & Yagloglou, C. P. (1923). Determining lines of equal comfort. *Transactions of the American Society of Heating and Ventilating Engineers, 29,* 163–176.

Houston, B. K. (1969). Noise, task difficulty, and Stroop color-word performance. *Journal of Experimental Psychology, 82*(2), 403–404.

Houston, B. K. & Jones, T. M. (1967). Distraction and Stroop color-word performance. *Journal of Experimental Psychology, 74,* 54–56.

Hovey, H. B. (1928). Effects of general distraction on the higher thought processes. *American Journal of Psychology, 40,* 585–591.

Howard, P. (1972). Office landscaping revisited. *Design & Environment, 3*(3), 40–47.

Howell, W. C. (1976). *Essentials of Industrial and Organizational Psychology.* Homewood, IL: Dorsey Press.

Howells, L. T. & Becker, S. W. (1962). Seating arrangement and leadership emergence. *Journal of Abnormal and Social Psychology, 64*(2), 148–150.

Hubbard, C. L. (1917). Recent developments in the theory of ventilation. *Architectural Record, 41*(1), 51–57.

Hubbard, C. T. (1921). Over the executive's desk. *System, 40,* 286ff.

Hubert, P. G. (1897). The business of a factory. *Scribner's Magazine, 21*(33), 310.

Hughes, P. C. (1976). Lighting the office. *The Office, 84*(3), p. 127ff.

Humes, J. F. (1941). The effects of occupational music on scrappage in the manufacture of radio tubes. *Journal of Applied Psychology, 25,* 573–587.

Hundert, A. J. & Greenfield, N. (1969). Physical space and organizational behavior: A study of an office landscape. *Proceedings of the 77th Annual Convention of the American Psychological Association,* pp. 601–602.

Industrial Recreation Association (1944). *Music in Industry.* Chicago: Industrial Recreation Association.

Ives, R. S. & Ferdinands, R. (1974). Working in a landscaped office. *Personnel Practice Bulletin, 30*(2), 126–141.

Jacobs, K. & Hustmeyer, F. E. (1974). Effects of four psychological primary colors on G.S.R., heart rate and respiration rate. *Perceptual and Motor Skills, 38*, 763–766.

Jaeger, D. (1979). In-depth planning, not "office landscape" is goal. *Contract, 12*(8), 60–61.

James, L. R. & Jones, A. P. (1976). Organizational structure: A review of structural dimensions and their conceptual relationships with individual attitudes and behavior. *Organizational Behavior and Human Performance, 16*, 74–113.

Jasinski, F. J. (1956). Technological delimitation of reciprocal relationships: A study of interaction patterns in industry. *Human Organization, 15*(2), 24–28.

Jerison, H. J. (1957). Performance on a simple vigilance task in noise and quiet. *Journal of the Acoustical Society of America, 29*(11), 1163–1165.

Jerison, H. J. (1959). Effects of noise on human performance. *Journal of Applied Psychology, 43*(2), 96–101.

Jockusch, P. (1982). Towards a redefinition of standards for the quality of working life. Unpublished paper presented at the 20th Congress of the International Association of Applied Psychology, Edinburgh.

Johns, E. & Sumner, F. C. (1948). Relation of the brightness differences of colors to their apparent distances. *Journal of Psychology, 26*, 25–29.

Johnson, R. (1983, June 19). Rush to cottage computer work falters despite advent of inexpensive technology. *The Wall Street Journal*, p. 37.

Joiner, D. (1971). Office territory. *New Society, 18*, 660–663.

Joiner, D. (1976). Social ritual and architectural space. In H. Proshansky, W. Ittelson & L. Rivlin (Eds.), *Environmental Psychology*, 2nd ed. (pp. 224–241). New York: Holt, Rinehart, & Winston.

Jones, J. W. (1978). Adverse emotional reactions of nonsmokers to secondary cigarette smoke. *Environmental Psychology and Nonverbal Behavior, 3*, 125–127.

Jones, J. W. & Bogat, A. (1978). Air pollution and human aggression. *Psychological Reports, 43*, 721–722.

Jones, R. D. (1970). Effects of thermal stress on human performance: A review and critique of existing methodology. Aberdeen Proving Ground, MD: Human Engineering Laboratories, U.S. Army Research & Development Center.

Justa, F. C. & Golan, M. B. (1977). Office Design: Is privacy still a problem? *Journal of Architectural Research, 6*(2), 5–12.

Katz, D. & Kahn, R. L. (1966). *The Social Psychology of Organizations*. New York: Wiley.

Katz, D. & Kahn, R. L. (1978). *The Social Psychology of Organizations*, 2nd ed. New York: Wiley.

Kalff, L. C. (1971). *Creative Light*. New York: Van Nostrand-Reinhold.

Keighley, E. C. (1970). Acceptability criteria for noise in large offices. *Journal of Sound and Vibration, 11*(1), 83–93.

Keighley, E. C. (1973a). Visual requirements and reduced fenestration in office buildings – A study of window shape. *Building Science, 8*, 311–320.

Keighley, E. C. (1973b). Visual requirements and reduced fenestration in offices – A study of multiple apertures and window area. *Building Science, 8*, 321–331.

Kelvin, P. (1973). A social-psychological examination of privacy. *British Journal of Social and Clinical Psychology, 12*, 248–261.

Kenrick, D. T. & Johnson, G. A. (1979). Interpersonal attraction in aversive environments: A problem for the classical conditioning paradigm? *Journal of Personality and Social Psychology, 37*, 572–579.

Kerr, W. A. (1942). Psychological effects of music as reported by 162 defense trainees. *Psychological Record, 5*(7), 205–212.

Kerr, W. A. (1944). Psychological research in industrial music and plant broadcasting. *Journal of Psychology, 17*, 243–261.

Kerr, W. A. (1945). Experiments on the effects of music on factory production. *Applied Psychology Monographs, 5*, 1–40.

Kilpatrick, J. J. (1981, October 1). Industrial homework: Good or bad? *Knoxville News Sentinel*, p. 22.

Kirk, R. E. & Hecht, E. (1963). Maintenance of vigilance by programmed noise. *Perceptual and Motor Skills, 16*, 553–560.

Kirkpatrick, F. H. (1943a). Music in industry. *Personnel Journal, 20*(2), 88–94.

Kirkpatrick, F. H. (1943b). Take the mind away. *Personnel Journal, 22*(6), 225–228.

Kleeman, W. B. (1981). *The Challenge of Interior Design*. Boston, MA: CBI Publishing.

Kleeman, W. B. (1982). The future of the office. *Environment and Behavior, 14*(5), 593–610.

Knowles, E. S. (1983). Social physics and the effects of others: Tests of the effects of audience size and distance on social judgments and behavior. *Journal of Personality and Social Psychology, 45*(6), 1263–1279.

Konar, E. & Sundstrom, E. (1985, in press). Status demarcation in the office. In J. Wineman (Ed.), *Behavioral Issues in Office Design*. New York: Van Nostrand.

Konar, E., Sundstrom, E., Brady, C., Mandel, D. & Rice, R. (1982). Status markers in the office. *Environment and Behavior, 14*(3), 561–580.

Konecni, V. J. & Sargent-Pollock, D. (1976). Choice between melodies differing in complexity under divided-attention conditions. *Journal of Experimental Psychology: Human Perception and Performance, 2*(3), 347–356.

Konz, S. (1979). *Work Design*. Colombus, OH: Grid Publishing.

Korman, A. K. (1977). *Organizational Behavior*. Englewood Cliffs, NJ: Prentice-Hall.

Kornbluth, M. (1982, June). The electronic office. *The Futurist*, pp. 37–42.

Korte, C., Ypma, I. & Toppen, A. (1975). Helpfulness in Dutch society as a function of urbanization and environmental input level. *Journal of Personality and Social Psychology, 32*(6), 996–1003.

Kraemer, Sieverts & Partners (1977). *Open-Plan Offices: New Ideas, Experience and Improvements* (English translation by J. L. Ritchie). London: McGraw-Hill.

Kryter, K. D. (1970). *The Effects of Noise on Man.* New York: Academic Press.

Kuller, R. (1970). The perception of an interior as a function of its colour. In B. Honikman (Ed.), *Proceedings of the Architectural Psychology Conference at Kingston Polytechnic* (pp. 49–53). Kingston: RIBA Publications.

Lacey, J. & Lacey, B. (1958). Verification and extension of the principle of autonomic response stereotypy. *American Journal of Psychology, 71*, 50–73.

Laird, D. A. (1933). The influence of noise on production and fatigue, as related to pitch, sensation, level, and steadiness of the noise. *Journal of Applied Psychology, 17*, 320–330.

Landy, F. & Trumbo, D. (1976). *Psychology of Work Behavior.* Homewood, IL: Dorsey Press.

Lang, J., Burnette, C., Moleski, W., Vachon, D. (Eds.). (1974). *Designing for Human Behavior: Architecture and the Behavioral Sciences.* Stroudsburg, PA: Dowden, Hutchinson, and Ross.

Langdon, F. J. (1966). Modern offices: A user survey. National Building Studies Research Paper No. 41. Ministry of Technology, Building Research Station. London: H. Majesty's Stationery Office.

Lazarus, R. S. (1966). *Psychological Stress and the Coping Process.* New York: McGraw-Hill.

Leavitt, H. J. (1951). Some effects of certain communication patterns on group performance. *Journal of Abnormal and Social Psychology, 46*, 38–50.

Leffingwell, W. H. (1925). *Office Management: Principles and Practice.* New York: McGraw-Hill.

Leffingwell, W. H. & Robinson, E. M. (1943). *Textbook of Office Management*, 2nd ed. New York: McGraw-Hill.

Lentz, E. (1950). Morale in a hospital business office. *Human Organization, 9*(3), 17–25.

Lerner, L. (undated). Exploring the criteria for the office of the future. New York: Environetics International.

Lescohier, D. D. & Brandeis, E. (1935). *History of Labor in the United States 1896–1932.* New York: Macmillan.

Lewis, L. L. (1975). The office-landscaping concept. In C. Fetridge & R. S. Minor (Eds.), *Office Administration Handbook* (pp. 827–841). Chicago: Dartnell.

Lewis, P. T. & O'Sullivan, P. E. (1974). Acoustic privacy in office design. *Journal of Architectural Research, 3*(1), 48–51.

Lieberman, L. (1969). Management expert discounts office landscape concept. *Contract, 10*(5), 10–12.

Lifson, K. A. (1957). Production welding in extreme heat. *Ergonomics, 1*(1), 345–346.

Likert, R. (1961). *New Patterns of Management*. New York: McGraw-Hill.

Link, J. M. & Pepler, R. D. (1970). Associated fluctuations in daily temperature, productivity and absenteeism. *ASHRAE Transactions, 76*(2), 326–337.

Lipman, A. (1969). The architectural belief system and social behavior, *British Journal of Sociology, 20*, 190–204.

Lipman, A., Cooper, I., Harris, R. & Tranter, R. (1978). Power: A neglected concept in office design? *Journal of Architectural Research, 6*(3), 28–37.

Locke, E. (1983). The nature and causes of job satisfaction. In M. Dunnette (Ed.), *Handbook of Industrial and Organizational Psychology* (pp. 1297–1349). New York: Wiley.

Locke, E. A. & Schweiger, D. M. (1979). Participation in decision-making: One more look. In B. Staw (Ed.), *Research in Organizational Behavior*, Vol. 1 (pp. 265–339). Greenwich, CT: JAI Press.

Loeb, M. & Jones, P. D. (1978). Noise exposure, monitoring and tracking performance as a function of signal bias and task priority. *Ergonomics, 21*(4), 265–272.

Logan, A. (1961, October 21). Onward and upward with the arts: Building for glory. *The New Yorker*, p. 39ff.

Loquial, C. (1891). Engine-room chat. *The Engineering Magazine, 1*(4), 539–543.

Longmore, J., & Ne'eman, E. (1974). The availability of sunshine and human requirements for sunlight in buildings. *Journal of Architectural Research, 3*(2), 24–29.

Lord, C. B. (1917). Influence of environment on the woman worker. *Transactions of the American Society of Mechanical Engineers, 39*, 1141–1148.

Lorenz, K. (1966). *On Aggression*. New York: Harcourt, Brace & World.

Lorenzen, H. J. (1967). The economic reasons behind landscaping. *Office Design, 5*(6), 22–25.

Lorenzen, H. J. & Jaeger, D. (1968). The office landscape: A "systems" concept. *Contract, 9*(1), 164–173.

Louis Harris & Associates, Inc. (1978). *The Steelcase National Study of Office Environments: Do They Work?* Grand Rapids, MI: Steelcase.

Louis Harris & Associates, Inc. (1980). *The Steelcase National Study of Office Environments No. II: Comfort and Productivity in the Office of the 80's.* Grand Rapids, MI: Steelcase.

Lublin, J. S. (1980, May 12). Privacy at work. *The Wall Street Journal*, Editorial page.

Luckiesh, M. (1924). *Light and work*. New York: Van Nostrand.

Luckiesh, M. (1931). Visual efficiency in quiet and noisy workplaces. *Electrical World, 98,* 472–473.

Lunden, G. (1972). Environment problems of office workers. *Build International, 1,* 90–93.

MacCord, C. W. (1894). The modern mechanical drawing-room. *The Engineering Magazine, 7*(6), 855–863.

Mackworth, N. H. (1948). The breakdown of vigilance during prolonged visual search. *Quarterly Journal of Experimental Psychology, 1,* 6–12.

Mackworth, N. H. (1950). Researches on the measurement of human performance. Medical Research Council, Special Report, Series 268. London: H. Majesty's Stationery Office.

Main, J. (1982, June). Work won't be the same again. *Fortune,* 58–65.

"Managers use a variety of tactics against time-wasters, nuisances." (1983, February 9). *The Wall Street Journal,* p. 33.

Manasseh, L. & Cunliffe, R. (1962). *Office Buildings.* New York: Reinhold.

Mandel, D. R., McLeod, W. P. & Malven, F. (1980). Seating and performance: An initial investigation. Unpublished manuscript, University of Connecticut.

Manning, P. (Ed.). (1965). *Office Design: A Study of Environment by the Pilkington Research Unit.* Liverpool: University of Liverpool Press.

Manning, P. (1968). Lighting in relation to other components of the total environment. *Transactions of the Illuminating Engineering Society, 33*(4), 159–166.

Marans, R. W. & Spreckelmeyer, K. F. (1982a). Evaluating open and conventional office design. *Environment and Behavior, 14,* 333–351.

Marans, R. W. & Spreckelmeyer, K. F. (1982b). Measuring overall architectural quality. *Environment and Behavior, 14*(6), 652–670.

Marbach, W. D., Lubenow, G. C. & Ghinby, F. (1981, December 28). Invasion of the computers. *Newsweek,* p. 57.

March, J. G. & Simon, H. A. (1958). *Organizations.* New York: Wiley.

Margulis, S. T. (1977). Conceptions of privacy: Current status and next steps. *Journal of Social Issues, 33*(3), 5–21.

Margulis, S. T. (1979). Privacy as information management: A social psychological and environmental framework. Report No. NBSIR 79-1793, Center for Building Technology, National Engineering Laboratory, U.S. National Bureau of Standards, Washington, DC.

Markus, T. A. (1967). The function of windows – A reappraisal. *Building Science, 2,* 97–121.

Markus, T. A. (1970, January 7). Building appraisal: St. Michael's Academy, Kilwinning. *Architects Journal Information Library, 7,* 9–50.

Markus, T. A., Whyman, P., Morgan, J., Whitton, D., Maver, T., Canter, D. & Fleming, J. (1972). *Building Performance.* New York: Wiley.

Marshall, N. J. (1970). Environmental components of orientations toward privacy. In J. Archea & C. Eastman (Eds.), *EDRA 2: Proceedings of the Second Annual Environmental Design Research Association Conference*, (pp. 246–251). Stroudsburg, PA: Dowden, Hutchinson & Ross.

Marshall, N. J. (1972). Privacy and environment. *Human Ecology, 1*(2), 93–110.

Martindale, D. A. (1971). Territorial dominance behavior in dyadic verbal interactions. *Proceedings of the 79th Annual Convention, American Psychological Association, 6*, 305–306.

Maslow, A. H. (1943). A theory of human motivation. *Psychological Review, 50*, 370–396.

Maslow, A. H. & Mintz, N. L. (1956). Effects of esthetic surroundings: I. Initial effects of three esthetic conditions upon perceiving "energy" and "well-being" in faces. *The Journal of Psychology, 41*, 247–254.

Mathews, K. E. & Canon, L. K. (1975). Environmental noise level as a determinant of helping behavior. *Journal of Personality and Social Psychology, 32*, 571–577.

Matthies, L. H. (1959). How to run a good meeting. *The Office, 50*(1), 14–15.

Matula, R. A. (1981). Effects of visual display units on the eyes: A bibliography (1972–1980). *Human Factors, 23*(5), 581–586.

McBain, W. N. (1961). Noise, the "arousal hypothesis," and monotonous work. *Journal of Applied Psychology, 45*(5), 309–317.

McCallum, R., Rusbult, C., Hong, G., Walden, T. & Schopler, J. (1979). Effect of resource availability and importance of behavior on the experience of crowding. *Journal of Personality and Social Psychology, 37*, 1304–1313.

McCann, P. H. (1969). The effects of ambient noise on vigilance performance. *Human Factors, 11*(3), 251–256.

McCarrey, M. W., Peterson, L., Edwards, S. & Von Kulmiz, P. (1974). Landscape office attitudes: Reflections of perceived degree of control over transactions with the environment. *Journal of Applied Psychology, 59*(3), 401–403.

McCarty, D. G. (1946). *Law Office Management*. New York: Prentice-Hall.

McCormick, E. J. (1976). *Human Factors in Engineering and Design*. New York: McGraw-Hill.

McCormick, E. J. & Tiffin, J. (1974). *Industrial Psychology*, 6th ed. Englewood Cliffs, NJ: Prentice-Hall.

McCullough, W. (1969). *Physical Working Conditions*. London: Gower Press.

McDaniel, R. (1945). How music increases office production. *American Business, 15*(4), 22–26.

"McDonald's Think Tank." (1976). *The Office, 84*(3), 115–119.

McGehee, W. & Gardner, J. (1949). Music in a complex industrial job. *Personnel Psychology, 2*(3), 405–417.

McGrath, J. E. (Ed.). (1970). *Social and Psychological Factors in Stress*. New York: Holt, Rinehart & Winston.

McGrath, J. E. (1976). Stress and behavior in organizations. In M. E. Dunnette (Ed.), *Handbook of Industrial and Organizational Psychology* (pp. 1351–1395). Chicago: Rand-McNally.

McGrath, J. E. & Altman, I. (1966). *Small Group Research: A Synthesis and Critique of the Field.* New York: Holt, Rinehart & Winston.

McGrath, J. J. (1963). Irrelevant stimulation and vigilance performance. In D. N. Buckner & J. J. McGrath (Eds.), *Vigilance: A Symposium* (pp. 3–19). New York: McGraw-Hill.

McGregor, D. (1960). *The Human Side of Enterprise.* New York: McGraw-Hill.

McGuire, W. (1969). The nature of attitudes and attitude change. In G. Lindzey & E. Aronson (Eds.), *The Handbook of Social Psychology*, 2nd ed., Vol. III (pp. 136–314). Reading, MA: Addison-Wesley.

McIntyre, D. A. (1980). *Indoor Climate.* London: Applied Science Publishers.

McNall, P. E. & Schlegel, J. C. (1968). Practical thermal environmental limits for young adult males working in hot, humid environments. *ASHRAE Transactions, 74*(2), 225–235.

McNelis, J. F., Williams, H. G. & Henderson, R. L. (1975). A survey and analysis of important visual tasks in offices – Part 2. *Lighting Design and Application, 5*, 16–23.

Meakin, B. (1905). *Model Factories and Villages: Ideal Conditions of Labour and Housing.* Philadelphia: George W. Jacobs.

Mehrabian, A. (1976). *Public Places and Private Spaces: The Psychology of Work, Play and Living Environments.* New York: Basic Books.

Mehrabian, A. & Diamond, S. (1971a). The effects of furniture arrangement, props, and personality on social interaction. *Journal of Personality and Social Psychology, 20*, 18–30.

Mehrabian, A. & Diamond, S. (1971b). Seating arrangement and conversation. *Sociometry, 34*, 281–289.

Melcher, A. J. (1976). *Structure and Process of Organizations: A Systems Approach.* Englewood Cliffs, NJ: Prentice-Hall.

Michelson, W. (1970). *Man and His Urban Environment: A Sociological Approach.* Reading, MA: Addison-Wesley.

Michelson, W. (1977). From congruence to antecedent conditions: A search for the basis of environmental improvement. In D. Stokols (Ed.), *Perspectives in Environment and Behavior* (pp. 205–219). New York: Plenum.

Mikol, B. & Denny, M. P. (1955). The effect of music and rhythm on rotary pursuit performance. *Perceptual and Motor Skills, 5*, 3–6.

Milgram, S. (1970). The experience of living in cities. *Science, 167*, 1461–1468.

Miller, J. G. (1960). Information input, overload and psychopathology. *American Journal of Psychiatry, 116*, 695–704.

Miller, J. G. (1964). Adjusting to overloads of information. *Disorders of Com-*

munication (Proceedings of the Conference of the Association for Research in Nervous and Mental Disease, December 7 and 8, 1962, New York, N.Y.), Vol. 42 (pp. 87–100). Baltimore, MD: Williams & Wilkins.

Mills, E. D. (1972). *The Changing Workplace*. London: George Godwin.

Mintz, N. L. (1956). Effects of esthetic surroundings: II. Prolonged and repeated experience in a "beautiful" and an "ugly" room. *The Journal of Psychology, 41*, 459–466.

"Mixed Reactions to First U. S. Office Landscape." (1968). *Contract, 9*(4), 74–79.

Moleski, W. H. (1974). Behavioral analysis and environmental programming for offices. In J. Lang, C. Burnette, W. Moleski & D. Vachon (Eds.), *Designing for Human Behavior* (pp. 302–315). Stroudsburg, PA: Dowden, Hutchinson & Ross.

Moleski, W. & Lang, J. (1982). Organizational needs and human values in office planning. *Environment and Behavior, 14*(3), 319–332.

"More Controversy Over Office Landscaping at IBD, BEMA Seminars in New York and Chicago" (1968). *Contract, 9*(12), 80–83.

Moreira, N. & Bryan, M. E. (1971). Noise annoyance susceptibility. *Journal of Sound and Vibration, 21*, 449–462.

Morgan, C. T., Cook, J. S., Chapanis, A. & Lund, M. W. (1963). *Human Engineering Guide to Equipment Design*. New York: McGraw-Hill.

Morgan, G. A., Goodson, F. E. & Jones, T. (1975). Age differences in the association between felt temperatures and color choices. *American Journal of Psychology, 88*(1), 125–130.

Morgan, J. J. (1916). The overcoming of distraction and other resistances. *Archives of Psychology, No. 35, 24*(4), 1–84.

Morgan, J. J. (1917). The effect of sound distraction upon memory. *American Journal of Psychology, 28*, 191–208.

Morrow, P. C. & McElroy, J. C. (1981). Interior office design and visitor response: A constructive replication. *Journal of Applied Psychology, 66*(5), 646–650.

Most, B. W. (1981, May). Color scheming. *American Way*, p. 26ff.

Mourant, R. R., Lakshmanan, R. & Chantadisai, R. (1981). Visual fatigue and cathode ray tube display terminals. *Human Factors, 23*(5), 529–540.

Mullee, W. R. (1933). They sit or stand and are better operators for the change in posture. *Factory Management and Maintenance, 91*(8), 313–314.

Munsterberg, H. (1913). *Psychology and Industrial Efficiency*. Boston: Houghton Mifflin.

Munsterberg, H. (1915). *Business Psychology*. Chicago, IL: La Salle Extension University.

Murrell, K. F. H. (1965). *Human Performance in Industry*. New York: Reinhold.

"Muzak Theory and Practice." (1959). *Engineering* [weekly], *188*(4888), 689.

Myers, C. S. (1925). *Industrial Psychology*. New York: The Peoples' Institute.

Nadler, D. A., Hackman, J. R. & Lawler, E. E. (1979). *Managing Organizational Behavior.* Boston: Little, Brown.

Naisbett, J. (1982). *Megatrends: Ten New Directions Transforming Our Lives.* New York: Warner Books.

Ne'eman, E. (1974). Visual aspects of sunlight in buildings. *Lighting Research and Technology, 6*(3), 159–164.

"The Neglected Network." (1965, March). *Office Design, 3*(2), 18–20.

Nelson, D. (1974). Scientific management, systematic management, and labor, 1880–1915. *Business History Review, 48*(4), 479–500.

Nelson, D. (1975). *Managers and Workers: Origins of the New Factory System in the United States, 1880–1920.* Madison, WI: University of Wisconsin Press.

Nemecek, J. & Grandjean, E. (1973). Results of an ergonomic investigation of large-space offices. *Human Factors, 15*(2), 111–124.

Newhall, S. M. (1941). Warmth and coolness of colors. *Psychological Record, 4*(15), 198–212.

Newman, R. I., Hunt, D. L. & Rhodes, F. (1966). Effects of music on employee attitude and productivity in a skate board factory. *Journal of Applied Psychology, 50*(6), 493–496.

Nimmons, G. C. (1919). Modern industrial plants. Part VII. *Architectural Record, 45*(6), 506–525.

Norman, R. D. & Scott, W. A. (1952). Color and affect: A review and semantic evaluation. *Journal of General Psychology, 36*, 185–223.

Nunneley, S. A., Dowd, P. J., Myhre, L. G., Stribley, R. F. & McNee, R. C. (1979). Tracking-task performance during heat stress simulating cockpit conditions in high performance aircraft. *Ergonomics, 22*(5), 549–555.

"Office Landscape Gives Olsten Future Flexibility." (1970). *Contract, 11*(4), 62–67.

"Office Landscape: Pro & Con" (1968). *Contract, 9*(4), 80–85.

Oldham, G. R. & Brass, D. J. (1979). Employee reactions to an open-plan office: A naturally occurring quasi-experiment. *Administrative Science Quarterly, 24*, 267–284.

Oliver, T. (Ed.). (1902). *Dangerous Trades: The Historical, Social, and Legal Aspects of Industrial Occupations as Affecting Health, by a Number of Experts.* London: J. Murray.

O'Malley, J. J. & Poplawsky, A. (1971). Noise-induced arousal and breadth of attention. *Perceptual and Motor Skills, 33*, 887–890.

Osmond, H. (1957). Function as the basis of psychiatric ward design. *Mental Hospitals, 8*, 23–30.

Packard, V. (1959). *The Status Seekers.* New York: David McKay.

Palmer, A. E. & Lewis, M. S. (1977). *Planning the Office Landscape.* New York: McGraw-Hill.

Park, J. F. & Payne, M. C. (1963). Effects of noise level and difficulty of task in performing division. *Journal of Applied Psychology, 47*(6), 367–368.

Parsons, H. M. (1974). What happened at Hawthorne? *Science, 182*, 922–932.

Parsons, H. M. (1976). Work environments. In I. Altman & J. F. Wohlwill (Eds.), *Human Behavior and Environment: Advances in Theory and Research* (pp. 163–209). New York: Plenum.

Patterson, M. L. (1973). Compensation in nonverbal immediacy behavior: A review. *Sociometry, 36*, 237–252.

Patterson, M. L. (1976). An arousal model of interpersonal intimacy. *Psychological Review, 83*, 235–245.

Paulus, P. B., Annis, A. B., Seta, J. J., Schkade, J. K. & Matthews, R. W. (1976). Crowding does affect task performance. *Journal of Personality and Social Psychology, 34*, 248–253.

Paulus, P. W. & Matthews, R. W. (1980). When density affects task performance. *Personality and Social Psychology Bulletin, 6*(1), 119–124.

Paulus, P. B., McCain, G. & Cox, V. (1978). Death rates, psychiatric commitments, blood pressure and perceived crowding as a function of institutional crowding. *Environmental Psychology and Nonverbal Behavior, 3*, 107–116.

Payne, R. L., Fineman, S. & Wall, T. D. (1974). Organizational climate and job satisfaction: A conceptual synthesis. *Organizational Behavior and Human Performance, 16*, 45–62.

Payne, R. L. & Pugh, D. S. (1983). Organizational structure and climate. In M. D. Dunnette (Ed.), *Handbook of Industrial and Organizational Psychology* (pp. 1125–1174). New York:Wiley.

Pennock, J. R. & Chapman, J. W. (1971). *Privacy*. New York: Atherton Press.

Pepler, R. D. (1958). Warmth and performance: An investigation in the tropics. *Ergonomics, 2*(1), 63–88.

Pepler, R. D. (1959). Extreme warmth and sensoriomotor coordination. *Journal of Applied Psychology, 14*, 383–386.

Pepler, R. D. (1963). Performance and well-being in heat. In C. M. Herzfeld (Ed.), *Temperature: Its Measurement and Control*. Vol. III, Part 3. (pp. 319–336). New York: Rinehold.

Pepler, R. D. (1973). A study of productivity and absenteeism in an apparel factory with and without air-conditioning. *ASHRAE Transactions, 79* (2), 81–86.

Pepler, R. D. & Warner, R. E. (1960). Warmth, glare, and a background of quiet speech: A comparison of their effects on performance. *Ergonomics, 3*(1), 68–73.

Pepler, R. D. & Warner, R. E. (1968). Temperature and learning: An experimental study. *ASHRAE Transactions, 74*(2), 211–224.

Peters, T. J. & Waterman, R. H. (1982). *In Search of Excellence: Lessons from America's Best-Run Corporations*. New York: Warner Books.

Phillips, R. E. (1900). The betterment of working life. *The World's Work, 1*, 157–159.

Pierson, W. H. (1949). Notes on an early industrial architecture in England. *Journal of the Society of Architectural Historians, 8*(1), 1–32.

Pile, J. F. (1969). The nature of office landscaping. *American Institute of Architects Journal, 52*(1), 40–48.

Pile, J. F. (1976). *Interiors 3rd Book of Offices.* New York: Whitney Library of Design.

Pile, J. F. (1978). *Open Office Planning.* New York: Whitney Library of Design.

"Piped-in Music Is Money to Employers." (1971). *Administrative Management, 32,* 66.

Planas, R. (1978, March). Perfect open plan priority: The human element. *Buildings,* pp. 74–75.

Plutchik, R. (1959). The effects of high intensity intermittent sound on performance, feeling and physiology. *Psychological Bulletin, 56*(2), 133–151.

Plutchik, R. (1961). Effect of high intensity intermittent sound on compensatory tracking and mirror tracing. *Perceptual and Motor Skills, 12,* 187–194.

Pollock, K. G. & Bartlett, F. C. (1932). Psychological experiments on the effects of noise. Industrial Health Research Board, Report No. 65. London: H. Majesty's Stationery Office.

Poock, G. K. & Wiener, E. L. (1966). Music and other auditory backgrounds during visual monitoring. *Journal of Industrial Engineering, 17*(6), 318–323.

Poppel, H. L. (1982). Who needs the office of the future? *Harvard Business Review, 60*(6), 146–155.

Porter, L. W., Lawler, E. E. & Hackman, J. R. (1975). *Behavior in Organizations.* New York: McGraw-Hill.

Poulton, E. C. (1970). *Environment and Human Efficiency.* Springfield, IL: Charles C Thomas.

Poulton, E. C. (1976a). Arousing environmental stresses can improve performance, whatever people say. *Aviation, Space and Environmental Medicine, 47,* 1193–1204.

Poulton, E. C. (1976b). Continuous noise interferes with work by masking auditory feedback and inner speech. *Applied Ergonomics, 7*(2), 79–84.

Poulton, E. C. (1977). Continuous intense noise masks auditory feedback and inner speech. *Psychological Bulletin, 84*(5), 977–1001.

Poulton, E. C. (1980). *The Environment at Work.* Springfield, IL: Charles C Thomas.

Poulton, E. C. & Edwards, R. S. (1974). Interactions and range effects in experiments on pairs of stresses: Mild heat and low-frequency noise. *Journal of Experimental Psychology, 102*(4), 621–628.

Poulton, E. C. & Kerslake, D. (1965). Initial stimulating effect of warmth upon perceptual efficiency. *Aerospace Medicine, 36,* 29–32.

Pressy, S. L. (1921). The influence of color upon mental and motor efficiency. *American Journal of Psychology, 32,* 326–356.

Propst, R. (1968). *The Office – A Facility Based on Change*. Elmhurst, IL: The Business Press.

Proshansky, H., Ittelson, W. & Rivlin, L. (Eds.). (1970). *Environmental Psychology: Man and His Physical Setting*. New York: Holt, Rinehart & Winston.

Proshansky, H. Ittelson, W. & Rivlin, L. (Eds.). (1976). *Environmental Psychology: People and Their Physical Settings*, 2nd ed. New York: Holt, Rinehart & Winston.

Provins, K. A. & Bell, C. R. (1970). Effects of heat stress on the performance of two tasks running concurrently. *Journal of Experimental Psychology, 85*, 40–44.

Quinn, R. P. & Staines, G. L. (1979). *The 1977 Quality of Employment Survey*. Ann Arbor, MI: Institute for Social Research, University of Michigan.

Rabbitt, P. (1968). Recognition: Memory for words correctly heard in noise. *Psychonomic Science, 6*(8), 383–384.

"The Ragtime Laundry." (1916). *Illustrated World, 251*, 599–600.

Rapoport, A. & Watson, N. (1967). Cultural variability in physical standards. *Transactions of the Bartlett Society, 6*, 63–83.

Reilly, R. E. & Parker, J. F., Jr. (1968). Effect of heat stress and prolonged activity on perceptual-motor performance. U.S. National Aeronautics and Space Administration, Report No. NASA CR-1153, Arlington, VA: Biotechnology, Inc.

Renwick, P. A. & Lawler, E. E. (1978, May). What you really want from your job. *Psychology Today*, pp. 53–65.

Rhee, H. A. (1968). *Office Automation in Social Perspective*. Oxford: Basil Blackwell.

Rice, A. K. (1963). *The Enterprise and Its Environment*. London: Tavistock.

Richards, C. B. & Dobyns, H. F. (1957). Topography and culture: The case of the changing cage. *Human Organization, 16*, 16–20.

Riland, L. H. & Falk, J. Z. (1972, April). Employee reactions to office landscape environment. Psychological Research & Services, Personnel Relations Department, Eastman Kodak Company.

Ripnen, K. H. (1974). *Office Space Administration*. New York: McGraw-Hill.

Robichaud, B. (1958). *Selecting, Planning and Managing Office Space*. New York: McGraw-Hill.

Robinson, J. B. (1891). Tall office buildings of New York. *The Engineering Magazine, 1*(2), 185–202.

Roethlisberger, F. J. & Dickson, W. J. (1941). *Management and the Worker: An Account of a Research Program Conducted by the Western Electric Company, Hawthorne Works, Chicago*. Cambridge, MA: Harvard University Press.

Roethlisberger, F. J. & Dickson, W. J. (1949). *Management and the Worker*. Cambridge, MA: Harvard University Press.

Rosow, I. (1961). The social effects of the physical environment. *Journal of the*

American Institute of Planners, 27, 127–133.

Ross, L. (1977). The intuitive psychologist and his shortcomings: Distortions in the attribution process. In L. Berkowitz (Ed.), *Advances in Experimental Social Psychology,* Vol. 10 (pp. 174–220). New York: Academic Press.

Rotton, J., Barry, T., Frey, J. & Soler, E. (1978). Air pollution and interpersonal attraction. *Journal of Applied Social Psychology, 8,* 57–71.

Rotton, J., Olszewski, D., Charleton, M. & Soler, E. (1978). Loud speech, conglomerate noise, and behavioral aftereffects. *Journal of Applied Psychology, 63*(3), 360–365.

Rout, L. (1980, October 5). Designers modify the open office to meet complaints of workers. *The Wall Street Journal,* p. 33.

Ruff, C. & Associates (1978). Tomorrow's working environment. *Fortune, 97*(10), p. 23ff.

Russell, W. (1957). Effects of variations in ambient temperature on certain measures of tracking skill and sensory sensitivity. U.S. Army Medical Research Laboratory, Project No. 6-95-20-001, Report No. 300, Fort Knox, KY.

Ruys, T. (1970). Windowless Offices. Master's thesis, Architecture, University of Washington.

Saegert, S., Mackintosh, B. & West, S. (1975). Two studies of crowding in urban public spaces. *Environment and Behavior, 7*(2), 159–184.

Samuel, W. M. S. (1964). Noise and the shifting of attention. *Quarterly Journal of Experimental Psychology, 16,* 264–267.

Sanders, M., Gustanski, J. & Lawton, M. (1976). Effect of ambient illumination on noise level of groups. *Journal of Applied Psychology, 59*(4), 527–528.

Santamaria, A. (1970). Background Music on a Mental Task: Influence of Playing Time on Performance and Heart Variability. Master's thesis, Industrial Engineering, Kansas State University.

Saunders, J. E. (1969). The role of the level and diversity of horizontal illumination in an appraisal of a simple office task. *Lighting Research and Technology, 1*(1), 37–46.

Sauser, W. I., Arauz, C. G. & Chambers, R. M. (1978). Exploring the relationship between level of office noise and salary recommendations: A preliminary research note. *Journal of Management, 4*(1), 57–63.

Sawyer, K. (1979, May 14). Systems furniture closes in on Mr. Big. *The Washington Post,* p. C1ff.

Schaie, K. W. (1961). Scaling the association between colors and mood tones. *American Journal of Psychology, 74,* 266–273.

Schein, E. H. (1972). *Organizational Psychology,* 2nd. ed. Englewood Cliffs, NJ: Prentice-Hall.

Schiffenbauer, A. I., Brown, J. E., Perry, P. L., Schulack, L. K. & Zanzola, A. M. (1977). The relationship between density and crowding: Some architectural modifiers. *Environment and Behavior, 9,* 3–14.

Schoenberger, R. W. & Harris, C. S. (1965). Human performance as a function of changes in acoustic noise levels. *Journal of Engineering Psychology, 4*(4), 108–119.

Schneider, B. (1975). Organizational climates: An essay. *Personnel Psychology, 28,* 447–479.

Schulyer, M. & Nolan, T. (1912). A modern publishing house (Part 1). *Architectural Record, 31*(3), 275–308.

Schulze, J. W. (1919). *Office Administration.* New York: McGraw-Hill.

Schumann, A. (1974). Keeping blight from the open office. *Administrative Management, 35*(10), 26–28.

Scott, L. (1905). Better conditions for workers. *World's Work, 10*(3), 6408–6413.

Scott, W. D. (1916). *Increasing Human Efficiency in Business.* New York: Macmillan.

Scott, W. E. (1966). Activation theory and task design. *Organizational Behavior and Human Performance, 1,* 3–30.

Seiler, J. A. (1967). *Systems Analysis in Organizational Behavior.* Homewood, IL: Irwin-Dorsey.

Sells, S. B. (1970). On the nature of stress. In J. McGrath (Ed.), *Social and Psychological Factors in Stress* (pp. 134–139). New York: Holt, Rinehart & Winston.

Shackel, B., Chidsey, K. D. & Shipley, P. (1969). The assessment of chair comfort. *Ergonomics, 12*(2), 269–306.

Shannon, C. & Weaver, W. (1949). *The Mathematical Theory of Communication.* Urbana, Il: University of Illinois.

Sharpe, D. T. (1974). *The Psychology of Color and Design.* Chicago: Nelson-Hall.

Shaw, M. E. (1964). Communication Networks. In L. Berkowitz (Ed.), *Advances in Experimental Social Psychology,* Vol. 1, (pp. 111–147). New York: Academic Press.

Shaw, M. E. (1981). *Group Dynamics: The Psychology of Small Group Behavior,* 3rd ed. New York: McGraw-Hill.

Shepherd, R. D. & Walker, J. (1957). Absence and the physical conditions of work. *British Journal of Industrial Medicine, 14,* 266–274.

Sherrod, D. R. & Downs, R. (1974). Environmental determinants of altruism: The effects of stimulus overload and perceived control on helping. *Journal of Experimental Social Psychology, 10,* 468–479.

Shoshkes, L. (1976). *Space Planning: Designing the Office Environment.* New York: Architectural Record Books.

Shultz, E. & Simmons, W. (1959). *Offices in the Sky.* Indianapolis: Bobbs-Merrill.

Shuttleworth, G. (1972). Convertible space in office buildings. *Building Research, 9*(2), 9–15.

Slesin, S. (1977, October 31). Office, sweet office. *New York,* p. 55ff.

Sloan, S. A. (1972). Translating psycho-social criteria into design determinants.

In W. J. Mitchell (Ed.), *Environmental Design: Research and Practice. Proceeding of EDRA3/AR8 Conference, UCLA, January, 1972* (pp. 14-5-1 to 14-5-10). Los Angeles: University of California.

Sloan, S. A. (undated). FAA Tenant GSA Landlord Maslov Love Participation Satisfaction Offices Personal Space Work Production Social Needs Designers Users Product Process. Spokane, WA: People Space Architecture Company.

Smith, H. C. (1947). *Music in Relation to Employee Attitudes, Piecework, and Industrial Production.* Palo Alto, CA: Stanford University Press.

Smith, K. R. (1951). Intermittent loud noise and mental performance. *Science, 114*, 132–133.

Smith, M. (1944). *Handbook of Industrial Psychology.* New York: Philosophical Library.

Smith, M. J., Cohen, B. G. F., Stammerjohn, L. W. & Happ, A. (1981). An investigation of health complaints and job stress in video display operations. *Human Factors, 23*(4), 387–400.

Smith, P. C. (1983). Behaviors, results, and organizational effectiveness: The problem of criteria. In M. D. Dunnette (Ed.), *The Handbook of Industrial and Organizational Psychology* (pp. 745–775). New York: Wiley.

Smith, S. (1978). Is there an optimum light level for office tasks? *Journal of the Illuminating Engineering Society, 7*, 255–258.

Smith, W. A. (1961). Effects of industrial music in a work situation requiring complex mental activity. *Psychological Reports, 8*, 159–162.

Snow, W. B. (1891). Healthful air in factory buildings. *The Engineering Magazine, 1*(4), 539–543.

Solly, C. M. (1969). Effects of stress on perception attention. In B. P. Rourke (Ed.), *Explorations in the Psychology of Stress and Anxiety* (pp. 1–14). Ontario: Longmans.

Solon, L. V. & Hopf, H. A. (1927). The Fidelity Mutual Life Insurance Company Building. *Architectural Record, 63*(1), 1–16.

Sommer, R. (1959). Studies in personal space. *Sociometry, 22*, 247–260.

Sommer, R. (1961). Leadership and group geography. *Sociometry, 24*, 99–109.

Sommer, R. (1962). The distance for comfortable conversation: A further study. *Sociometry, 25*, 111–116.

Sommer, R. (1965). Further studies of small group ecology. *Sociometry, 28*, 337–348.

Sommer, R. (1969). *Personal Space: The Behavioral Basis of Design.* Englewood Cliffs, NJ: Prentice-Hall.

Sommer, R. (1974). *Tight Spaces: Hard Architecture and How to Humanize It.* Englewood Cliffs, NJ: Prentice-Hall.

Sommer, R. & Ross, H. (1958). Social interaction on a geriatrics ward. *Interpersonal Journal of Social Psychiatry, 4*, 128–133.

Spacapan, S. & Cohen, S. (1983). Effects and aftereffects of stressor expectations. *Journal of Personality and Social Psychology, 45*(6), 1243–1254.

Steele, F. I. (1971). Physical settings and organization development. In H. Hornstein, W. Burke, B. Benedict, R. Lewicki & M. Hornstein (Eds.), *Strategies of Social Change: A Behavioral Science Analysis* (pp. 244–254). Glencoe, IL: The Free Press.

Steele, F. I. (1973a). Physical settings and social interaction. In W. Bennis, D. Berlew, E. Schein & F. I. Steele (Eds.), *Interpersonal Dynamics: Essays and Readings on Human Interaction* (pp. 439–447). Homewood, IL: Dorsey Press.

Steele, F. I. (1973b). *Physical Settings and Organization Development.* Reading, MA: Addison-Wesley.

Steele, F. I. & Jenks, S. (1977). *The Feel of the Work Place: Understanding and Improving Organizational Climate.* Reading, MA: Addison-Wesley.

Steers, R. M. (1975). Problems in the measurement of organizational effectiveness. *Administrative Science Quarterly, 20*, 546–558.

Steers, R. M. & Porter, L. W. (1975). *Motivation and Work Behavior.* New York: McGraw-Hill.

Steffans, J. L. (1897). The modern business building. *Scribner's Magazine, 22,* 37–61.

Steinzor, B. (1950). The spatial factor in face to face discussion groups. *Journal of Abnormal and Social Psychology, 45,* 552–555.

Stephens, S. D. G., & Anderson, C. M. B. (1971). Experimental studies on the uncomfortable loudness level. *Journal of Speech & Hearing Research, 14,* 262–270.

Stevens, S. S. (1972). Stability of human performance under intense noise. *Journal of Sound and Vibration, 21*(1), 35–56.

Stevens, S. S., Egan, J. P., Waterman, T. H., Miller, J., Knapp, R. H. & Rome, S. C. (1941). The effects of noise on psychomotor efficiency. Report 274, Psycho-acoustic Laboratory, Harvard University, Cambridge, MA. (U.S. Dept. of Commerce Report PB8334.)

Stewart, J. (1979, June 23). Computer shock: The inhuman office of the future. *Saturday Review*, pp. 14–17.

Stokols, D. (1972). On the distinction between density and crowding: Some implications for future research. *Psychological Review, 79,* 275–277.

Stokols, D. (1976). Social unit analysis as a framework for research in environmental and social psychology. *Personality and Social Psychology Bulletin, 2,* 350–358.

Stramler, C. S., Kleiss, J. A. & Howell, W. C. (1983). Thermal sensation shifts induced by physical and psychological means. *Journal of Applied Psychology, 68*(1), 187–193.

Strodtbeck, F. & Hook, H. (1961). The social dimensions of a 12-man jury table. *Sociometry, 24,* 397–415.

Sturgis, R. (1904). *A Dictionary of Architecture and Building,* Vol. 2. New York: Macmillan.

Sucov, E. W. (1973, February). European research. *Lighting Design & Application*, pp. 39–43.

Sundstrom, E. (1975a). Toward an interpersonal model of crowding. *Sociological Symposium, No. 14*, 129–144.

Sundstrom, E. (1975b). An experimental study of crowding: Effects of room-size, intrusion, and goal-blocking on nonverbal behavior, self-disclosure, and self-reported stress. *Journal of Personality and Social Psychology, 32*(4), 645–654.

Sundstrom, E. (1978). Crowding as a sequential process: Review of research on the effects of population density on humans. In A. Baum & Y. Epstein (Eds.), *Human Response to Crowding* (pp. 31–116). Hillsdale, NJ: Lawrence Erlbaum.

Sundstrom, E. (1984). Physical environment and social behavior. In K. Deaux and L. Wrightsman, *Social Psychology in the Eighties*, 4th ed. (pp. 430–457). Monterey, CA: Brooks/Cole.

Sundstrom, E. & Altman, I. (1974). Field study of territorial behavior and dominance. *Journal of Personality and Social Psychology, 30*, 115–124.

Sundstrom, E. & Altman, I. (1976). Interpersonal relationships and personal space: Research review and theoretical model. *Human Ecology, 4*(1), 47–67.

Sundstrom, E., Burt, R. & Kamp, D. (1980). Privacy at work: Architectural correlates of job satisfaction and job performance. *Academy of Management Journal, 23*(1), 101–117.

Sundstrom, E., Herbert, R. K. & Brown, D. W. (1982). Privacy and communication in an open plan office: A case study. *Environment and Behavior, 14*(3), 379–392.

Sundstrom, E., Town, J., Brown, D., Forman, A. & McGee, C. (1982a). Physical enclosure, type of job, and privacy in the office. *Environment and Behavior, 14*(5), 543–559.

Sundstrom, E., Town, J., Osborn, D., Rice, R., Konar, E., Mandel, D. & Brill, M. (1982b). Office noise, satisfaction, and performance. Unpublished paper presented at the annual conference of The American Psychological Association, Washington, DC.

Sundstrom, E., Town, J., Rice, R., Konar, E., Mandel, D. & Brill, M. (1982c). Physical enclosure of workspaces and privacy in the office. Unpublished paper presented at the Congress of The International Association of Applied Psychology, Edinburgh.

Sundstrom, E., Town, J., Rice, R. W., Konar, E., Mandel, D. & Brill, M. (1982d). Privacy in the office, satisfaction, and performance. Unpublished paper presented at the annual conference of the American Psychological Association, Washington, DC.

Szilagyi, A. & Holland, W. (1980). Changes in social density: Relationships with functional interaction and perceptions of job characteristics, role stress, and work satisfaction. *Journal of Applied Psychology, 65*(1), 28–33.

Tagiuri, R. & Litwin, G. H. (1968). *Organizational Climate: Explorations of a Concept*. Boston: Harvard University Press.

Tausky, C. (1978). *Work Organizations: Major Theoretical Perspectives*. Itasca, IL: Peacock.

Taylor, F. W. (1895). A piece rate system being a step toward partial solution of the labor problem. *Transactions of the American Society of Mechanical Engineers, 16*, 856–903.

Taylor, F. W. (1911). *Scientific Management Comprising Shop Management, the Principles of Scientific Management, Testimony Before the Special House Committee*. New York: Harper & Row.

Taylor, R. B. (1982). On ignoring the physical environment. *Population & Environmental Psychology Newsletter, 9*(3), 20–21.

Taylor, R. B. & Lanni, J. C. (1980). Territorial dominance: The influence of the resident advantage on triadic decision making. *Journal of Personality and Social Psychology, 41*, 909–915.

Teichner, W. H., Arees, E. & Reilly, R. (1963). Noise and human performance, a psychophysiological approach. *Ergonomics, 6*(1), 83–97.

Teichner, W. H. & Wehrkamp, R. F. (1954). Visual-motor performance as a function of short-duration ambient temperature. *Journal of Experimental Psychology, 47*, 447–450.

Terry, G. R. (1975). *Office Management and Control*. Homewood, IL: Richard D. Irwin.

Thackray, R. I. & Touchstone, R. M. (1970). Recovery of motor performance following startle. *Perceptual and Motor Skills, 30*, 279–292.

Thackray, R. I., Touchstone, R. M. & Jones, K. N. (1972). Effects of simulated sonic booms on tracking performance and autonomic response. *Aerospace Medicine, 43*(1), 13–21.

Theologus, G. C., Wheaton, G. R. & Fleischman, E. A. (1974). Effects of intermittent, moderate intensity noise stress on human performance. *Journal of Applied Psychology, 59*, 539–547.

Throstle, T. (1847). Factory life in New England. *The Knickerbocker, 30*, 511–518.

Tinker, M. A. (1925). Intelligence in an intelligence test with an auditory distractor. *American Journal of Psychology, 36*, 467–468.

Tinker, M. A. (1938). Effect of stimulus-texture upon apparent warmth and affective value of colors. *American Journal of Psychology, 51*, 532–535.

Toffler, A. (1980). *The Third Wave*. New York: Bantam Books.

Town, J. P. (1982). Effects of Participation in Office Design on Satisfaction and Productivity. Doctoral dissertation, Psychology, University of Tennessee, Knoxville.

Trist, E. L. & Bamforth, K. W. (1951). Some social and psychological consequences of the long-wall method of coal-getting. *Human Relations, 4*, 3–38.

Trist, E., Higgins, G., Murray, H. & Pollack, A. (1963). *Organizational Choice*. London: Tavistock.

"The Trouble With Open Offices." (1978, August 7). *Business Week*, p. 84ff.

Tushman, M. L. & Moore, W. L. (1982). *Readings in the Management of Innovation*. Boston: Pitman.

Uhlig, R., Farber, D. J. & Bair, J. H. (1979). *The Office of the Future*. New York: North-Holland.

Uhrbrock, R. S. (1961). Music on the job: Its influence on worker morale and production. *Personnel Psychology, 14*, 9–38.

"Using Color and Design to Increase Efficiency." (1979, April 9). *Business Week*, p. 112–H.

Uttal, B. (1982). What's detaining the office of the future? *Fortune, 105*(9), 176–196.

Vail, H. (1978). The automated office. In E. Cornish (Ed.), *1999: The World of Tomorrow* (pp. 30–33). Washington, DC: World Future Society.

Valciras, D. J. M. C. L. (1976). Office lighting in a total environment. *Lighting Design and Application. 6*(10). 35–37.

"The Value of Music in Factories." (1913). *The Outlook, 105*, 9–10.

Vaughn, J. A., Higgins, E. A. & Funkhouser, G. E. (1968). Effects of body thermal state on manual performance. *Aerospace Medicine, 39*(12), 1310–1315.

Vaughn, R. C. (1977). *Introduction to Industrial Engineering*, 2nd ed. Ames, IA: Iowa State University.

Vernon, H. M. (1918). An investigation of the factors concerned in the causation of industrial accidents. British Ministry of Munitions, Health of Munition Workers Committee, Memo 21. London: H. Majesty's Stationery Office.

Vernon, H. M. (1919). The influence of hours of work and of ventilation on output in tinplate manufacture. Industrial Fatigue Research Board, Report No. 1, London: H. Majesty's Stationery Office.

Vernon, H. M. & Warner, C. G. (1932). Objective and subjective tests for noise. *Personnel Journal, 11*(3), 141–149.

Vicker, R. (1981, August 4). Computer terminals allow more people to work at home instead of commuting. *The Wall Street Journal*, p. 56.

Vinsel, A., Brown, B. B., Altman, I. & Foss, C. (1980). Privacy regulation: Territorial displays and effectiveness of individual functioning. *Journal of Personality and Social Psychology, 39*, 1104–1115.

Viteles, M. S. & Smith, K. R. (1946). An experimental investigation of the effect of change in atmospheric conditions and noise upon performance. *Heating Piping & Air Conditioning, 18*, 107–112.

Wagner, K. C. (1954). Those annoying "human factors." *The Journal of Industrial Engineering, 5*(2), p. 3ff.

Wahba, M. A. & Bridwell, L. G. (1975). Maslow reconsidered: A review of research on the need hierarchy theory. In K. N. Wexley & G. A. Yukl (Eds.), *Organizational Behavior and Industrial Psychology: Readings With Commentary* (pp. 5–11). New York: Oxford University Press.

Walker, C. R. & Guest, R. H. (1952). *The Man on the Assembly Line*. Cambridge, MA: Harvard University Press.

Walton, W. E., Guilford, R. B. & Guilford, J. P. (1933). Color preferences of 1,279 university students. *Journal of Psychology, 45*, 322–328.

Wandersman, A. (1979a). User participation: A conceptual framework. *Environment and Behavior, 11*, 465–482.

Wandersman, A. (1979b). User participation: A study of types of participation, effects, mediators, and individual differences. *Environment and Behavior, 11*, 185–208.

Warner, H. D. (1969). Effects of intermittent noise on human target detection. *Human Factors, 11*(3), 245–250.

Warner, H. D. & Heimstra, N. W. (1971). Effects of intermittent noise on visual search tasks of varying complexity. *Perceptual and Motor Skills, 32*, 219–226.

"Wasted Opportunities" (1893). *Architectural Record, 3*(1), 72–86.

Watkins, W. H. (1964). Effect of certain noises upon detection of visual signals. *Journal of Experimental Psychology, 67*(1), 72–75.

Webb, E., Campbell, D. T., Schwartz, R. D. & Sechrest, L. (1966). *Unobtrusive Measures: Nonreactive Research in the Social Sciences*. Chicago: Rand-McNally.

Weber, M. (1947). *The Theory of Social and Economic Organization* (translated by A. M. Henderson & T. Parsons). New York: The Free Press.

Webster, J. C. (1959). The skyscraper: Logical and historical considerations. *Journal of the Society of Architectural Historians, 18*(4), 126–139.

Weick, K. (1979). *The Social Psychology of Organizing*, 2nd ed. Reading, MA: Addison-Wesley.

Weinstein, A. & Mackenzie, R. S. (1966). Manual performance and arousal. *Perceptual and Motor Skills, 22*, 498.

Weinstein, N. D. (1974). Effect of noise on intellectual performance. *Journal of Applied Psychology, 59*(5), 548–554.

Weisman, W. (1953). New York and the problem of the first skyscraper. *Journal of the Society of Architectural Historians, 12*(1), 13–21.

Welford, A. T. (1973). Stress and performance. *Ergonomics, 16*(5), 567–580.

Wells, B. (1964). Office Design and the Office Worker. Doctoral dissertation, University of Liverpool.

Wells, B. (1965a). Subjective responses to the lighting installation in a modern office building and their design implications. *Building Science, 1*, 57–68.

Wells, B. (1965b). The psycho-social influence of building environments: Sociometric findings in large and small office spaces. *Building Science, 1*, 153–165.

Westin, A. (1967). *Privacy and Freedom.* New York: Atheneum.

Weston, H. C. (1921). A study of efficiency in fine linen weaving. Industrial Health (Fatigue) Research Board, Report No. 20. London: H. Majesty's Stationery Office.

Weston, H. C. (1945). The relation between illuminance and visual performance. Industrial Health Research Board, Report No. 87. London: H. Majesty's Stationery Office.

Weston, H. C. (1952). Essentials of good lighting in places of work. *Psychology at Work, 4,* 2–9.

Weston, H. C. and Adams, S. (1935). The performance of weavers under varying conditions of noise. Industrial Health Research Board, Report No. 70. London: H. Majesty's Stationery Office.

Weston, H. C. & Taylor, A. (1926). The relation between illumination and efficiency in fine work – typesetting by hand. Industrial Fatigue Research Board and Illumination Research Committee. London: H. Majesty's Stationery Office.

Wexner, L. B. (1954). The degree to which colors (hues) are associated with mood-tones. *Journal of Applied Psychology, 38,* 432–435.

White, A. G. (1953). The patient sits down: A clinical note. *Psychosomatic Medicine, 15*(3), 256–257.

Wicker, A. W. (1973). Undermanning theory and research: Implications for the study of psychological and behavioral effects of excess populations. *Representative Research in Social Psychology, 4,* 185–206.

Wicker, A. W. (1979). *An Introduction to Ecological Psychology.* Monterey, CA: Brooks/Cole.

Widgery, R. & Stackpole, C. (1972). Desk position, interview anxiety, and interviewer credibility: An example of cognitive balance. *Journal of Counseling Psychology, 19*(3), 173–177.

Wiener, N. (1948). *Cybernetics.* New York: Wiley.

Wilkinson, R. T. (1963). Interaction of noise with knowledge of results and sleep deprivation. *Journal of Experimental Psychology, 66,* 332–337.

Wilkinson, R. T. (1969). Some factors influencing the effect of environmental stressors upon performance. *Psychological Bulletin, 72*(4), 260–272.

Wilkinson, R. T. (1974). Individual differences in response to the environment. *Ergonomics, 17*(6), 745–756.

Wilkinson, R. T., Fox, R. H., Goldsmith, R., Hampton, I. F. G. & Lewis, H. E. (1964). Psychological and physiological responses to raised body temperature. *Journal of Applied Physiology, 19*(2), 287–291.

Wilson, G. D. (1966). Arousal properties of red versus green. *Perceptual and Motor Skills, 23,* 947–949.

Wineman, J. (1982). Office design and evaluation: An overview. *Environment and Behavior, 14*(3), 271–298.

Wing, J. F. (1965). A review of the effects of high ambient temperature on mental performance. Report No. AMRL-TR-65-102. Aerospace Medical Research Laboratories, Wright-Patterson Air Force Base, OH.

Witten, M. (1978, June). Towards the liberated office. *Canadian Business*, p. 61ff.

Wofford, J. C., Gerloff, E. A. & Cummins, R. C. (1977). *Organizational Communication: The Keystone to Managerial Effectiveness*. New York: McGraw-Hill.

Wohlwill, J. F. (1974). Human adaptation to levels of environmental stimulation. *Human Ecology, 2*(2), 127–147.

Wohlwill, J. F. (1975). Behavioral response and adaptation to environmental stimulation. In A. Damon (Ed.), *Physiological Anthropology* (pp. 295–334). Cambridge, MA: Harvard University Press.

Wohlwill, J. F., Nasar, J. L., DeJoy, D. M. & Foruzani, H. H. (1976). Behavioral effects of a noisy environment: Task involvement versus passive exposure. *Journal of Applied Psychology, 61*(1), 67–74.

Wolgers, B. (1973). Study of office environment-attitudes to office landscapes and open-plan offices. *Build International, 6*, 143–146.

Woodhead, M. M. (1959). Effect of brief loud noise on decision making. *Journal of the Acoustical Society of America, 31*, 1329–1331.

Woodhead, M. M. (1964a). The effect of bursts of noise on an arithmetic task. *American Journal of Psychology, 77*, 627–633.

Woodhead, M. M. (1964b). Searching a visual display in intermittent noise. *Journal of Sound and Vibration, 1*(2), 157–161.

Woodhead, M. M. (1969). Performing a visual task in the vicinity of reproduced sonic bangs. *Journal of Sound and Vibration, 9*(1), 121–125.

Woods, R. A. (1903). The human touch in industry. *Munsey's Magazine, 29*(3), 321–328.

Woodson, W. G. (1981). *Human Factors Design Handbook*. New York: McGraw-Hill.

"Work in America." (1977, July 5). C.B.S. Television Special.

Wotton, E. (1976). Some considerations affecting the inclusion of windows in office facades. *Lighting Design and Application, 6*(2), 32–40.

Wright, B. (1962). The influence of hue, lightness, and saturation on apparent warmth and weight. *American Journal of Psychology, 75*, 232–241.

Wright, B. & Rainwater, L. (1962). The meanings of color. *The Journal of General Psychology, 67*, 89–99.

Wundt, W. (1893). *Grundzouge dur Physiologischen Psychologie*. Leipzig: W. Engelmann.

Wyatt, S. & Langdon, J. N. (1937). Fatigue and boredom in repetitive work. Industrial Health Research Board, Report No. 77. London: H. Majesty's Stationery Office.

Wylie, H. L. (1958). *Office Management Handbook*, 2nd ed. New York: Ronald Press.

Wyon, D. P. (1974). The effects of moderate heat stress on typewriting performance. *Ergonomics, 17*, 309–318.

Yerkes, R. M. (1919). Report of the Psychology Committee of the National Research Council. *Psychological Review, 26*, 83–136.

Yerkes, R. M. & Dodson, J. D. (1908). The relation of strength of stimulus to rapidity of habit formation. *Journal of Comparative Neurology and Psychology, 18*, 459–482.

Zager, R. & Rosow, M. I. (Eds.). (1982). *The Innovative Organization: Productivity Programs in Action*. New York: Pergamon.

Zajonc, R. B. (1965). Social facilitation. *Science, 149*, 269–274.

Zalesny, M., Farace, R. V. & Kurchner-Hawkins, R. (1985, in press). Perceived work environment and organizational level as determinants of employee work perceptions and attitudes. *Environment and Behavior*.

Zeisel, J. (1981). *Inquiry by Design: Tools for Environment-Behavior Research*. Monterey, CA: Brooks/Cole.

Zeitlin, L. R. (1969). A comparison of employee attitudes toward the conventional office and the landscaped office. Unpublished report, Port of New York Authority.

Zenardelli, H. A. (1967). Testimonial to life in a landscape. *Office Design, 5*(6), 30–36.

Zenhausern, R., Pompo, C. & Ciaiola, M. (1974). Simple and complex reaction times as a function of subliminal and supraliminal accessory stimulation. *Perceptual and Motor Skills, 38*, 417–418.

Zermeno, R., Moseley, R. & Braun, E. (1980). The robots are coming – slowly. In T. Forester (Ed.), *The Microelectronics Revolution* (pp. 184–197). Oxford: Basil Blackwell.

Zimny, G. H. & Weidenfeller, E. W. (1963). Effects of music upon *GSR* and heart-rate. *American Journal of Psychology, 73*, 311–314.

Zweigenhaft, R. L. (1976). Personal space in the faculty office: Desk placement and the student–faculty interaction. *Journal of Applied Psychology, 61*(4), 529–532.

NAME INDEX

SUBJECT INDEX

1756859R0030

Printed in Great Britain
by Amazon.co.uk, Ltd.,
Marston Gate.